Rediscovering Gouache

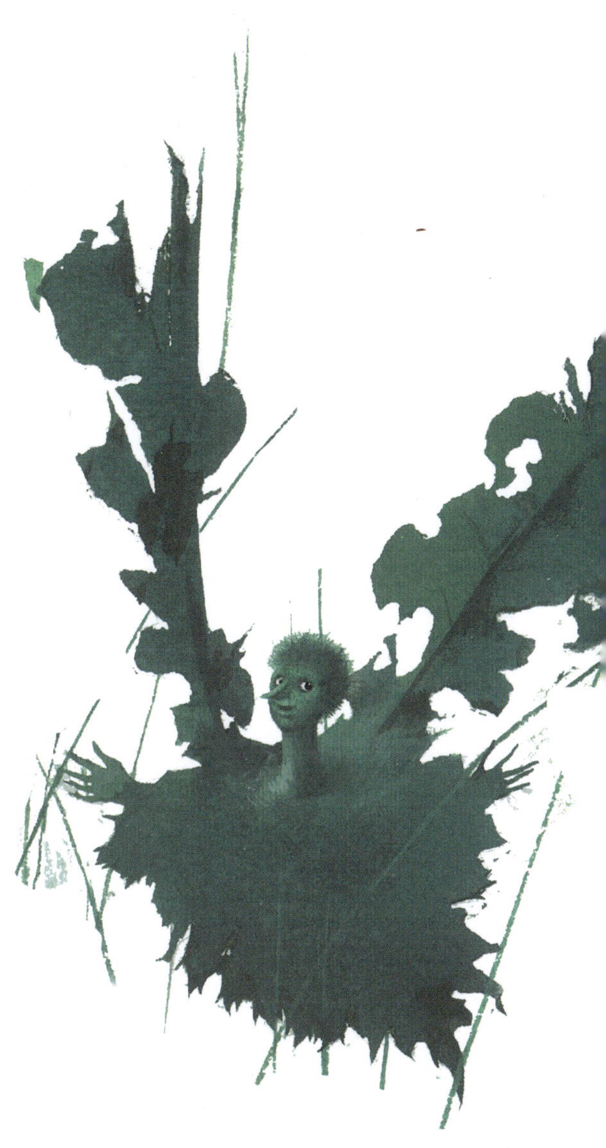

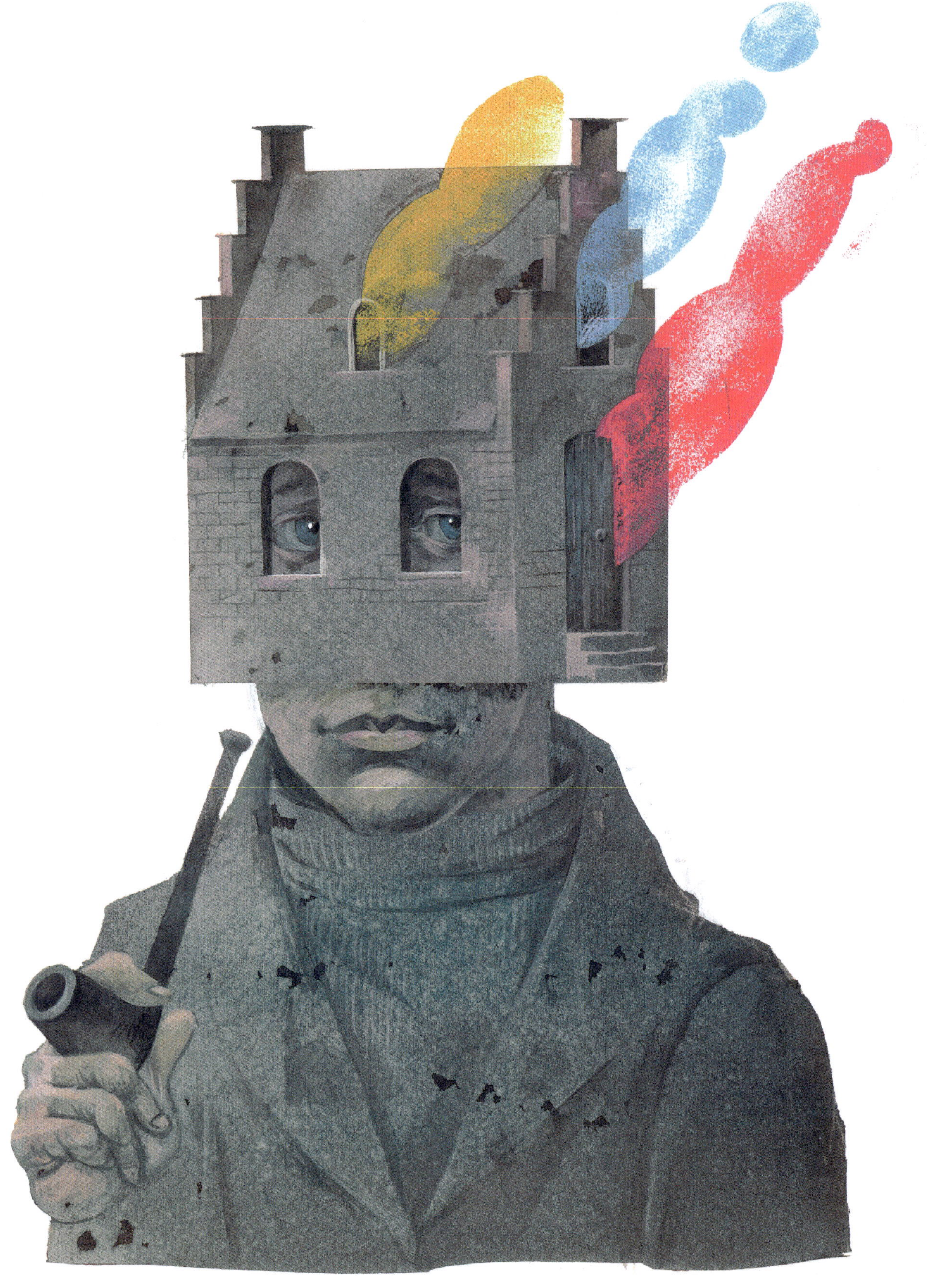

Rediscovering Gouache

A New Approach to a Versatile Technique for Contemporary Artists and Illustrators

Aljoscha Blau

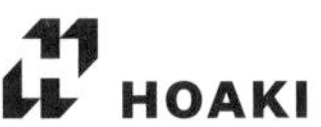

HOAKI

Big Brother

Gouache is like the "big brother" of watercolour. The technique eliminates the boundaries between "proper painting" and the spontaneous charm of watercolours, combining the advantages of both techniques. You could say gouache is watercolour that's caught on in studios. Watercolour with added time– that's outgrown quick sketches– and is able to do quite wonderful things. But doing wonderful things and teaching wonderful things is not the same thing.

A good teacher needs two things: Firstly, he must be a real expert who is capable of creating something new and interesting. Secondly– and this is just as important–, he must have the willingness to share his knowledge. Both don't come naturally but Aljoscha Blau possesses both traits in a great way. Aljoscha has been a source of inspiration for me since our days as students together in Hamburg– and he's a shining, genuine artist.

So it's not surprising to me that he wrote this fantastic book about the "big brother" of watercolours, a book that I'm sure will be a great benefit to you– as the fabulous work of Aljoscha has been to me.

In this spirit, I wish you much enjoyment with this book and the great technique of gouache.

Felix Scheinberger

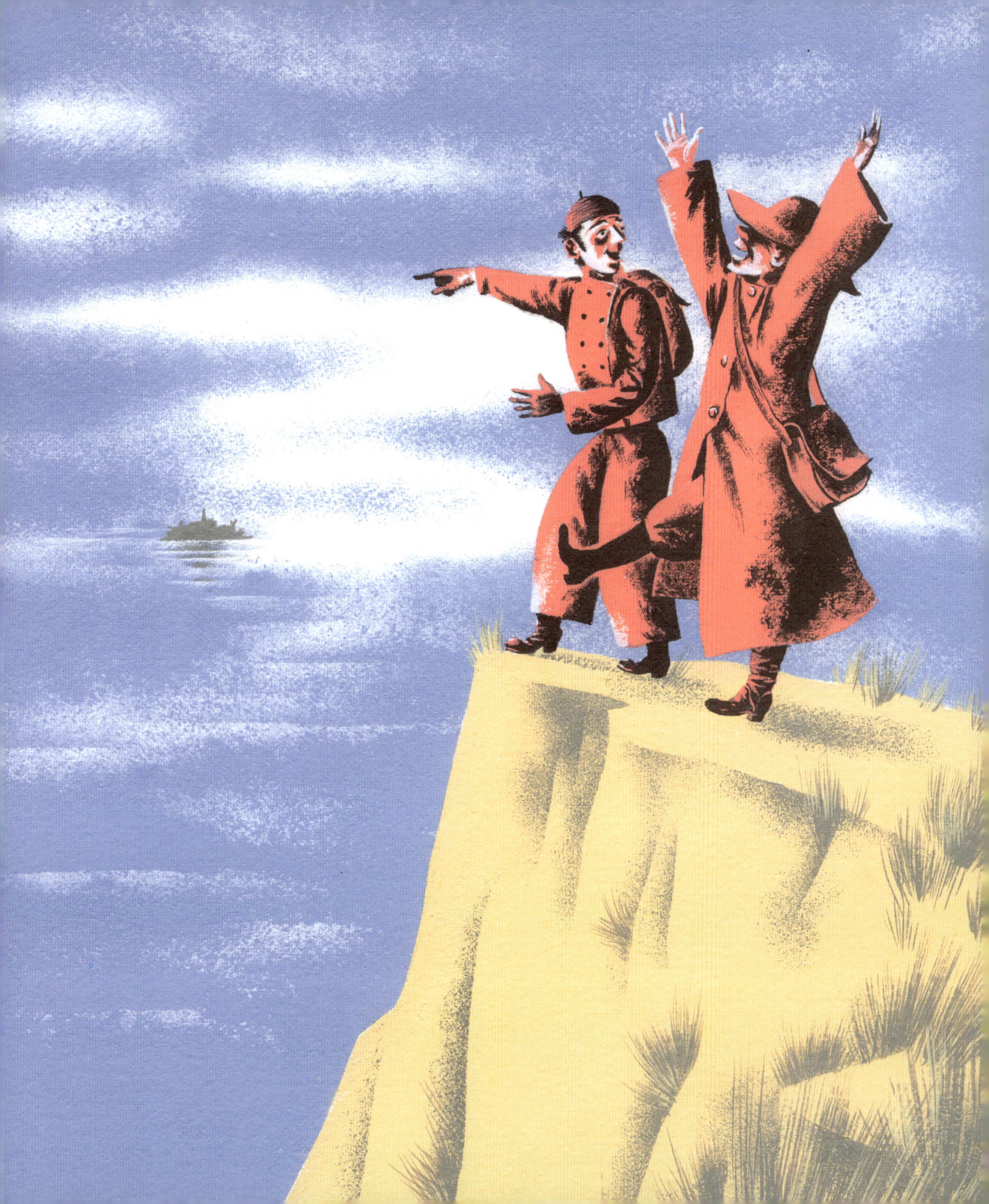

A Peek into the Kitchen

Artists seldom divulge their secrets. They rarely talk about their techniques and almost never write books about how their pictures are made. What a pity! Because when I look back on my student days, I really would have enjoyed reading books by my favourite artists so I could, in a way, watch them at work.

That's why *Rediscovering Gouache* is intended as a gift to the young art student who didn't have a book like this. And especially to you, who hopefully could use a few tips on gouache painting here and now. It may sound paradoxical for an author, but I believe that you only learn from books to a limited extent. Yet I firmly believe that learning with a book and a pen (or a brush in this case) in one's hand can work just fine.

Be inspired by what you discover in this book and if a particular technique appeals to you, try it out. Feel free to copy, in other words, fake it till you make it! And if it helps you make better pictures, it'll make the world a little bit more beautiful. And so that you understand how the book is structured, I'm offering up a little analogy from the kitchen. If this was a cookbook, say, about baking (and painting is only slightly different from cooking or baking) I would explain the structure of the book like this:

Part I: The introduction explains why people like to bake and all the delicious things that have been produced from dough since ancient times. Famous bakers.

Part II: Materials. Here we'll walk through the kitchen; you'll learn the proper ingredients for the dough and about special baking trays, rolling pins and ovens as well as how to use them and where to buy them.

Part III: First steps. Tips on how to optimally design your workplace so that baking is really fun. It's also about planning the process.

Part IV: Techniques. Baking bread, cakes, crepes, cookies, pies and pierogi. This is where you'll learn about different types of baking and their combinations.

Part V: Tips from the chef. Here are some recipes with step-by-step instructions and tips on how to make quick progress in baking.

And one more brief comment before we begin: Everything in this book is true because it comes from practice. But it's also quite subjective because it comes from me. That's why I'm sure that you will gradually fill up this book, which is filled with my pictures, with your own. And now–have fun, enjoy gouache!

Aljoscha Blau

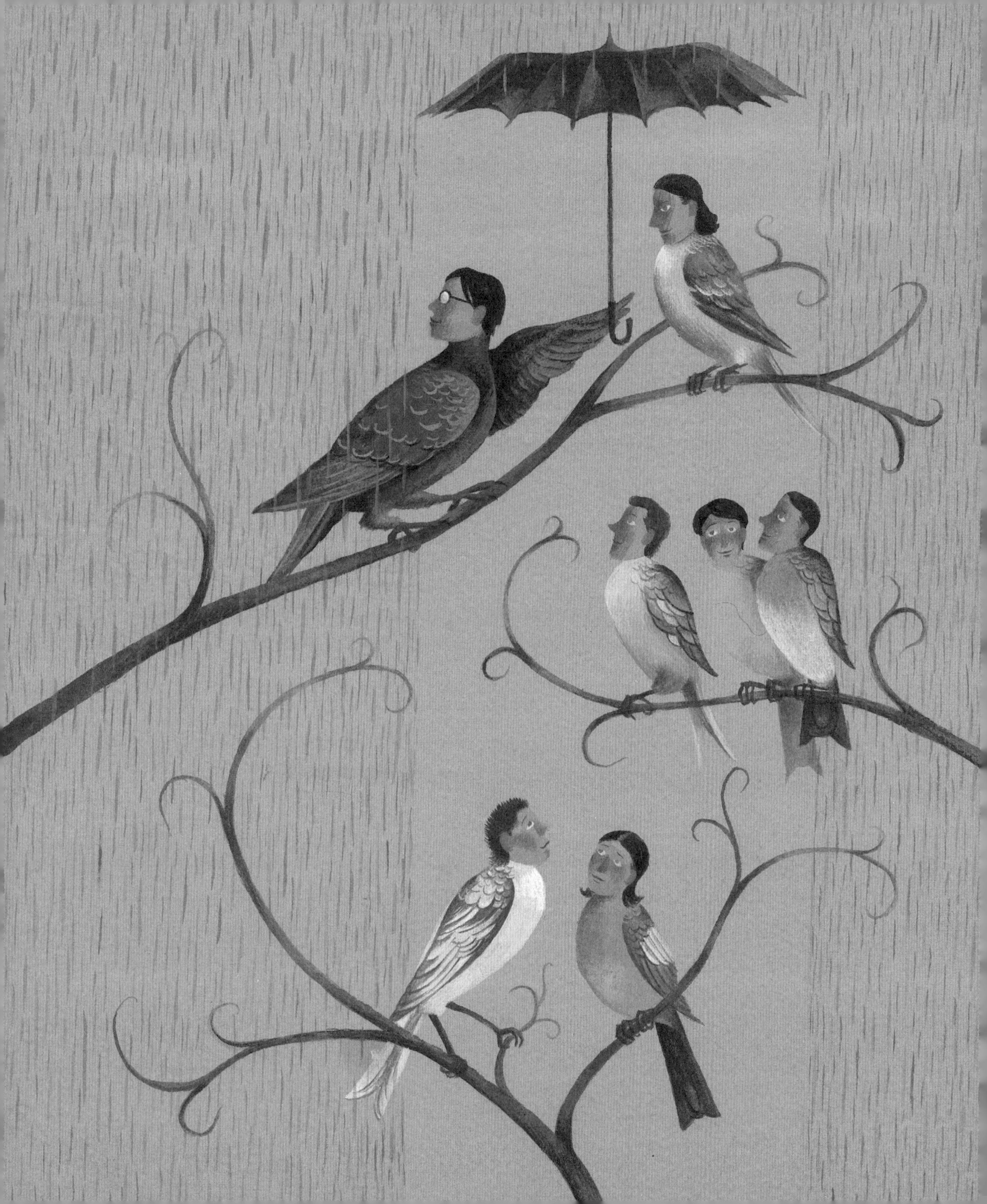

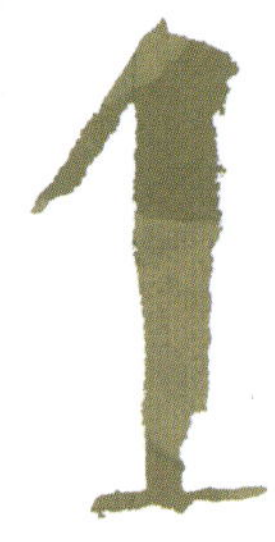

What is Gouache? The basics for pros and amateurs

The Nitty-Gritty. Materials

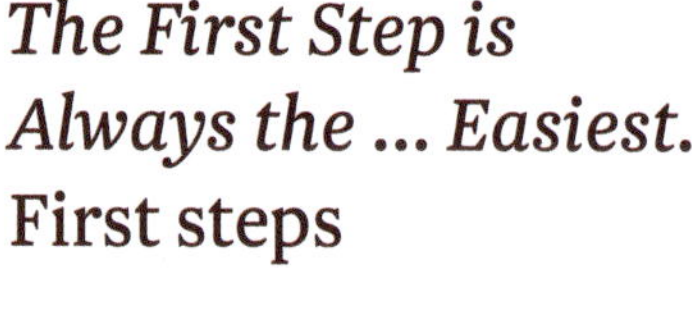

The First Step is Always the ... Easiest. First steps

Nothing is Impossible. Gouache techniques

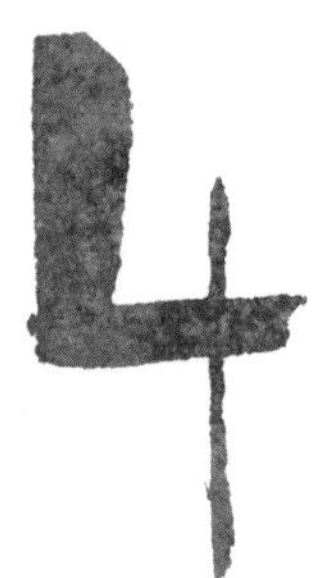

Portrait of a Banana Tree. Apply and develop

5

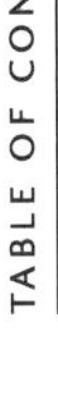

What is Gouache? The basics for pros and amateurs

How do you pronounce "gouache"? What was gouache paint made of in the past and today? Where did artists of all eras employ gouache? Answers to these questions and lots of important facts about gouache can be found in this chapter.

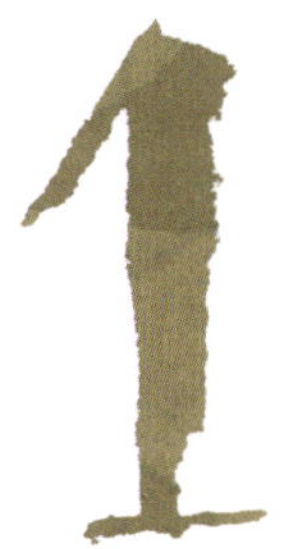

The other watercolour. Balancing act of composition: Pigments, gum arabic & co

Gouache is my absolute favourite technique. It's been around since people were writing scriptures on parchment skins and illustrating them, and had portraits of their loved ones painted on tiny medallions. Gouache is paint for the delicate – old and modern masters like Dürer, Matisse and Chagall painted in this technique and also appreciated its finesses. Children usually make their first painting attempts with these paints because no prior knowledge is needed to enjoy painting with it. And despite all the gouache paintings already painted, just as many are still waiting to be painted!

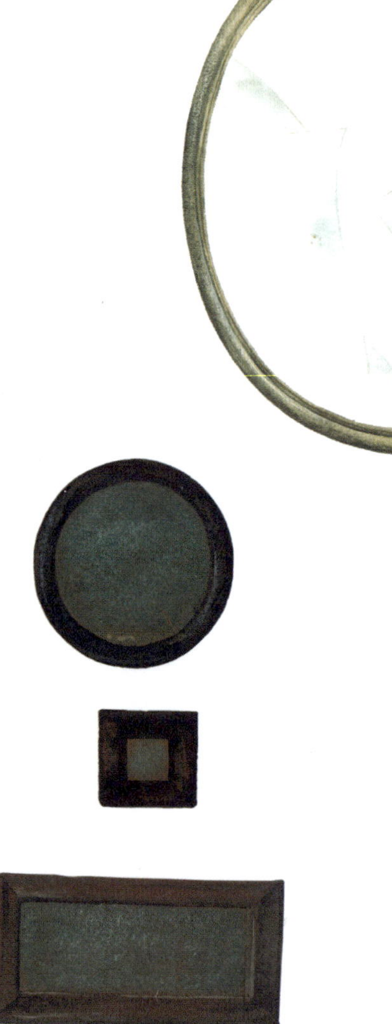

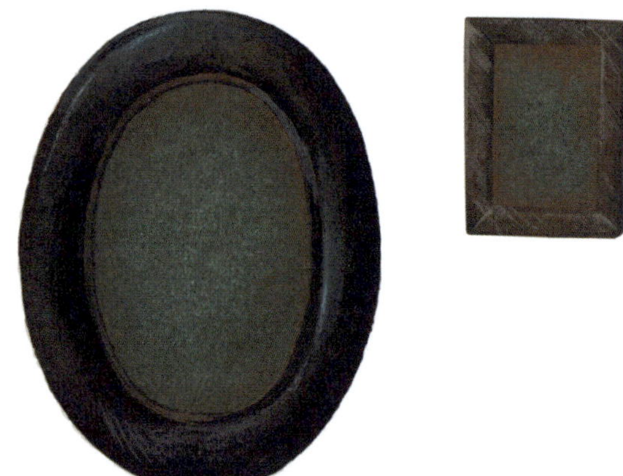

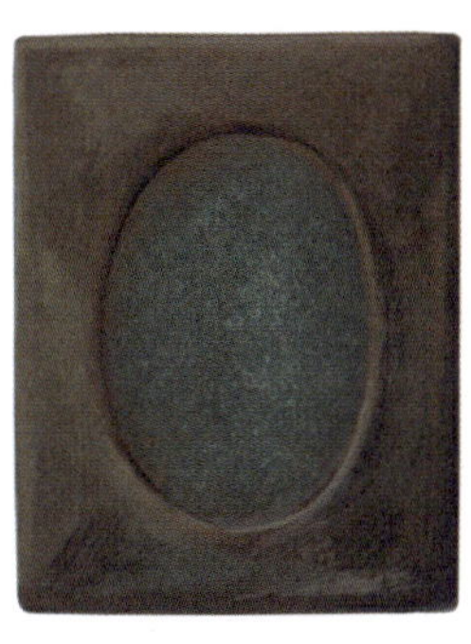
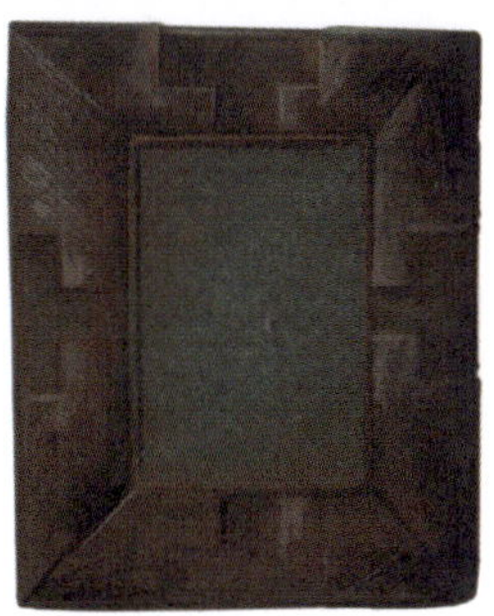
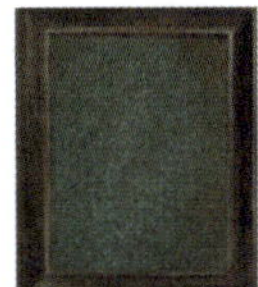
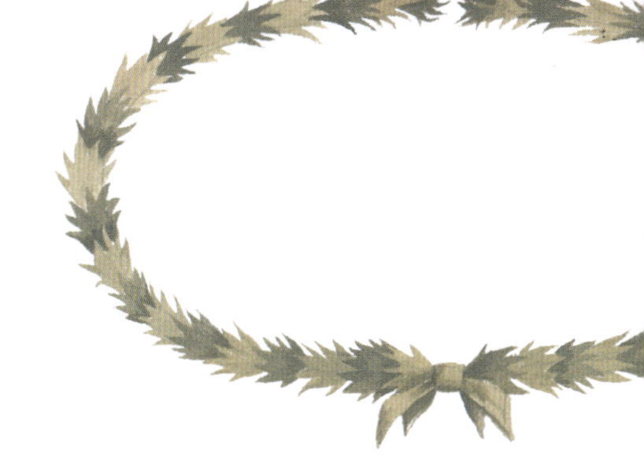

Composition

When we speak about a single painting technique through an entire book, it's important to talk about the terminology right from the start. Gouache, pronounced **[gu:aʃ]**, is the name for opaque watercolours with gum arabic as a binder. Most manufacturers also mix chalk or kaolin with the pigments to increase opacity. The hygroscopic addition of propylene glycol or glycerine is also a characteristic of some paints. In the past, honey was mixed into the paints instead of glycerine so that they dry more smoothly. It's an all-round sensitive matter and like for perfumes, no manufacturer will tell us their exact recipes. So when choosing paints we can only rely on empirical comparisons, manufacturer information and, of course, our budget.

In Part Two of this book we will try out the most important gouache brands and examine their behaviours and properties. But first of all, you need to know that real gouache usually differs from inexpensive school watercolours in that it contains more colour pigments and no cheap binders and extenders, such as dextrin and starch. This is reflected in the price, but also in the properties. Paints of so-called "academy" or "student quality" are made to appeal to beginners or hobby painters. High quality gouache for professionals is offered in "artist quality."

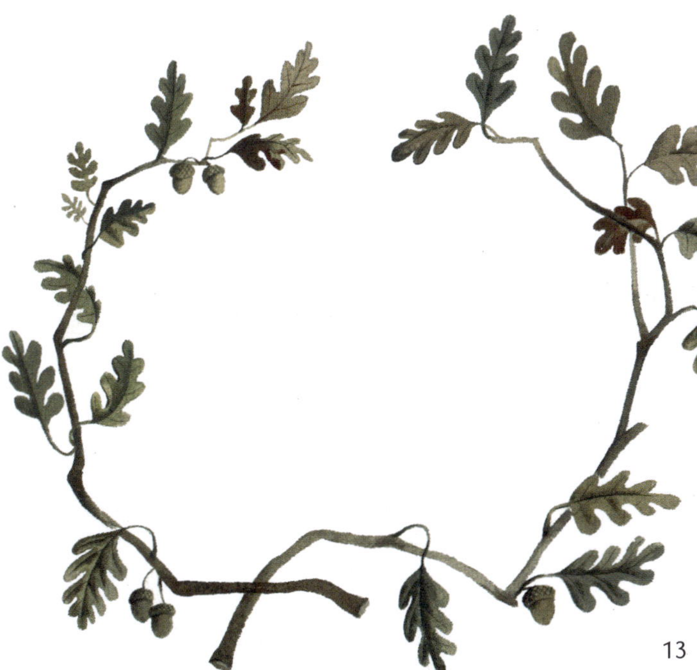

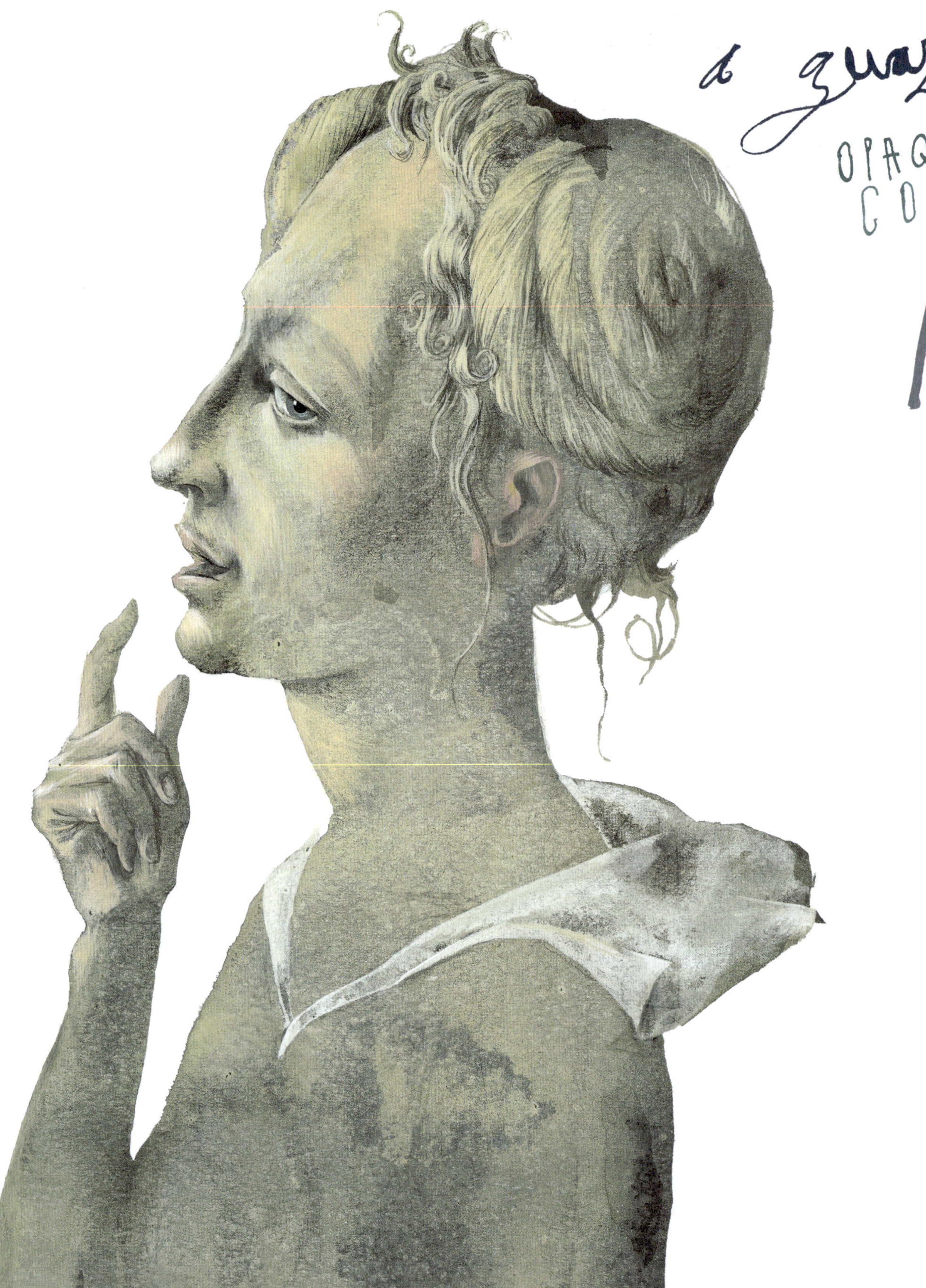
OPAQUE

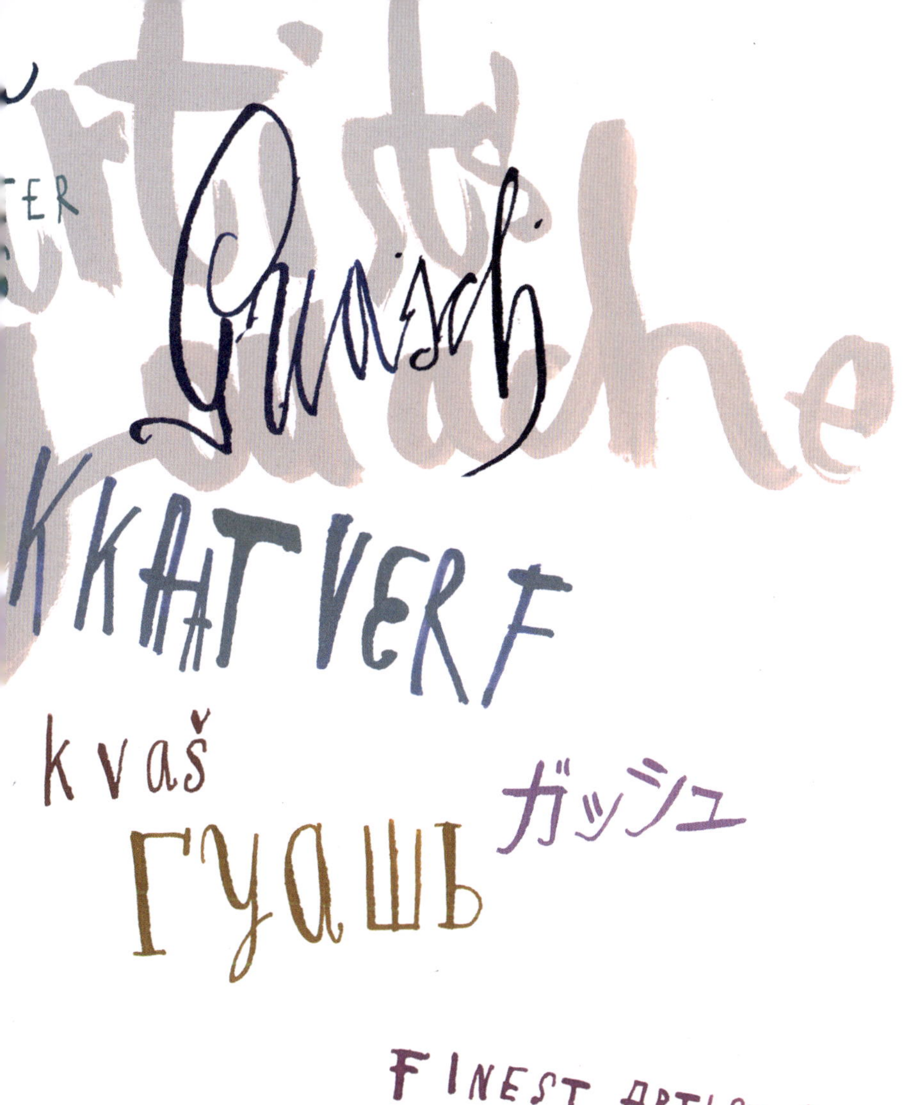

A guazzo

It's not precisely documented, but most art historians suggest that the original French term gouache was derived from *guazzo* (Italian for puddle, pool). Some think it is related to wash. At any rate, it's clear that any plausible etymology of the word should include the reference to water. Anyone researching further mentions of the Italian word will encounter reports by the two great Renaissance chroniclers Giorgio Vasari and Paolo Pino.

In the mid-sixteenth century, they actually used the term a guazzo to describe painting with watery glue- or plant-based opaque paints. The technique, which is quite inferior to Italian oil painting, was used for landscapes or festive decorations by artists *oltramontani*, or "beyond the mountains." This mainly referred to Dutch and German artists, from whom their Italian counterparts adopted the technique. Although "gouache" or "gouaches" was the name in common use since the nineteenth century to describe painting with opaque watercolours and opaque white, it took until the 1930s before the opaque watercolours used for art and design were manufactured under this name by Winsor & Newton.

GOUACHE

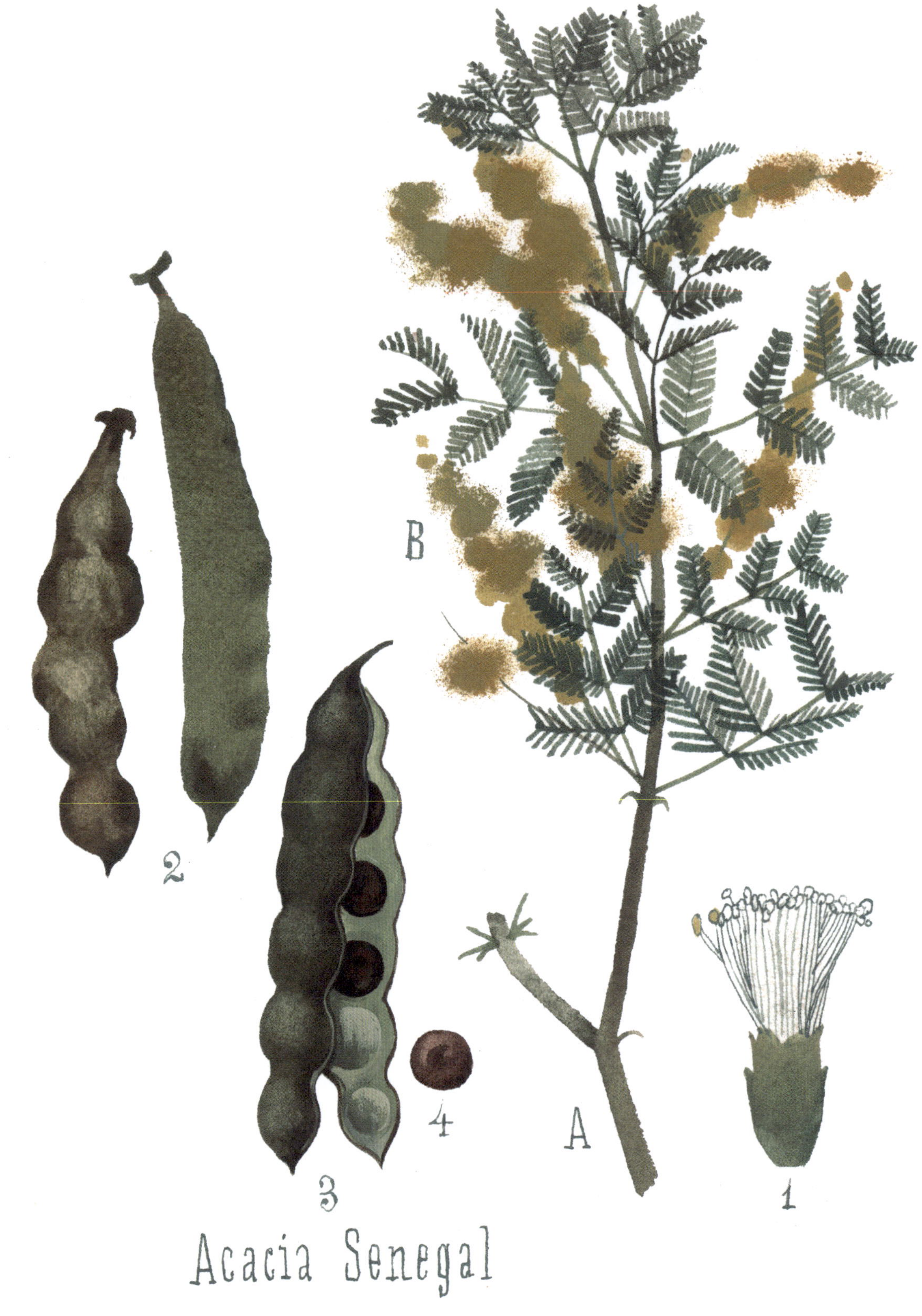
B
2
3
4
A
1
Acacia Senegal

A unique sap

"Acacia gum" or gum arabic is used for the production of premium quality gouache. This substance, essential for gouache and watercolours, is the dried sap of a few African acacia varieties. It is collected by scratching the bark and gathering the resin that drips out. It is transparent, well soluble in water, non-toxic and has no taste. Even in biblical times, this tree sap saved the people of Israel from starvation when they left Egypt. The same substance feeds us today as food additive E414. We encounter it daily in gummy bears, biscuits, but also in medicinal pills. It glues our envelopes and cigarette papers together and has been used as a binder for watercolours for at least two thousand years.

Much has been tried, but so far there is no synthetic substitute that is of a similar quality and comparably priced. When a discussion broke out among Italian artists about suitable binders for watercolours in 1598, it was decided that of all the gums that were known, it was unsurpassed.

Thus gum arabic prevailed in cultural history and won out over other plant and animal glues such as cherry-tree gum, tragacanth, dextrin or rabbit-skin glue. The best gum arabic comes from the Acacia senegal from Sudan, all other varieties are less popular and are obtained in other African countries in the Sahel from Senegal to Somalia. They only cost a quarter of the price of real gum arabic resin.

The light colour, adhesive strength and odourlessness of the solution are decisive for quality and price. When there were bottlenecks in the supply of gum arabic in European history, for example over a long period during the Second World War, the paint manufacturers replaced it with inferior cherry-tree gum or potato starch.

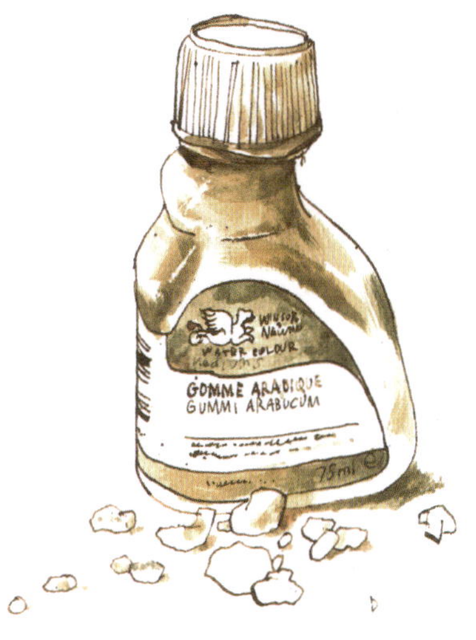

Almost half of the world's gum arabic production comes from the Sudanese war zone of Darfur. When the United States imposed economic sanctions on Sudan in 1997, it soon, under pressure from industry, had to make an exception for the natural resin. Rumour has it that the embargo primarily endangered the supply to Coca-Cola plants.

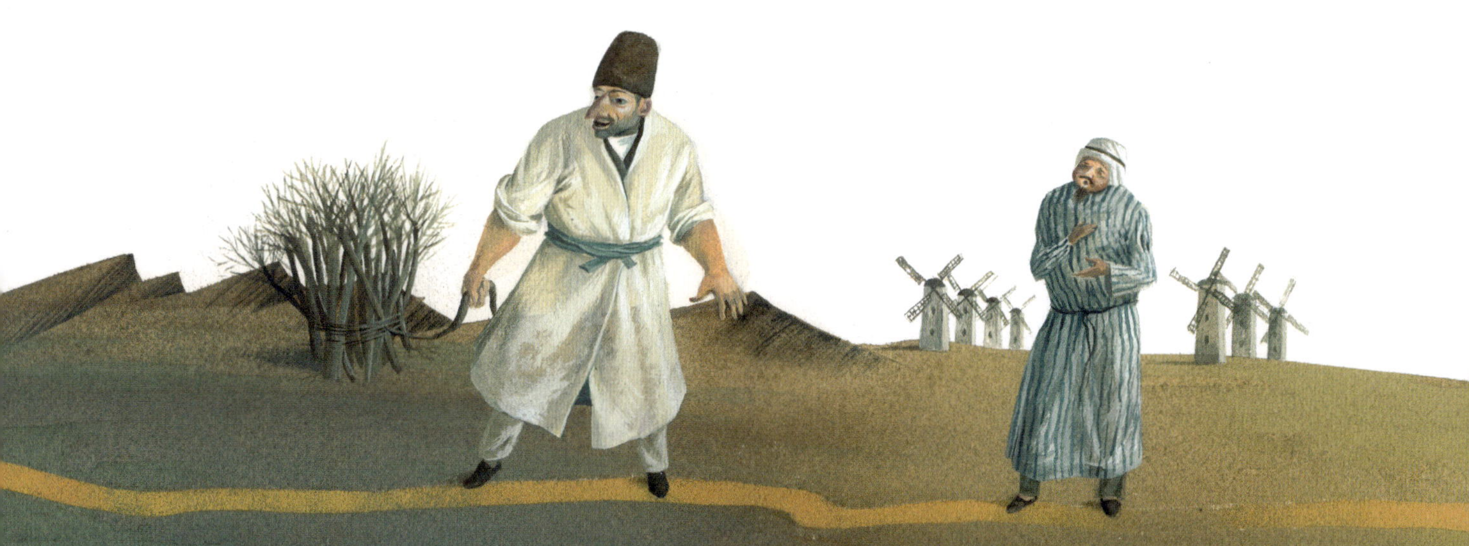

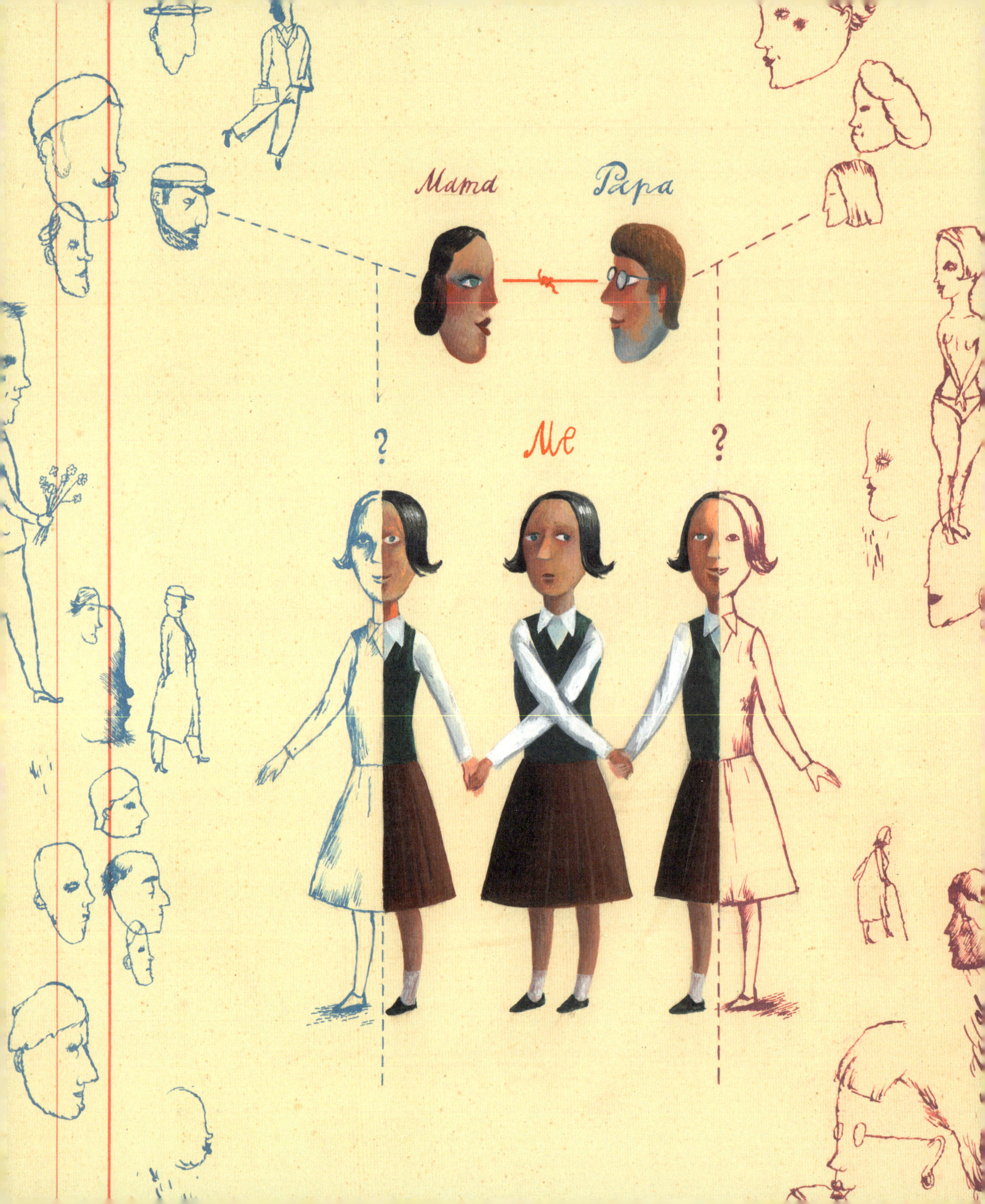
Mama
Papa
Me
?
?

Siblings and cousins.
Gouache vs. other paints: Watercolour, acrylic, tempera, oil and pastel

> *"...pure watercolour with strict avoidance of white is practiced little more these days; it was in fashion in the 1860s and 1870s. The English, in particular, had achieved great perfection in it. We prefer gouache. This type of painting uses the opaque white together with the watercolour paints. This is mixed in everywhere, giving such a picture a chalky, dry character. It is lustreless and doesn't rely on sidelight, as oil painting mainly is..."*
>
> LOVIS CORINTH *"Das Erlernen der Malerei" (Learning to Paint), 1920*

My artistic "evolution" – at least as far as the use of watercolours is concerned – was not much different from the history of this technique in the nineteenth century as described by Lovis Corinth. At the time, I really didn't care whether the painting technique we used in the preparatory courses for the art academy in the Soviet Union were categorized more as "gouache" or "watercolour." A watercolour box and a large tin of opaque white – it was only watercolours that we grappled with three times a week. It's astonishing, but the strict division between watercolour and gouache taken for granted today has only been around for a short time. Specifically since 1804, when the British Society of Painters in Watercolours included in its statutes that only pictures that were painted without opaque white or other opaque colours are considered true "watercolours" and can thus be accepted in their exhibitions. However, many artists continued and enjoyed painting with opaque watercolours, which were called "body colours" to distinguish them. And while watercolour painting became a highly respected occupation in England, gouache played an important role particularly in France and especially in poster art at the end of the nineteenth century.

What exactly is its relationship with other painting techniques? What is the difference between them and gouache? Some basic information will help here.

Watercolour

is the closest relative, you could almost say a twin sister of gouache. Since the same gum arabic binder is included in both paints, the difference is in other details. The pigments in watercolour paints are more finely ground, but their proportion is much higher in gouache. Because of this, and also thanks to the mixed opaque white or chalk, gouache paints achieve an opacity that is completely lacking in watercolours.

Acrylic paint

arrived in the middle of the twentieth century as a new alternative to existing painting techniques. Acrylic quickly became popular (both among hobby artists and professionals) and supplanted, albeit not entirely, traditional and complex techniques such as gouache or oil paints. Like gouache, acrylic can be applied both in glazed layers (usually with the addition of the acrylic binder) and opaque. The main difference to gouache, however, is that the acrylic paints become completely waterproof after drying and form an elastic, plastic-like layer. An acrylic painting dries comparatively quickly, but not as quickly as a gouache, and can withstand an almost infinite amount of overpainting.

Tempera

is a collective term for many, sometimes very old painting techniques that are still known to us from antiquity, for example from the mummy portraits of Fajum. The term comes from temperare, which in Latin means temper or moderate. In order to produce these colours, oily and watery substances are "tempered" to an emulsion that by nature cannot last long. With egg tempera it is egg yolk with linseed oil and water, with casein tempera it is the casein made from milk by denaturation, mild lye and water. These colours dry very quickly and become more and more water-insoluble over time. Before oil painting gradually replaced tempera around 1500, it was the most popular technique of the late Middle Ages and the Renaissance. For example, most of Botticelli's pictures were painted in tempera.

Pastel

is also an important painting technique, although it is a "dry" technique. In the production of pastel chalks, the pigments are first ground, then soaked in binders and pressed into sticks. White chalk or kaolin is also added, just as with gouache. This also explains the relationship and visual similarity of the pictures in both techniques; the dull surface and the "pastel" of the colours are created by the added chalk. This "softness" is very typical for both pastel and gouache.

Oil

Linseed oil is the eponymous binder for oil paints, which is why these paints have almost nothing in common with gouache. Developed in the Middle Ages, this technique took several centuries to replace tempera as the supreme discipline of painting, first in Northern Europe, the Netherlands and only later in Italy. The techniques of oil painting are very complex. Traditionally it is begun with a primer, followed by a preparatory coat, which is often done in tempera or gouache. This is used to sketch out the lighting conditions and the general atmosphere in earth tones. From this basis, the painter works both to the light and to the dark: a technique that we use in a similar way with gouache. Only then are many colour glazes applied. Since oil paints take a very long time to dry, it can take several months to create a painting.

One stunning example of such a preparatory work is Leonardo's "The Adoration of the Magi," an unfinished painting in the Uffizi Gallery, which fortunately for us never got beyond the background coat. Here we can see how an oil painting is created from a huge painted drawing. From rough sketches to detailed but monochrome figures, we can see all the steps that the painter has gone through.

→ TIP: If your paint jar says both gouache and tempera, one of the terms is guaranteed to be out of place. But it's not difficult to tell the two techniques apart. Tempera is always based on a "temporary" oil-water mixture. This is where the name comes from, which means a "tempered," that is, moderate and short-lived mixture. Paints that are bound with gum arabic – gouache and watercolours – contain neither emulsion nor fat. They therefore have nothing in common with "tempera."

Comparison chart
Gouache / Acrylic / Tempera / Oil / Pastel / Watercolour

	GOUACHE	ACRYLIC	TEMPERA	OIL	PASTEL	WATERCOLOUR
How difficult is it to learn the painting technique?	▲▲	▲▲	▲▲▲▲	▲▲▲▲▲	▲▲▲	▲▲▲
How sensitive are pictures painted using this technique?	▲▲▲	▲	▲▲	▲	▲▲▲▲▲	▲▲
How expensive are the paints?	▲▲	▲▲▲▲	▲▲▲	▲▲▲▲▲	▲▲	▲▲▲
How harmful is the painting technique to the environment and health?	▲	▲▲	▲	▲▲▲▲	▲	▲

Not very much ▲
Very much ▲▲▲▲▲

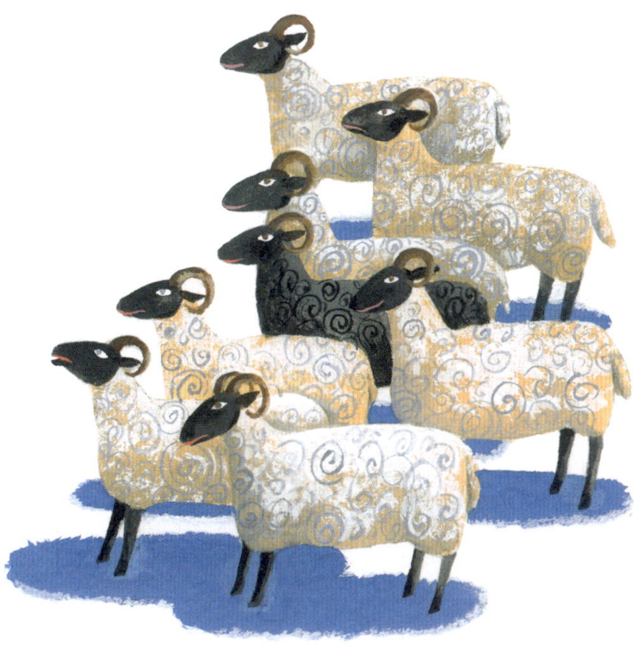

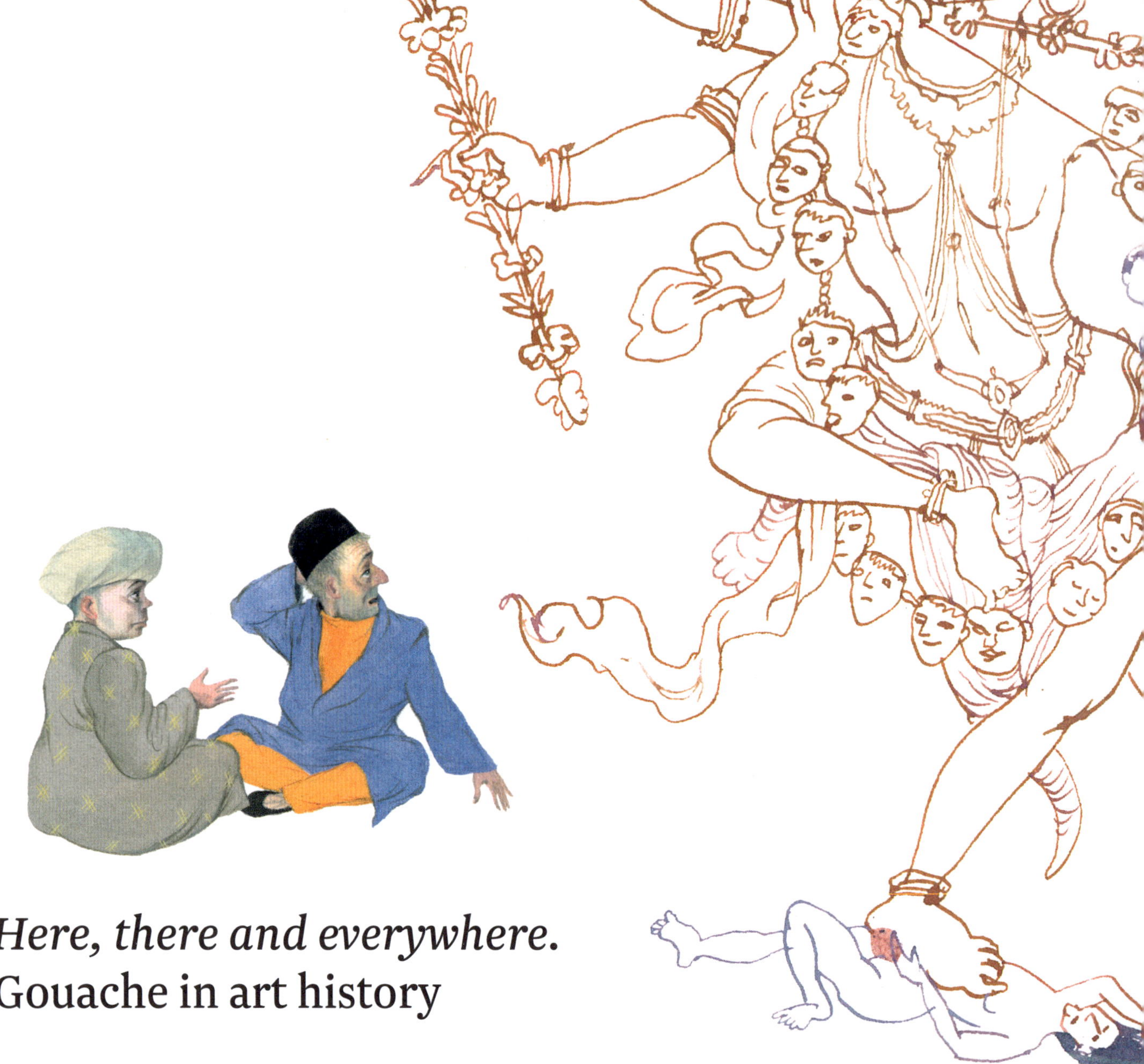

Here, there and everywhere. Gouache in art history

People were painting with opaque watercolours, which we now refer to as gouache, long before many other painting techniques emerged. It happened in many corners of the world and independently. Sometimes it was done on parchment, sometimes on palm leaves and many of these pictures survived for hundreds of years.

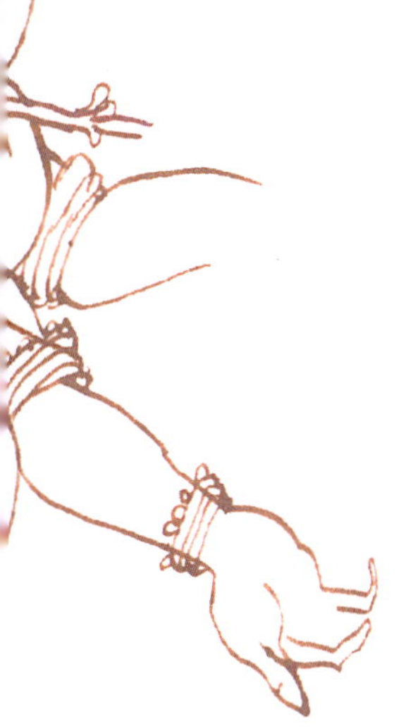

It is the turn of the millennium around 1000 AD. Long before oil, watercolour and certainly acrylic paints take to the stage and become popular, Buddhist monks in the Himalayas are working in great detail on thangka rolls with green, red or white taras. At the same time, monks of the Benedictine order are painting in the scriptoria of Piacenza and Monte Cassino with almost the same paints on large, lavishly illustrated Bibles and Alexander romances. When, beginning in the early Middle Ages, European artists used opaque and transparent watercolours to paint the Bible or books of hours, it was called "illuminating." The book illustrators at that time were mostly monks and were skilled not only in painting but in gilding and calligraphy. But what we admire beyond gold in the gorgeous Book of Kells and the Gutenberg Bible is consistently gouache.

Islamic book art also uses the same watercolours and has experienced several climaxes since its inception. Many religious, but also scientific works were illustrated – sometimes realistically and sometimes breathtakingly. The oldest surviving illustrated book is dated 1009 and is an astronomical treatise by Abd al-Rahman al-Sufi. But we think first of all of the beautiful gouaches in the books of the Persian masters. The heyday of the Persian miniature began around 1300 after the Mongol conquest of Baghdad. At that time, the spiritual and cultural centre of Islam shifted to Tabriz and Shiraz. Everything that comes later in Islamic miniature painting from India or the Ottoman Empire is significantly influenced by the Persian tradition, which originated in these two cities.

At the time of the Renaissance, gouache advanced to became more than it used to be – the preferred technique for miniatures. They are also beginning to use them for large paintings on cardboard, often as preparatory studies for oil paintings or to design festive decorations. But we also know of many independent gouache paintings by great artists from the time: for example the famous brown hare by Albrecht Dürer in the Albertina, probably the most famous gouache in the world!

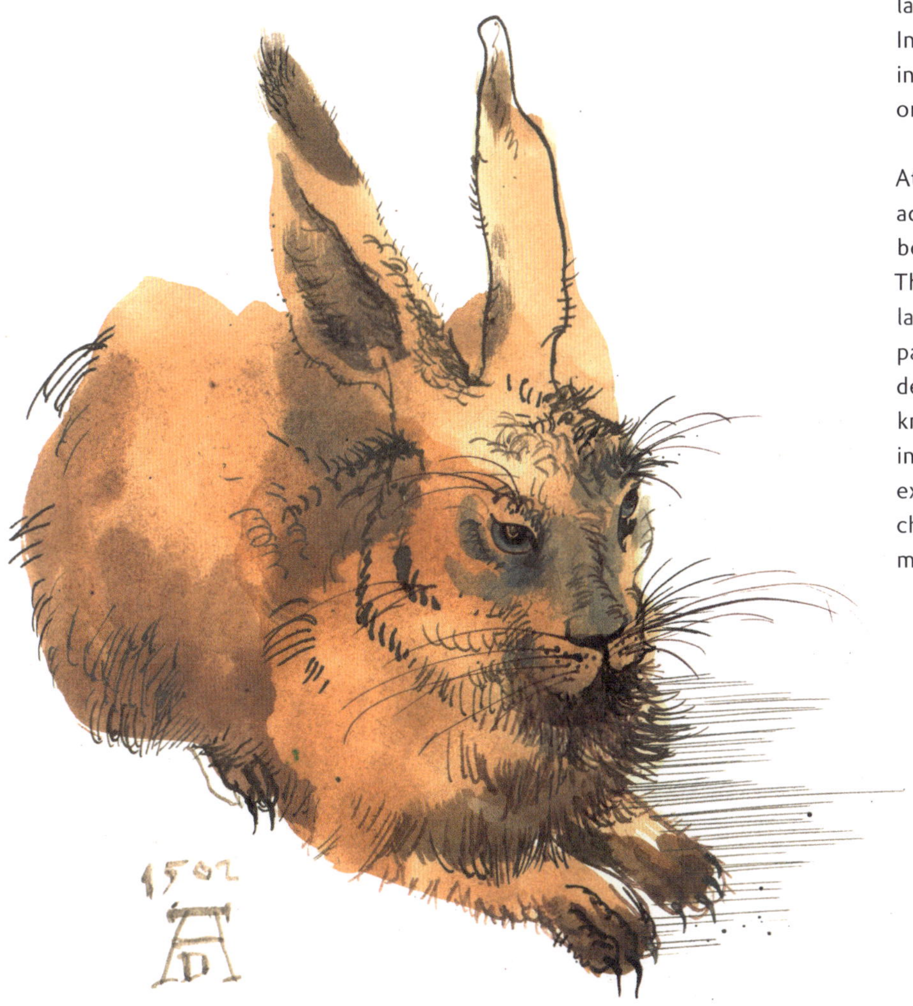

People continued to paint with gouache, but it would take centuries before the paints were produced under their current name and in the form we know. Until the end of the eighteenth century, artists used their watercolours in the form of a "cake" that they dipped into water and then rubbed bits into a suitable container, such as an oyster shell. Starting in 1830, porcelain bowls were used instead of shells. A small revolution occurred in 1846 when William Winsor, an artist with a scientific background, and water-colourist Henry Newton launched watercolours in metal tubes.

Another major innovation came from England when Winsor & Newton introduced their patented zinc oxide pigment called "Chinese White." This fine permanent colour increased the popularity of gouache among artists. William Turner, Peter de Wint and William Blake are a few of the British painters who experimented a great deal with watercolours and gouache.

Looking at nineteenth century Germany, Adolf von Menzel was the greatest master of gouache there. The painter always studied his surroundings in drawings and used the rapid technique of gouache in the time before photography to record his spontaneous ideas and observations of his hometown of Berlin, fellow citizens, as well as animals as in his "Children's Album." Lovis Corinth said of him, "Menzel accomplished his greatest achievements in gouache painting... I myself have always remembered one of his own hands, holding the ink cup, as one of the greatest masterpieces of our time."

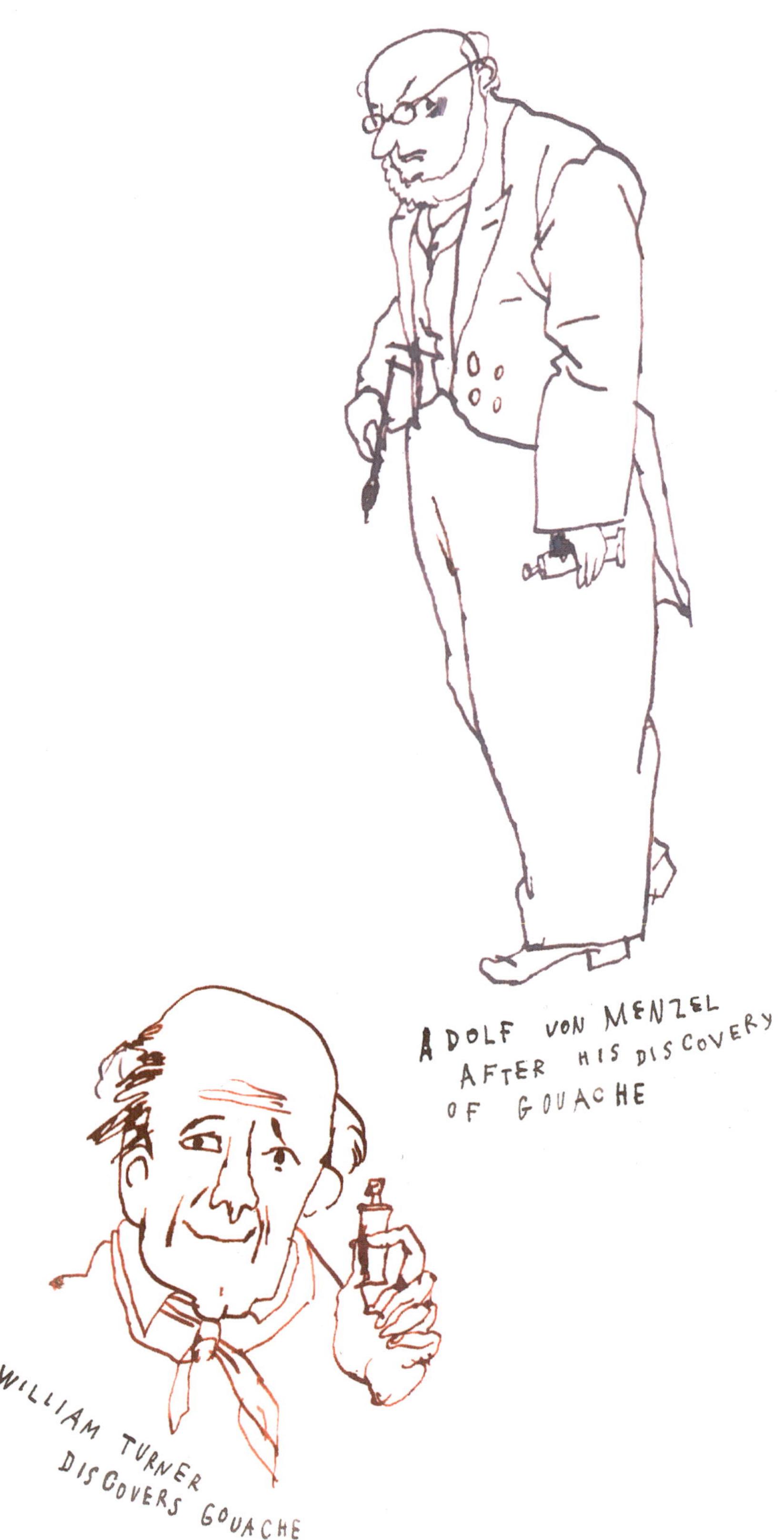

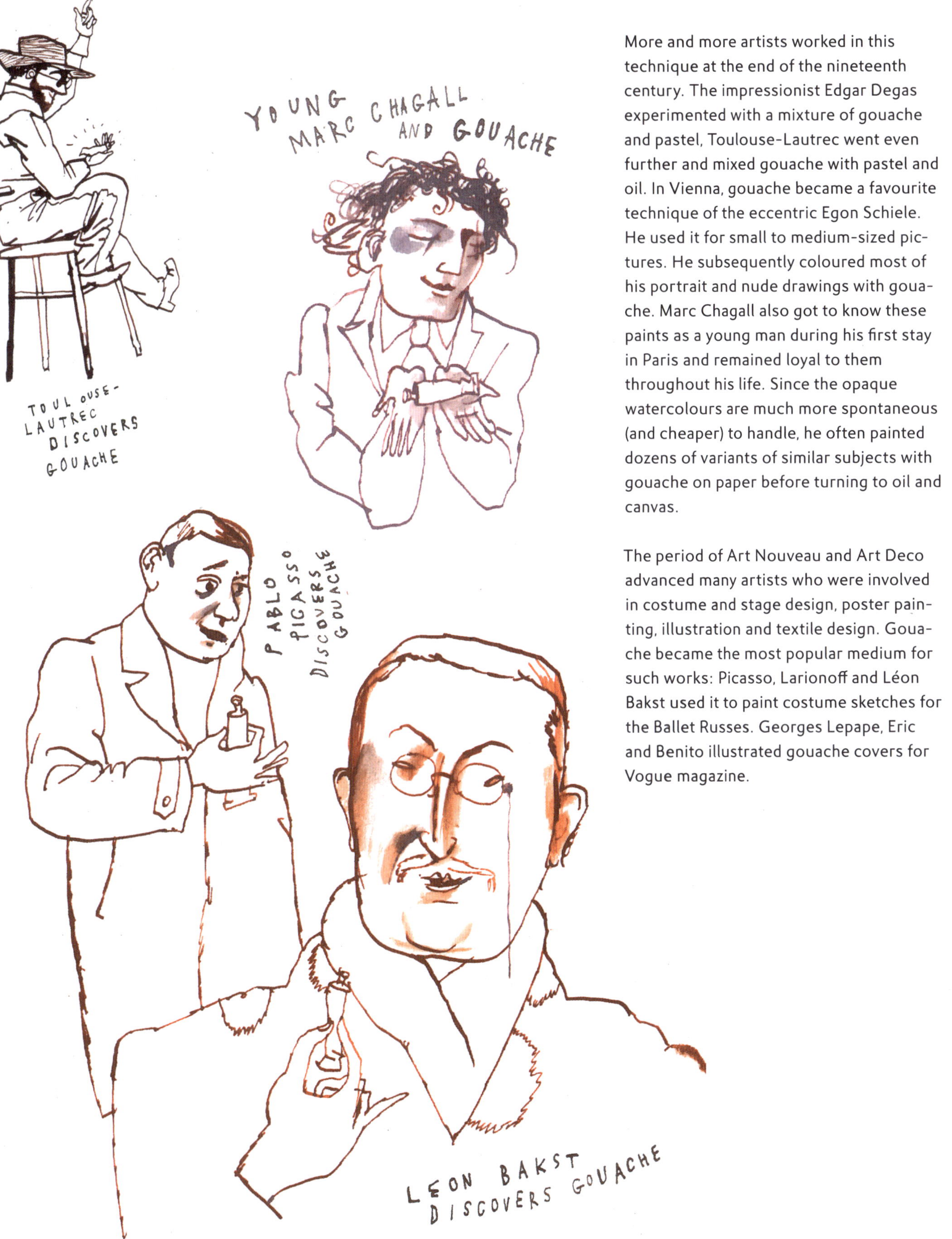

More and more artists worked in this technique at the end of the nineteenth century. The impressionist Edgar Degas experimented with a mixture of gouache and pastel, Toulouse-Lautrec went even further and mixed gouache with pastel and oil. In Vienna, gouache became a favourite technique of the eccentric Egon Schiele. He used it for small to medium-sized pictures. He subsequently coloured most of his portrait and nude drawings with gouache. Marc Chagall also got to know these paints as a young man during his first stay in Paris and remained loyal to them throughout his life. Since the opaque watercolours are much more spontaneous (and cheaper) to handle, he often painted dozens of variants of similar subjects with gouache on paper before turning to oil and canvas.

The period of Art Nouveau and Art Deco advanced many artists who were involved in costume and stage design, poster painting, illustration and textile design. Gouache became the most popular medium for such works: Picasso, Larionoff and Léon Bakst used it to paint costume sketches for the Ballet Russes. Georges Lepape, Eric and Benito illustrated gouache covers for Vogue magazine.

Since the mid-twentieth century, gouache has become THE paint for illustrators and book artists around the world. Not too long ago, Tomi Ungerer, Étienne Delessert, Eric Carle and Binette Schroeder; Maira Kalman, Igor Oleynikov and Rébecca Dautremer today (to name just a few great artists) use gouache in their very own way for artistic picture books. Today, when many illustrators work digitally, you can use painting and drawing programs like Procreate to produce very sophisticated gouache imitations with hundreds of different brushes and grounds.

Gouache is not just reserved for illustrators. Many contemporary artists continue to use this technique. Among the most important of them: David Hockney, who paints many of his portraits and large-scale landscapes with gouache and uses it for sketches and preliminary designs for his acrylic paintings. Canadian Marcel Dzama merges plants, animals and humans into small and subtle, mostly very surreal drawings. Walton Ford is an American artist who uses gouache to paint very large, bizarre, sometimes brutal animal allegories and provides them with stylized handwritten comments.

→ TIP: Don't throw away your sketches. I assure you, your friends, fellow artists, even collectors will often appreciate them much more than you think. David Hockney is paying attention. An approximately A3-sized gouache study for his famous "Pool with two Figures" was auctioned in 2016 for more than $2 million.

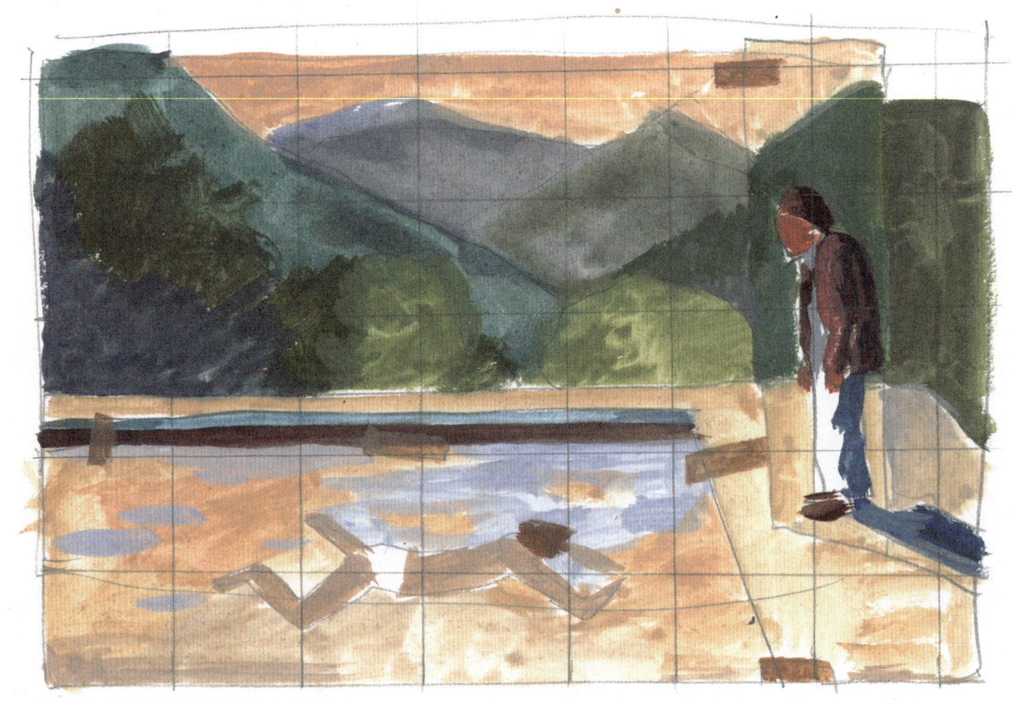

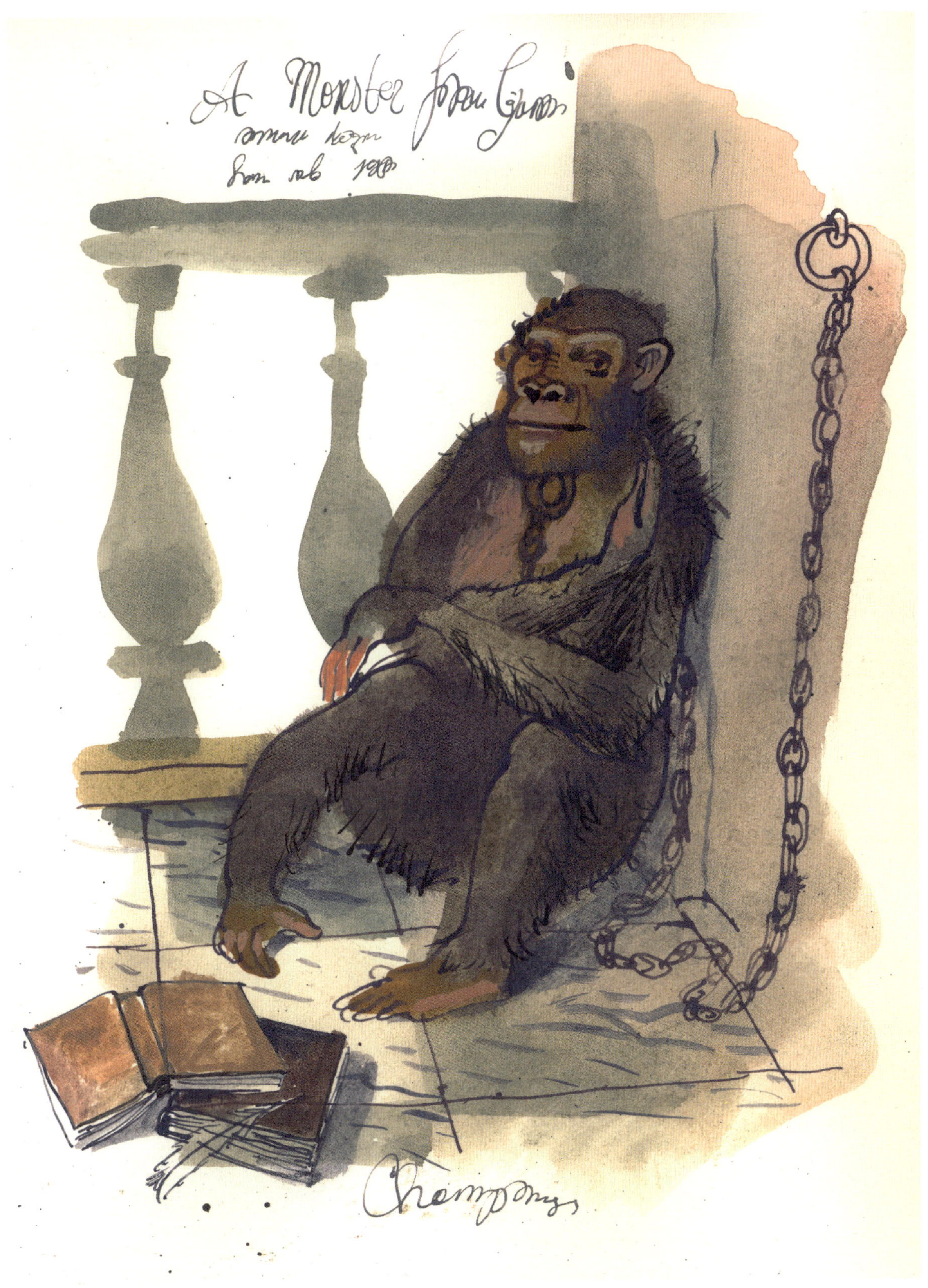
A Monster

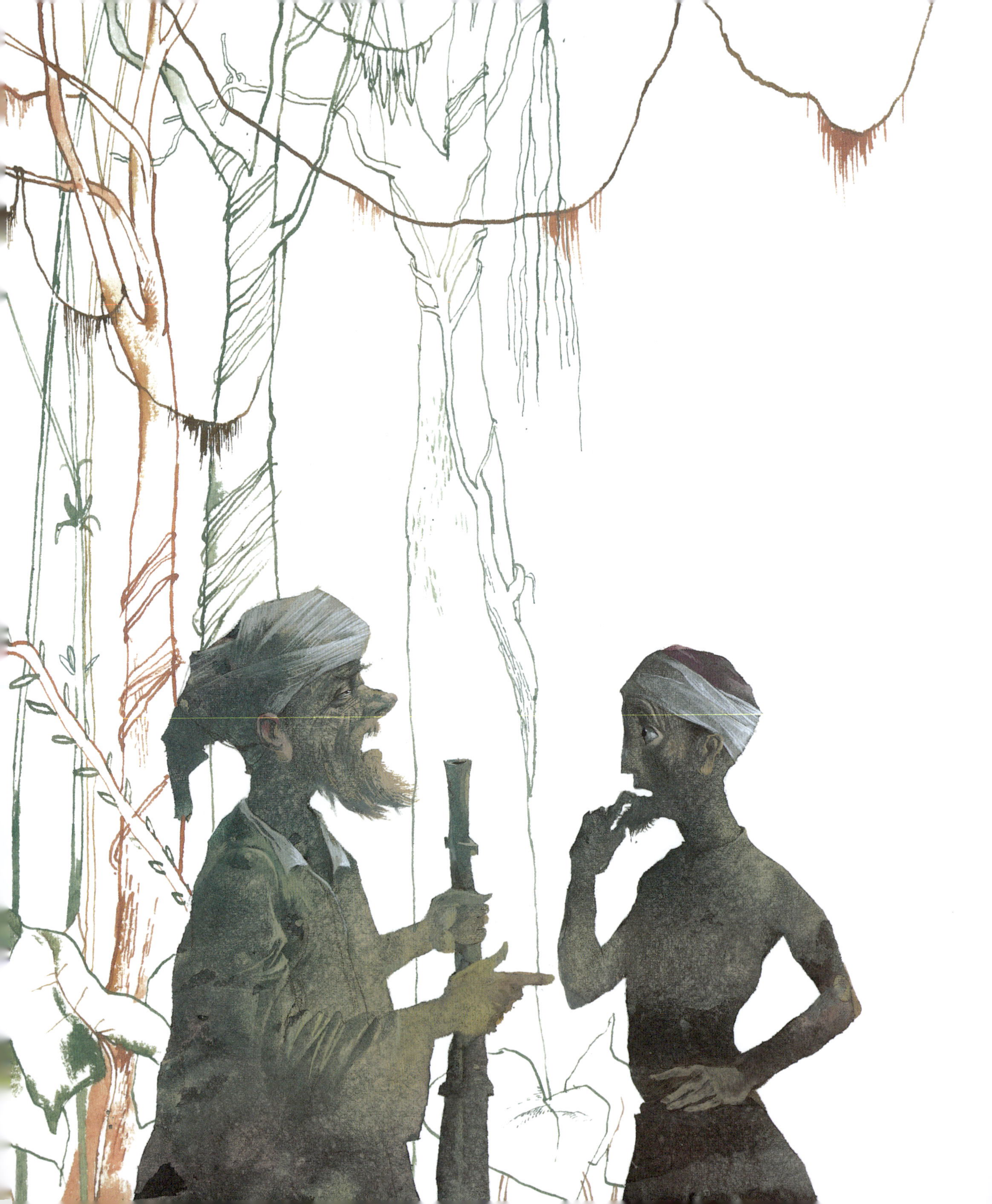

The gouache essentials at a glance

1. Changing consistency

You can dilute these paints with lots of water and apply them as a glaze, making them very similar to watercolours. If you use the paints when they're pasty and thick, you can paint in multiple opaque layers to cover the dark places with lighter ones.

2. Sensitivity

Gouache remains water-soluble after drying, so you can rework the dried paint layer, correct it or add to it.

3. Fast drying time

Compared to other paints – watercolour, acrylic and especially oil – gouache dries much faster. This makes it the favourite among artists who work outdoors and among professional cartoonists, illustrators and poster artists who work with deadlines and can't afford to wait weeks for paint to dry.

4. Details

Since the pigments are finely ground and the binder is very subtle, this technique allows us to achieve the finest details. This is one of the reasons that gouache became the preferred technique for portrait miniatures in the eighteenth and nineteenth centuries.

5. Dull surface

Due to the very high pigment content and the addition of opaque white or chalk, gouaches are characterized by their beautiful velvety surface, similar to pastel paintings. But just like pastels, they are very sensitive and difficult to fix.

6. Change of colours

Because of its chalk content, gouache often looks different after drying than when wet. Some bright colours darken and the dark colours lighten up a bit. The cheaper the paints, the more they lighten – because of the high proportion of extender, they change even more.

The Nitty-Gritty. Materials

This is where we take the necessary materials under the microscope. Which gouache brands are on the market? What are the key differences between them? Which utensils are essential and which are rarely used? First of all, we'll deal with the paints, paper and brushes. Then we'll explore other tools.

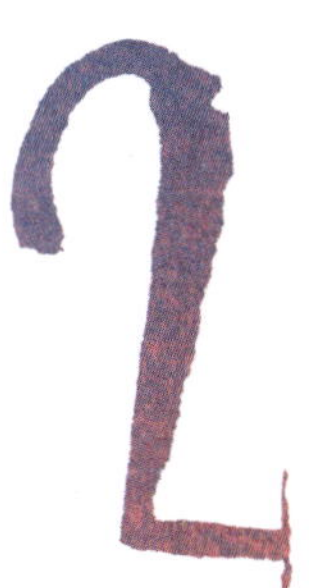

Top or flop. What makes good paints good?

First off, acceptable, "artist quality" gouache paints are never sold in 1-litre bottles at bargain basement prices. There's a lot that makes gouache fun to work with – its velvety surface, the even application, the glow of the highly pigmented colours or their high opacity. If we don't want to miss out on some or all of these great features, we shouldn't purchase cheap "student quality" paints. There are also opaque watercolours that you can call gouache under certain circumstances, but they are thinned with dextrose, kaolin, glycerol or starch and, unfortunately, contain little pigment. You'll have to dig deeper in your pockets, but it doesn't mean that the most expensive is always the best paint. What should we look for? What distinguishes good paints from those we should rather avoid? Let's go through the main features of gouache and how we can test it.

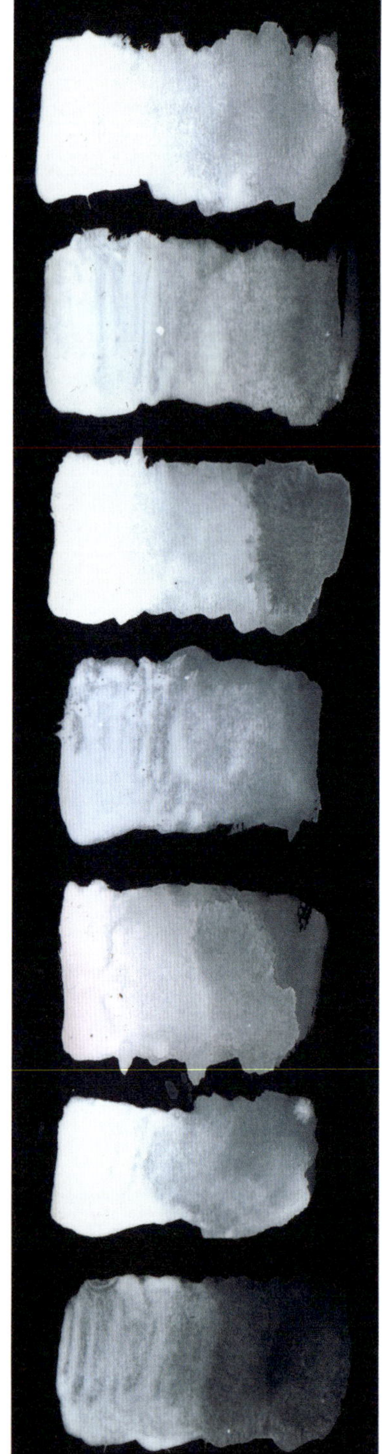

Royal Talens Deckweiss 106

Lascaux Weiss 327

Winsor & Newton Permanent white 512

Royal Talens Weiss 100

Holbein Permanent white G790

Schmincke Calligraphy SUPRA Deckweiß 101

Schmincke Akademie 100

Opacity

Gouache is an opaque watercolour. Therefore, *opacity* (covering power) is one of its most important characteristics. Good paints cover very well and not because they've been mixed with a lot of chalk or white parts, but because of a high concentration of real pigments. This concentration is much higher than in watercolours, for instance. To see how opaque one paint or another is you can try this test: Paint stripes over a black and white drawing or page of printed text and see if the drawing still shows through after drying. The opacity of different shades of white is best recognized by making stripes on black paper.

→ TIP: The most important thing in choosing the right paint brand is how it feels to you personally. The interaction of paint and paper, their smell and flow behaviour ... you can only discover all these features, and thus your favourite brand, through trial and error. So the decision as to what constitutes reasonable quality for you is always subjective. I always find it counterproductive if the paints are so inordinately expensive that you're too inhibited to even put them on paper. But it's just as little use when the paints are simply too dull or not opaque.

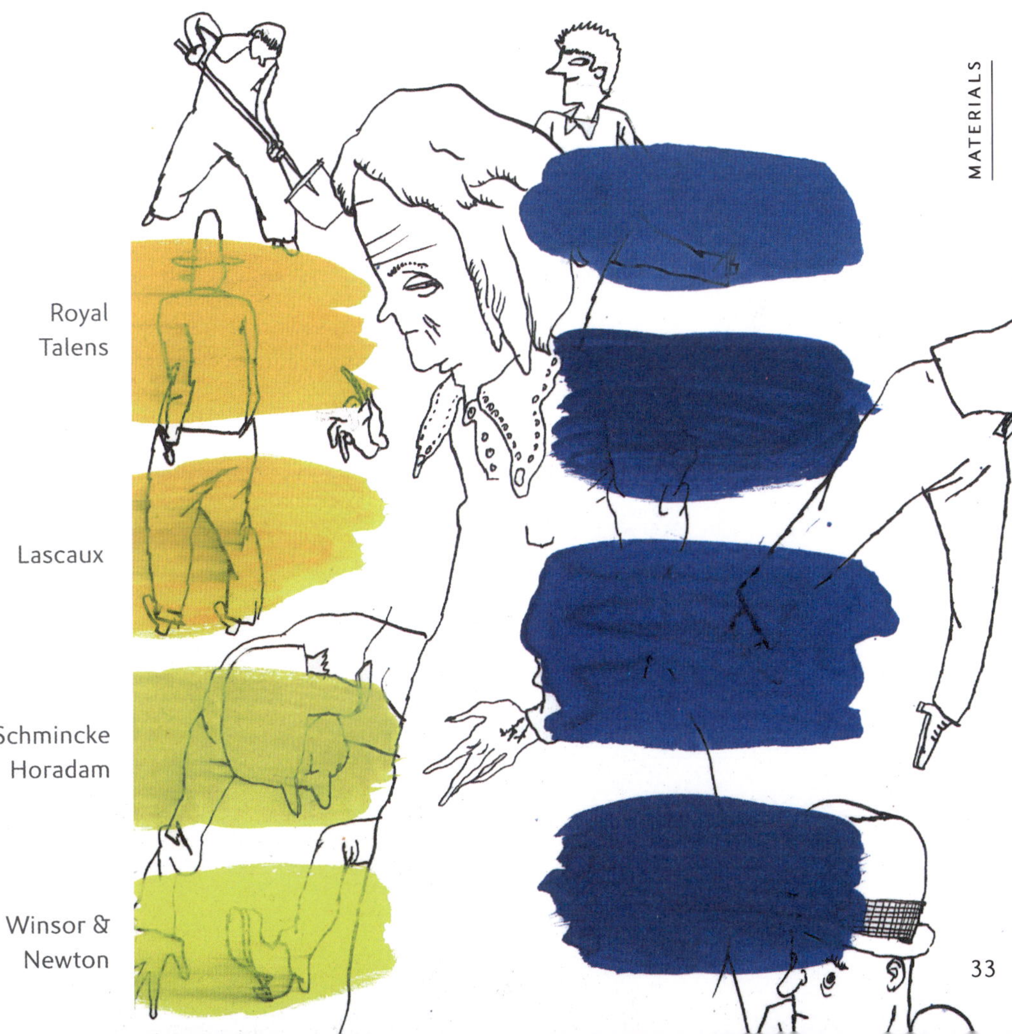

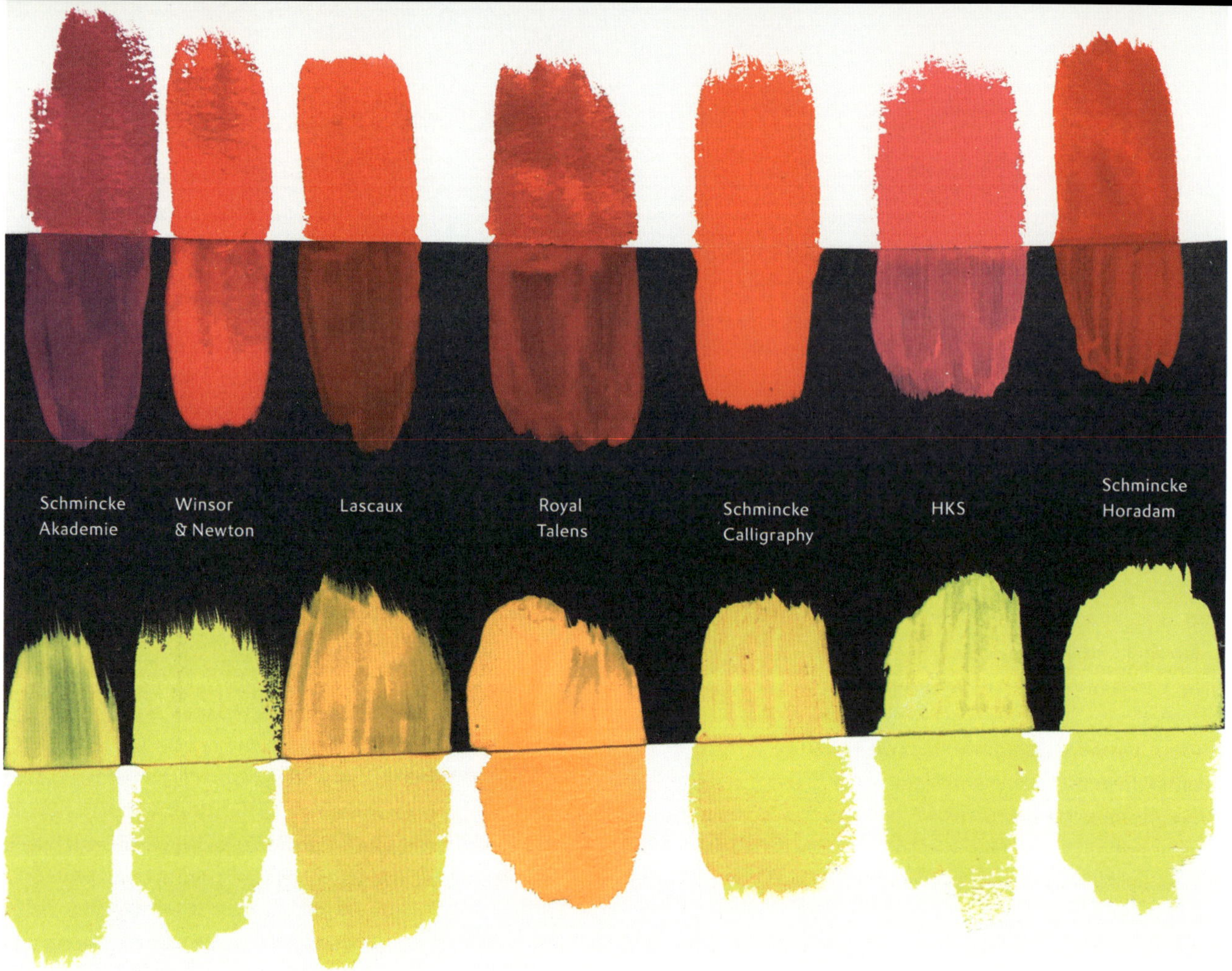

Schmincke Akademie

Winsor & Newton

Lascaux

Royal Talens

Schmincke Calligraphy

HKS

Schmincke Horadam

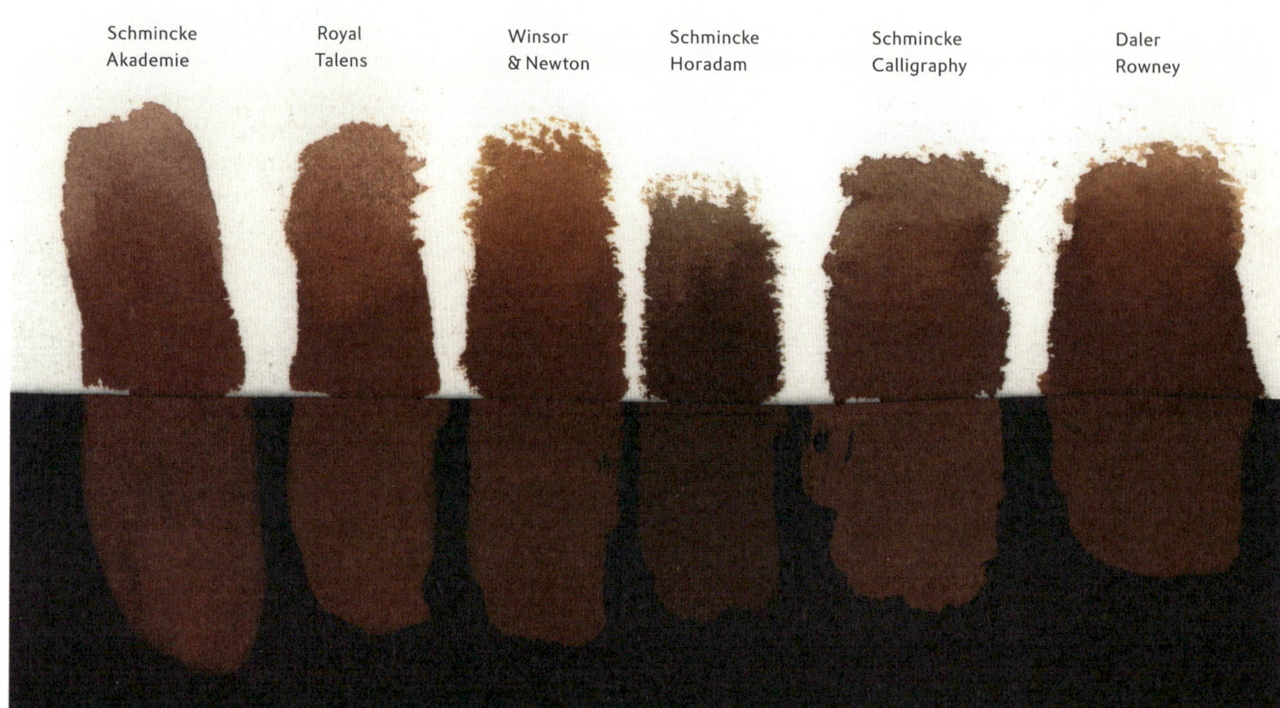

Brilliance

You can use another test to test how rich and bright the individual colours are. This characteristic is called brilliance. For testing, you can paint stripes over white (and definitely black) paper to see which of your paints have more luminosity. Good paints won't fade too much even after drying.

Lightfastness

Doesn't every artist want his pictures to outlast him and still look the same fifty, even a hundred years from now? That's why it's important to pay attention to the lightfastness of your paints. This means the durability of the paints in daylight. Lightfast paints remain unchanged for a long time; the less stable paints soon fade.

This feature is sometimes identified by asterisks* sometimes by + signs or the letter A on the label. Lightfastness is usually tested using strong xenon light in the laboratory. But there are manufacturers who go even further: Schmincke exposes its paint samples to the sun on the company roof for up to two and a half years and documents the fading of the pigments in real time. But you needn't worry too much: Better gouache paints all guarantee the highest or good lightfastness, which should meet our requirements.

Schmincke Calligraphy

Schmincke Akademie

Schmincke Horadam

Royal Talens

Lascaux

Winsor & Newton

Daler Rowney

Label, talk to me! Learning to interpret information

Take a tube of paint in your hand and take a closer look at the label. It's time to read the "fine print" and learn the meaning of the cryptic asterisks and squares. Schmincke, but also Winsor & Newton and Royal Talens reveal a great deal of information about the composition and properties of their paints. As an example, we'll use quinacridone violet from Schmincke Horadam® Gouache. Known in antiquity as purple, it was extracted from the gland of a snail called the purple dye murex. The colour cost between 10-300 times as much as gold and was very popular both in ancient Egypt and in Rome. It is said that Caesar's lover Cleopatra had the sail of her ship dyed purple, although wearing this colour was strictly reserved for the emperor on penalty of death! One gram of natural snail purple costs about $2,500 and £1,700 today and is only rarely used for rather exotic purposes. For example, Orthodox Jews still dye the threads of the tallit (prayer shawl) with the dye from snail glands because the Torah requires it.

Article numbers

The article number of every paint at Schmincke is not a random combination. The following information can be extracted from it. Using our example, No. 12 360 means:

12: Series 12 - Horadam® gouache (other series: e.g. 10 - mussini®, 11 - Norma® Professional, 13 - primacryl®, 14 - Horadam® aquarell etc.)

3: 300s are red (other colours: 100s white, 200s yellow, 300s red, 400s blue, 500s green, 600s brown, 700s black, 800s (usually) special-effect paints and 900s special colours)

60: An undefined number for more precise categorization

Pigment

This is based on the international colour index system and consists of a combination of letters and numbers. The letters at the beginning of the pigment name (e.g. PV19 for quinacridone violet) mean the following colour groups:

PW = Pigment white
PB = Pigment blue
PY = Pigment yellow
PG = Pigment green
PO = Pigment orange
PBr = Pigment brown
PR = Pigment red
PBk = Pigment black
PV = Pigment violet

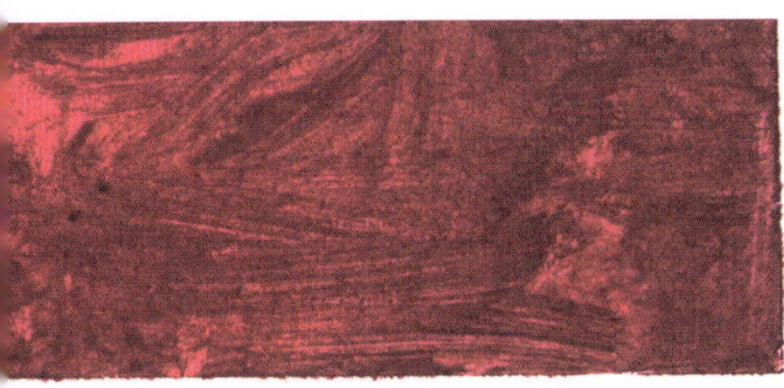

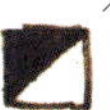

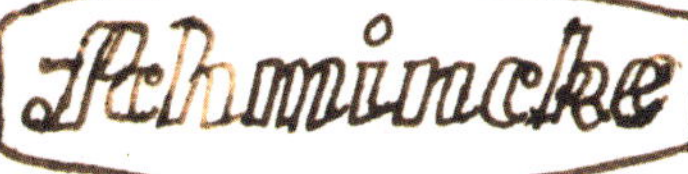

Opacity

All paints have different opacity or transparency properties. It depends, for example, on the surface distribution and particle size of the pigment and is identified with these symbols:

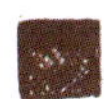 opaque

 semi-opaque

 semi-transparent

 transparent

Lightfastness

At Schmincke, lightfastness is classified according to a 5-star system as follows:

★★★★★ extremely lightfast
★★★★ good lightfastness
★★★ lightfast
★★ limited lightfastness
★ less lightfast

Price group

Horadam® Gouache is available in four price groups that are calculated depending on the pigment content. The price increases with the group number. Quinacridone violet is group 2.

A worthwhile purchase. Overview of the chief gouache brands

Since gouache paints all contain the same binder, you can (and should) put your palette together with paints by different manufacturers. The colours and pigments differ from brand to brand – thus, for example, sepia from Royal Talens may be different than sepia from Winsor & Newton. Your favourite brand might also not offer a few hues that you can find elsewhere. I'll present some paints by the common brands but will only look at high-quality gouache in "artist quality" and no cheap brands.

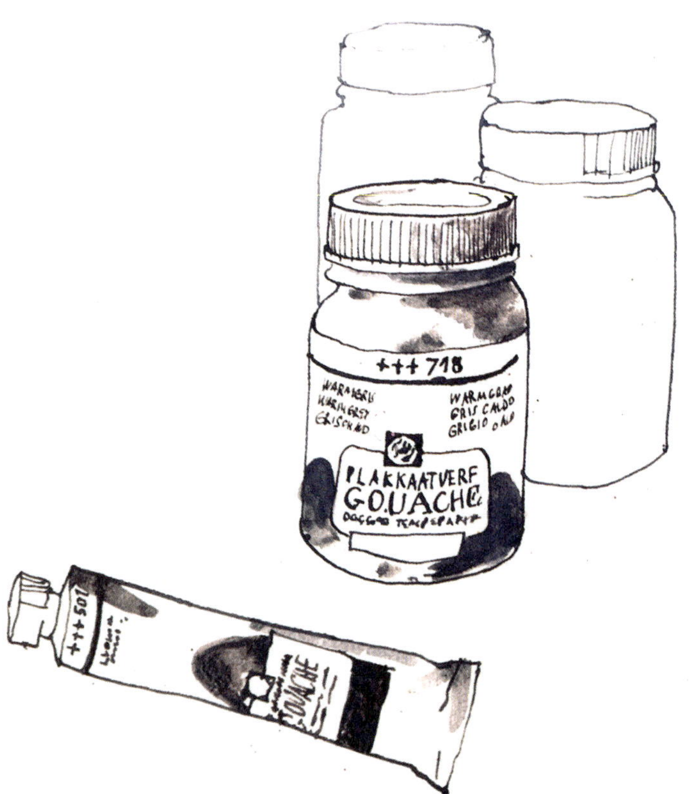

Royal Talens Gouache Extra Fine

Good and relatively inexpensive paints of solid artist quality from the Netherlands. I have been using these paints for over 20 years and I like them, among other things, because I can leave the open jars standing throughout the day. This avoids the annoying task of squeezing the paint from the tubes and keeping them moist. In addition, a jar of Royal Talens gouache lasts a long time and can be refilled. A clear recommendation, especially for beginners, because of the very good price-performance ratio. The range includes 45 colours in 50 ml jars or 60 colours in 20 ml tubes. Rating: good quality, moderate price.

The German brand Schmincke is serious about gouache and offers four different varieties. Three of them are in the upper premium segment and one is in the cheaper range of study paints.

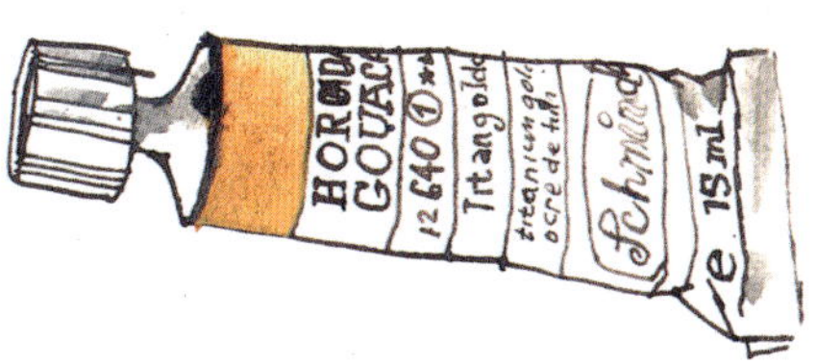

Schmincke Horadam® Gouache

is very good and expensive: they are simply the best paints on the market. Since no additional white components are added to this variety, these paints have a natural opacity of the pigments. Horadam® Gouache also produces most shades from pure pigments (and not pigment combinations). Of the 48 colours, 38 are one-pigment shades (for comparison: in Schmincke HKS® Designers' Gouache with 48 colours, there are only 8). Filled in 15 ml tubes. Rating: excellent quality, very high price.

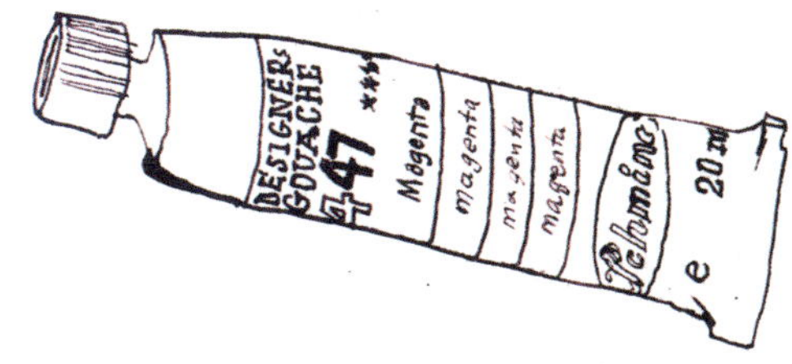

Schmincke HKS® Designers' Gouache

48 colours, also very good quality. Developed for commercial artists and designers, these paints reproduce essential HKS® tones. The last two digits of the article number of this type therefore correspond to the HKS® numbering (in the colour fan). Maximum opacity, sometimes with white additive in 20 ml tubes. Rating: good quality, high price.

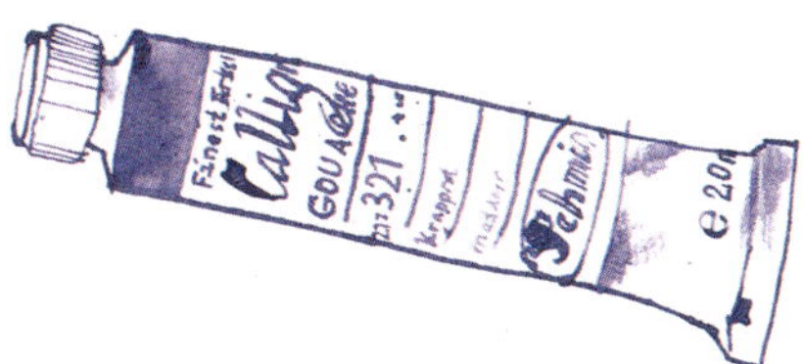

Schmincke Calligraphy Gouache

13 colours in 20 ml tubes. This opaque gouache was developed for different forms of calligraphy (drawing, poster, drawing pen, etc.) and is therefore particularly finely pigmented. Contains some interesting special colours such as supra opaque white, jet black, silver and gold. Rating: good quality, very high price.

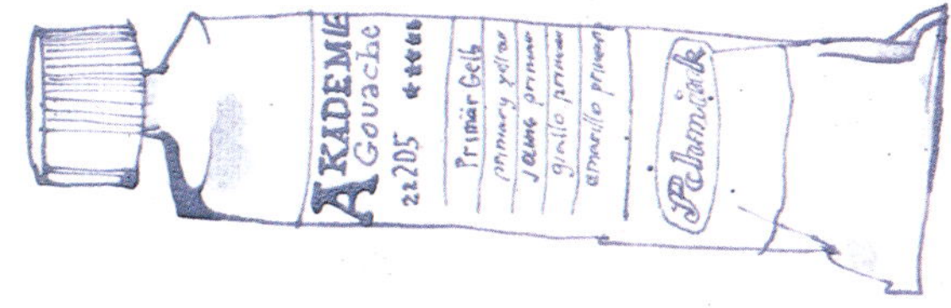

Schmincke Akademie® Gouache

30 colours available in 60 ml tubes and 250 ml bottles. They are quite inexpensive already, even cheaper if you buy the large 250 ml bottles. Although not in the segment of "artist paints", Schmincke has recently significantly improved the quality of this line, for example in terms of the opacity of some tones. Rating: moderate quality, low price.

→ TIP: If you're wondering which paints are the best for you to start with, I would recommend the very good, but relatively inexpensive Royal Talens Gouache, especially for a start. You can then always switch to more upmarket Winsor & Newton or Schmincke Gouache or add a few tins of exotic brands like ShinHan to your range. You can find out more about the tools you'll need and my paint recommendations in the chapter "Setting up your workplace."

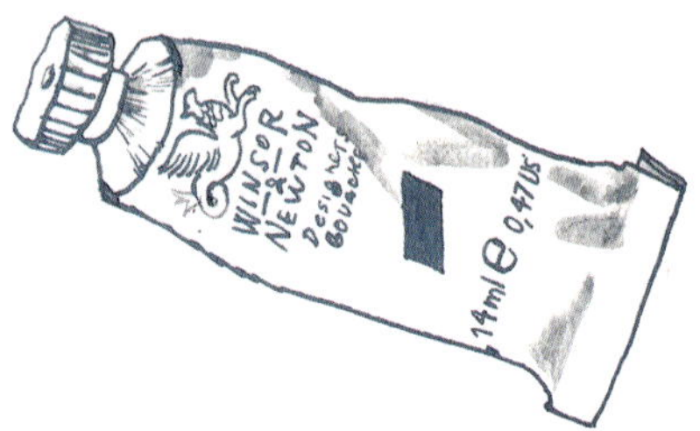

Winsor & Newton Designer's Gouache

Very good and expensive. A classic from Great Britain, W&N prides itself on being the inventor of modern gouache paints, which they launched in 1935 under the name "opaque watercolours." W&N has a very high pigment content and a wide range of 84 colours with 15 different shades of red alone (also 4 black, 4 white, gold and silver) in small 14 ml tubes. Rating: good quality, high price.

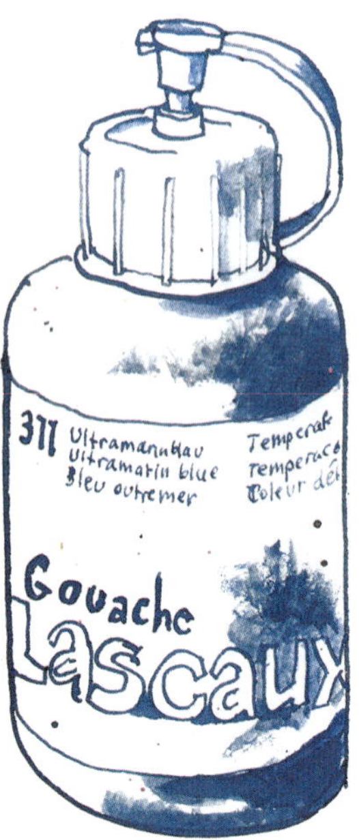

Lascaux Gouache

A good and medium-priced gouache from Switzerland. Although these paints are opaque and lightfast, they have a slightly "oily" texture, which is probably due to the addition of additives other than gum arabic, possibly also glycerine. The range includes 34 colours in 85 ml plastic bottles (some colours also in 250 or 500 ml).
Rating: good quality, moderate price.

I would like to mention a few other gouache brands that are good, but are difficult to find in many regions. You can buy most of them online.

Sennelier Extra Fine Gouache

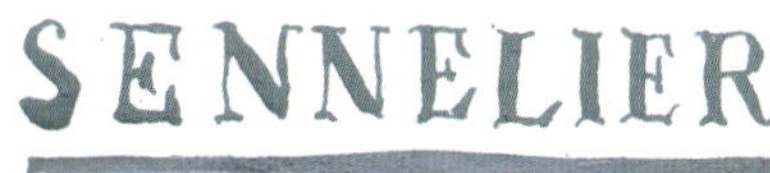

Good, long-standing French brand with a proud 59 colours in 21 ml tubes. Use your next visit to Paris to buy these paints directly in the old company shop at Quai Voltaire 3, opposite the Louvre! Rating: good quality, high price.

Pébéo Gouache Extra Fine T

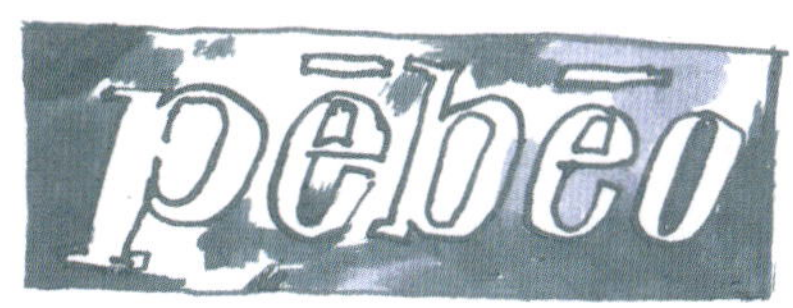

Another French brand that produces gouache in artist quality. 74 colours in 20 ml tubes. Rating: good quality, high price.

Linel Gouache Extra-Fine

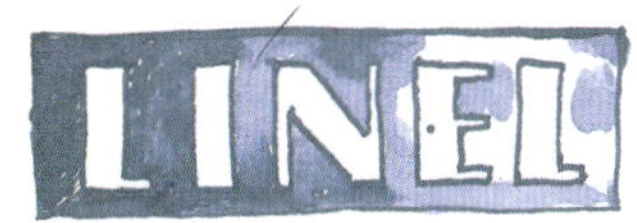

Another well-known French brand, unfortunately difficult to come by in some countries. In tubes of 15 ml with an incredible 122 colours. Rating: good quality, high price.

Holbein Gouache

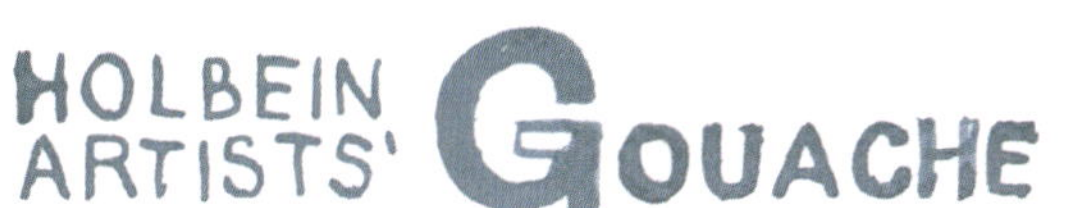

A very well-known Japanese brand, used mainly in the USA and Asia by designers and illustrators. 89 colours in 5 ml and 15 ml tubes. Rating: excellent quality, very high price.

Daler-Rowney Designers' Gouache

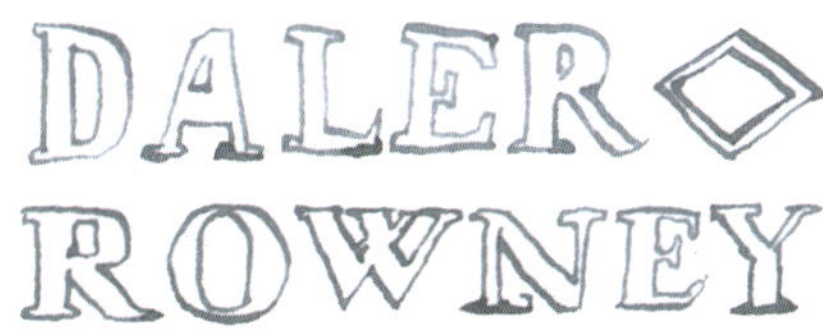

An artist-quality British brand with an amazing selection of 90 colours, available in 15 ml tubes (and an additional 5 selected colours in 38 ml tubes). Rating: good quality, high price.

→ TIP: "Treat yourself" to a few new paints for each new series of pictures or new book projects you begin. This way, you won't necessarily end up using your usual colour tones and your stock of paints will expand automatically!

ShinHan Poster Colour

ShinHan

South Korean brand with 69 colours in practical 40 ml plastic jars like those from Royal Talens and also for a similar price. The bright yellow, red and green tones are interesting! Rating: good quality, moderate price.

Invention from China. Choosing paper

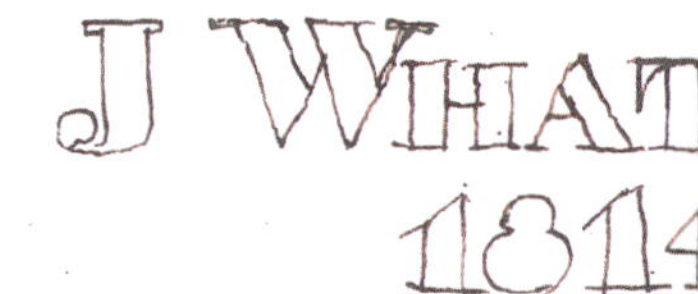

You may be surprised, but the very best paper you'll need for gouache painting is made without felling a single tree. It's made of 0% cellulose, 100% cotton. And that's important because many of the techniques described in this book (for example masking and reworking with water) only work when we use high quality paper. Provided you don't want your painting surface to curl, tear, crumble or otherwise let you down in an insidious way.

Paper, invented in ancient China, has always been used to preserve ancient knowledge. We know this because an imperial eunuch and official named T'sai Lun neatly wrote down the technology of papermaking in 105 AD. Specifically, he noted how the plant fibres are broken down and also how the paper was pressed.

It took some time for this Chinese know-how to reach Europe in the late Middle Ages where paper continued to be made mainly from old cloths until the nineteenth century. It wasn't until the 1780s that a special watercolour paper was produced by the English company J. Whatman. Until the twentieth century it was considered the best on the market and was so popular, it was even counterfeited. Today, pure cotton paper or paper made from rags is rather rare. But it is the paper we need to get the best out of gouache. The long cotton fibres make the paper strong, stretchy and pliable.

→TIP: Use better, thicker paper of 300 grams per square metre or more for pictures that are important to you. If you work with relatively little water, you may not even need to stretch the sheet onto a wooden plate!

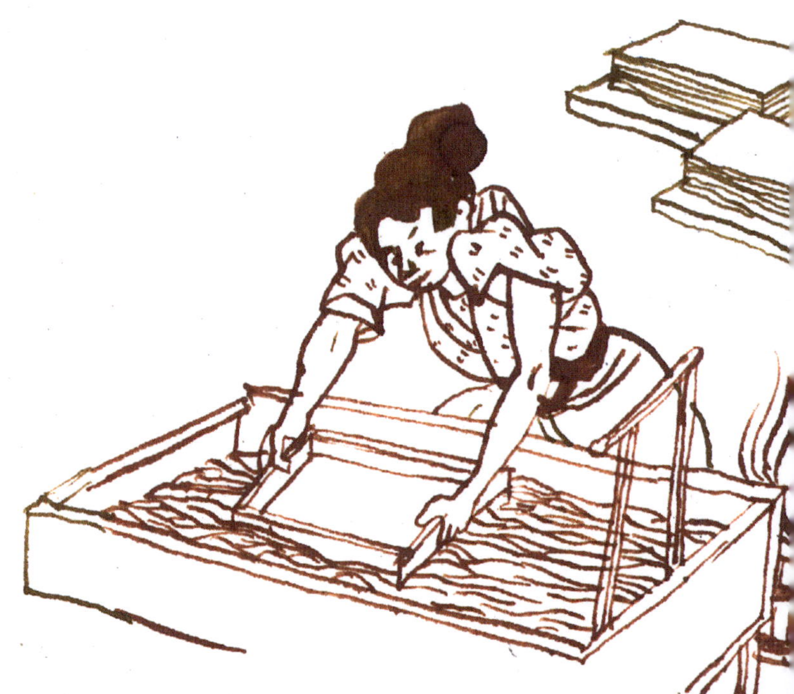

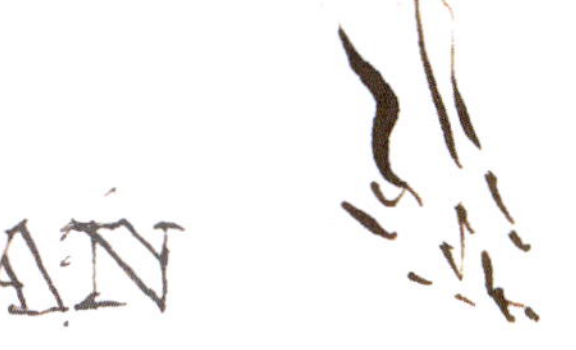

FABRIANO
dal 1264

fondé en l'An 1492
ARCHES
GRAIN TORCHON

Seek and you shall find, for all of the major paper manufacturers– Arche, Fabiano, Hahnemühle and Lana– include beautiful cotton papers for artists in their range. Lighter grades weigh between 180-300 grams per square metre (90 lb-140 lb) while the thicker (and more expensive) papers weigh 356-850 grams per square metre (156 lb-400 lb). The weight of a square metre of a certain type of paper is called grammages or volume and this is the first characteristic by which we differentiate the papers. In the United States, paper weight can instead be measured in pounds per 500 standard-sized sheets. A key point to look out for in this system is that papers intended for different purposes are cut to different sizes, meaning that two papers with the same apparent weight in pounds may not be the same at all. But there is a second and no less important feature: Watercolour papers also differ according to the nature of their surface. There are three levels:

Hot-pressed paper has a fairly smooth surface. Its advantage is that it's excellently suited for delicate details as well as for drawing with steel or reed pens. Its drawback is that the paint flow is not so easy to control.

Cold-pressed paper has a fine to medium grain and is suitable for details as well as for watercolour-like gradients.

Rough: The third surface quality is the roughest among watercolour papers. Pro: The pigments gather in the "valleys" and are often missing on the raised areas. This creates the typical watercolour effect, even when painting with gouache. Con: This paper is too uneven for fine details.

Watercolour paper is available both in sheets and in glued pads. The pads are of course more practical for painting on the go. However, if you work in the studio, I advise you to get your paper in loose sheets and cut it to the desired size (and then to stretch it). You'll get ideal smooth, non-wavy pictures and also save money!

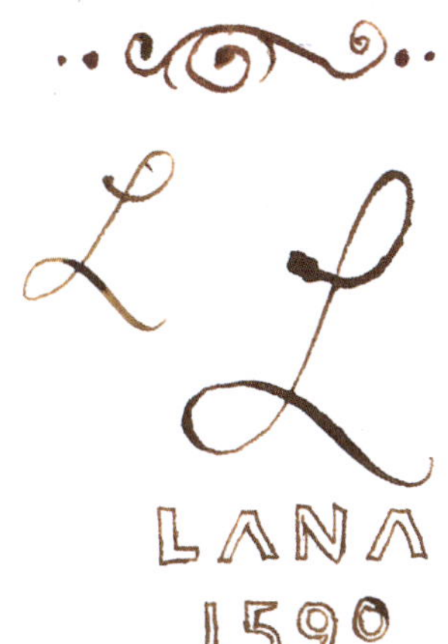

→TIP: Try out all three textures gradually. That way, you'll see which paper suits your painting style better. Experiment with different subjects on different painting surfaces! But you don't necessarily have to buy the more expensive 300 or 640 g/m² (140 lb or 300 lb) papers right away. Rather, stretch a lighter (but stable) 185 g/m² (90 lb) sheet onto a wooden board and paint on it.

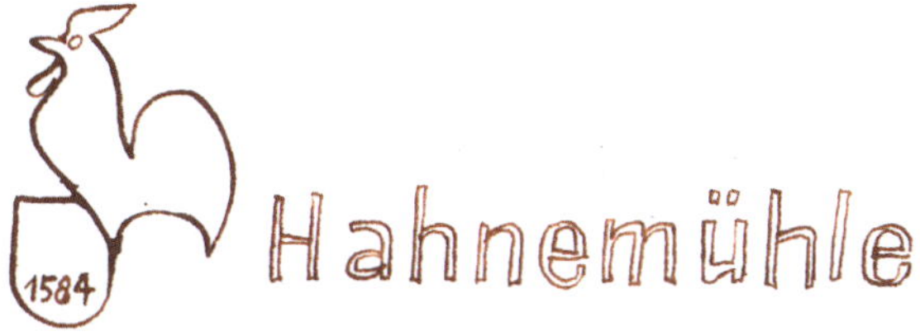

The Royal No. 7 and consorts. Comparing various brushes

Experience shows that at some point, every artist finds his or her choice of a few brushes that feel good in their hand (and are near and dear to them). To help guide you through the brush maze, we'll now go through all the brushes relevant for gouache.

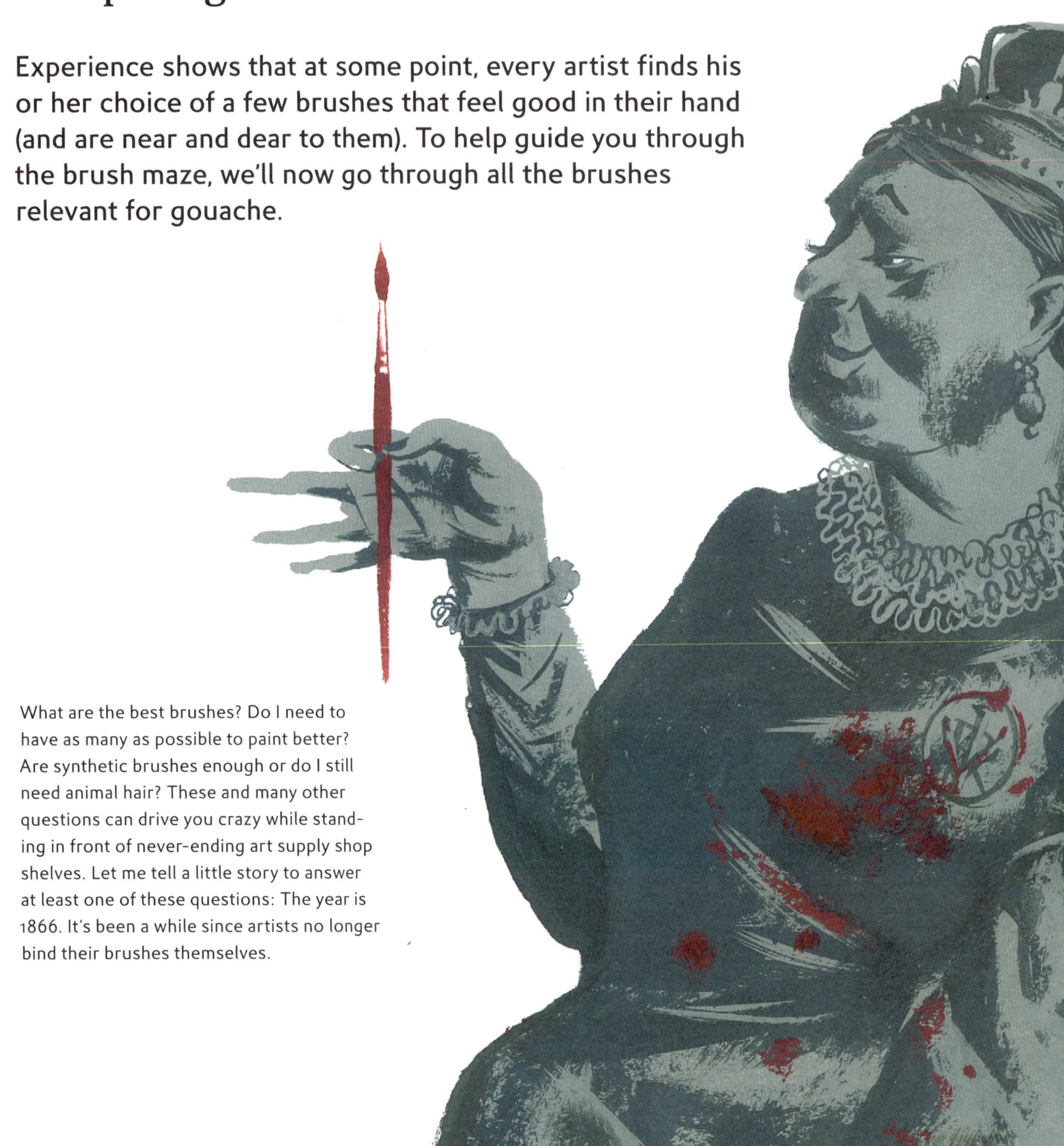

What are the best brushes? Do I need to have as many as possible to paint better? Are synthetic brushes enough or do I still need animal hair? These and many other questions can drive you crazy while standing in front of never-ending art supply shop shelves. Let me tell a little story to answer at least one of these questions: The year is 1866. It's been a while since artists no longer bind their brushes themselves.

In the seventeenth century this task was taken over by brush binders as they are called today. In England, Winsor & Newton became the court supplier for art materials. They were asked by Her Majesty Queen Victoria, herself a great lover of watercolours, to do no less than to produce the best watercolour brush in the world. The royal brush makers worked hard and could be proud of the result. In addition to the ivory handle and silver ferrule, the new brush in the queen's favourite size No. 7 had an incredibly fine tip of No. 00! The queen liked the product extremely well and it soon went into series production.

Even today, these brushes are made one at a time in the sleepy English fishing town of Lowestoft. No longer of ivory and silver, Series 7 is considered the best you can get on the market.

Brushes we can use today differ in their hair and shape. We'll start with hair: When do you use natural-hair brushes and when do you use synthetic brushes? Natural-hair brushes are expensive, but quite universal in use and are best suited for fine work such as hair and eyes, drawing thin lines or applying delicate transparent layers of paint and glazes. Thanks to its structure, natural hair absorbs more paint than synthetic hair. Synthetic brushes are suitable for rougher work. They are particularly good for mixing colours, blurring edges and for colour transitions. Synthetic brushes are usually cheaper and have greater suppleness.

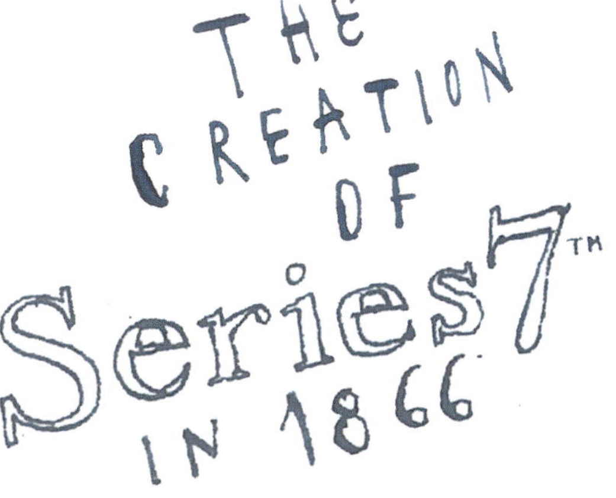

→ TIP: High-quality brushes made of natural hair should be washed out carefully. Gouache is much milder than acrylic or oil, but don't underestimate care and cleaning. Wash the brushes carefully with clear water and soap, because conventional detergent will degrease the hair over time. Rinse until the water runs clear. Take special care that no paint remains in the bottom of the brush head – otherwise the brush hair will spread more and more and the beautiful tip will soon be gone. Then, shape the tip and set the brush to dry. If you're careful, a good sable or squirrel-hair brush can serve you for several years.

Despite ever improving synthetic brushes, you can't do without natural-hair brushes. Let's take a closer look at what types of animals hair are used and what they are best suited for.

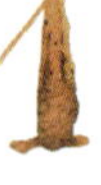

1. Kolinsky sable-hair

You don't have to paint everything using Series 7 brushes, but do try to purchase one or two Kolinsky brushes. For the brushes made of the winter fur of the male Siberian weasel (Mustela sibirica) remain the undisputed best. The combination of long life, high filling capacity, elasticity and a fine and stable tip make them the favourites of artists who work with watercolours.

2. Bristle brushes

round or flat, are very suitable for the dry brush technique when you paint with little water and very opaque layers.

3. Ox-hair brushes

have soft, elastic hair. They represent an inexpensive alternative to squirrel or sable-hair brushes. As rigger brushes, they are well suited for fine strokes, lines and calligraphy. The cat tongue or round shapes are good for washes.

4. Squirrel-hair brushes

are made of very fine bluish, black or brown hair. The tip is fine and the control of the paint flow is in no way inferior to that of a Kolinsky brush. The downside: These brushes are less elastic than sable-hair brushes, because squirrel hairs are thinner than those of the sable.

5. Sable/synthetic mix

In addition to pure sable-hair brushes, the modern manufacturers also offer blends with synthetic hair. They're better than pure synthetic brushes in terms of paint flow control. But they are not as good as the natural-hair brushes in terms of tips and elasticity.

6. Weasel-hair brushes

are an alternative to Kolinsky. The hair has a reddish-brown colour and a fine tip, the brushes fill well, but are usually shorter than Kolinsky brushes.

7. Goat-hair brushes

Wide, flat brushes made of goat hair on a natural wood handle are suitable for glazes and underpaintings, without leaving streaks or brush marks. Very soft hair!

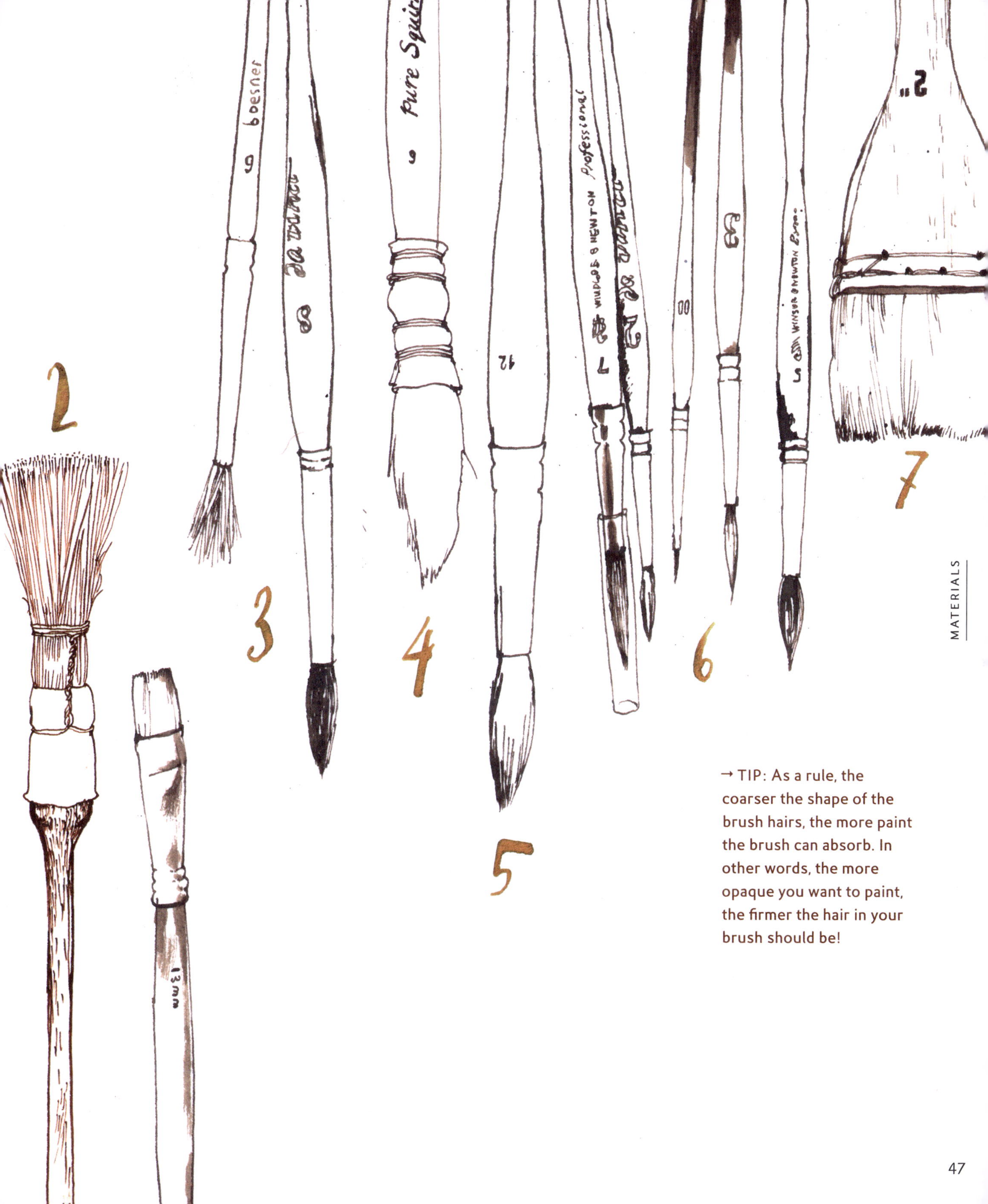

→ TIP: As a rule, the coarser the shape of the brush hairs, the more paint the brush can absorb. In other words, the more opaque you want to paint, the firmer the hair in your brush should be!

Brushes also differ in shape depending on their use.
On this double page you will find all the brushes relevant to gouache.

1. Flat brushes

distribute the paint well and can be used on the narrow side for relatively narrow lines and corners. They are preferred by artists who model wet-on-wet and desire a quick change between a wide and a narrow line.

2. Round brushes

Due to the long, closely spaced hair, round brushes can hold more paint than other shapes. They can be used universally and are therefore used for details as well as for large areas and glazes. Paint can be applied evenly by turning the brush.

3. Filbert brushes

are a type of flat brush with a rounded edge. They offer the advantages of both round and flat brushes. They are used to paint extensive areas and to make colour transitions, but they are also suitable for details.

4. Fan brushes

cannot take up a lot of paint and are therefore more suitable for creating "busy" structures, grains and patterns in the picture. There are fan brushes with more stable hair made of synthetic or bristles – they are good for colour gradients, textures and effects. The soft fan brushes made of badger hair are good for structures and to imitate textures.

5. Rigger brushes

are very long, thin brushes with or without a tip. They absorb a lot of paint and are well suited for lettering or elegant lines.

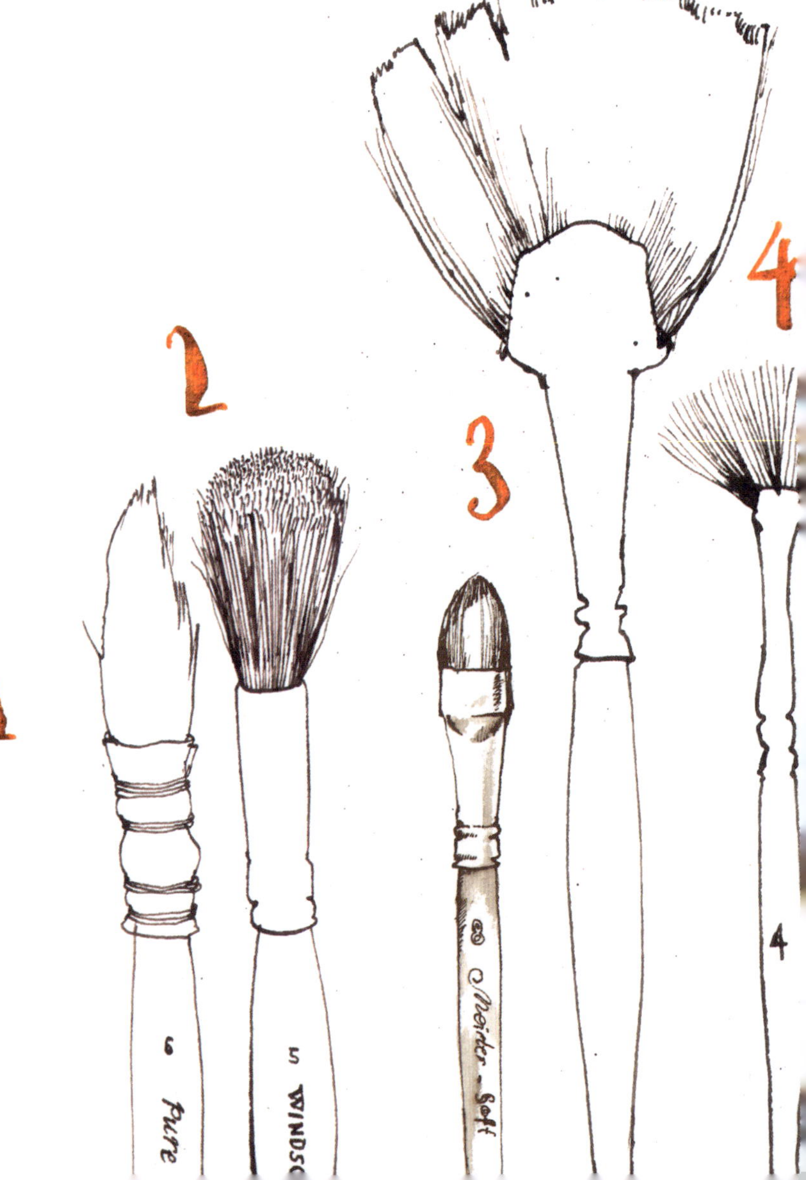

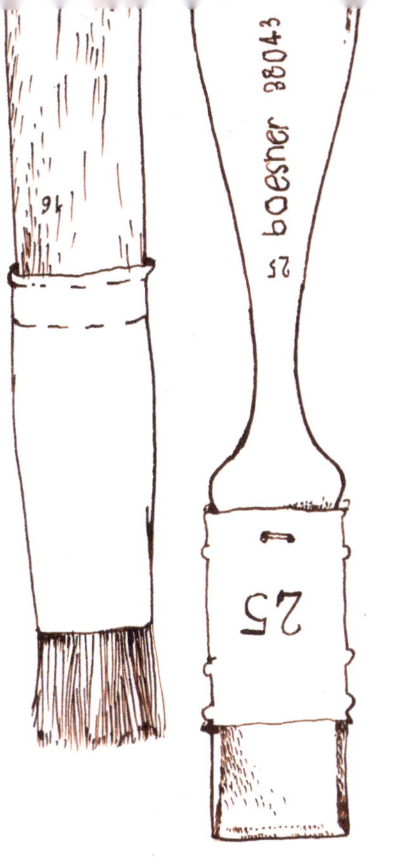

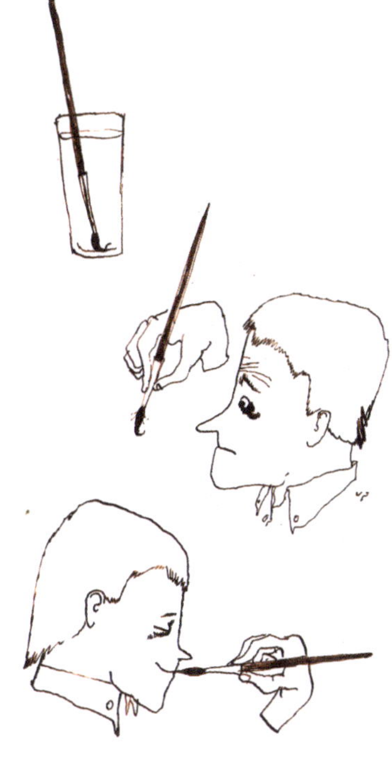

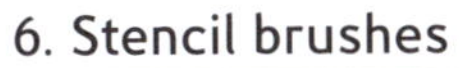

6. Stencil brushes

have dense white China bristles on a short handle and are cut flat. As the name suggests, they are designed for stippling and stencilling.

7. Silicone brushes

are suitable where the brush hair would otherwise stick together, for example to apply masking film.

8. Calligraphy brushes

Sadly, this Chinese brush made from fake "mountain lion hair" is not really suitable for gouache: the hair is too long and too soft! But I couldn't resist its extravagant appearance and also depicted it here.

→ TIP: Never leave your brush head down in the water cup, not even for a short time. Especially the sensitive sable-hair brushes with the fine tips will otherwise lose their shape, burst and become crooked. If it does happen, there's a rememdy. Hold the broken brush in previously boiled hot water for about 30 seconds and then shape the tip again. Dip the brush in gum arabic and let it stand overnight. If you're lucky, your brush will be ready to use again next time you paint (after washing out the gum arabic).

Not without my sponge!
Other utensils

After paints, paper and brush, it's time to look at the remaining tools. Here you'll find a few tips on basic equipment and what tools you need to come up with new ideas and techniques. Because new things often emerge when we put aside our usual tools and try to paint differently.

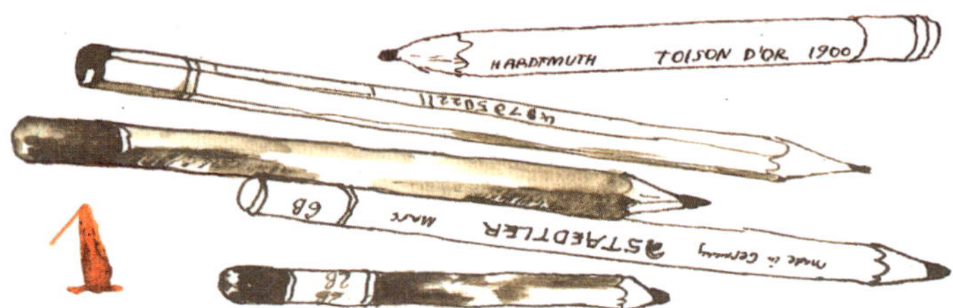

1. Pencils

You'll most likely need pencils for preliminary drawings. A pencil drawing can be easily corrected, erased and, if necessary, you can draw with a pencil on a layer of gouache paint. Just a tip: take the middle degrees of softness between H and 2B. Pencils over 3B smear easily and dirty the paper. And anything harder than 2H will scratch the paper.

2. Eraser

There are many types of erasers that are good for different purposes. Above all, you will need a soft eraser, which can be used, for example, to rub out the remains of the masking film without affecting the paint. Also have a second, harder eraser ready, which can remove the top paper layer with paint.

3. Knives

A good knife should not be missing in your workplace. It's best to get a cutter for the rough jobs (cutting paper to size) and a fine Martor or X-acto knife for the finer tasks (cutting out tape when masking, sharpening reed pens, etc.). A razor blade is also handy for scraping off small blobs of paint from the paper– a trick I learned from my grandmother, an architect, who used it to clean up her blueprints. But put the razor blade in the side of a cork so that you don't cut yourself.

4. Folding sticks

are used to break and fold the watercolour paper before cutting and stretching it.

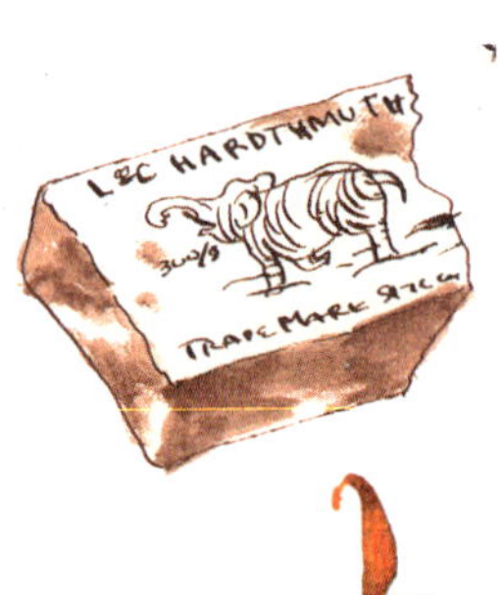

5. Palette

Your mixing palette is a very personal matter; every artist mixes paints their own way. Porcelain palettes are best suited for gouache. There are palettes of different sizes and shapes available, smooth or with wells to separate the colours. But it doesn't have to be an expensive palette from the art supply shop. Many artists (and I, too) use simple white porcelain plates, glass or Plexiglas panes. In the end, all that matters is that the paint doesn't drip off and that the mixing area is large enough.

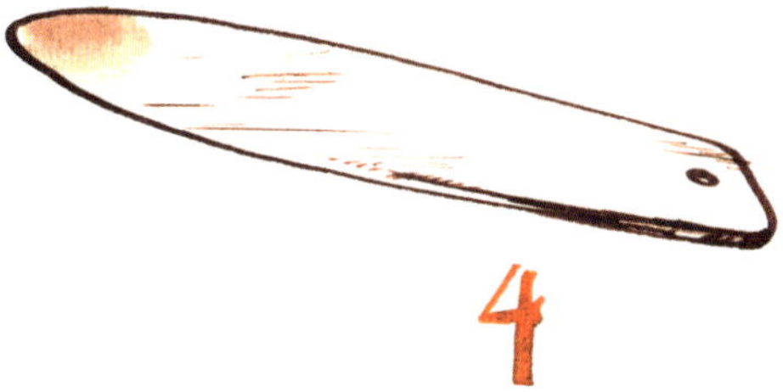

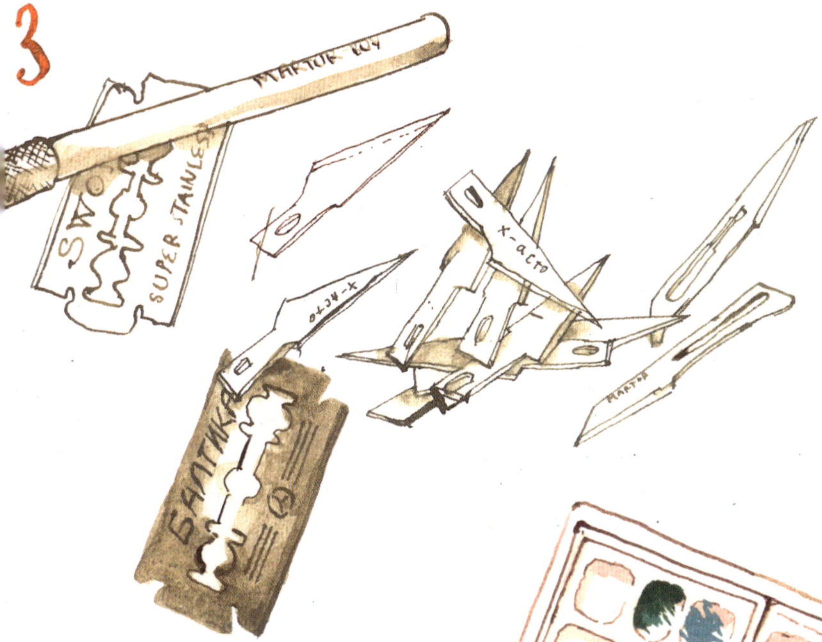

→ TIP: In order to mix a colour confidently, instead of a white porcelain palette some painters use a glass pane, which is painted with a medium grey (50:50 black/white) from below. This is good not only for beginners, because it makes it a lot easier to correctly estimate the grey value of the colour.

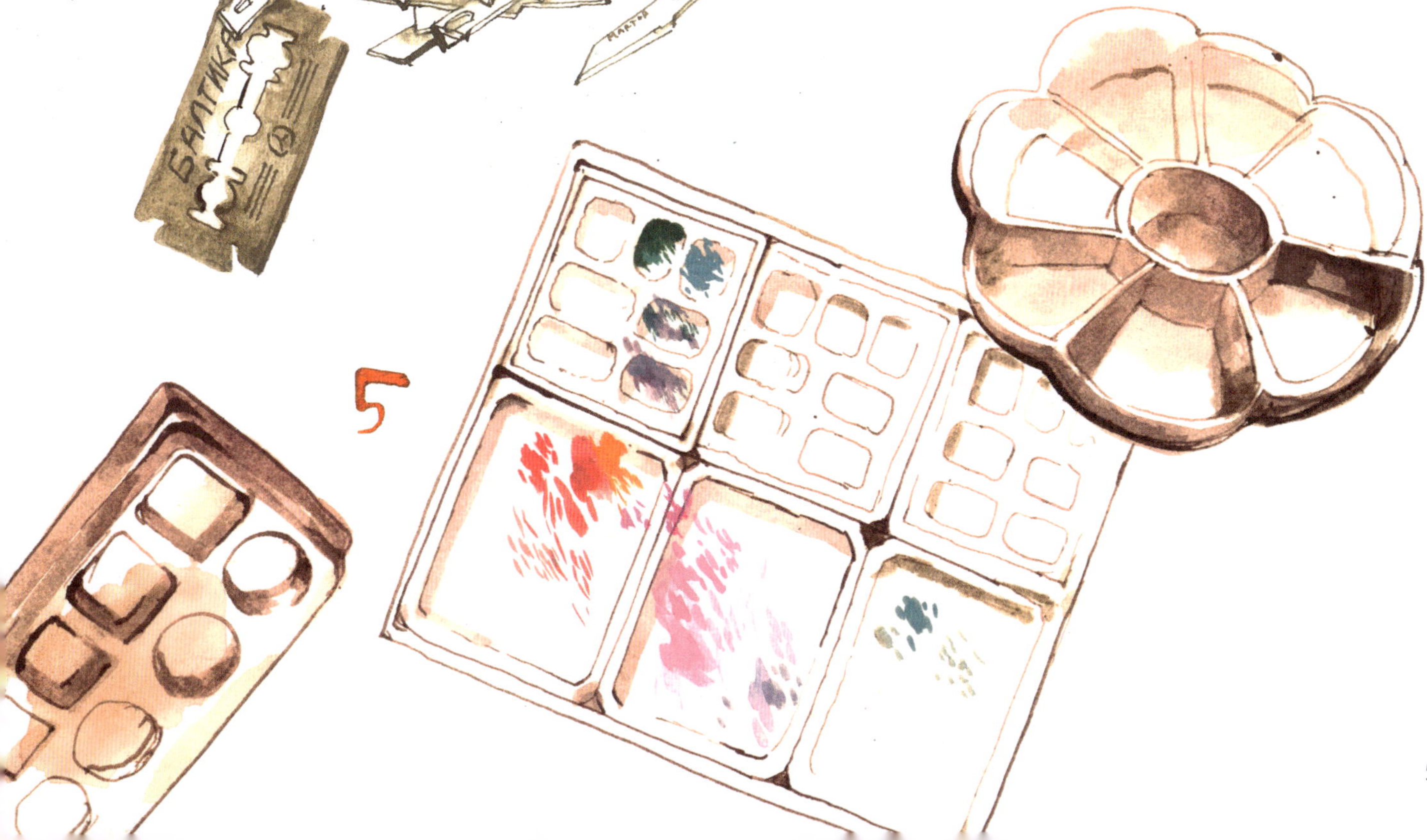

4

3

5

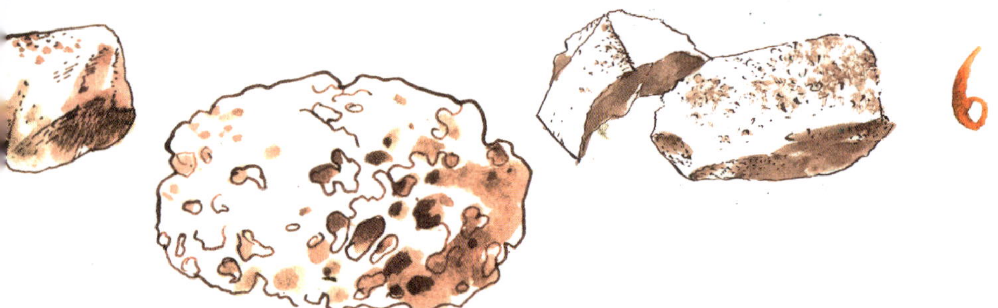

6. Sponges

are very good for dabbing structures or if you work with stencils. There are natural sea sponges that result in a slightly irregular texture. Small cosmetic sponges from the corner drugstore are also quite good. They're cheaper and can be easily cut to the required shape with scissors. It's worthwhile to collect several sponges for different structures. The sponges are also good for moistening the paper or for colouring large sections of the background.

7. Paper towels

are an important tool and should always be on your table. You don't need an entire roll next to your picture – one sheet will do. You can use it to dry the brush and dab excess paint or water away from the picture. More on this in the chapter on reworking.

8. Tape

You'll need three different kinds.

a) Watercolour wet adhesive tape made of paper, white or brown, for stretching the sheet on the board. More about this on p. 62 in the chapter "Stretching watercolour papers."

b) Parcel tape or scotch tape for masking the surfaces, see p. 120 "Masking with tape." 3M, Tesa or Scotch brands have proven to be very good.

c) If you've gotten into it and want more precision when masking, you should get more expensive masking tapes from the auto painters. I highly recommend Japanese tape made by Nichiban made of yellow rice paper. It adheres well, is water-repellent and can be removed easily. It's worth experimenting with how your paper and tape work together. If your watercolour paper is not glued well or if the tape is too sticky, it may tear strips when you peel it off. So always do a test before you start the picture!

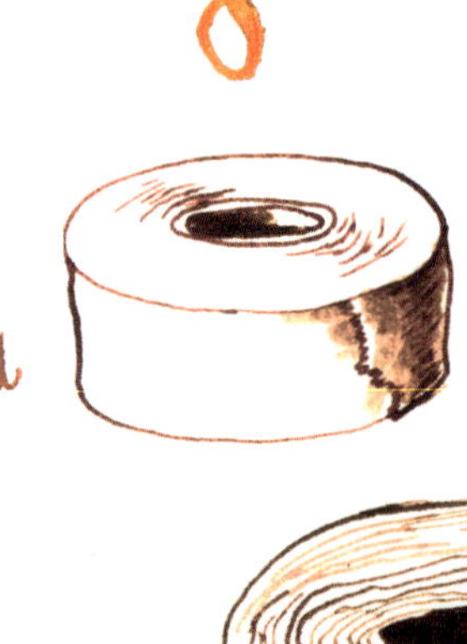

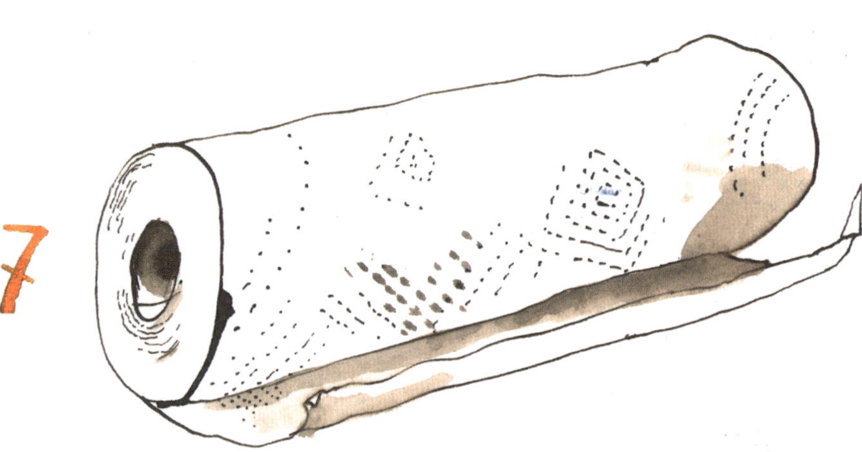

9. Brush washer with receptacle

A water receptacle is part of your basic equipment, of course. An empty 1-litre mason jar (better two) is actually enough, but if you want to work more professionally, I recommend using a stainless steel container with a spiral to hold the brushes. This will store your fine sable-hair brushes hanging nicely.

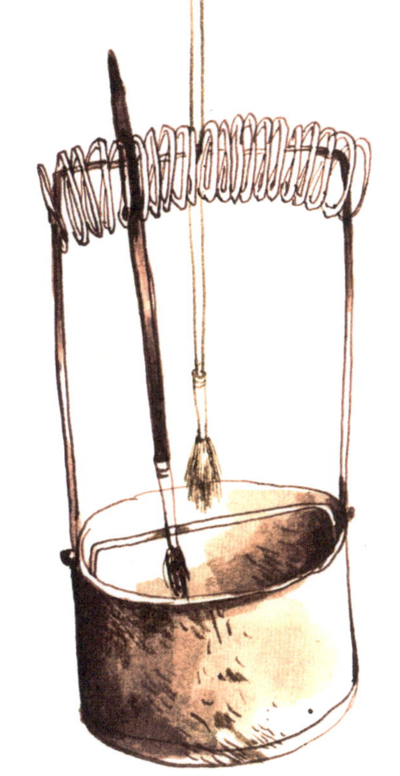

10. Hair dryer

If you work on several pictures at the same time or on a picture with many glazes, a hair dryer will be of great benefit. If you don't have an old one on hand and are about to rush out to get one, please make sure that it has a "cold air" function. Most of the time, this feature is identified by a snowflake. The paints dry more slowly in the "cold" wind, but much more gently.

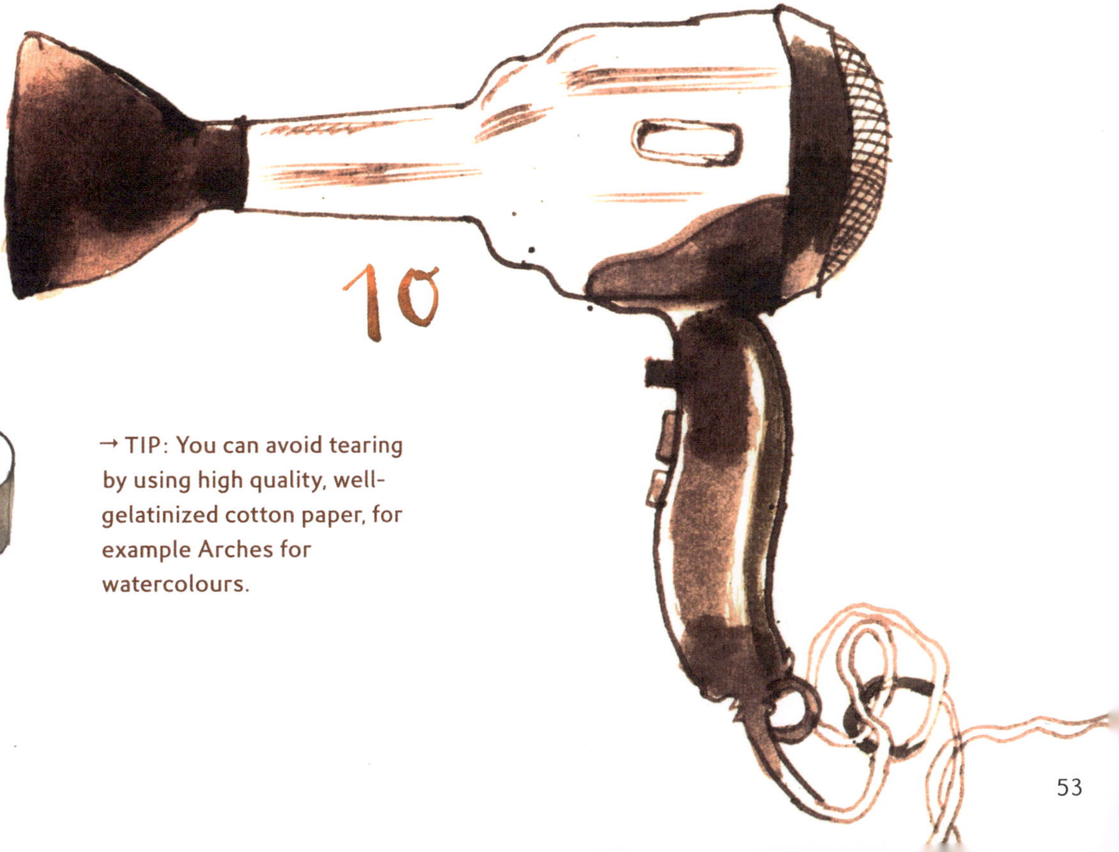

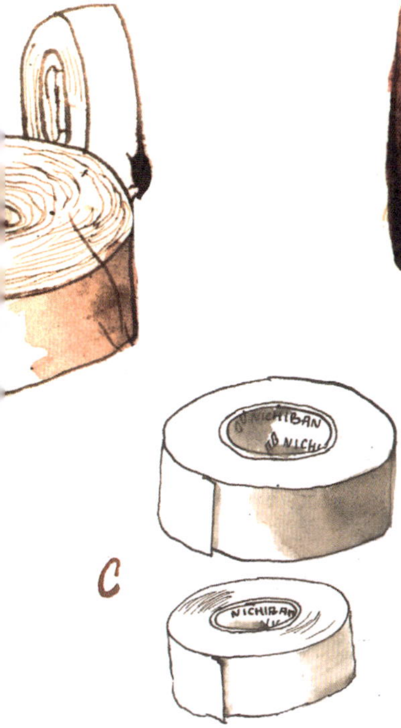

→ TIP: You can avoid tearing by using high quality, well-gelatinized cotton paper, for example Arches for watercolours.

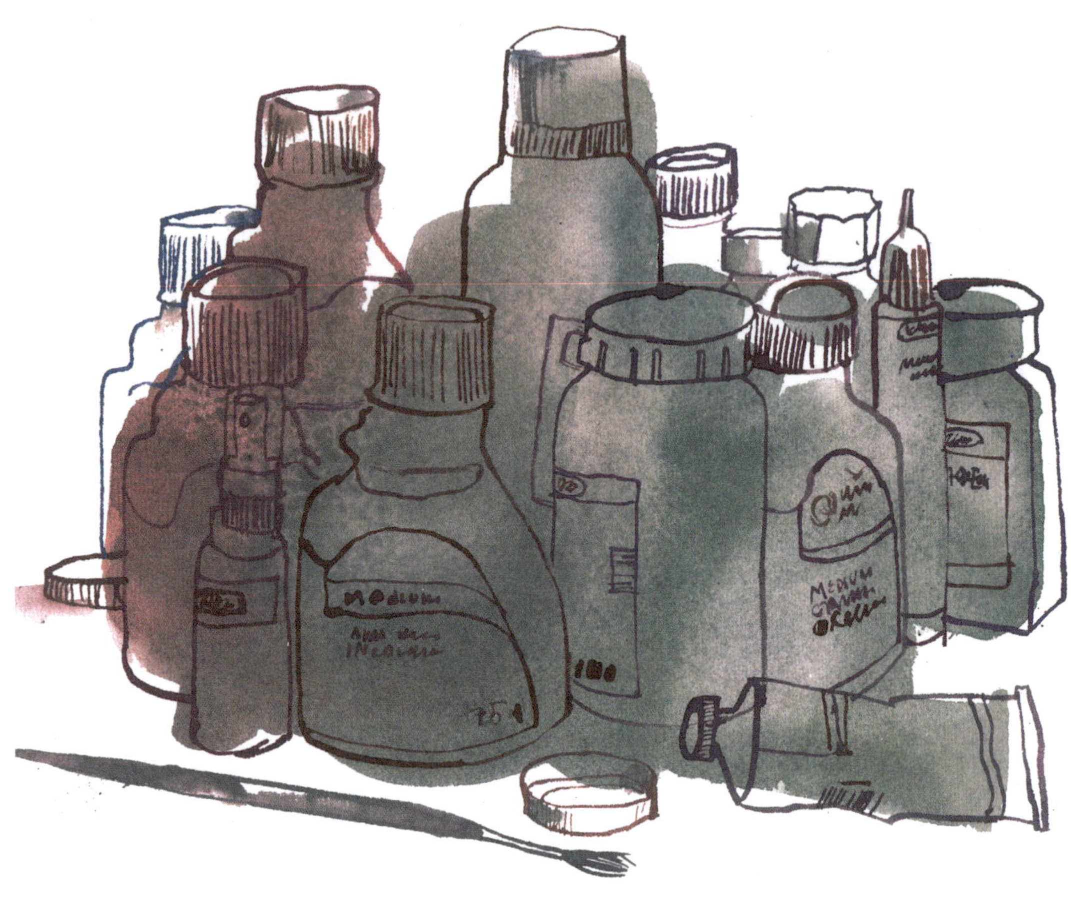

Painting helps. Other painting tools and what they're good for

Just unnecessary extras, nothing but tricks, you say? Of course you can create interesting pictures with just paints and water. But the use of an assortment of aids can enormously expand your painting technique. There's no rush! Don't try out different painting tools until you've already gotten some experience working with gouache. It always takes a little experimentation before you can integrate a new painting medium in your technique. Don't be afraid to experiment and make mistakes, because many an alleged garden path may lead to fascinating discoveries.

Masking fluid

Used correctly, this aid can work wonders. It makes it possible to leave out parts of the picture that you want to leave white or later paint very light colours. You can find step-by-step instructions on how this technique works in the chapter "Using masking fluid." But first a few words about what a masking fluid is. It's usually made of liquid rubber, also known as latex. After the film applied comes into contact with air, it hardens within a few minutes. This painting medium is produced under different names by all major paint manufacturers and is sometimes called liquid frisket (Schmincke), sometimes it's called masking fluid (Daler-Rowney and Sennelier), Abdeckmittel (Lukas) or art masking fluid (Winsor & Newton). I gradually tried out different brands and became particularly fond of Winsor & Newton's masking fluid. What should you look for when choosing this medium?

There are two different types: one is made *with ammonia* and latex. As a result, it stinks, but the area applied can be pulled off in one piece. This is the case with the masking films made by Winsor & Newton, Talens, Sennelier and some other manufacturers. The masking fluids *without ammonia*, often called liquid frisket, have a copolymer dispersion as a basis and are offered, for example, by Schmincke. They are odourless, but must be carefully rubbed off with an eraser.

What works with thin watercolour paints becomes a problem with opaque gouache: the paint smears easily when rubbed away. So, it's not easy. If you want to avoid the odour, you may end up having problems removing the frisket. Try both of them, I'll leave the agony of choice to you!

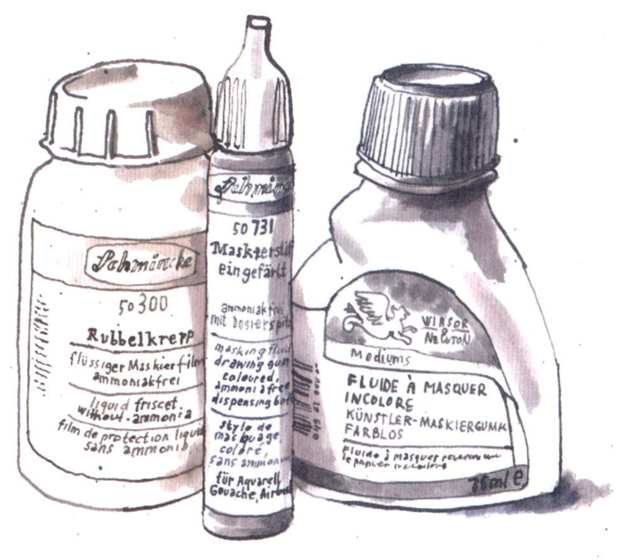

→ TIP: There are coloured masking fluids (Schmincke, Sennelier, Talens) or transparent (Winsor & Newton, Schmincke, Daler Rowney). The coloured ones stand out visually from the paper, so I prefer them to the colourless ones. By the way, you can dye a transparent masking fluid yourself with a few drops of gouache!

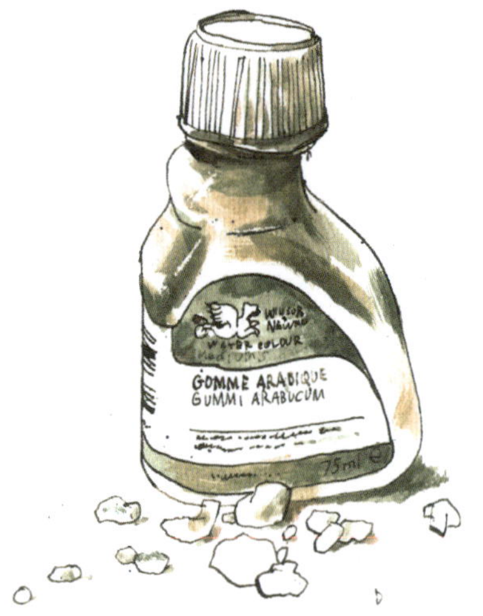

Gum arabic

As you already know, gum arabic is what holds the pigments together in gouache and watercolour paints. If you want to make your own gouache paints, you won't be able to do without this resin, which is made from African acacia. Those who use the finished paints from the art supply shops will still need gum arabic for the following uses:

When added to gouache, gum arabic slows down the drying process and increases its transparency. This can be useful for example when painting in wet-on-wet technique. The dry surface may shine a little, however. I also recommend gum arabic if you want to apply gouache in several thick layers. It prevents the paint from later cracking and peeling off, which can occur with "thick" painting styles. This happens because the lower, dry layers of paint absorb water from the layer just applied. Gum arabic is available in dry form as small yellowish lumps that are sold by weight – the original form – or bottled as a solution (for example from Winsor & Newton, Talens or Schmincke).

Fixatives

One special feature of gouache pictures is their matt, velvety surface. If you attempt to use fixative sprays on your originals, they'll quickly lose colour depth, contrasts and their beautiful "pastel" surface. I therefore advise against fixing the finished gouaches or working with varnishes. Instead, you should carefully wrap the pictures in rice paper during transport and frame them behind glass for display – and please, with a few millimetres of space! Nevertheless, fixatives can be useful. One interesting application is to add fixative "in between" layers, for example the first or the second layer of the picture. This allows us to continue painting over a layer without dissolving it. I myself don't use this "cheat" very often because the paints, once fixed, are actually difficult to rework if necessary. But when I do, I like to use these sprays: Universal fixative No. 50401 from Schmincke, Royal Talens Protecting Spray 680 Gouache/Watercolour or Fixative Spray 2070 from Lascaux.

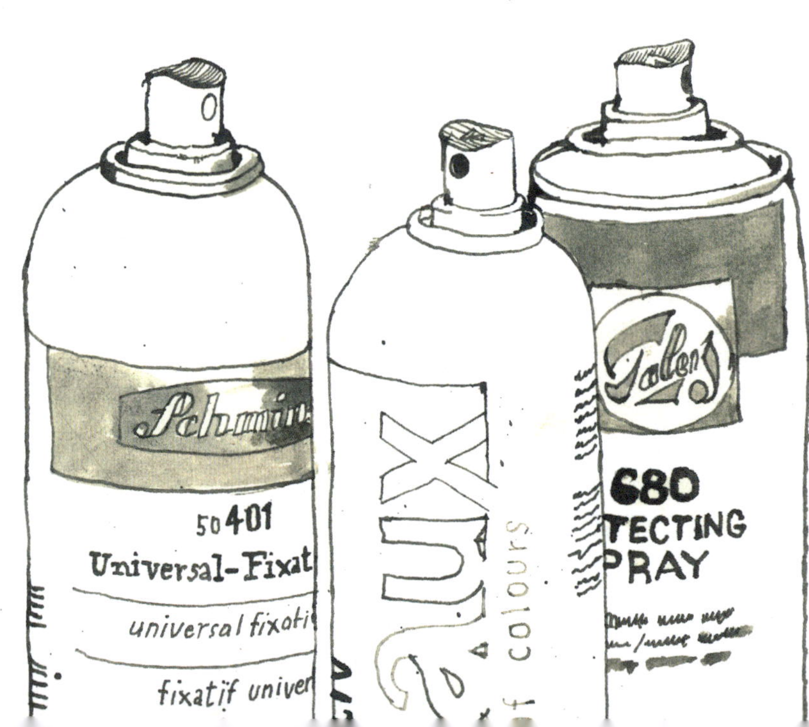

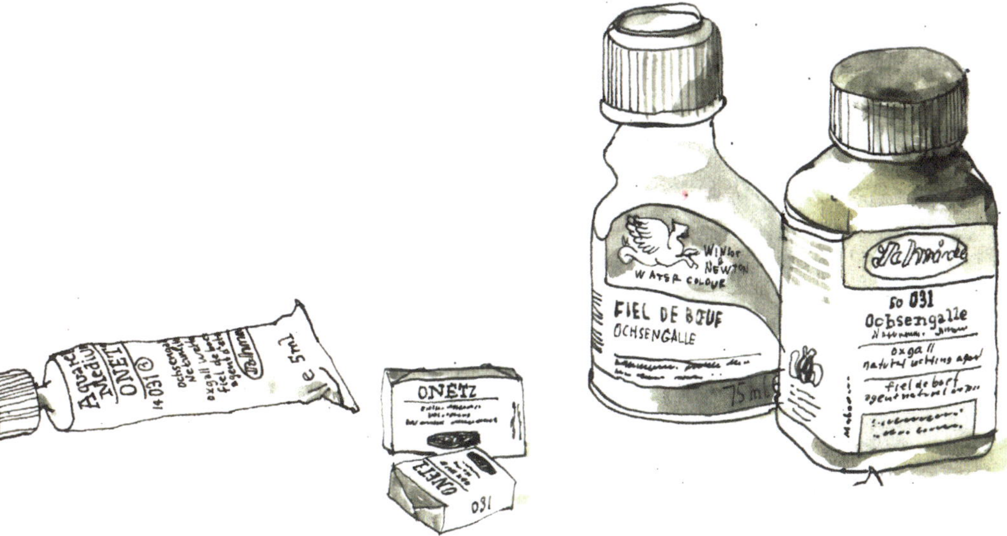

Ox gall

Sounds disgusting and this painting medium is bitter, but it doesn't stink and is completely transparent. Ox gall, which has been in use since Roman times, is first purified for use by painters. We owe the procedure for this to Peltro William Tomkins of London. From his tract "On the Preparation and Properties of a Colourless Refined Ox-Gall, for rendering Drawings in Water-Colours more bright and permanent" we know that he presented his method of rendering this animal product colourless and odourless to the Society of Arts in 1812. The society members must have been thrilled by this discovery and the demonstrations, because Mr. Tomkins left the room with a gold medal around his neck.

What is it good for? On the one hand, ox gall is useful when painting on backgrounds that are slightly oily and where watercolours might roll off. So it is used to wet and degrease painting surfaces and to improve the flow properties of the paint.

Ox gall also slows down the drying of the paint. It also has another property: adding it slightly fixates the otherwise water-soluble paints. This can be very helpful when painting several glazed layers.

Mr Tomkins raved over it, writing, "... (ox gall) prevents the gum from cracking; and the colours are so completely fixed in the paper itself, that subsequent tints can be washed over them without any risk of their becoming foul...." If you use ox gall, add it to the washout water – the more concentrated, the greater the effect. This bitter medium is sold as a liquid in tins and tubes (for example from Winsor & Newton, Talens and Schmincke) or in dry form in watercolour cups (onetz from Schmincke).

→ TIP: If you want to apply large areas evenly, you will often face the problem that individual brushstrokes remain visible. This is because gouache dries quickly and the transitions between the strokes don't blur. Approximately 10 drops of ox gall per jar of washing-up water will be enough to slow down the drying process and get rid of this annoying effect.

Iridescent painting media

If you like glitter or want part of your picture to have a mother-of-pearl shine, I would use an "iridescent painting medium." You can use it two ways: either add it to the paint or apply it over the paint that has already dried. The more painting medium you add to the paint, the more the paint will glisten after drying. If you use the second technique, the glitter layer will shine the most, but it will be less even. The small glitter particles are not reproducible and so this technique should only be used for pictures that are shown in their original form (which is also why it can't be reproduced here). Iridescent painting media are manufactured by Winsor & Newton and Schmincke (under the name aqua-Shine).

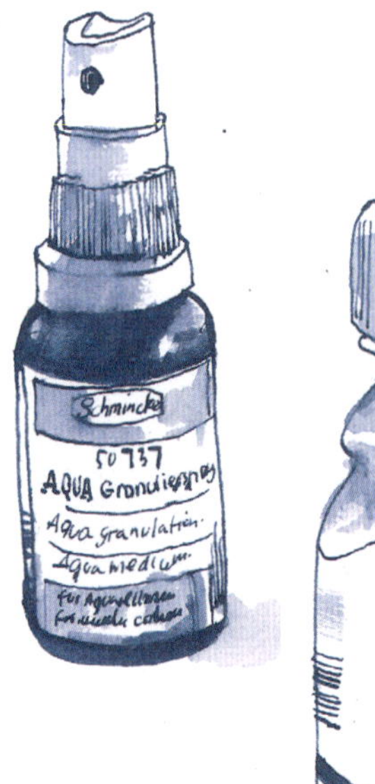

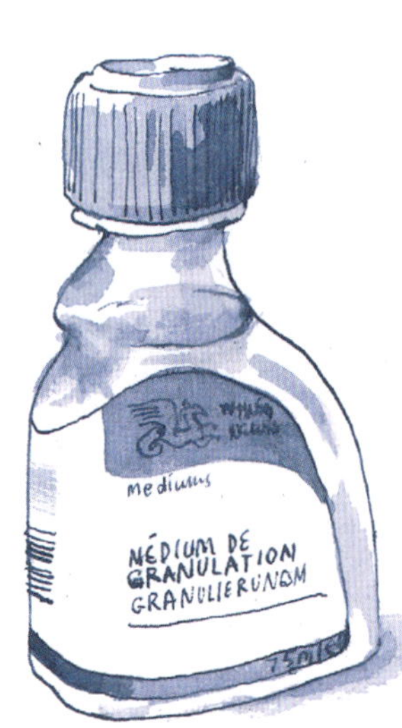

Granulation medium

In gouache, this medium makes the pigments contract or "granulate." The better the paint quality, the stronger the effect. In other words, paints with high pigment content are more sensitive to it than cheap paints with a lot of fillers and extenders. I will reveal a little secret here: Since the main component of most granulation media is alcohol, you can try the effect of "granulating" first with high-proof alcohol (vodka, schnapps, etc.) or even better with ethanol from the pharmacy. But I recommend having a second palette and a second water cup ready for "granulating" to avoid contaminating your other paints.

Granulation media are sold by Winsor & Newton in 75-ml bottles. Schmincke found a practical solution: They offer two granulation fluids as a spray, aqua-effect spray in 100 ml and aqua-granulating spray in 15 ml bottles. They can easily be sprayed onto the applied, still-damp paint.

Granulation medium
W&N

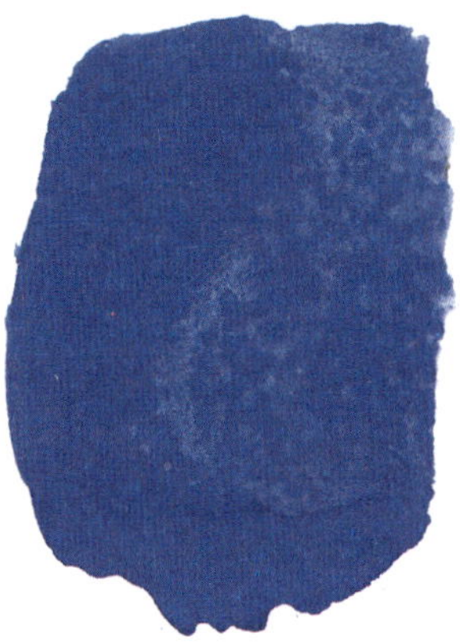

AQUA-Granulating spray
Schmincke

AQUA-Effect spray
Schmincke

Texture medium

This painting medium is produced by Winsor & Newton and contains fine particles, which, according to the manufacturer, "give the impression of depth and structure." Just like iridescent painting medium, the effect only comes into play on original pictures and is therefore not very useful for illustrators or artists whose pictures are printed.

Painting medium to increase water resistance

In addition to the traditional means that make gouache less water-soluble (ox gall, fixatives), there are also specially developed preparations for this. aqua-Fix by Schmincke – mixed with the paint – makes the gouache water-resistant after drying, similar to acrylic paint. This would lead to the question why not use acrylic paints in the first place. The ability to tame gouache this way, as well.

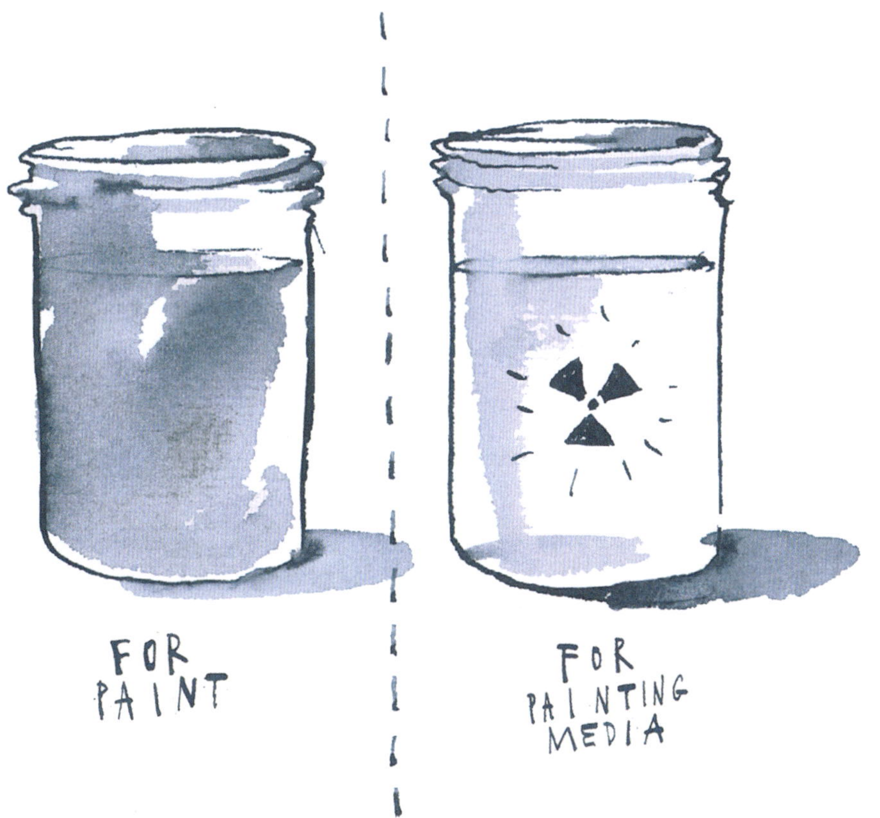

→ TIP: Since most painting media are substances that affect your paints, I advise that you always use a different water glass and a clean separate palette for them. Wash the brushes carefully if you use painting media. It's important that the paints in the tins or tubes don't come into contact with and get contaminated by the painting medium!

The First Step is Always the ... Easiest. First steps

In this chapter you'll find practical tips for setting up your workplace as well as for handling the paper being mounted. You'll also learn important things about composing colour sounds and why it's better to keep analogue and digital separate at your desk.

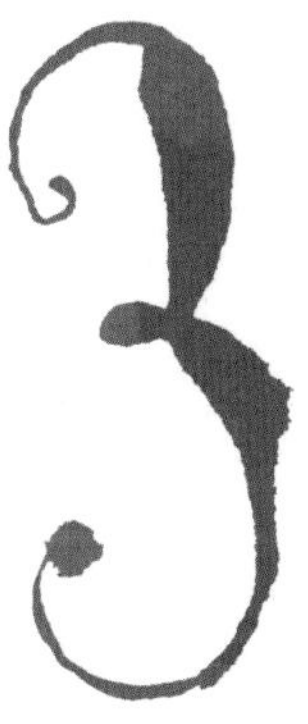

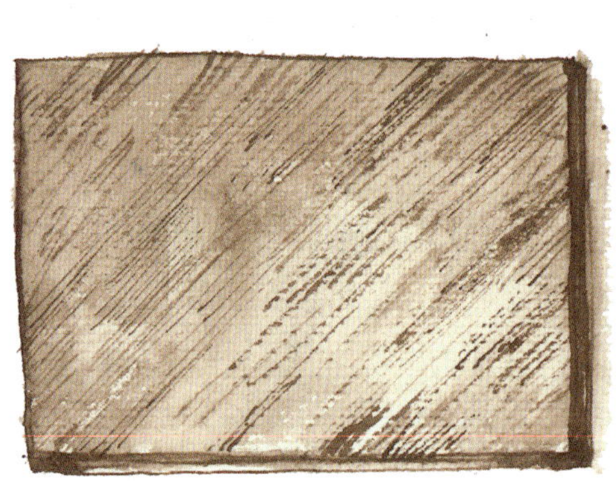

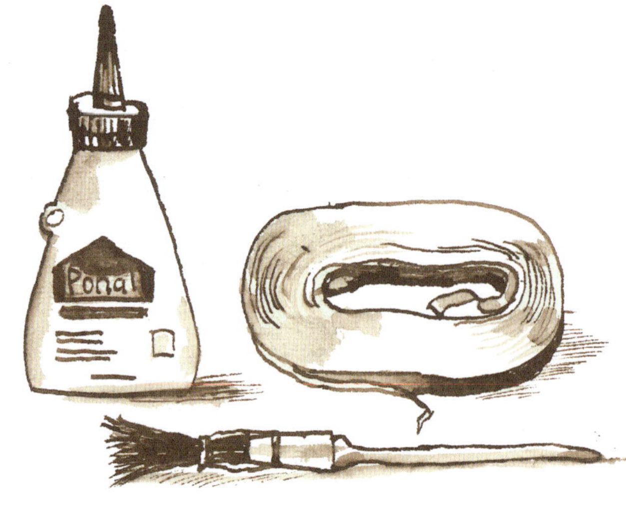

It's all about the tension. Stretching watercolour papers

Without stretching, even a good watercolour paper will eventually warp and form ugly troughs. As described in the chapter on the materials, there are a variety of papers that are suitable for gouache. In addition to single sheets, all major paper manufacturers also have painting pads of different sizes, and if you use them stretching isn't required. But if you want to determine the sizes yourself or put a lot of paint on the paper, you should definitely prefer single sheets to pads. It's also much less expensive!

You'll need:

- a board (from approx. 7 mm thickness, not thinner, otherwise it can warp)
- brown or white wet adhesive tape from an art supply shop
- wood glue (e.g., Ponal)
- a large bristle brush

1.

1. First, let the paper soak in cold water for about 10 minutes. The thicker the paper, the longer it should stay in the water. If you're in a hurry you can shorten the water treatment to 3-5 minutes. Then let the water drain off briefly and place the sheet on your board.

2. Cut four strips from the wet adhesive tape. Each strip should extend just over one side of the sheet in length.

3. Now take wood glue that you've already diluted 1:1 with water in a small jar. From experience, the glue layer on the wet adhesive tape is not sufficient and the tape will detach from the board. Now take the brush and first apply the glue solution to one strip of tape.

4. Then glue it so that it lays half on the board and half on the sheet. Immediately go to the second strip and do the same. Then the third and fourth. If the paper is still really wet, you can dab off the residual moisture with a paper towel.

Now set the board up to dry; it will take 30 minutes to one hour, depending on the volume of the paper, air humidity and room temperature. If it's summer put your board in the sun. That will shorten your wait quite a bit!

→ TIP: If you want to treat yourself or don't feel like stretching paper, I'd suggest you use higher volumes. From 450 g/m^2 (210lb) you can be sure that your paper won't curl – even without stretching. If you paint with relatively little water, this may work with a thickness of 300 g/m^2 (140lb).

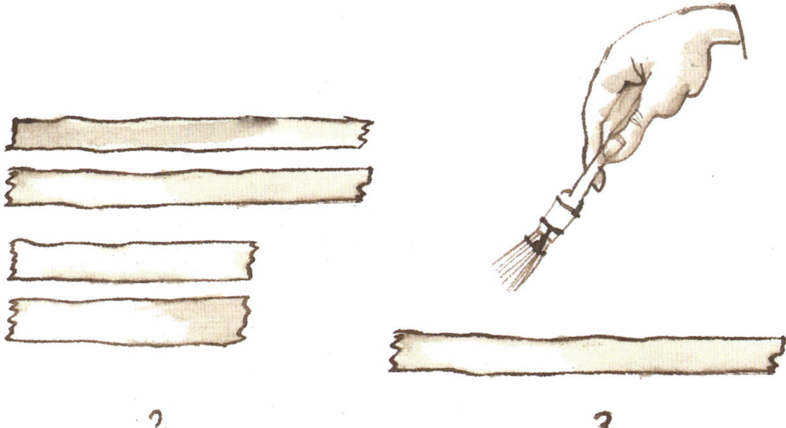

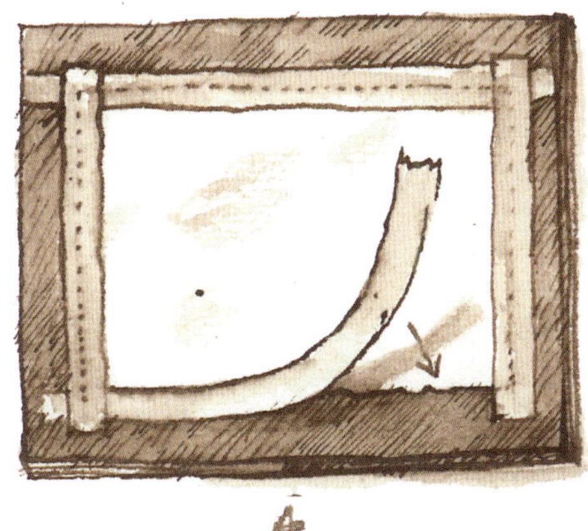

The power of triads.
An excursion in colour theory

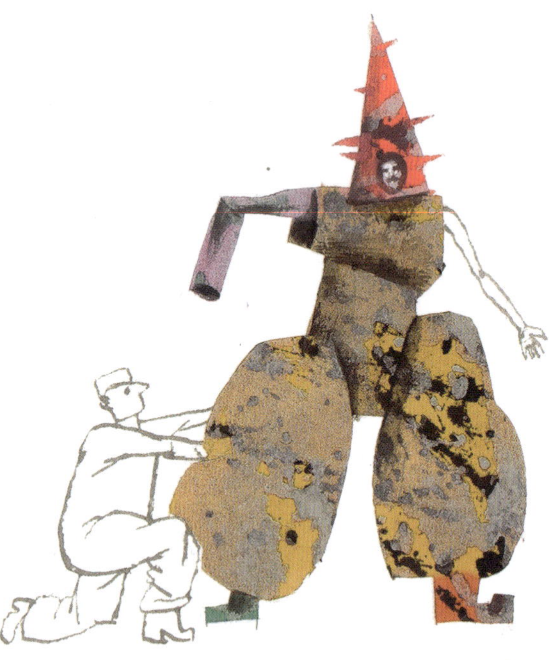

Colours are like music. You don't just hit all 88 piano keys to make it. It's music when you know how to strike a combination of three keys, which then merge into a major or minor chord. Depending on their "colouring," sounds create a certain mood. And it seems to me that in painting, our declared goal is also to convey feelings or atmospheres by using certain colour combinations. Since colour expresses emotions, combining different colours needs sensitivity whether you paint in gouache or are putting an outfit together to go out. Above all, rely on your instincts, but don't skip this chapter. You'll see, once you've understood it (even better, tried it!) this theoretical knowledge helps tremendously.

There are three colour properties that can be used to determine all colours. The hue or colour value describes a single distinguishable colour, for example yellow or red (Fig. 1). Brightness or tonal value describes the luminosity of a colour itself or its increased or decreased luminosity, which results from the addition of black or white components, whereby 0% brightness of any colour means black and 100% means white (Fig. 2). Saturation or depth of colour describes the intensity of a colour and is seen in its purity and brilliance. Saturation can be reduced by adding a neutral grey (Fig. 3).

Light colours and body colours

or RGB vs. CMYK

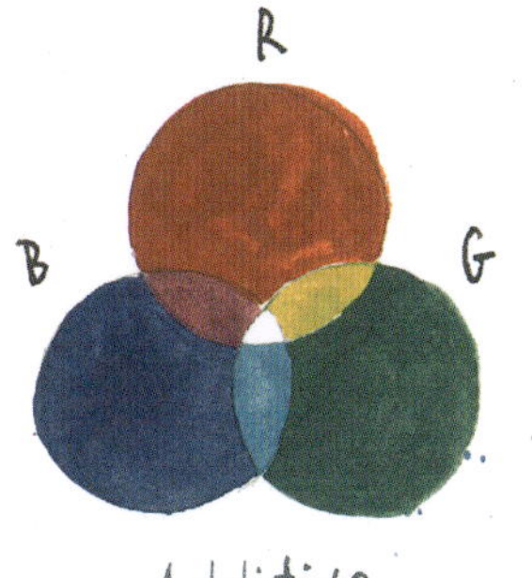

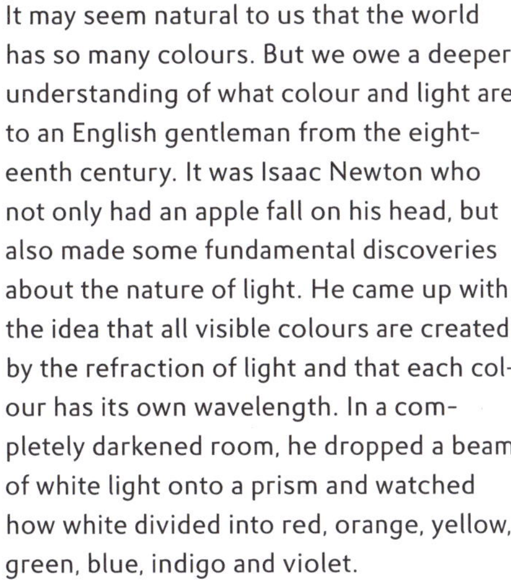

It may seem natural to us that the world has so many colours. But we owe a deeper understanding of what colour and light are to an English gentleman from the eighteenth century. It was Isaac Newton who not only had an apple fall on his head, but also made some fundamental discoveries about the nature of light. He came up with the idea that all visible colours are created by the refraction of light and that each colour has its own wavelength. In a completely darkened room, he dropped a beam of white light onto a prism and watched how white divided into red, orange, yellow, green, blue, indigo and violet.

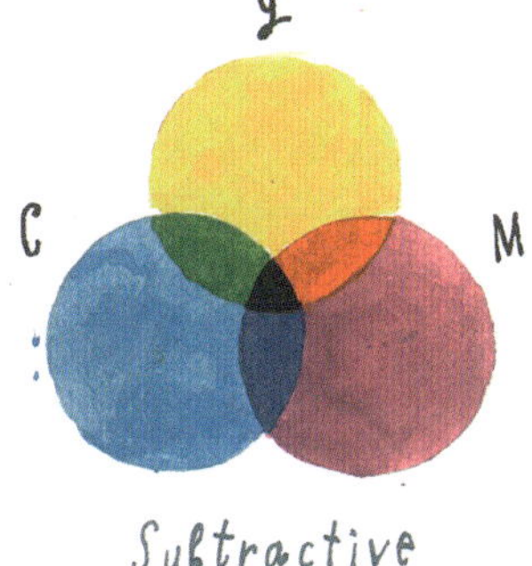

And not only that: He then proceeded to bundle the resulting spectral colours back to white light. In this process, which is called *additive* colour mixing, the brightness increases as each new colour is added. Newton experimented here with *light colours*, that is, with colours that emanate from luminous objects, such as sunlight, but also the light from colourful lanterns. The basic colours of light are red, green and blue; when put together they make white.

Since we're not dealing with pure light when painting, but with pigments mixed into the paint, it's not a matter of light colours, but of so-called *body colours*. Body or painter colours are our colour sensations that emanate from non-luminous objects, such as a yellow lemon or a black cat. These sensations arise because the object absorbs part of the light from the light source that illuminates the object.

When mixing body colours, a process called "subtractive," the brightness decreases more and more. This is because the colours extract other colour components from the white spectrum and "weaken the light" in this way. The primary colours in this case are cyan, magenta and yellow. When placed on top of each other, they result in black.

The basic difference between light and body colours can be seen in a simple example. When you look at an image on the computer screen, you see nothing but the glow of thousands of miniature LCD lights. They are coloured red, green and blue and additively form a picture. This colour model is called RGB. Now if you print out the same picture, you'll see the subject no longer glows, but is composed of thousands of colour dots. They lie on the paper and blend subtractively from cyan, magenta, yellow and black. Modelling this process with body colours is called CMYK.

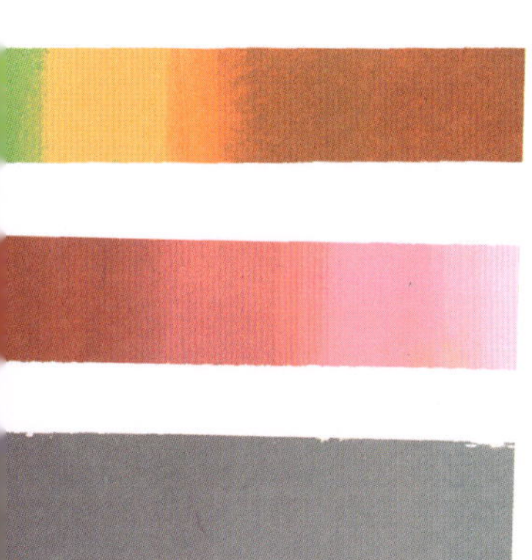

The colour wheel

The idea of arranging the visible colours in a circle also goes back to universal genius Sir Newton. The idea came to him when he noticed that the colours red and violet came very close to each other at the top and bottom of the spectrum. This new arrangement made it possible, on the one hand, to see the colours in context with one another and, on the other hand, to clearly distinguish the opposite colour pairs, the complementary colours. Johann Wolfgang von Goethe also developed his own colour theory and the colour wheel, which influenced both his contemporaries and later generations of artists. Goethe was less interested in the scientific side, but more in the "sensory and moral" effect of colours on people. The colour wheels according to Adolf Hölzel, Johannes Itten or Harald Küppers that are used today are based on Goethe's colour wheel.

What is important to know about the colour wheel? Firstly, that there are three primary colours that cannot be mixed. These are red, yellow and blue. Three secondary colours result from their mixture. And six tertiary colours are created from the mixture of neighbouring secondary and primary colours. Each colour mixture has its respective complementary colour, which is opposite it on the colour wheel. Understanding complementary colours is crucial for painting. It is very important to develop a feeling for which colours complement each other and which are analogue, or close to each other.

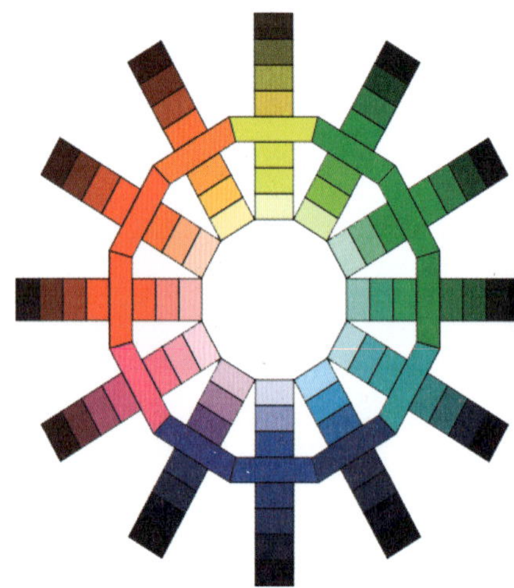

Küppers's colour wheel

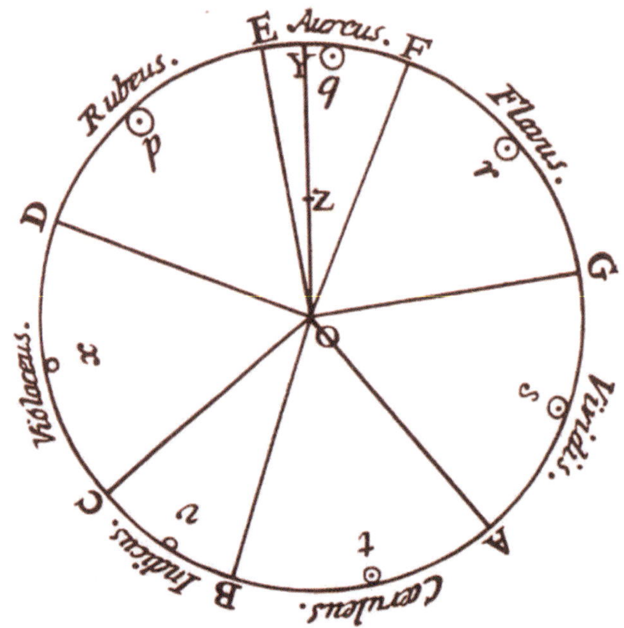

The first colour wheel (after Newton)

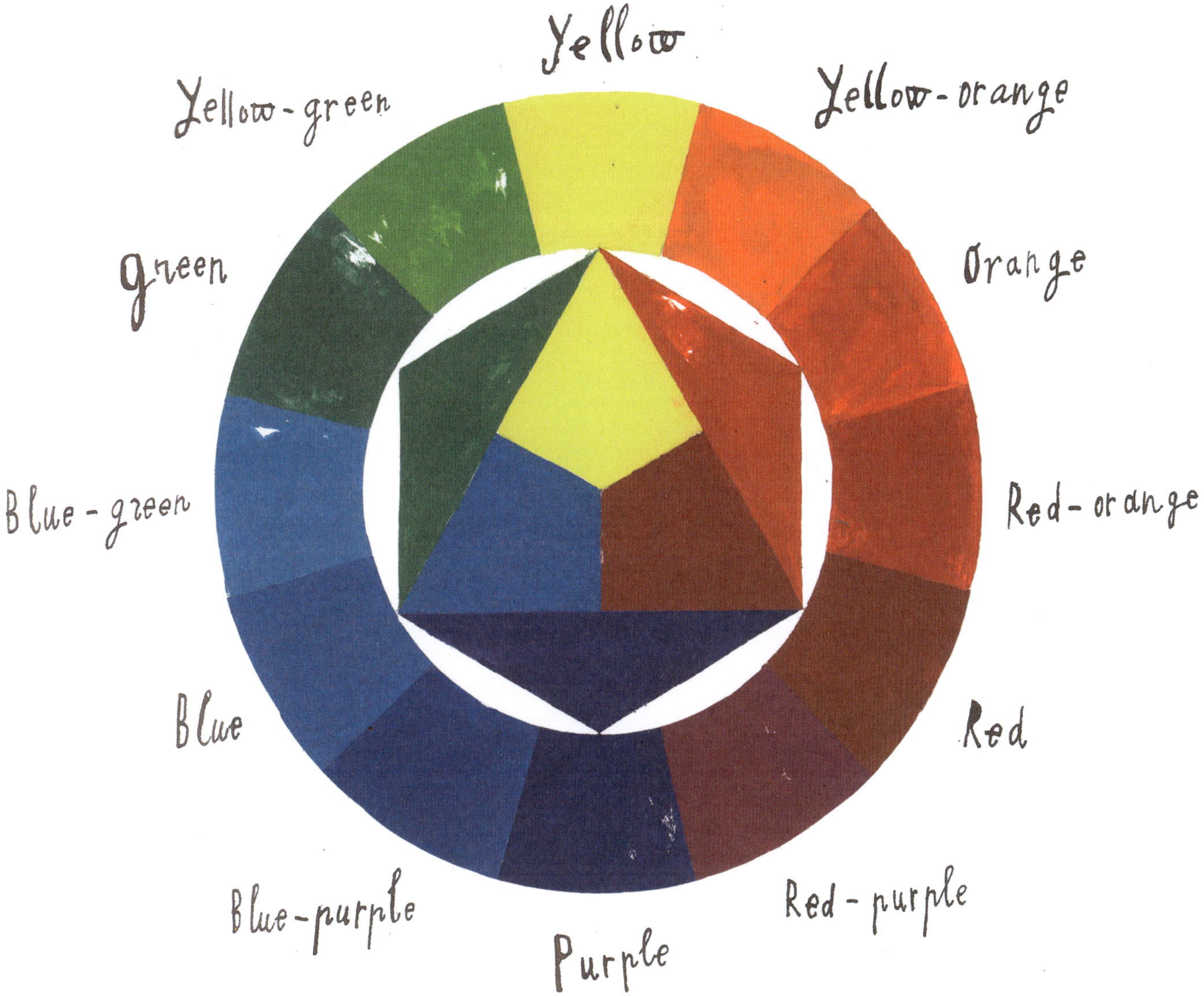

Yellow

Yellow-green

Yellow-orange

Green

Orange

Blue-green

Red-orange

Blue

Red

Blue-purple

Red-purple

Purple

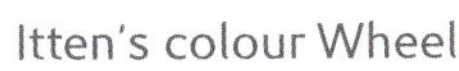

Itten's colour Wheel

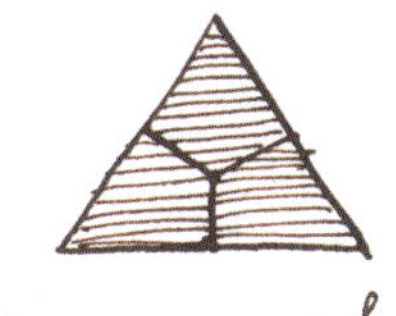

Primary colours
1

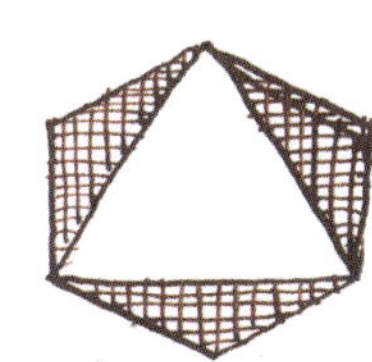

Secondary colours
2

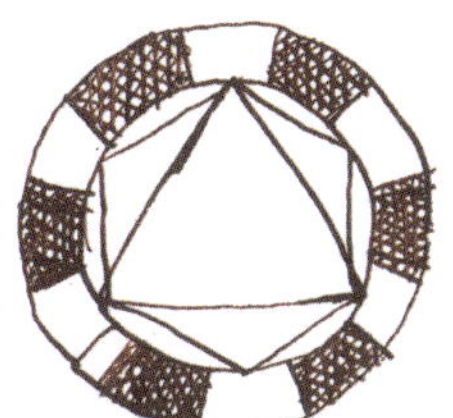

Tertiary colours
3

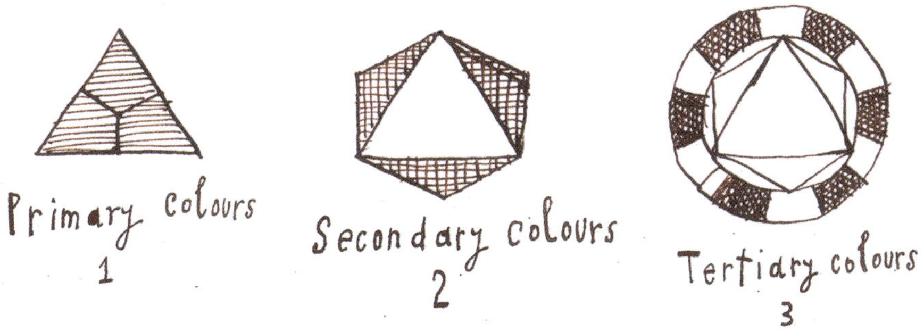

Colour contrasts

Now we come to the area that is directly related to painting and the interaction of colours. Being able to see colour contrasts and to recognize each of them separately is an important part of colour theory. However, you will rarely see a picture where there is only one colour contrast; they are usually mixed. In order to differentiate them better, I tried to use only one contrast each in the dog examples.

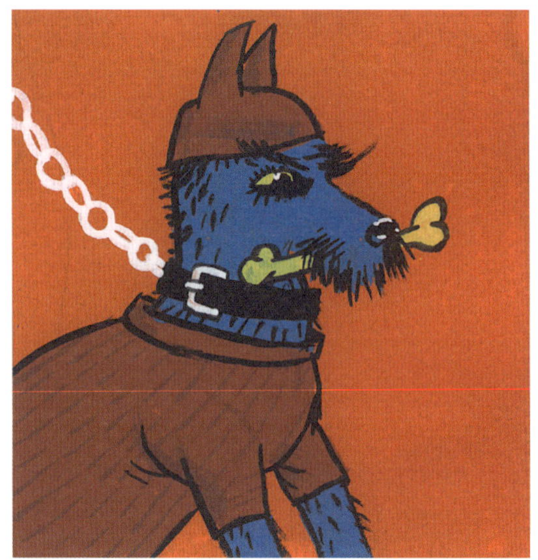

1. Colour-in-itself contrast

This contrast is the simplest of all and means that pure unmixed colours are juxtaposed. You can use primary, secondary and tertiary colours; it is also possible to use pure black or white, which increases the contrast. If black lines separate the individual colours, it increases the contrast effect (see illustration or think of pictures by Piet Mondrian). And if the dividing lines are white, the effect is weakened. It can generally be said that this type of contrast gives the impression of determination and strength.

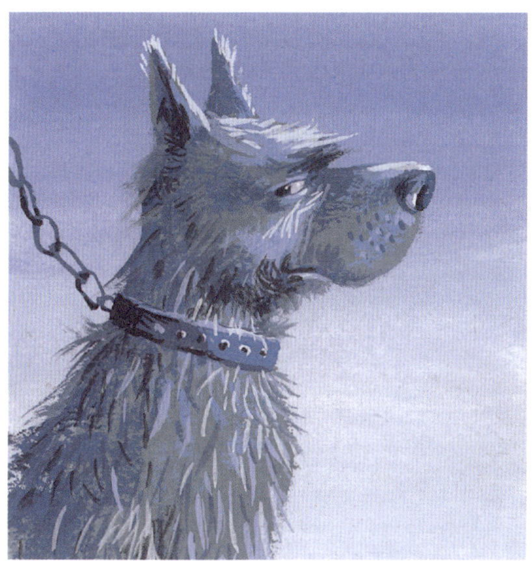

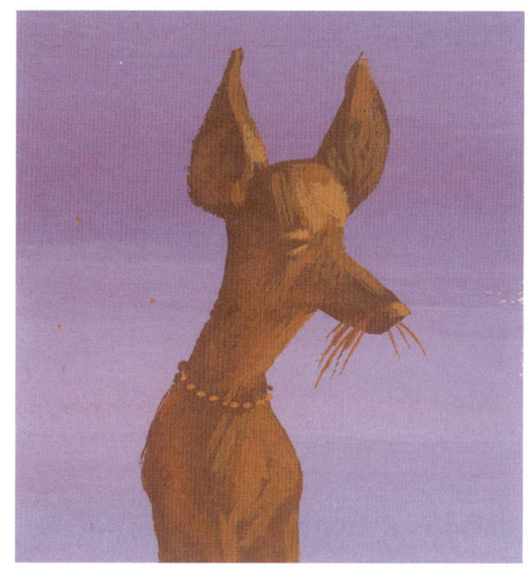

2. Light-dark contrast

This type of contrast is based on the interplay of colours with different tonal values. You can achieve light-dark contrast a) by juxtaposing colours that have different luminosity per se, for example, yellow is the lightest colour and violet is the darkest, and b) by adding it to a hue of white for lightening or black for darkening.

The best way to see the light-dark contrast is to narrow your eyes. This makes the colouration recede and the grey values can be better recognized!

3. Cool-warm contrast

This contrast arises from the simple fact that we humans like to associate colours with sensations. All colours that remind us of water, snow and moisture are perceived as cool and those that make us think of sun and fire as warm.

This principle is clearly integrated in Itten's colour wheel. All warm colours are on the right side and all cool colours are on the left. The warmest hue of red-orange and the coolest hue of teal lie on the horizontal centre line. The cool-warm contrast is an important means of expression in painting. It speaks directly to the viewer's emotions and is ideally suited to indicate possible dualities. For example, these could be such pairs as near/far, cool/warm, open/closed, cheerful/sad, easy/difficult and so on.

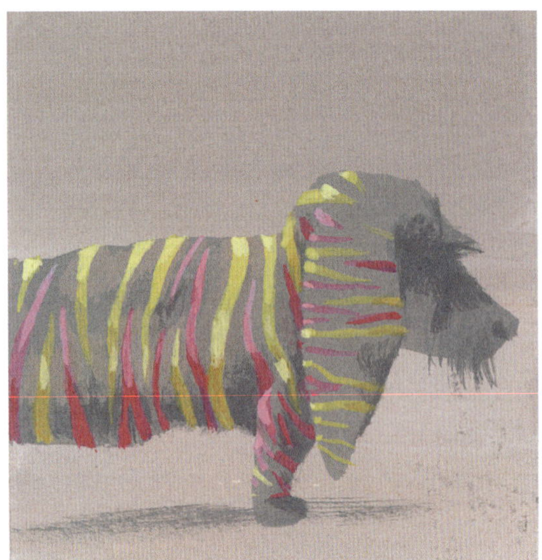

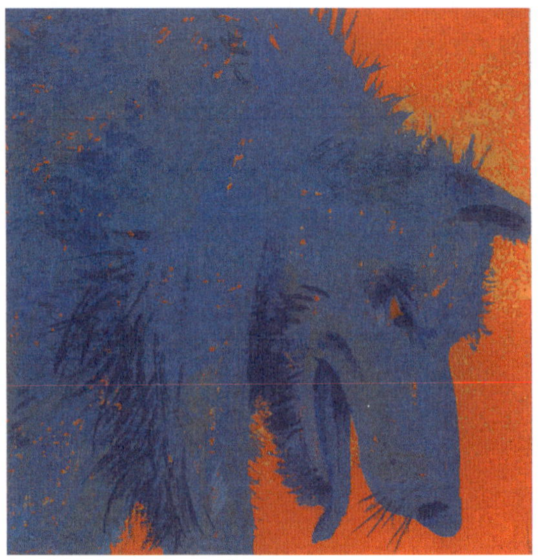

4. Quality contrast

This contrast is based on the interplay between pure, saturated colours and more dull and broken hues. A variation of this is chromatic-achromatic contrast, where saturated "colourful" colours contrast with those of black and white, that is, "achromatic" colours. It is also an effective tool for painting, which can be used to create accents and express moods. You can always change the degree of saturation of a colour by adding the following colours:

1. **Black:** the hue gets darker
2. **White:** the hue gets brighter, more pastel-like, cooler
3. **Grey:** the hue gets cloudy
4. **Complementary colour:** the hue usually gets darker and more broken

5. Quantity contrast

This contrast is also called proportion contrast, because it's about the relationships between the areas of individual colours. Whether it's a tiny dot or a large area of colour– the colour works not only through its presence, but also through its quantity. Contrast theory assumes that a balanced surface design should be based on the inversely proportional ratio of the light values of individual colours.

This means that with the combination of yellow (light value 9) and violet (light value 3), where yellow is three times as bright, one part of yellow would appear harmonious to three parts of violet. However, since a "harmonious" design often appears boring, you should try to bring more tension into the picture through more interesting arrangements. By the way, the light values of the colours are: yellow 9, orange 8, red 6, green 6, blue 4, violet 3.

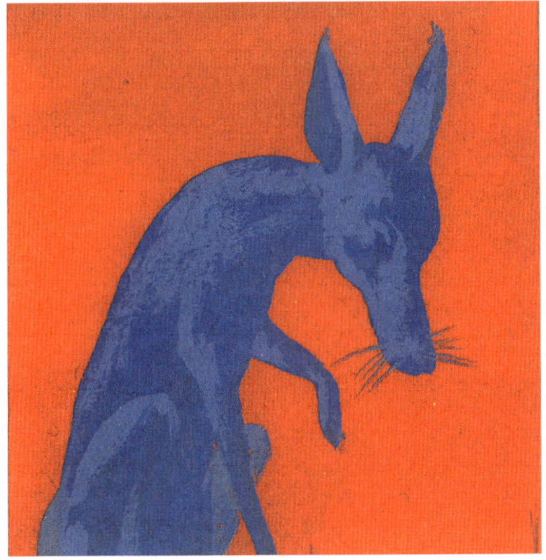

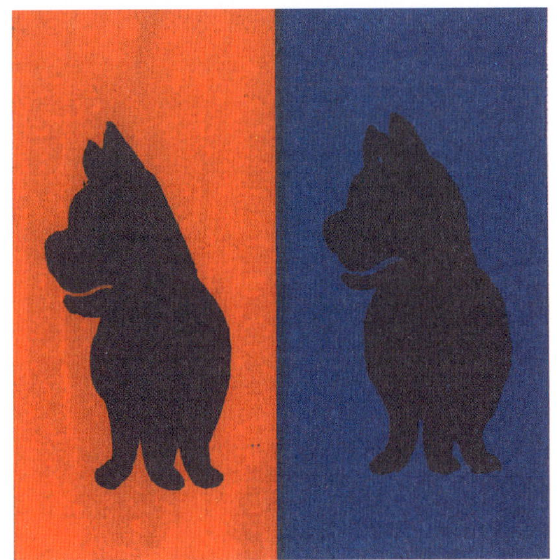

6. Complementary contrast

Complementary colours are always directly opposite one another in the colour wheel. Not only pure hues, but also broken and cloudy colours have their complementary opponents. There's something like a magnetic attraction because the closer two complementary colours come, the stronger their effect grows to the highest intensity. But as soon as they touch and mix, a neutral grey is created.

For example, to precisely determine a complementary colour, you can use a colour wheel, a rotatable cardboard disc that also shows lightened or darkened colours, blends and colour harmonies. Or google "colour calculator" or "colour wheel." Among countless colour generators, I recommend Adobe Color, a clearly structured website where you can play through and save all the well-known colour harmonies (color.adobe.com). But I assure you that your own intuition will help you more in painting than the Internet!

7. Simultaneous contrast

Simultaneous contrast is based on the knowledge that the human eye simultaneously creates a complementary colour to the colour seen. As a result, the same colour– whether it is isolated on white or on differently coloured backgrounds– is always perceived differently. In a picture, therefore, there is permanent mutual influence of the colours that we should be aware of.

Simultaneous contrasts come into their own precisely when complementary colours are not juxtaposed, but rather those that are adjacent to one of the complementary colours in the colour wheel. So, for example, instead of violet vs. yellow, we would put blue-violet vs. yellow together. This is why the identical grey puppy looks bluish on the orange background. Surrounded by blue, it seems to get an orange tinge.

Colour harmonies

You'll notice that when we paint, we always move between tension and balance. And where colour contrasts result in restlessness and explosiveness, there are colour chords that have a harmonizing effect when they occur. According to the laws of colour theory, a chord or a harmony is a relationship of colours that stand in certain positions in the twelve-part colour wheel. A distinction is made between the following options:

- monochrome harmonies
- analogue harmonies
- dyads (two-tone, complementary harmonies)
- triads (three-tone harmonies)
- tetrads (four-tone harmonies)

The effects of different colour combinations have been researched intensively for a long time and most of the knowledge we use today can be traced back to Johannes Itten. But here, too, the motto is: Feeling comes before accuracy. Because while graphic designers can determine the colour of each pixel on the screen and calculate their complementary colour, as well as possible dyads, triads and tetrads, when painting we rely on our intuition and experience.

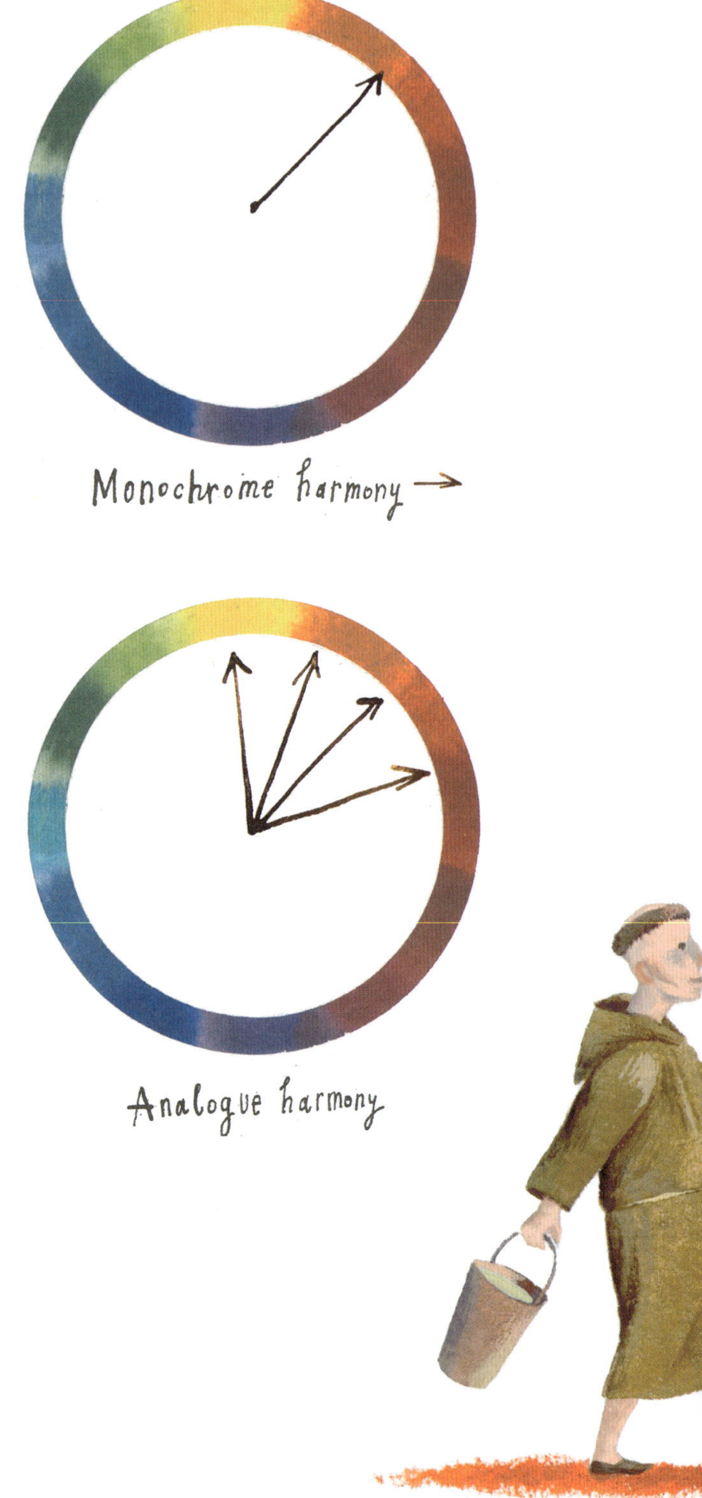

1. Monochrome harmony

If your painterly talents are not yet in top form, try to keep the ball flat and get to the goal with simple design tools. This simply means that you work with fewer colours, so "less colourful". It could even be that reducing the palette spurs your creativity. And you will also be certain of the effect of your colours. This is where you'll need the first kind of harmony, monochrome harmony. It is created when you take a single colour and combine it with its darkened or lightened variants. Your picture may live in a monochrome world, but you can be sure you can't make any major mistakes!

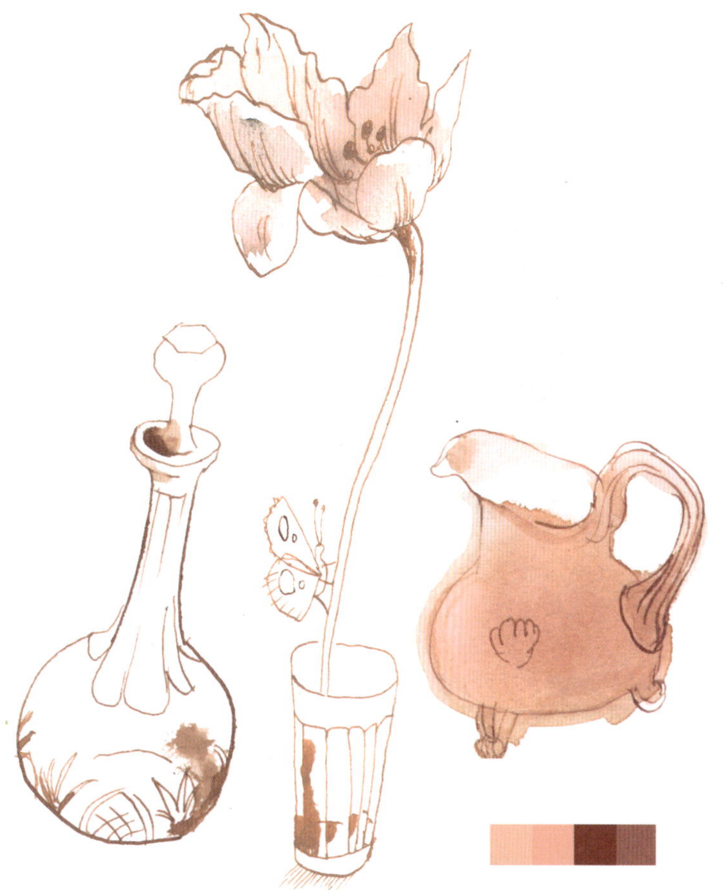

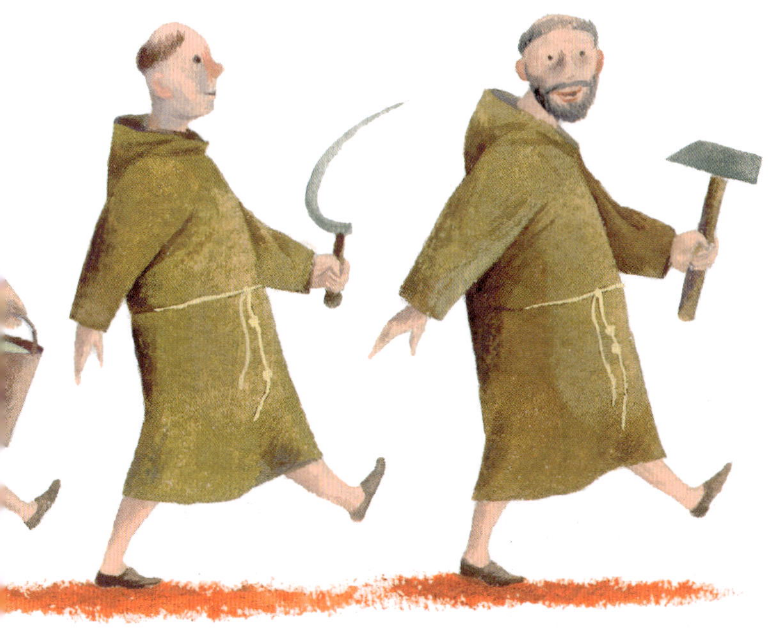

2. Analogue harmony

With analogue *harmony*, you go a step further and combine some colours that are the closest neighbours on the colour wheel. Some colours may be weakened in their saturation; others may appear as full tones. If you use this type of colour chord, it is often the area proportions of individual colours that are important, see quantity contrast.

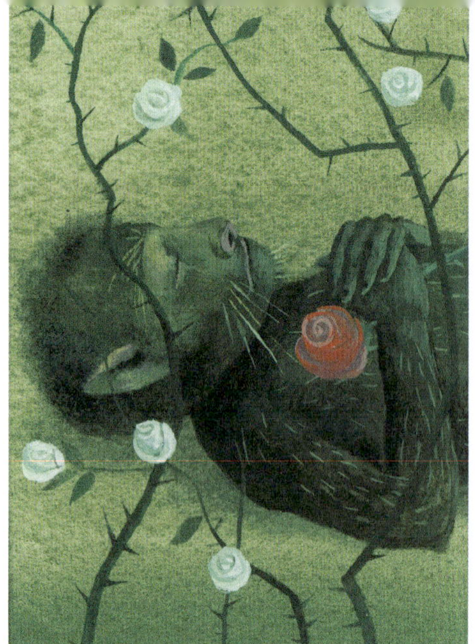

4. Triadic harmony

The next possibility for creating colour chords is to pick three colours equidistant from each other on the colour wheel. Connected by lines, they form an equilateral triangle. When this principle is applied, it's called *triadic harmony*. For example, solid blue-green, yellow-orange and red-violet – but also in variants tinged with black and white – form such triads. A modified version is when the triangle doesn't have three equal sides, but only two: thus an isosceles acute-angled triangle.

3. Complementary harmony

To use this next principle you don't have to be an expert in the colour harmonies. It's quite simple: Just take colours from the opposite areas of the colour wheel. Just as analogue colour chords have a calming effect, complementary colours attract each other and have an invigorating, and at the same time harmonious, effect. This type of colour chord is called a *dyad* or *complementary harmony* and is particularly effective, for example for placing accents. Again, it's important to deal with the area ratios inventively to create more tension and play between the two colour poles.

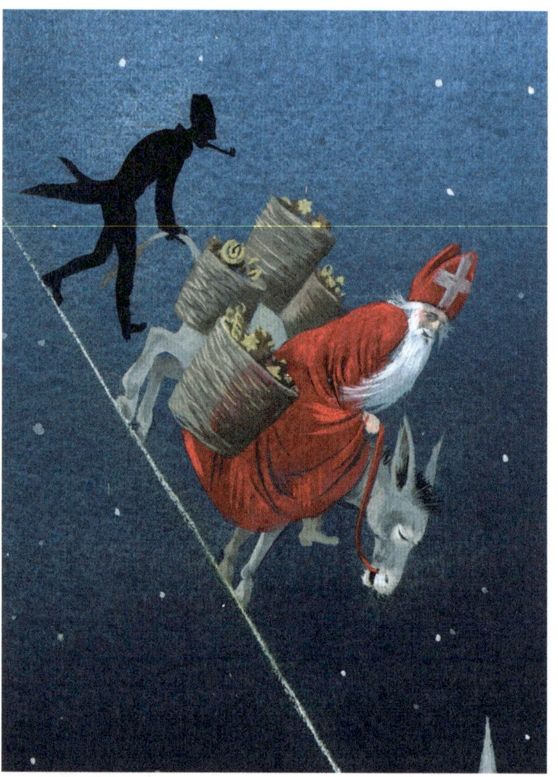

5. Tetradic harmony

A *tetradic* or *four-tone harmony*, as the name implies, is a matter of combinations of colours that are in the colour wheel in a square, a rectangle or, more rarely, a trapezoid. It sounds quite cerebral, but in practice it's not that complicated. Tetrads are like an extension of complimentary harmonies, where instead of each colour, two colours are taken from the left and right of the colour wheel. They may seem busy, so pay attention to the quantity contrasts.

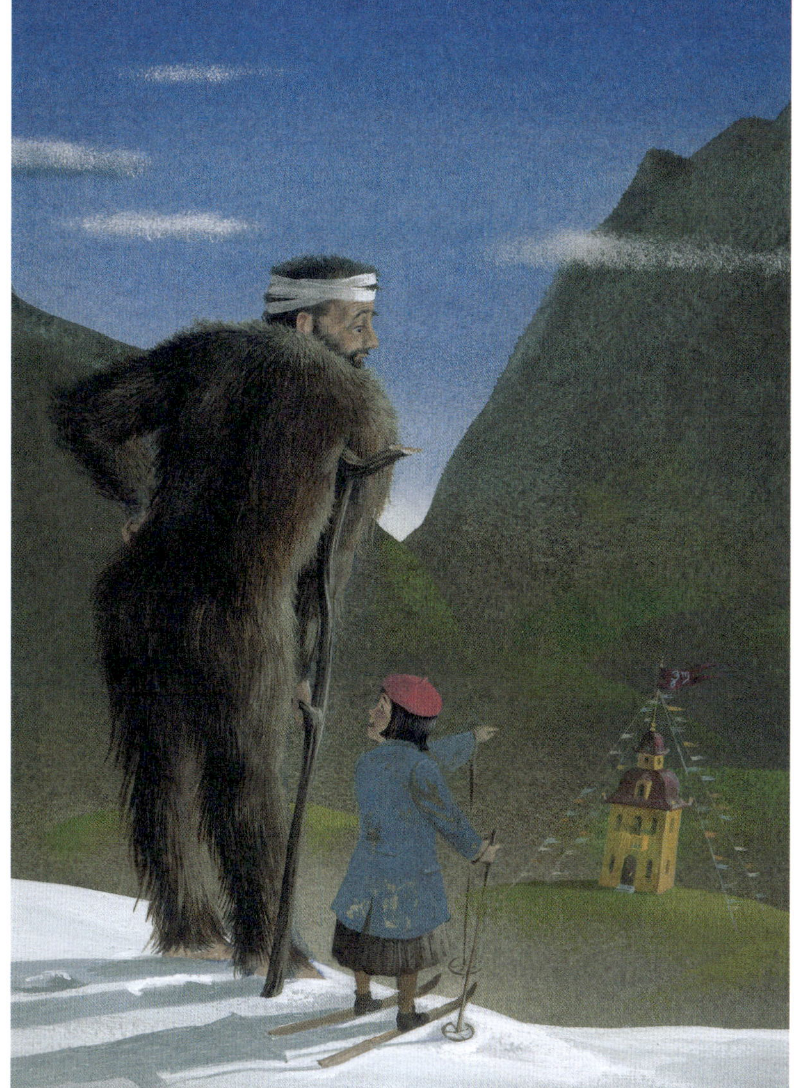

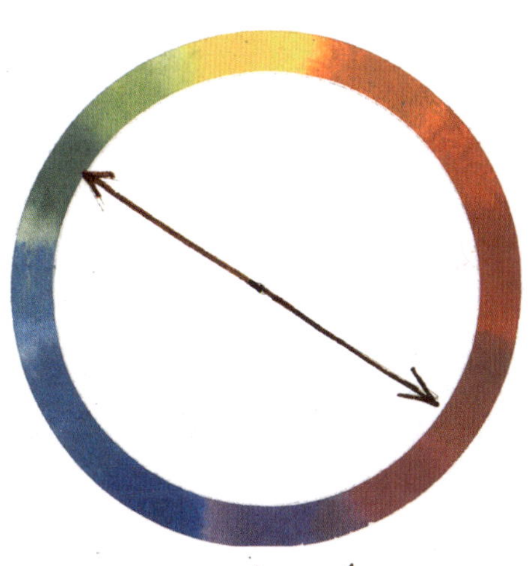

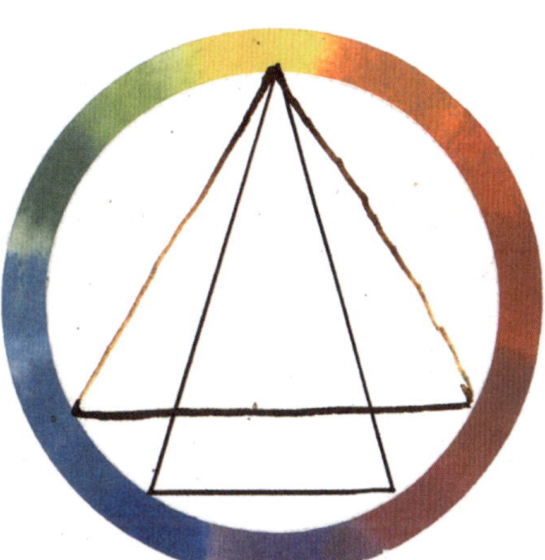

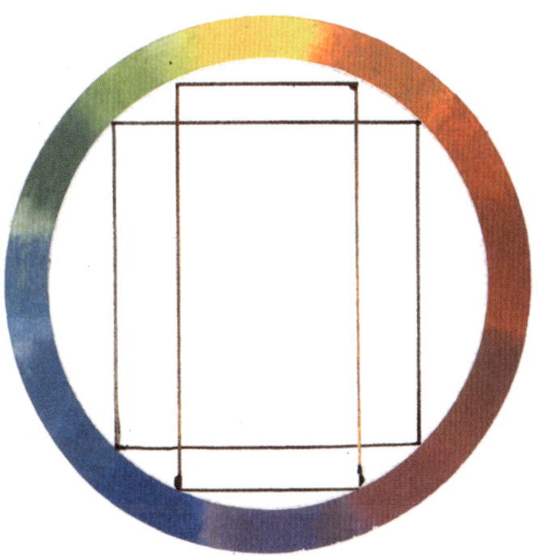

The home studio. Setting up your workplace

A good workplace is worth a mint. Did you know that the novel Lolita was written in the back seat of a car because Vladimir Nabokov felt protected there from noise and hullabaloo? Agatha Christie also didn't need a study and preferred to write her crime novels at the kitchen table between meals, or sometimes in the bedroom. We all have our quirks, which usually remain well hidden, so I'm fascinated by the idea that our living and working spaces are a fairly accurate reflection of what is going on in our heads. But artists' studios always look surprisingly different. See for yourself how chaotic or tidy things are on your desk. I'm just going to offer a few tips on what I've found to be the minimum or simply most practical when setting up a workspace for painting with gouache.

Let's start with the main question: the paints. What options do you have when you buy your first set of gouache paints or put together your own paint palette?

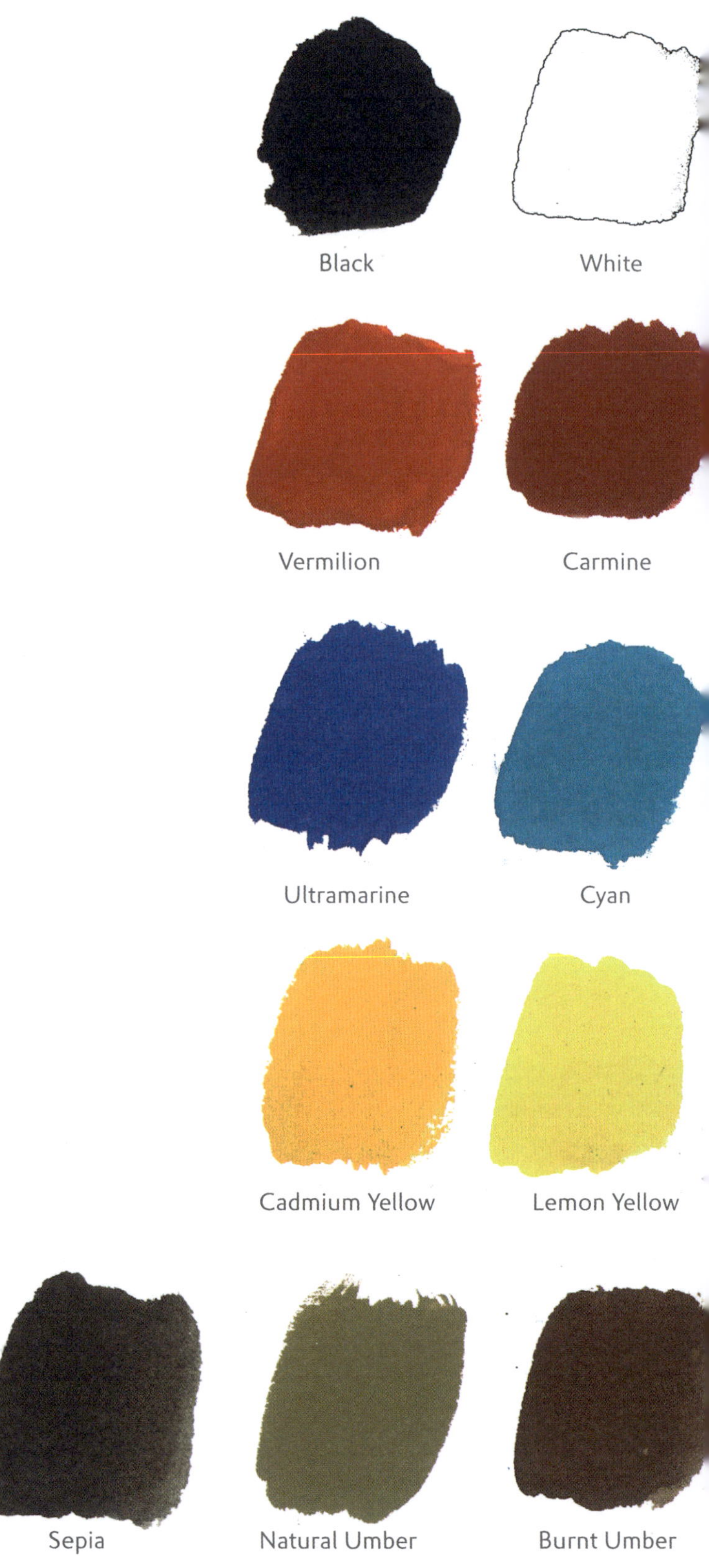

Grey

Magenta

Prussian Blue

Chrome Green

Emerald Green

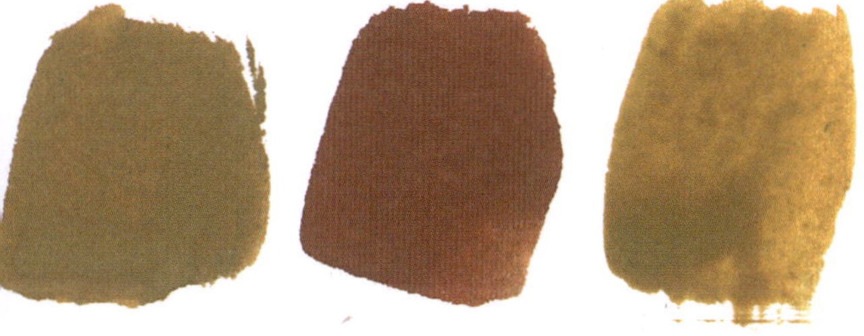
Sienna Natural Burnt Sienna Ochre

Your first set of gouache paints

If you want it the easy way, I recommend buying a set in artist quality from Royal Talens (jars or tubes), Schmincke (Horadam or HKS®) or Winsor & Newton. Depending on your budget, you can choose between several brands. Royal Talens sells good beginner sets with 12 small, 16-ml jars that don't cost a fortune, or 10 larger, 20-ml tubes for a proportionate cost increase. Winsor & Newton offers 10 paint tubes of 14 ml each if you're willing to spend a little more; Schmincke HKS® is available in a wooden box with 12 larger, 20-ml tubes at a similar price point. At the top end of the pricing spectrum, Schmincke offers a selection of 10 Horadam® 15-ml gouache tubes in a stylish metal tin.

Another nice option is to choose your own paints. Start with at least 12 colours – the first two being black and white (possibly with a grey). Then add at least two shades of red, a warm and a cool. I suggest vermilion and carmine or magenta, for example. Two or three shades of blue, such as ultramarine, cyan and Prussian blue. Two shades of yellow, also warm and cool: cadmium and lemon yellow. A nice shade of green, either chrome or emerald green. Then choose a few beautiful earth tones, depending on your preference – sepia, natural umber or burnt umber, natural sienna, burnt sienna and ochre yellow. This will take you to the first 12-18 shades that can (and should!) be expanded later.

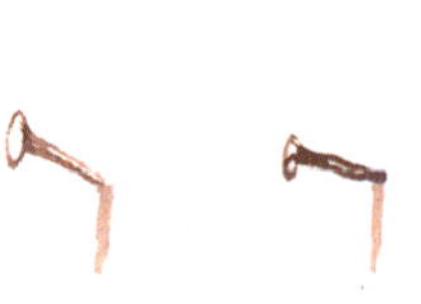

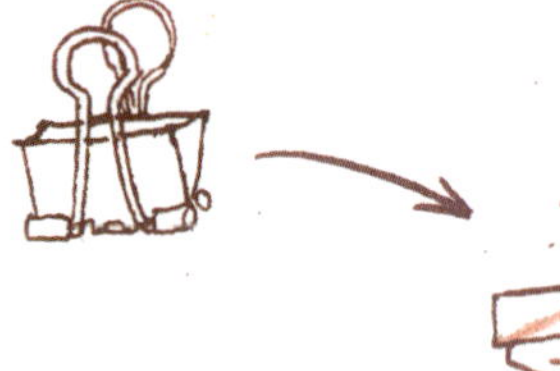

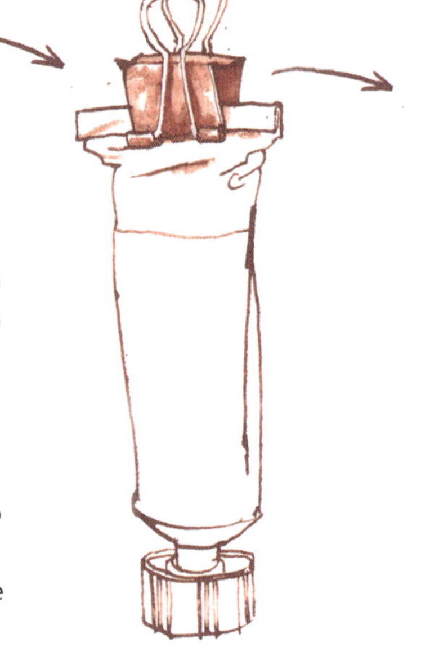

You probably won't use all of your paint tubes at once. So choose the tubes (or jars) that you really use and place them behind the pallet. I rarely have more than 8-10 jars on my desk at the same time. But what about all my other paints? There is a nicer method than storing them in a tin. I picked it up in my cousin's studio. It creates a better overview but it only works with tubes and not with glass jars.

Find a bit of empty wall space or a wooden board. Then hammer about 2 cm-long thin nails in at a distance of about 3 cm horizontally and 8 cm vertically from each other, as many as you have tubes of paint, and some more for new paints you'll add later. Now clip each tube with a binder clip (available from an art supply shop) on the seam edge and hang it upside down on the nails. Now you can sort the paints as you like, for example by the colour wheel for better orientation.

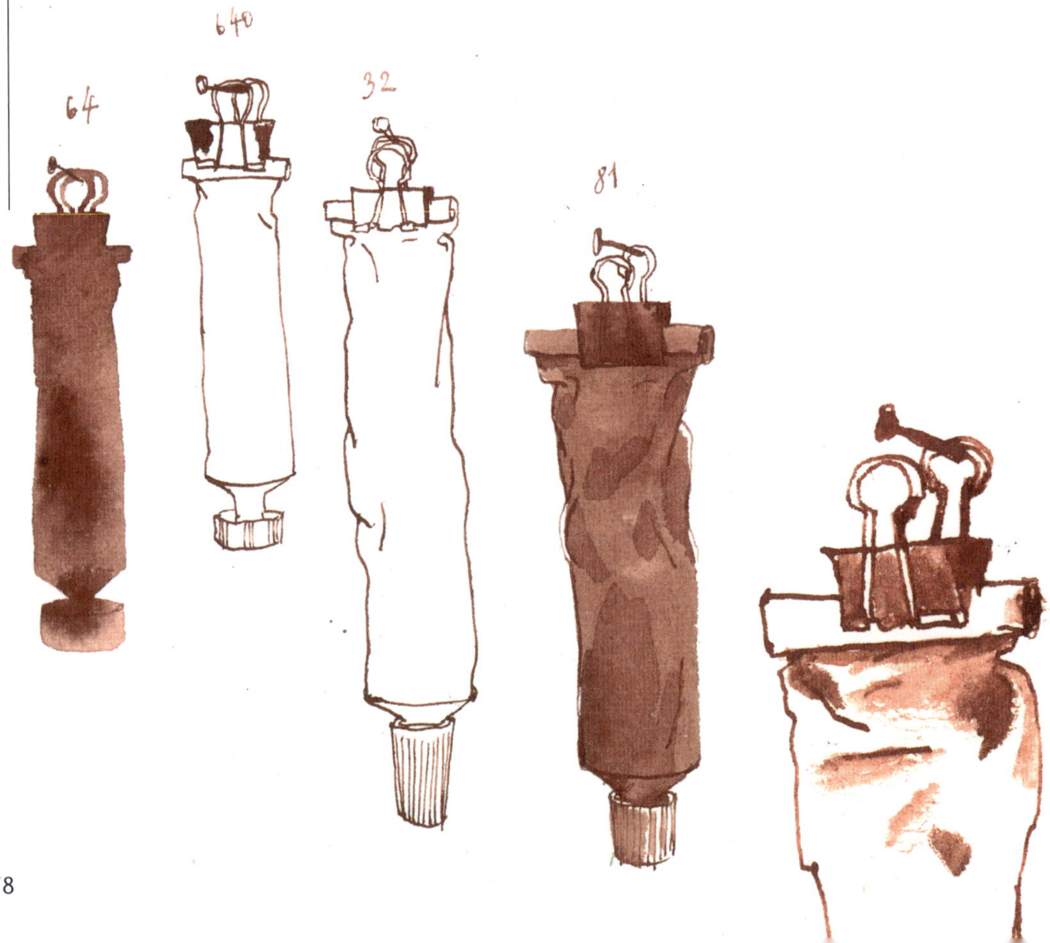

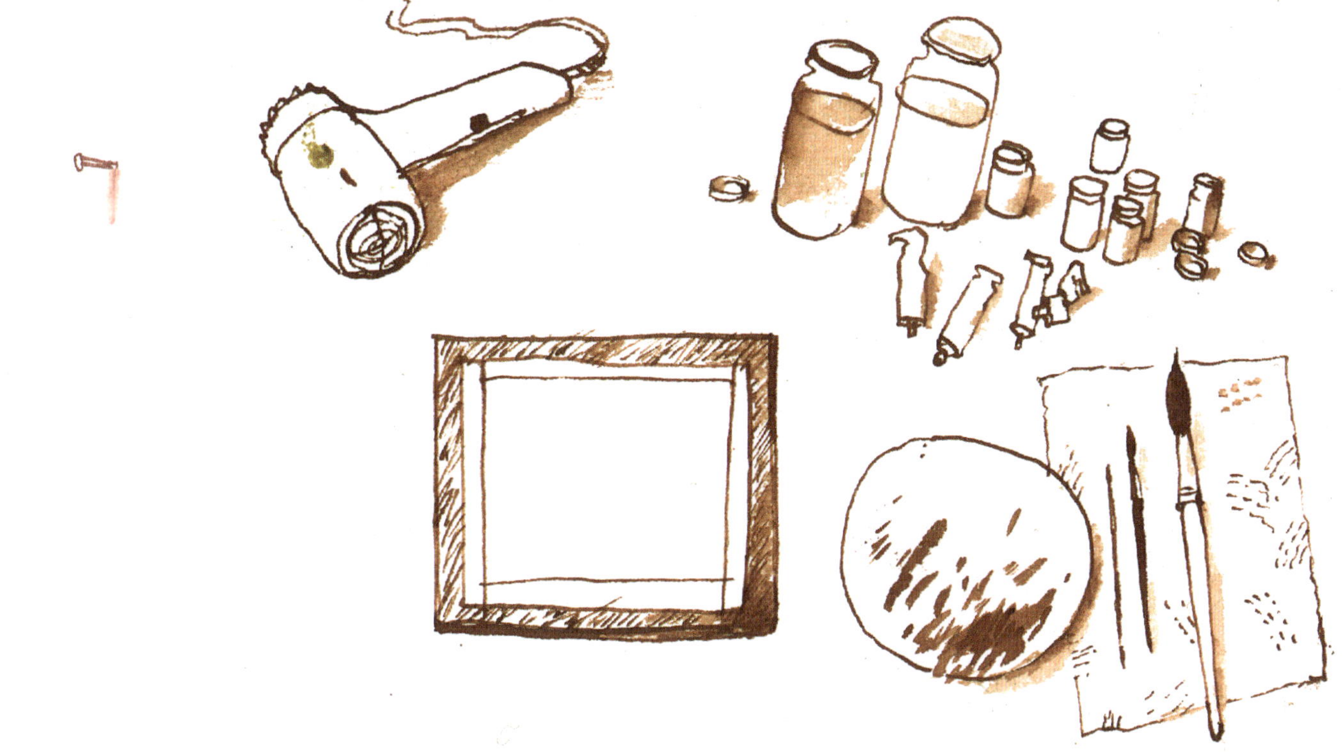

Next you need the *brushes*. You should put a small selection right next to the paints. The basic assortment includes two at first: small and large. The smaller one, your No. 3, 4 or 5 – should be made of Kolinsky sable-hair or be a brush made of a blend with a good tip. The larger one – from No. 12 – can be made from squirrel or ox-hair, alternatively from a blend. You'll use the small brush for details and the large one for backgrounds and glazing washes. Later you can get a bristle brush (for working with pasty paints) and a medium size brush of approx. No. 6, 7 or 8 made of sable-hair, synthetic or a blend.

Depending on how "wet and slushy" you paint, you may need to shorten your drying time. Then your *hair dryer* should be close by and at hand.

And last but not least, you need a *paper towel* next to the paints and the mixing palette for cleaning the brushes and quickly dabbing off excess paint.

All other painting materials, such as sponges, fixatives or masking fluid, can be kept tidily away from the battlefield and await their turn.

→ TIP: Since the water you'll be using to dilute or rework the paints will quickly get dirty, I recommend that you set a second cup of water next to the first. It will be used as soon as your brush has to be really clean again (for example to mix very light colours such as yellow or white).

Minor intermezzo.
Analogue vs. digital

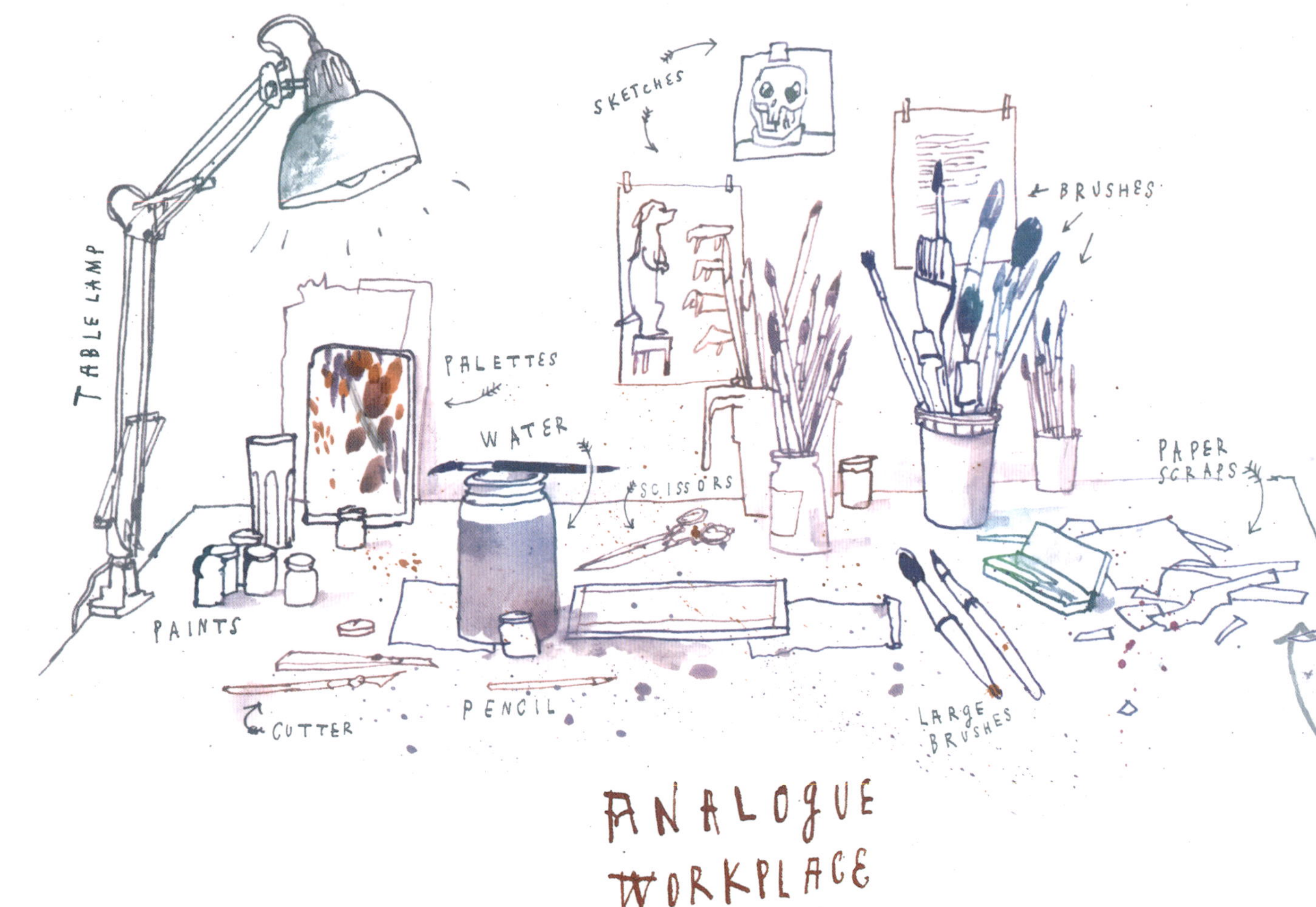

While we're talking about the optimal workplace, I would like to make a case for visual hygiene at the desk. Anyone who paints is exposed to digital media sooner rather than later: at the earliest when searching for references and at the latest when the finished picture is scanned and put online or emailed. That's why it is commonplace for a laptop to be part of the standard equipment of designers who also work in analogue fashion. And it seems only practical if the device with the subject you just googled is right in front of you to paint.

It took awhile until I had to admit to myself that although everyone did it, I wasn't so happy with hopping back and forth between painting, writing emails or editing pictures in Photoshop. My ability to multitask, which the computer in the workplace strained more and more, robbed me of the calm and concentration that are so important for painting. The nearby computer turned from a useful tool into a distraction. So I decided to spatially separate the digital from the analogue in my workplace. That means that my laptop has no business being wherever there are paints, scraps of paper, etc. And there is no painting, spraying or whittling in a corner with a computer, scanner and printer. I've set up two areas in my studio that are a few metres apart. Every time a painted picture moves into the digital world, I get up and go from the drawing to the computer desk, where the printer and scanner are also located. And if, for example, I don't know what a guinea fowl feather looks like, I google it and print out the image. Only then do I hang it on the wall as a reference.

You don't have to be dogmatic, but perhaps your computer is also butting in to help where it's not needed. In any case, not blindly mixing the brush and mouse in the workplace works best for me. Just like the way we separate the main course from the dessert and enjoy one after the other.

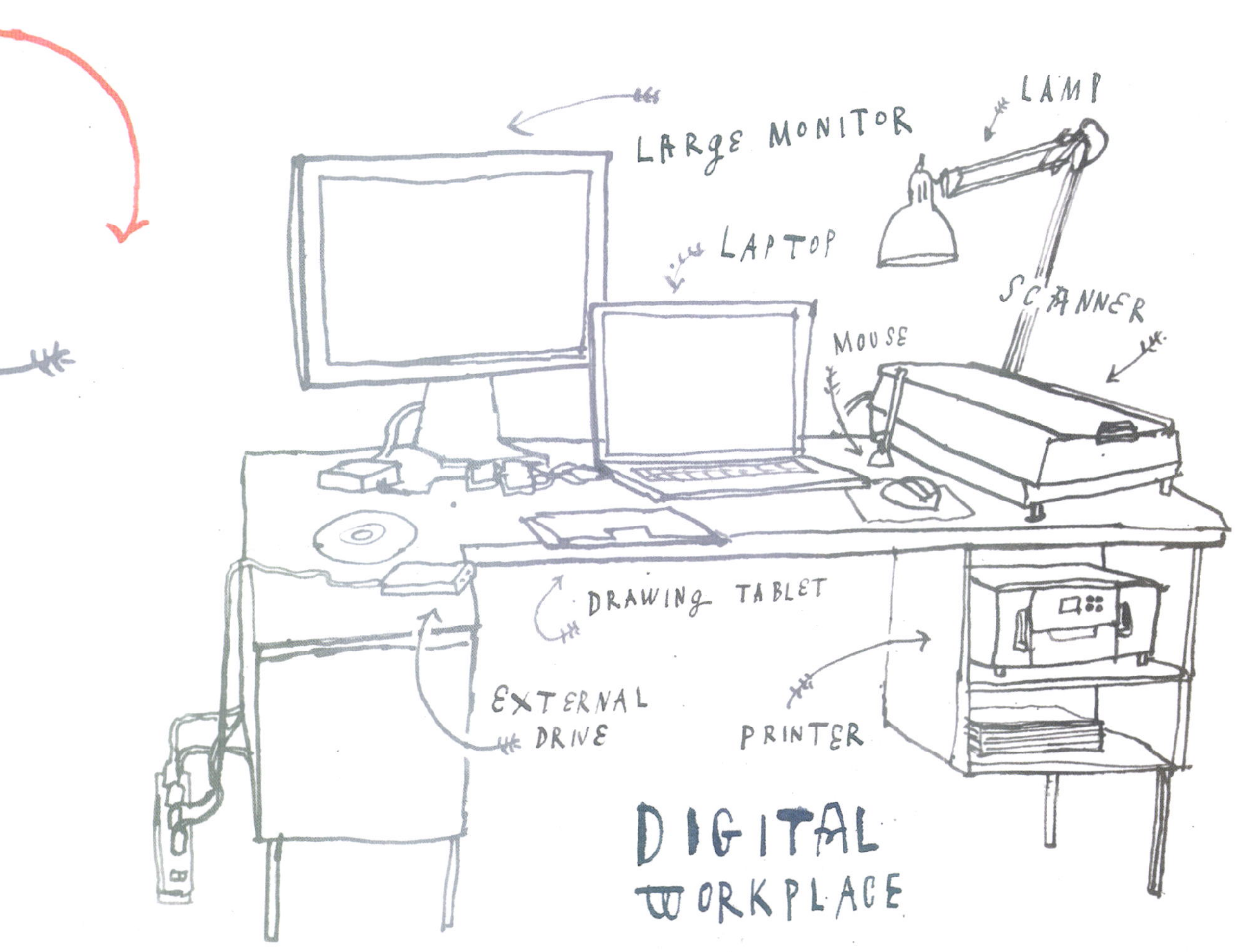

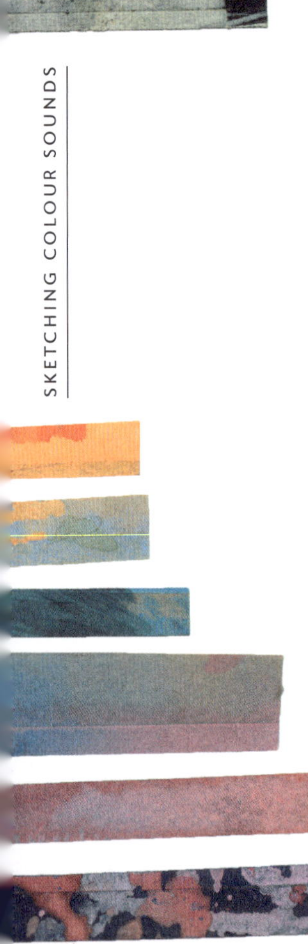

What does this yellow sound like? Sketching colour sounds

There is a phenomenon called synaesthesia. Some people have the ability to "see" sounds as colours or, conversely, to hear certain colour sounds as tones or melodies. Or even to taste them. Even if most of us are not true synaesthetes, we draw parallels between painting and making music. A description of music often speaks of timbres, of dark and light, warm and cool sounds.

As early as 1900 many artists were looking for correlations and rules of perception and expressed them as total works of art. For example, the composer Alexander Scriabin with his clavier à lumières or the founder of abstract painting Wassily Kandinsky, whose stage compositions with Thomas de Hartmann's The Yellow Sound (1912) and the "colour-tone drama" Violet (1914) are today considered to be the forerunners of Expressionist drama.

I don't think you have to be Kandinsky to recognize the importance of colour and sound combinations. Because colour can bring fleeting emotions as well as complex moods into our pictures that a monochrome or even black and white picture cannot convey. I therefore find it very important to determine the main colours of my planned picture in advance.

In order to feel out the right colour mood, it helps to make many samples with different colours. Then cut them out in snippets with a cutter and put them together into several groups of four or five. This way, the "wrong" hues can be sorted out quickly. New combinations thus form and soon you've got a new colour palette!

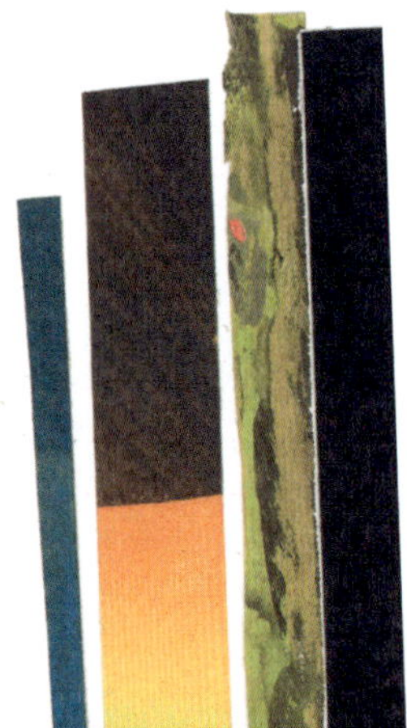

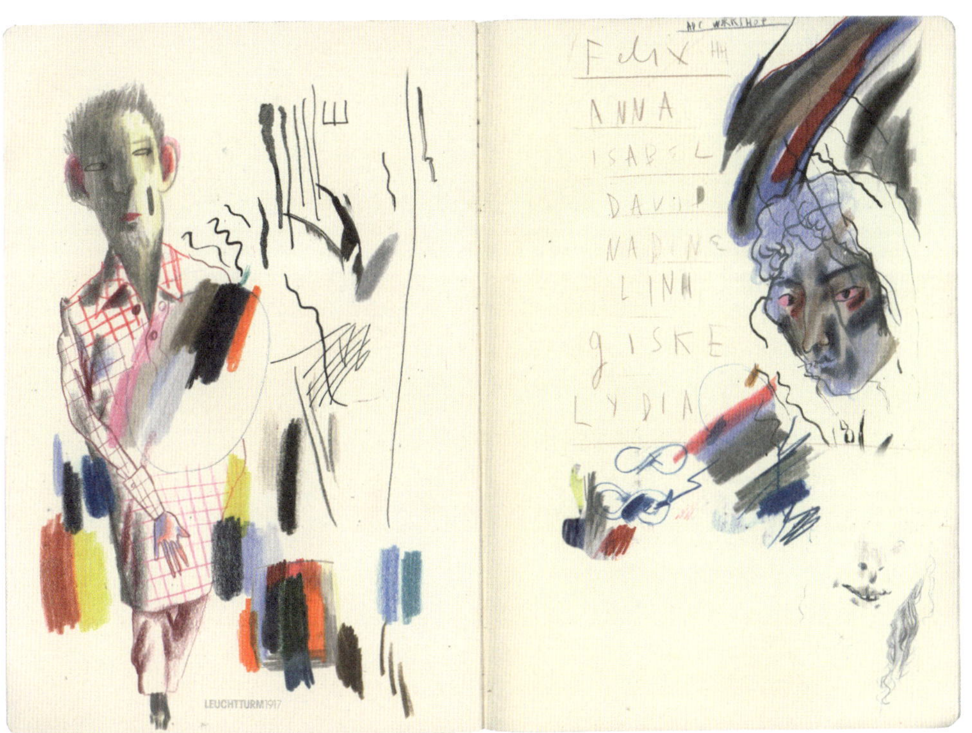

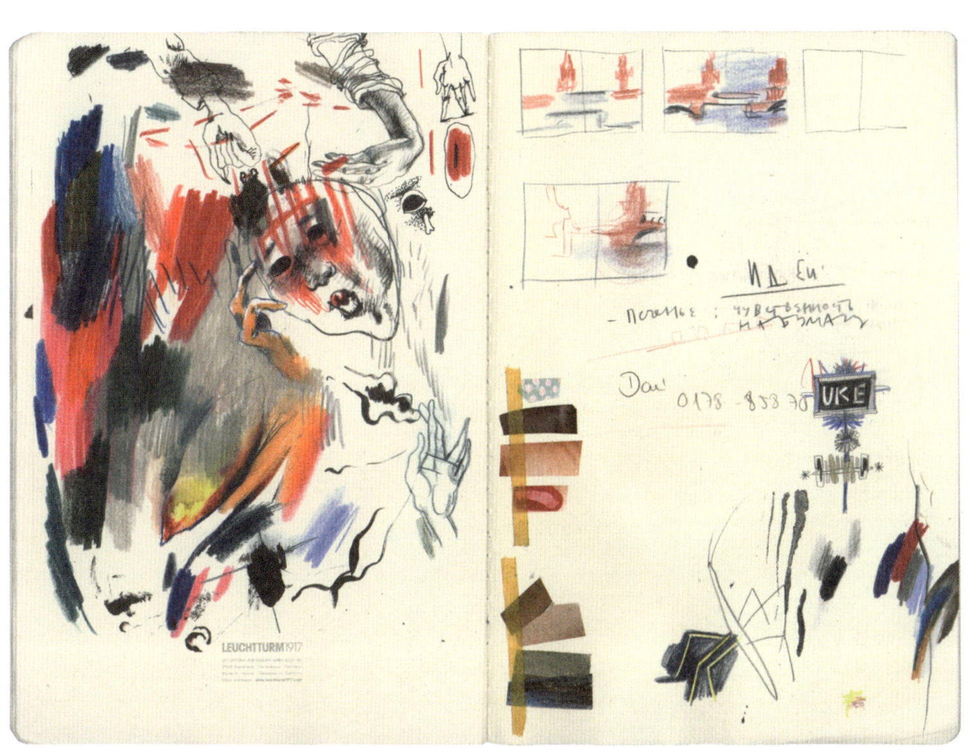

→TIP: The colour snippets can be painted. I also recommend sharpening your sense of interesting and unusual colour combinations in everyday life. What works very well is to rummage through books, magazines or advertising brochures, and when attractive colour combinations appear, simply cut them out and glue them in your sketchbook.

A little planning goes a long way. Thinking about work steps in advance

You'll see that painting in this technique is also a mental adventure. Gouache won't allow you to do everything you want with it, but it rewards anyone who is considerate of its minor foibles. So what's the right order when painting with gouache? Do I start with the details in the foreground and then go over the picture with a transparent glaze? Or should I paint the background first and then paint the figures on it? The answer is: It depends. So a little planning is a good idea.

When considering your picture, try to keep the following features of gouache in mind. It will help you achieve your desired results more easily.

Reworking. The paints can be re-dissolved with water and reworked. Sometimes removing one layer of paint spares you from having to apply several layers later on.

Opacity. Light hues can cover up the dark ones, but there's always a risk that the lower layer will dissolve or "bleed through." Therefore, you should avoid painting on very dark backgrounds with very light colours.

Number of paint layers. You'll want fewer if you paint with watery glazes and definitely with a pasty style of painting with a dry brush: You cannot layer infinite amounts of paint– like you can with acrylic– without adding special painting media. The paint is likely to crack and crumble. Think about how you can achieve the desired result with up to four or five layers of paint.

Employ transparency. In theory, you can mix any light tone with opaque white, but in practice it's often advisable to let the paper shine through (as with watercolour painting). Try to use gouache transparently and don't paint over the paper completely, especially at the beginning.

→ TIP: A picture like this Moby Dick painted using a mixed technique needs to be planned. First, the background was applied as a wash with a transparent turquoise blue, which turned darker on the bottom. Then came the white whale with all its dimples and wrinkles painted in light colours, partly transparent, partly opaque. And then the entire picture was given a yellowish glaze, which again minimized all the light-dark and colour contrasts. This gave the picture the desired "underwater look."

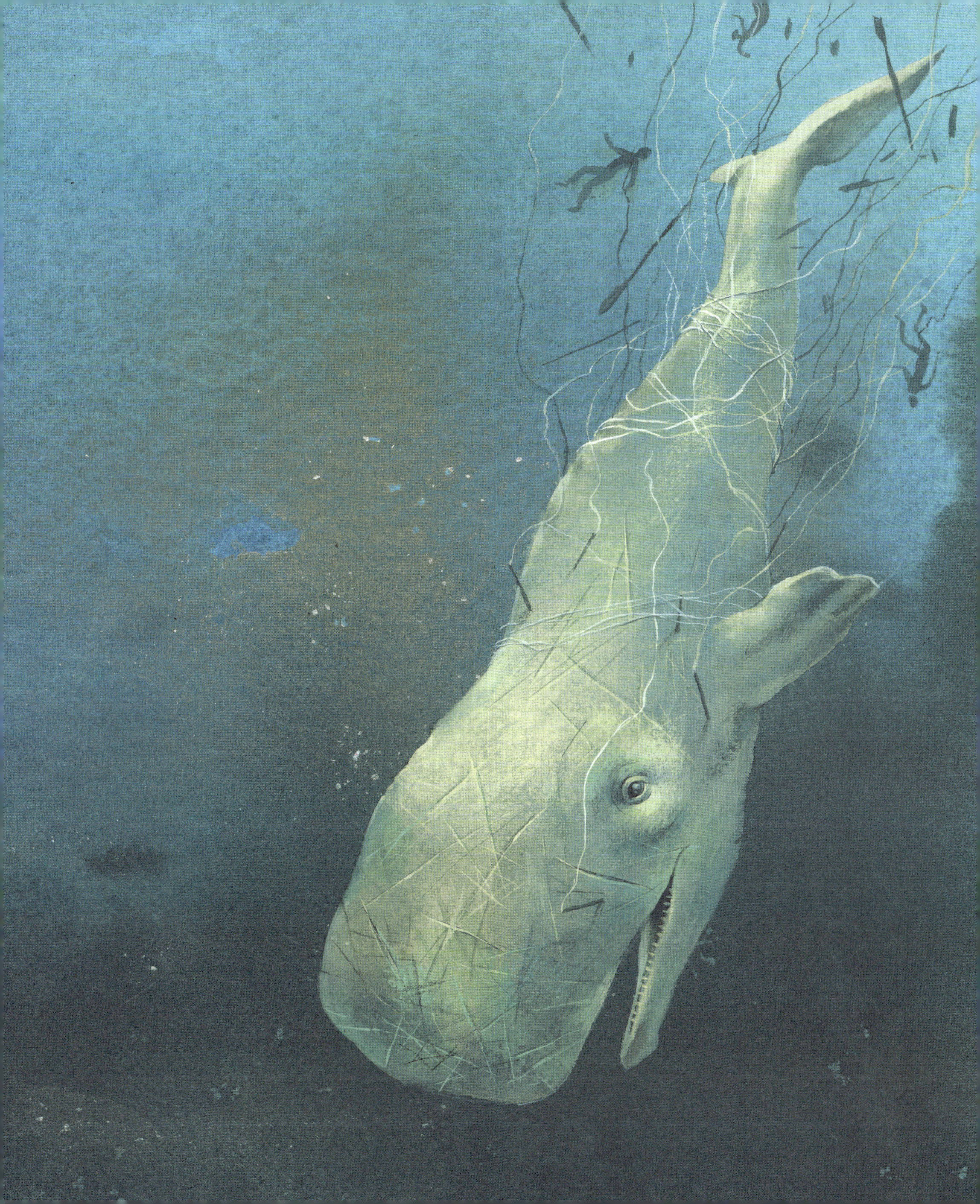

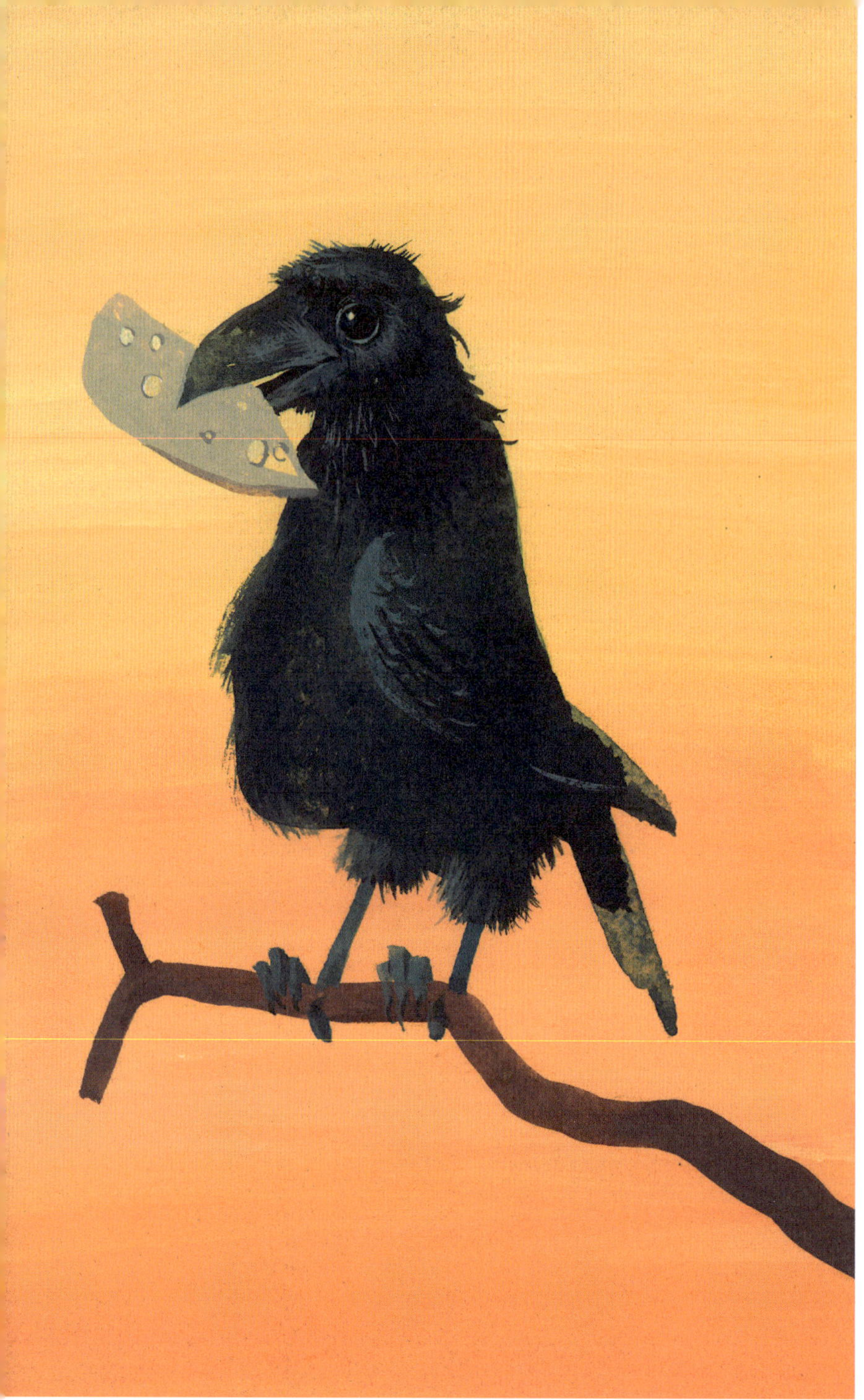

For an example of different painting styles, I painted a raven, once black and once white. (And both have fairly been given a piece of cheese). Take a close look at how different colours influence the work steps. Because when painting picture no. 1 they are very different than its "negative," no. 2.

With black raven no. 1 it was simple to start with the light background and to paint over it in more (ever-darker) layers. The usual process of working from the background to foreground and later to add details works great here.

The black raven was painted like this:

1. Create the yellow background
2. Paint the branch, black raven silhouette
3. Dab away the superfluous black with a paper towel
4. Paint the feathers on the body, model the head with light grey
5. Paint the fuzz on the feet and the cheese

For the white raven, the same sequence would mean that we would have to apply white (raven) and light brown (branch) over the black background. That could be problematic, because black is easy to dissolve and rework, which we don't want to happen in this case. Therefore, the white of the paper was left blank prior to priming with the masking fluid. This meant that after removing the latex film it was possible to finish painting the plumage with a few brush strokes. And all that without having to paint over the black in the background!

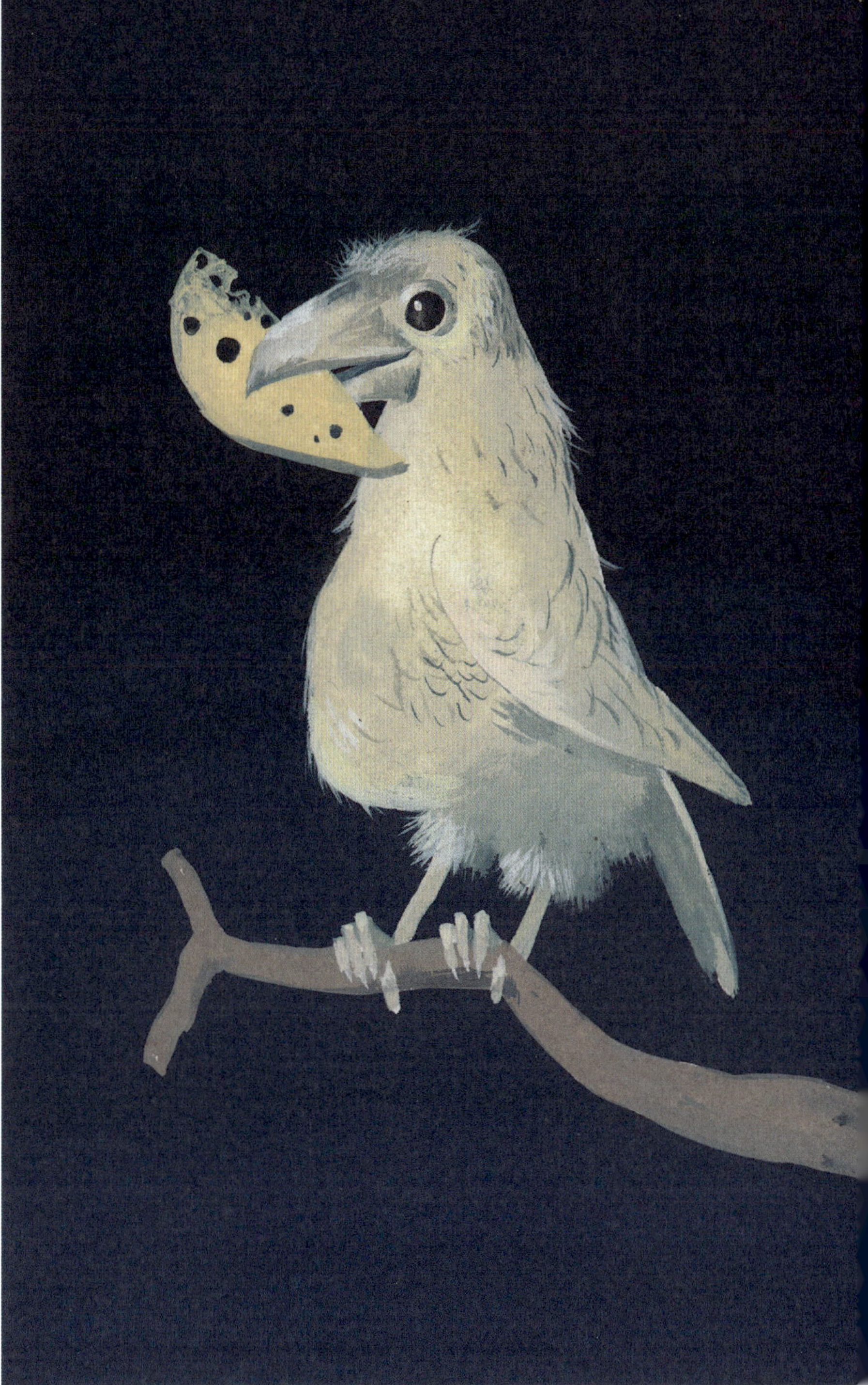

For this picture it was a bit different:

1. Cover the light silhouette of the raven, the cheese and the branch with masking fluid
2. Apply background loosely in black/Prussian blue
3. Remove masking fluid
4. Paint the branch and raven in transparent greyish-yellow, then the darker plumage
5. Model the eye and head
6. Paint the fuzz on the feet and the cheese

Nothing is impossible. Gouache techniques

Gouache can be painted both transparently as with watercolour, but also opaquely, comparable to oil or acrylic. We can cover with gouache or moisten and rework the dried paint. In this chapter we'll go through the broad repertoire of techniques that make gouache so unique and try them out step by step.

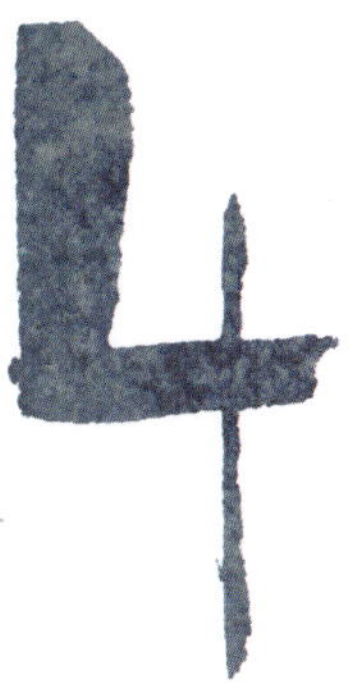

Almost like watercolour, but not quite. Glazing and washes

You already learned at the beginning of this book that gouache and watercolour have a lot in common. Now let's take a closer look at what we can do with this knowledge. Gouache paints are, by definition, opaque watercolours. But that's only partly true, because gouache can also be painted transparently. As soon as we use plenty of water, gouache doesn't differ significantly in its application from watercolour at all. So we'll first familiarize and try out glazing and washing, two basic techniques of watercolour painting, in gouache.

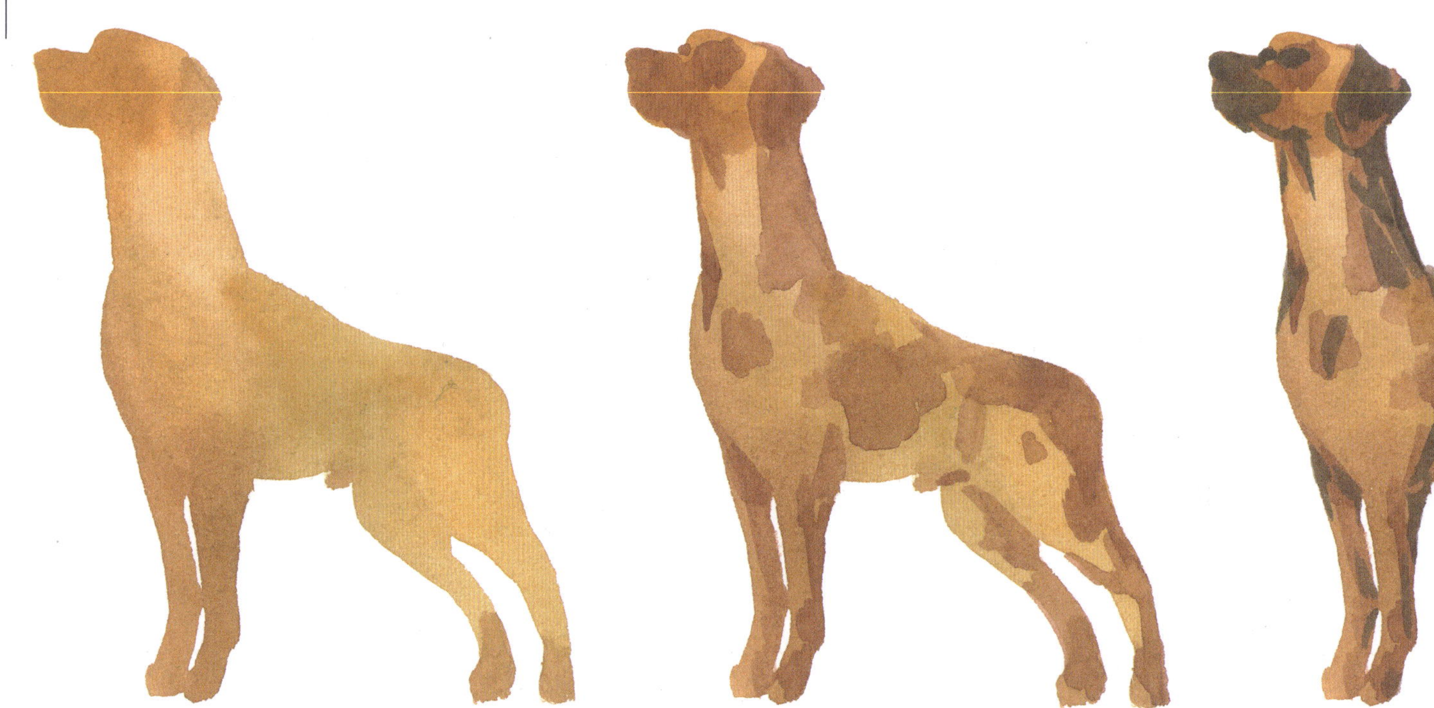

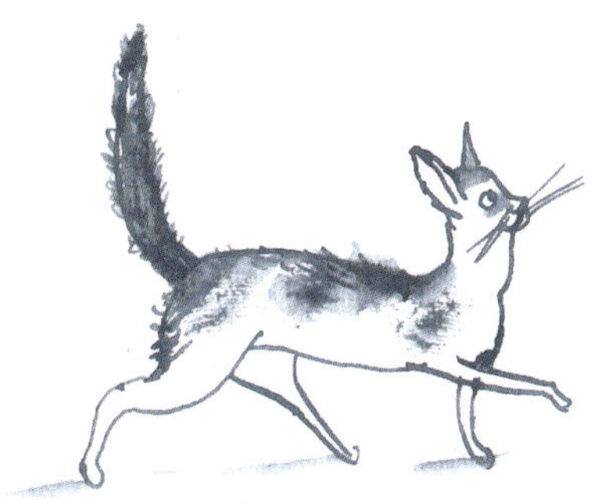

Glazing

Glazing is when we paint in transparent layers. Each layer should be allowed to dry completely before going over it with a new layer. The colours created by layering paint in this manner are usually deeper and more complex than if we would paint a similar tone alla prima, all at once. You move from light to dark, starting with a first light coat of paint. The picture gets darker and fuller the more new layers are painted over it.

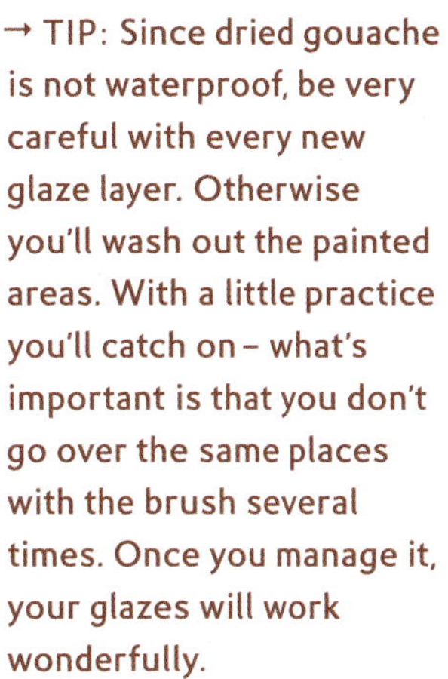

→ TIP: Since dried gouache is not waterproof, be very careful with every new glaze layer. Otherwise you'll wash out the painted areas. With a little practice you'll catch on – what's important is that you don't go over the same places with the brush several times. Once you manage it, your glazes will work wonderfully.

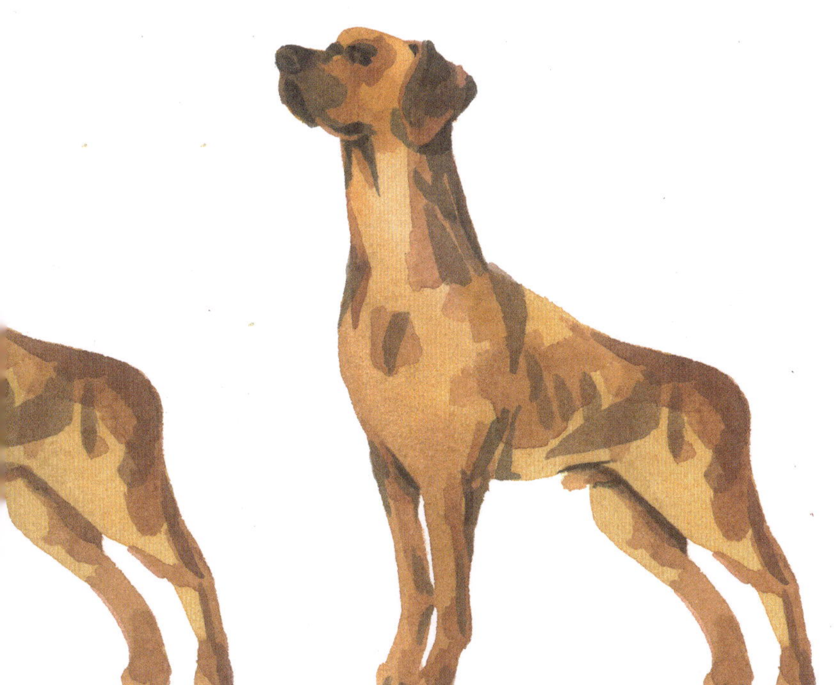

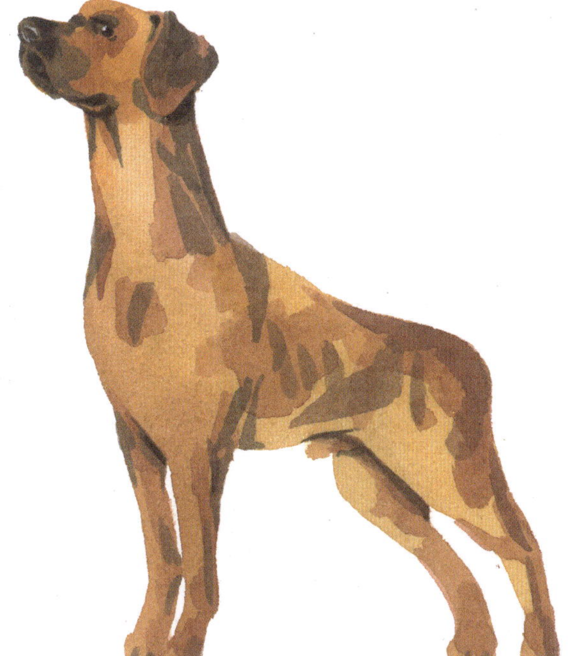

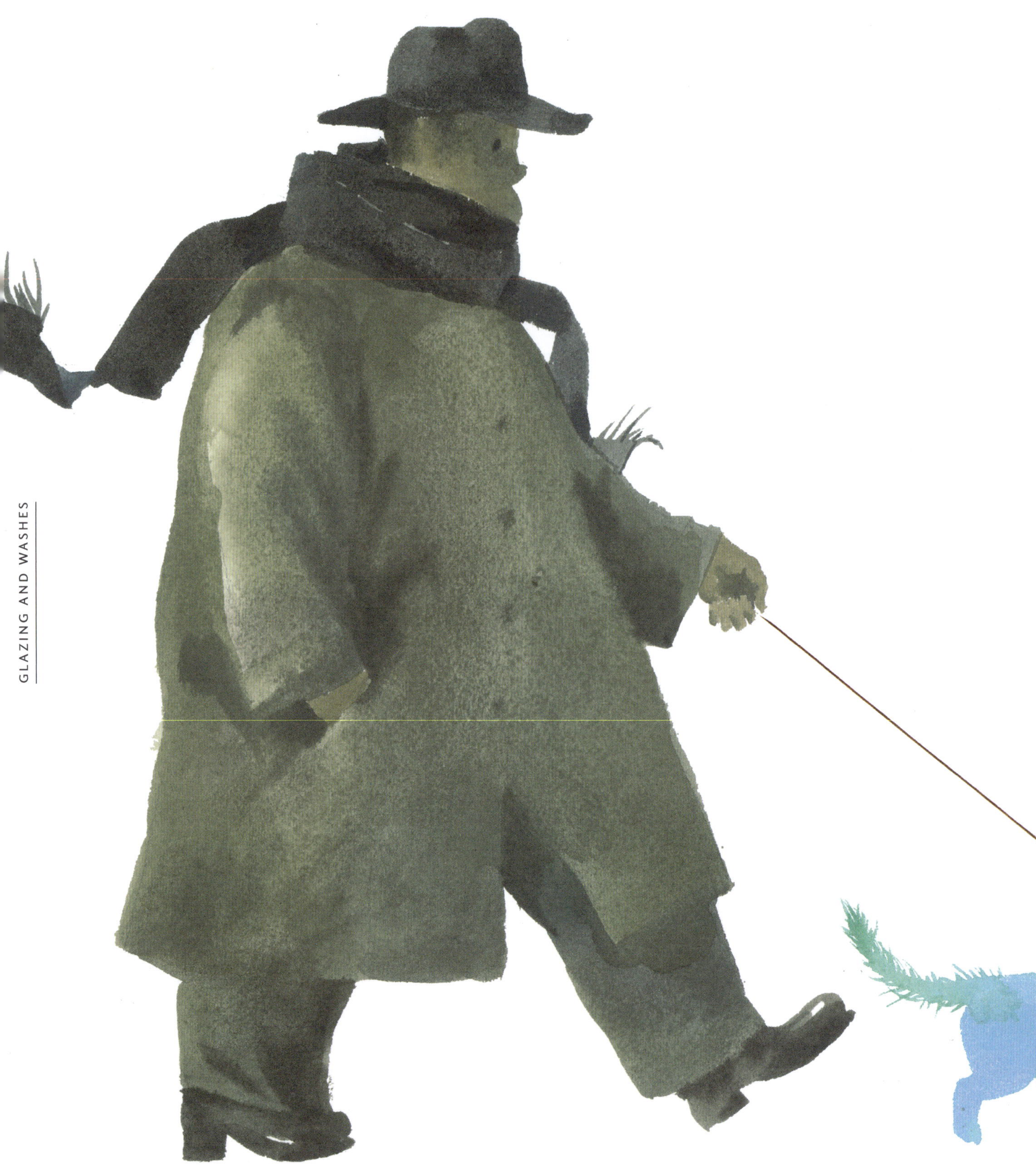

Washing

Unlike with glazing, you don't wait here until a layer of paint is dry, but continue to work with highly diluted paint in seamless transitions. The resulting colour gradients are more difficult to control than with the slow "step-by-step" build-up of a glaze. In washing, the anarchic and unpredictable side of the watercolours comes into its own. On the one hand, paper is important for this technique: the paint flow depends on its colour absorption and texture. On the other hand, a soft, large brush, flat or round, is very helpful. Washing is also used to colour a drawing in such a way that it remains clearly visible. Think for example of drawings by Goya or Rembrandt...

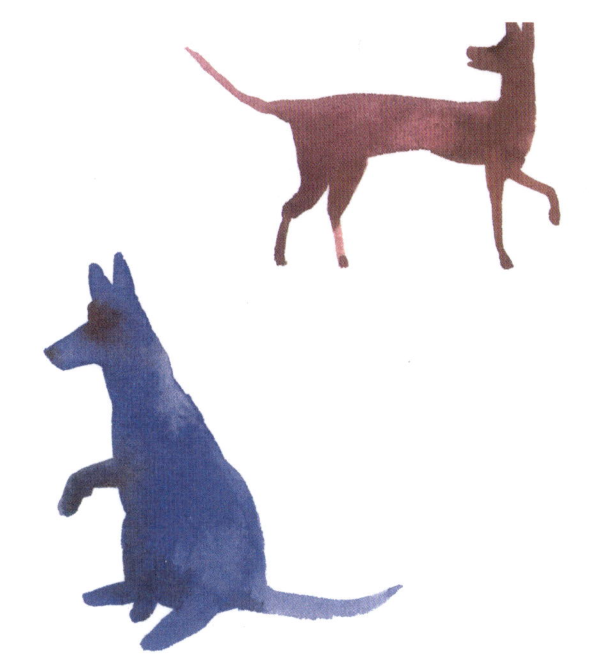

The most interesting effects can be achieved by combining glazing and washing. See the two techniques as building blocks that complement each other perfectly. A washed background can be a great counterpoint to accurately elaborated glazed figures in the foreground.

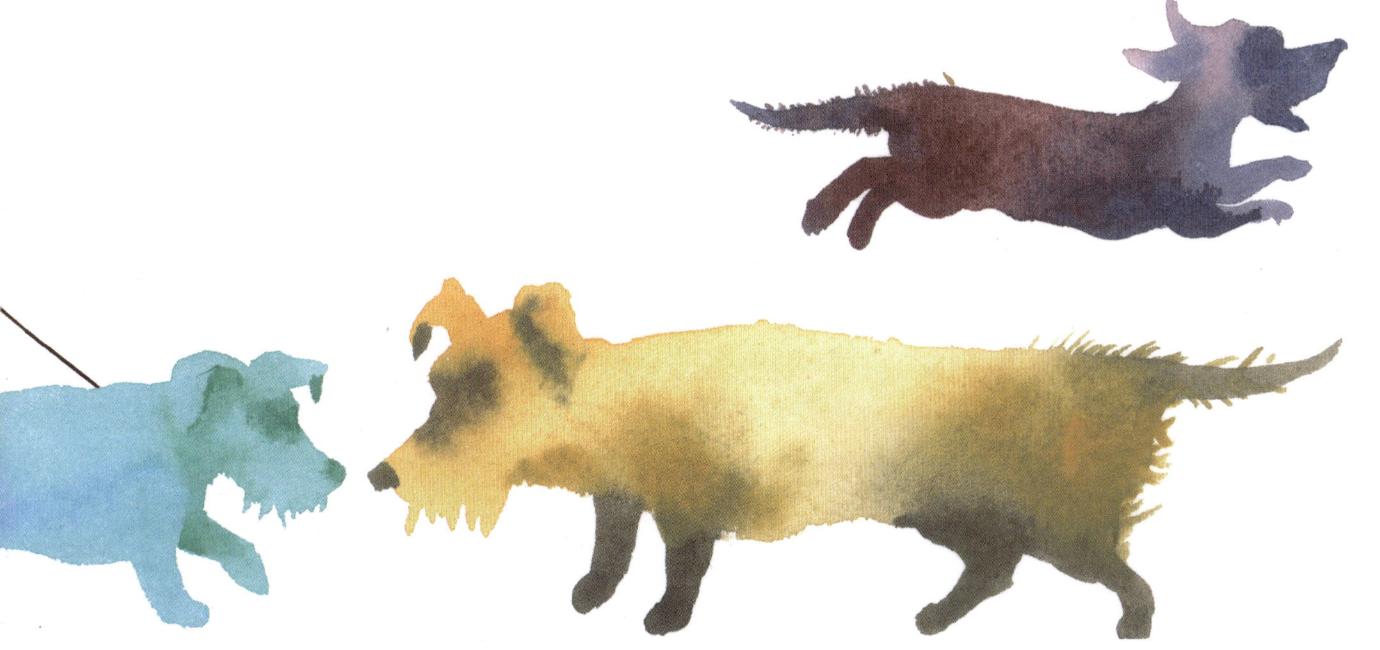

Pulling moods from the depths. Opaque or transparent painting, from dark to light

No matter whether you're a beginner or an experienced professional– everyone is familiar with the famed fear of the blank page. This technique, which I am presenting to you here, is ideally suited to cheat your *horror vacui*. No more white desert to cross. Start right away with a colourful background or completely prime your picture in black!

This technique is often used in oil painting. For me, there has always been something very natural about it. Because it's about bringing your subject out of the unknown, the darkness and more and more into the light. Faces painted in this way shine magically as if from the inside. Think of very expressive portraits from the Renaissance by Petrus Christus or Hans Holbein. With the first layer of deep primer you create a hue that is decisive for the atmosphere of your later picture. A bluish background will immerse the picture in a rather distant, cool mood and a brownish-red background will colour everything more warmly and emotionally.

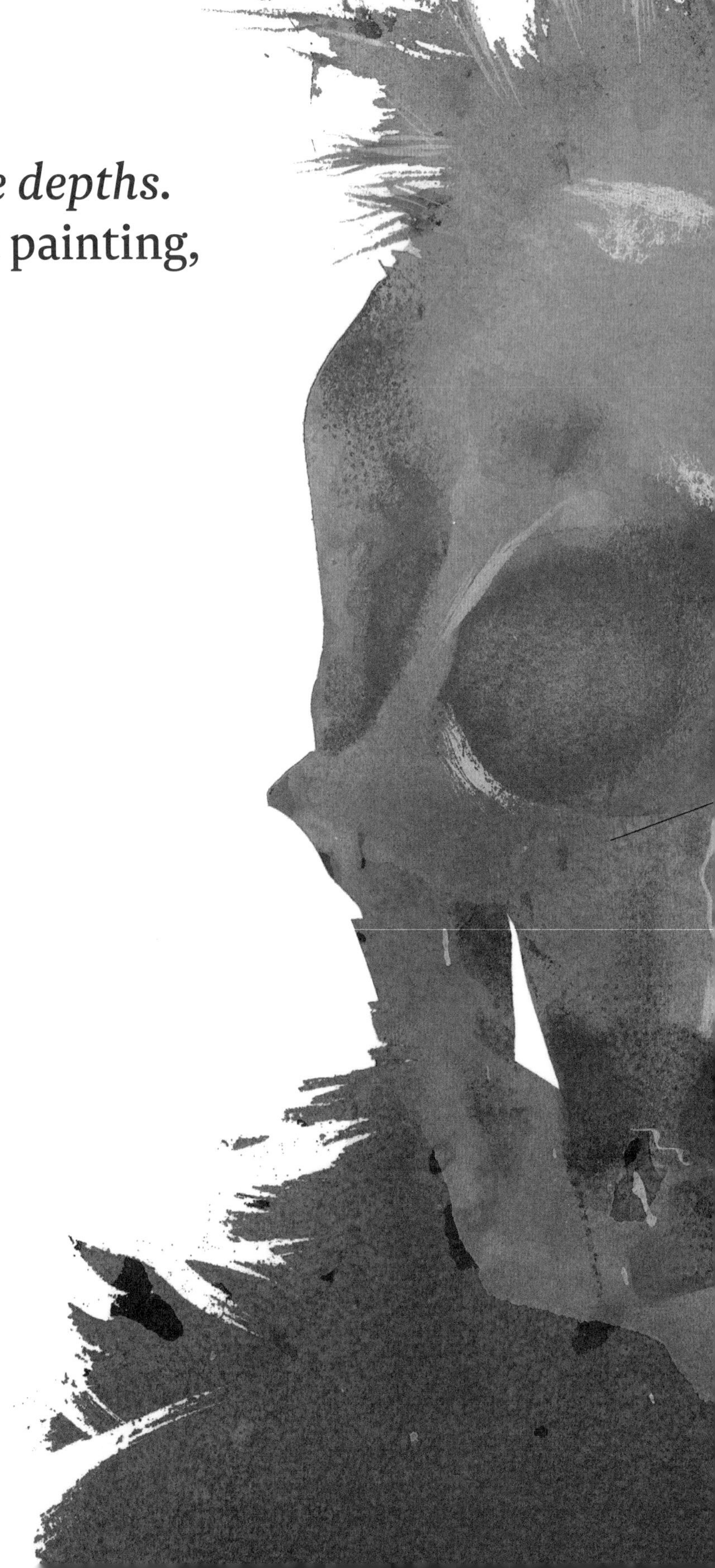

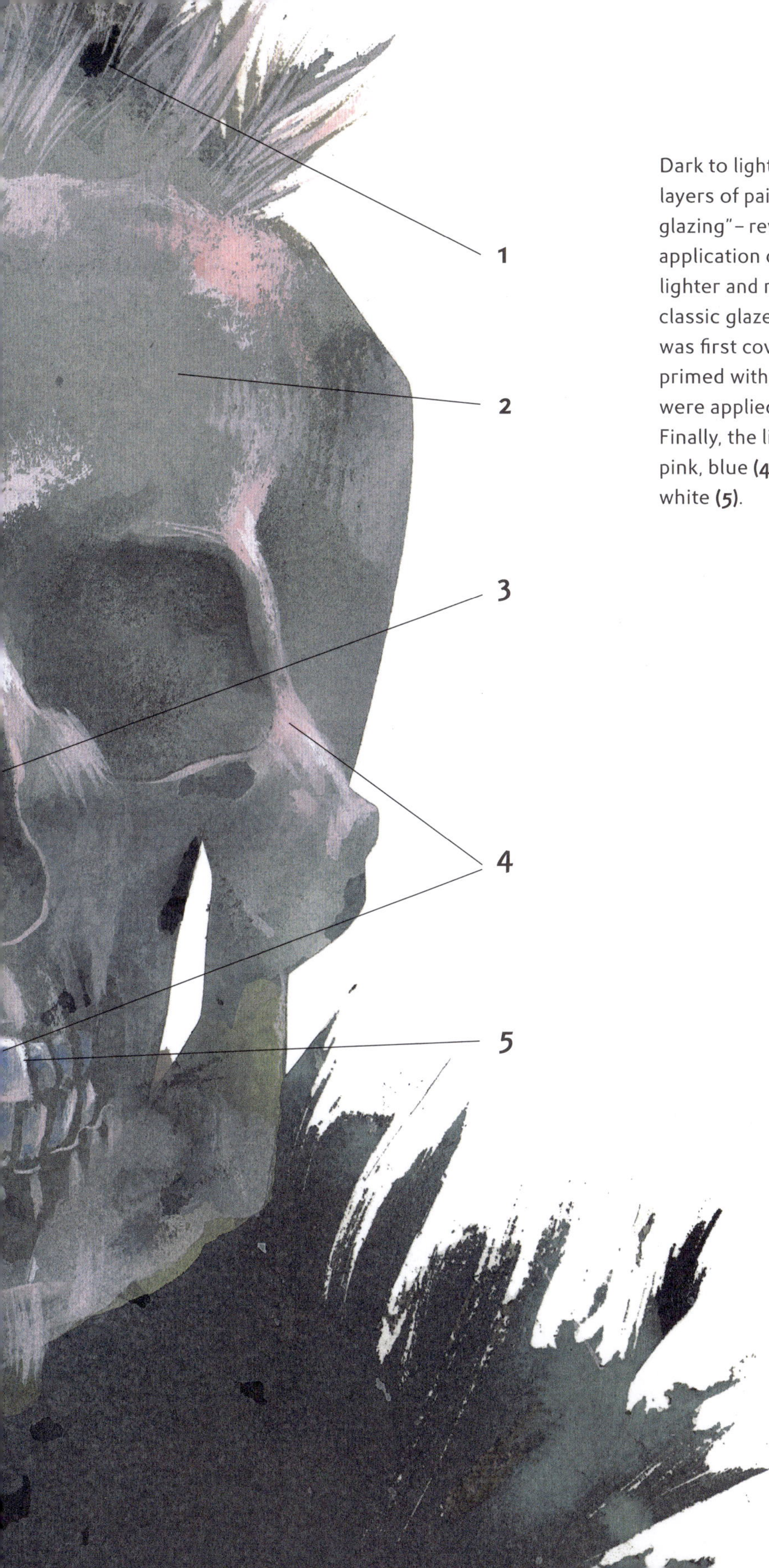

Dark to light also works with transparent layers of paint– then it's a kind of "reverse glazing"– reverse because with every new application of paint we make the picture lighter and not darker, as is the case with a classic glaze. In this picture, the silhouette was first covered with masking fluid and primed with black **(1)**. Then glazed layers were applied in grey **(2)**, then beige **(3)**. Finally, the lights were painted with opaque pink, blue **(4)** and at the very end with white **(5)**.

→ TIP: Regardless of whether you apply ever-lighter layers with pasty or with diluted paints: sooner or later the regular transparent white won't cover enough. Therefore it is advisable to get a "permanent" white or "opaque white." Paints of these names are more pigmented and mostly consist of titanium dioxide, which has a higher opacity than zinc white. And if that's not enough: Look for the super-opaque "bleed-proof white" paints that some manufacturers (for example Daler-Rowney or Dr. Ph. Martin's) offer. They easily cover all conceivable water-soluble paints and inks.

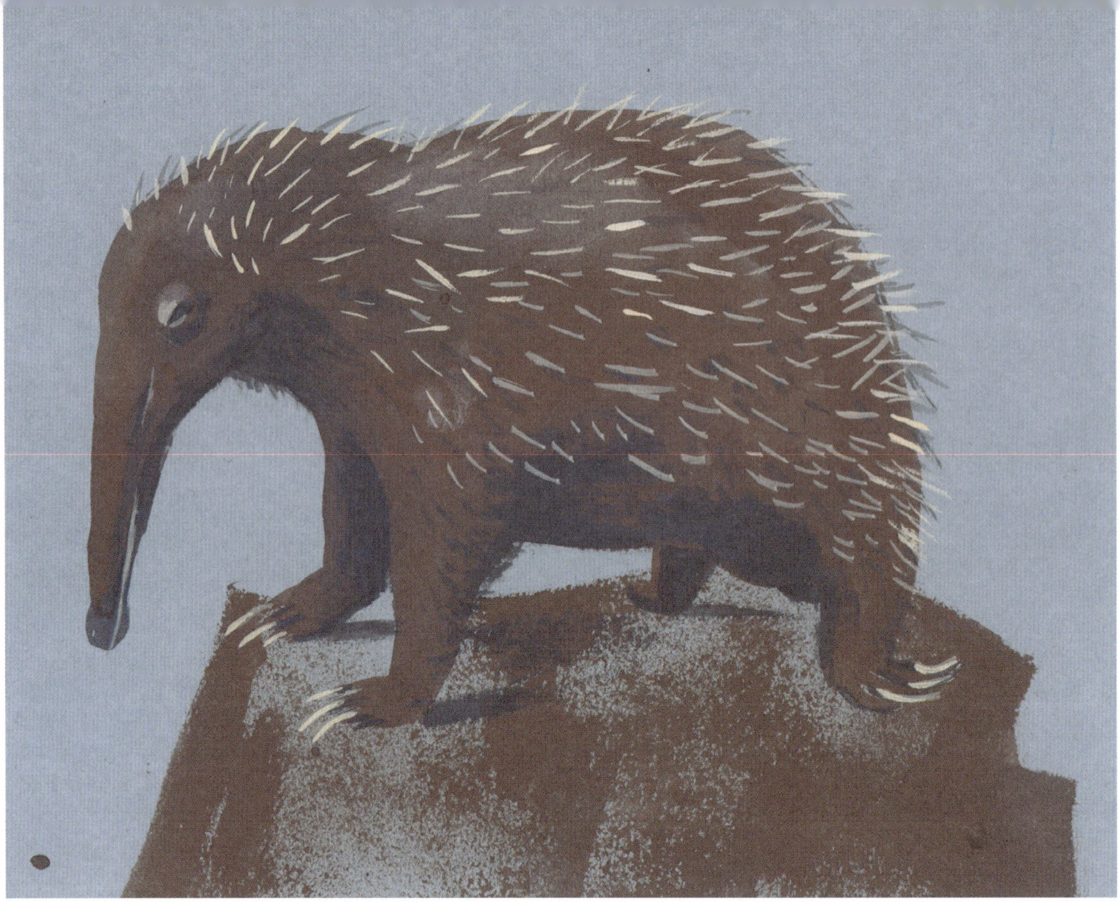

When painting from dark to light– similar to glazing– it's important to let the layer just painted dry completely. Many artists use coloured paper in order not to have to prime it first. This saves time and looks good. High-quality gouache paints retain their brilliance and opacity when diluted, so they will continue to shine beautifully on black or dark-coloured paper. Unfortunately, coloured watercolour papers are rare, but it is still possible to find them in delicate grey, blue or cream, as offered for example by Bockingford from England. If you're looking for other rich or dark colours, you can resort to Canson's Mi Teintes, which can pass as watercolour paper (both animal pictures were painted on Canson paper).

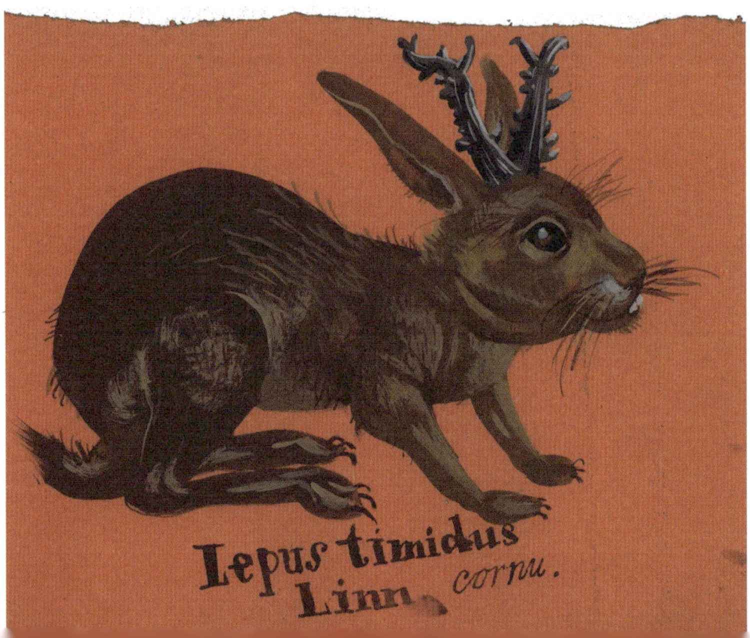

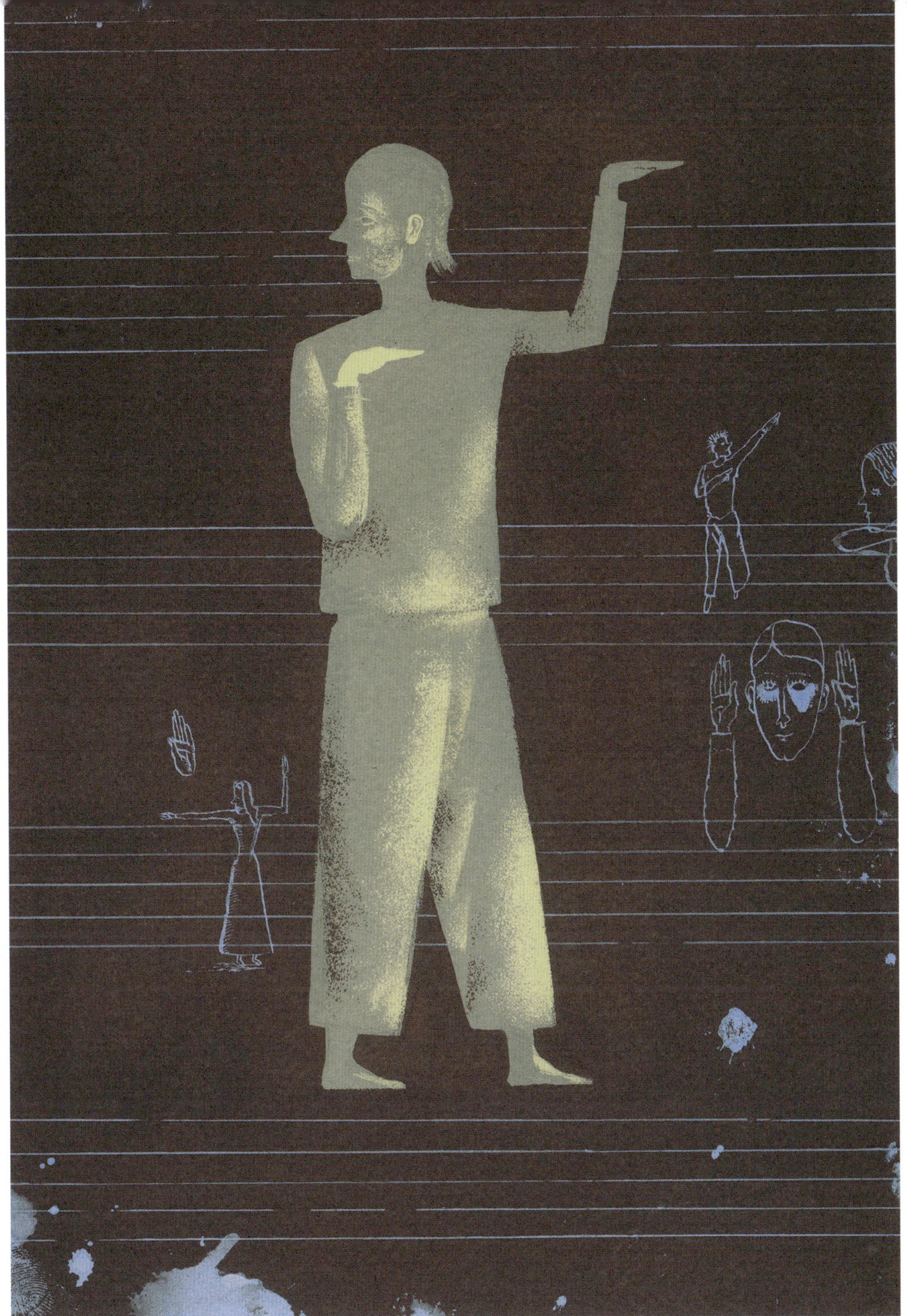

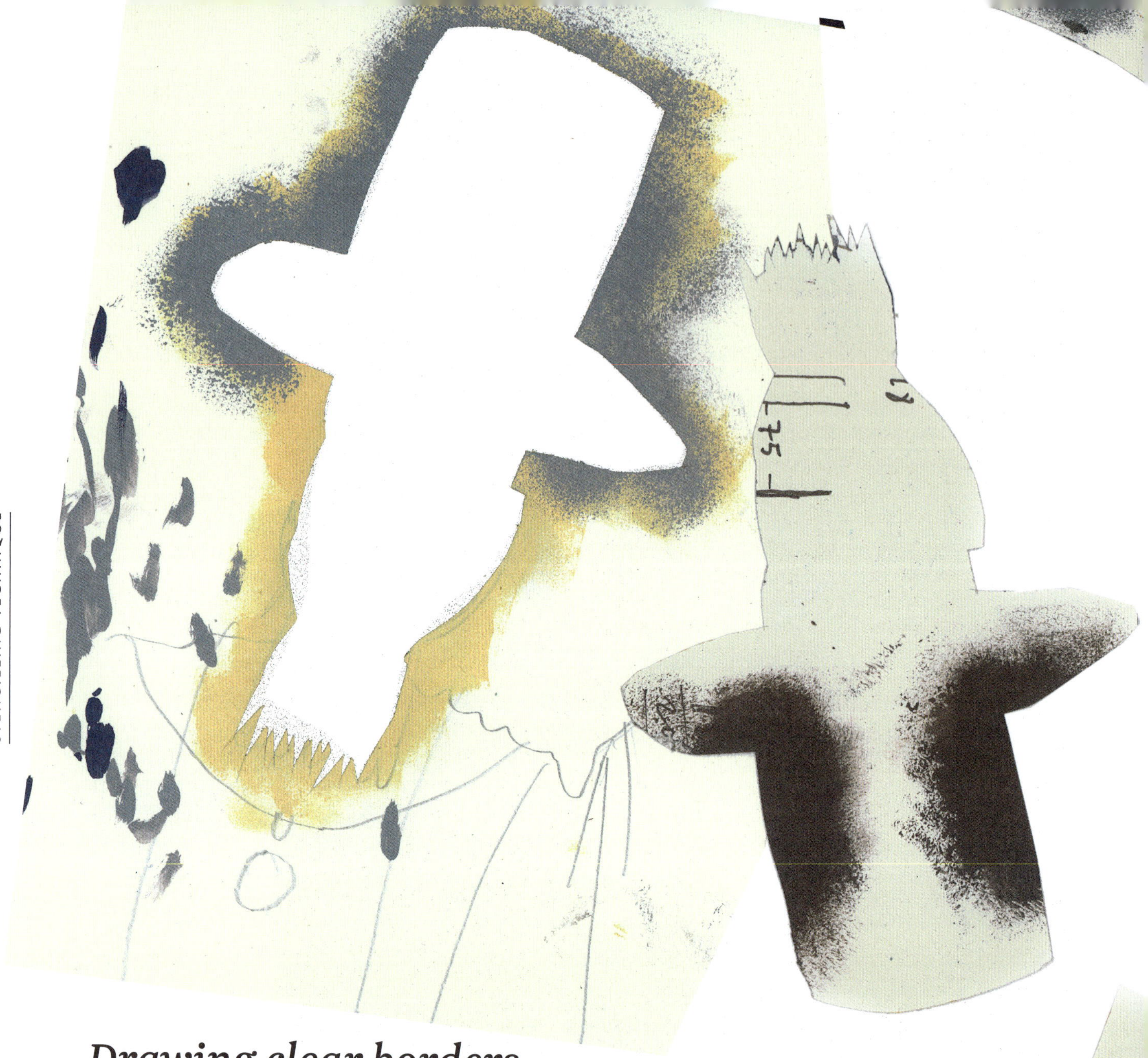

Drawing clear borders. Stencilling technique

It's great fun to put your brush aside to continue working on the picture with scissors and a knife. Often a few cuts and light dabs are enough and you've saved yourself a great deal of time. And it looks great too.

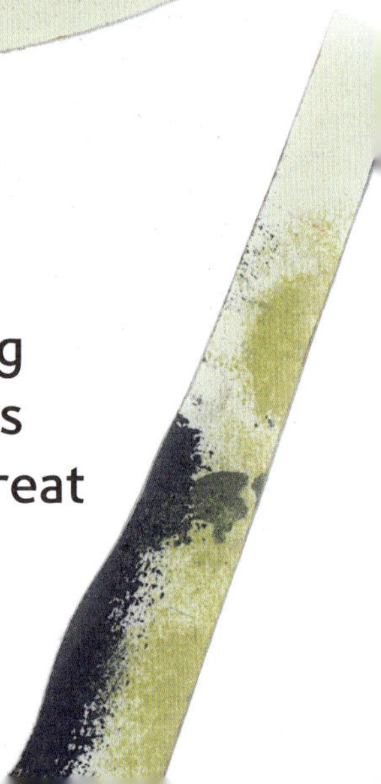

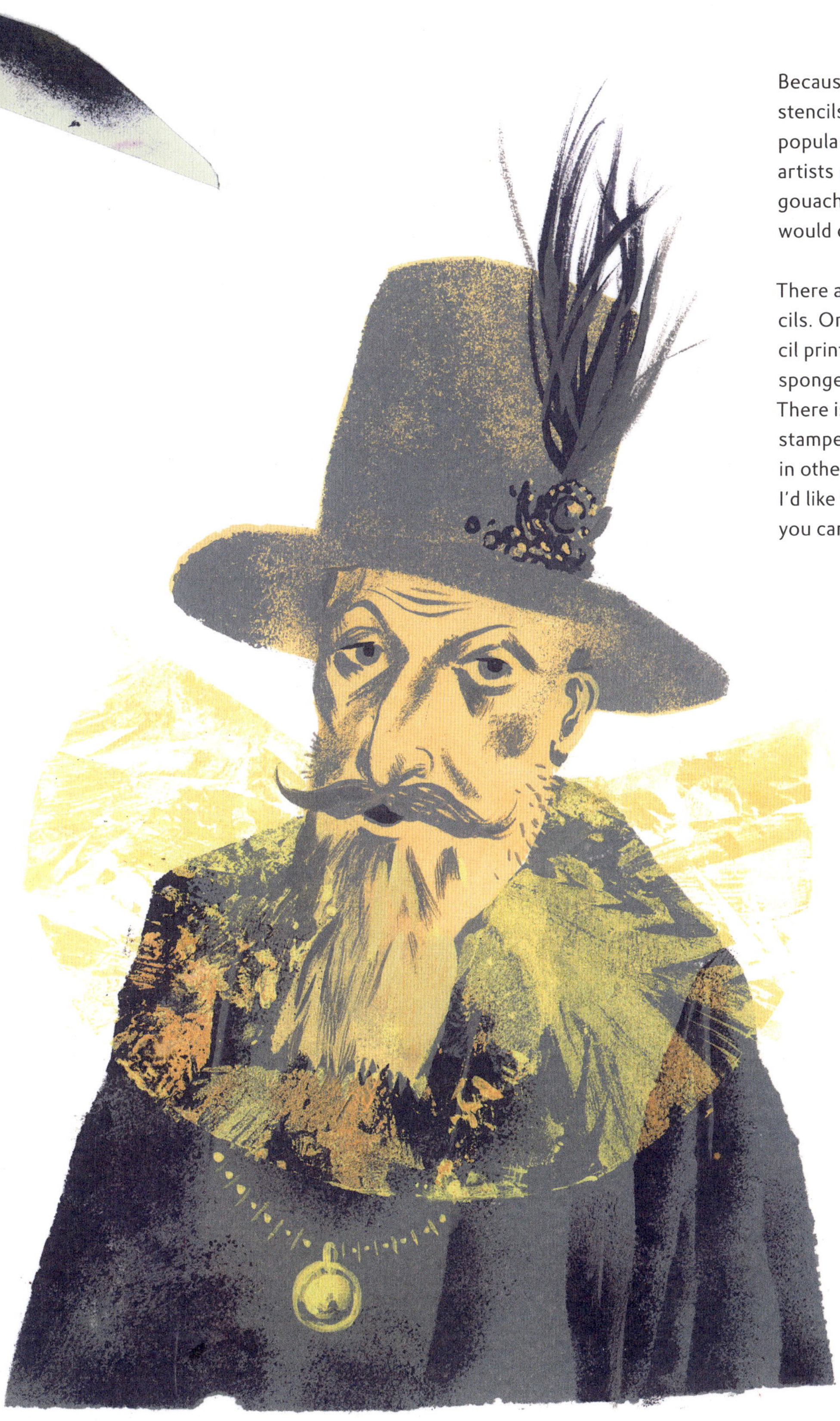

Because of their speed and simplicity, stencils have become one of the most popular techniques in street art. Graffiti artists use completely different paints than gouache, of course, because the pictures would only last until the next rain!

There are many different ways to use stencils. One possibility is to make a pure stencil print, that is, to apply all paints with a sponge or brush through cut out shapes. There is another way, too: You can use the stamped curves or straight edges as an aid in otherwise classically painted pictures. I'd like to show you a few examples of how you can use this effective technique.

Alternatives to artist sponges with different textures:

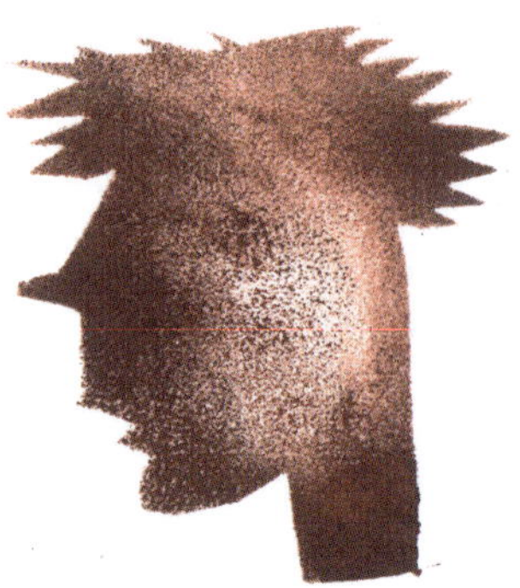

Cosmetic sponge: very fine

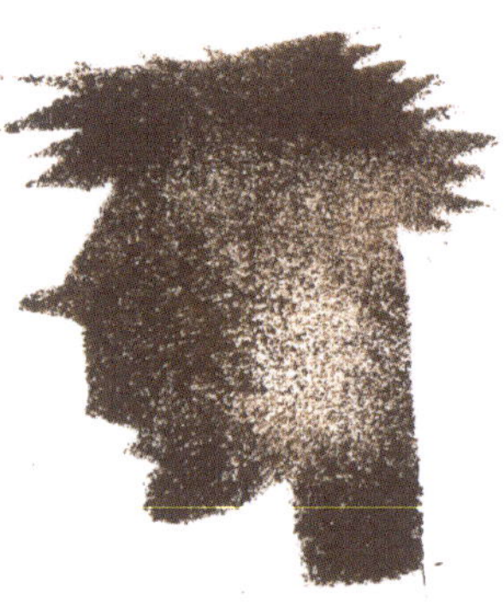

Pot sponge: medium

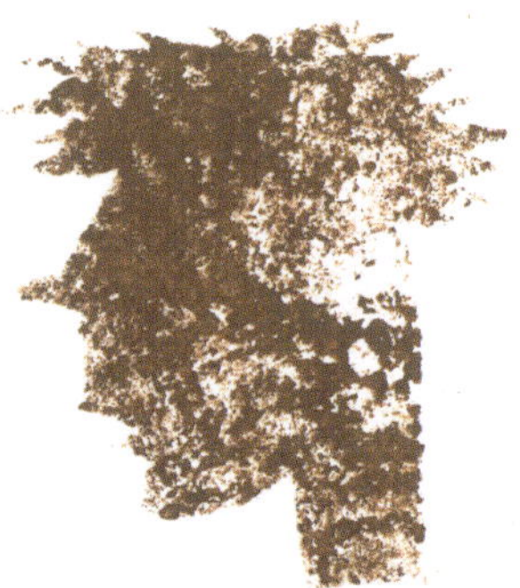

Natural sponge: coarse and irregular

First you create your stencil. A pencil sketch in advance usually helps and leaves room for corrections when cutting. For cutting itself, it is enough if you get paper, a cutter and a cut-resistant surface and be very careful– that's all you need. When the stencil is finished, go to the second step: apply paint. We have two main tools at our disposal: stencil brushes (see chapter "Comparing various brushes") or different sponges. An enormous selection of "artist and painting sponges" with or without handles, made of foam or synthetic, awaits you in your art supply shop and on the Internet. In my opinion, just because "art" is on the packaging it doesn't necessarily guarantee better pictures. Feel free to try cheaper, but not lesser options from the drugstore on the corner.

→ TIP: You can use scissors to cut the sponges to the shape you want. Give it a try and find out for yourself what works best for you.

Guide to stencilling

1. Use little water

When dabbing with a sponge or stencil brush, you always use pasty paints, i.e. undiluted or with just a little water. If the gouache is too liquid, it will run under the stencil edge and soften it. In addition, you won't have the beautiful texture and the paints are very likely to smear.

2. Paint application with a brush

If you're working with a sponge, you should apply the paint to it with a brush. This may seem odd, because it would feel more natural to press the sponge against the paint! However, you will quickly notice that the paint behaves much more delicately when carefully applied with a brush. Dabbing is also easier to control.

3. Robust stencils

If you use harder cardboard for the stencil, it will definitely last longer. Thin paper soaks through quickly, but can be applied more precisely, so that the edges come out razor-sharp. If you're cutting stencils for extended use, you can use transparent PVC or acetate film. It's waterproof and lasts forever.

4. Experiment with other tools

Once you've gotten familiar with the classic tools of sponges and stencil brushes, go a step further and experiment with large bristle brushes, rags, twigs or scrub-brushes – in short, with anything you can use to splash, dribble, dab or stamp the paints ...

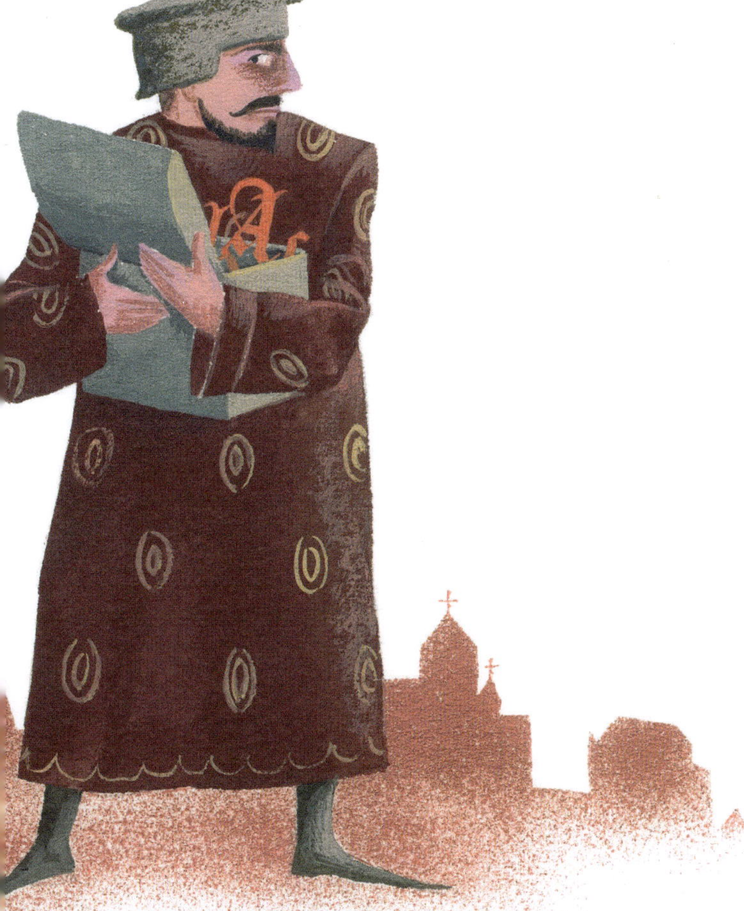

Dry spell. The beauty of dry brushing

Another method that is used very similarly in acrylic painting is the so-called "dry brush." The paint is applied in layers so that the paper texture remains visible. With this technique, dip the brush into the semi-wet gouache. The most important thing is you should not add any additional water. Then you can brush away excess paint from the brush (on a paper towel or rag) so that about a third of the paint remains in the brush. Now you can paint in quick strokes over the picture surface.

With this technique, it's easy to avoid affecting and washing out the lower layers of paint. Therefore, you should try to paint with the dry brush with as little water as possible. It's important that you apply the paint firmly and don't go back and forth over the same places several times. The more pasty the paint, the more robust the brush hairs can be. So bristle brushes, and not the fine sable-hair brushes, are advisable, especially for medium and large formats. Save your sable-hair brushes for details and watery glazes!

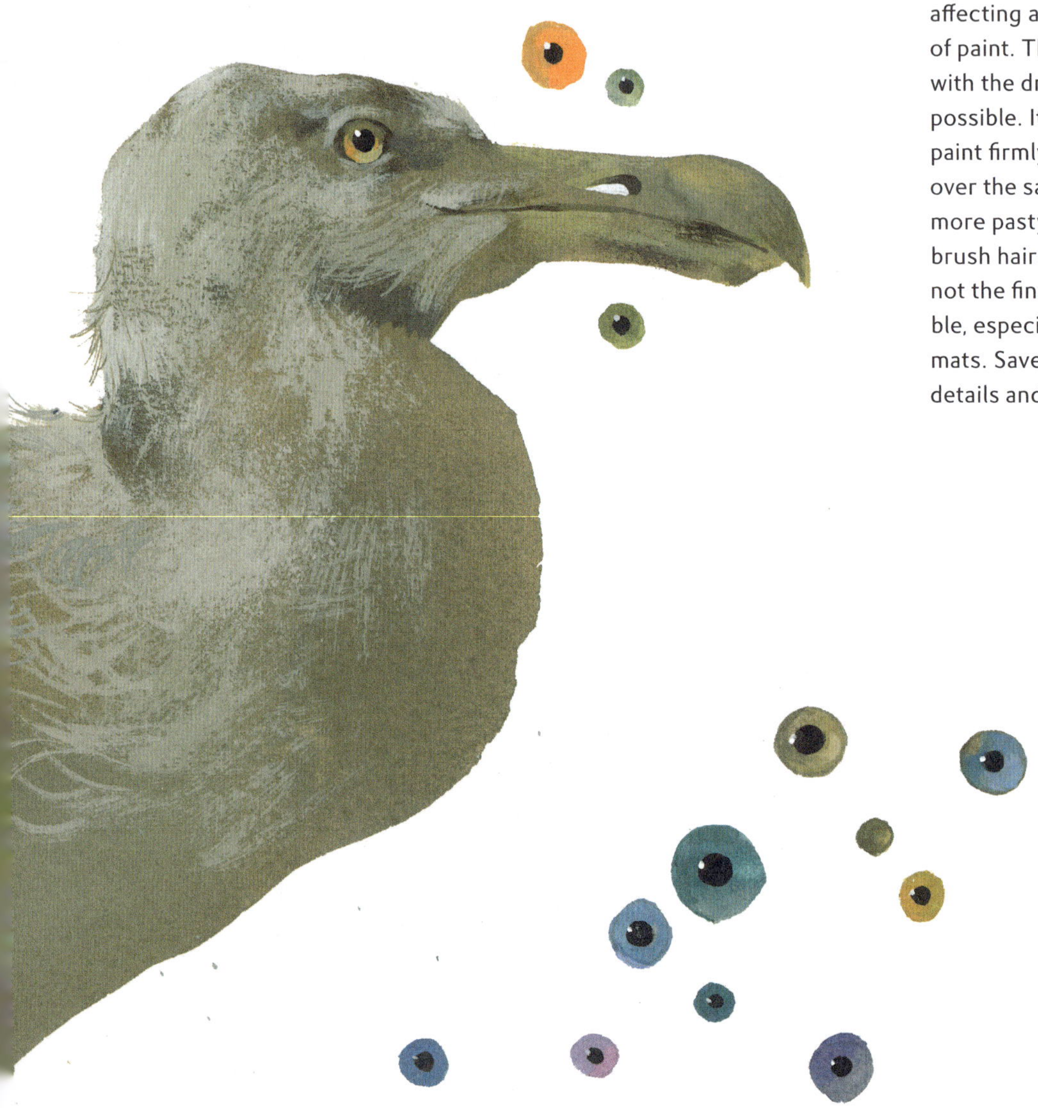

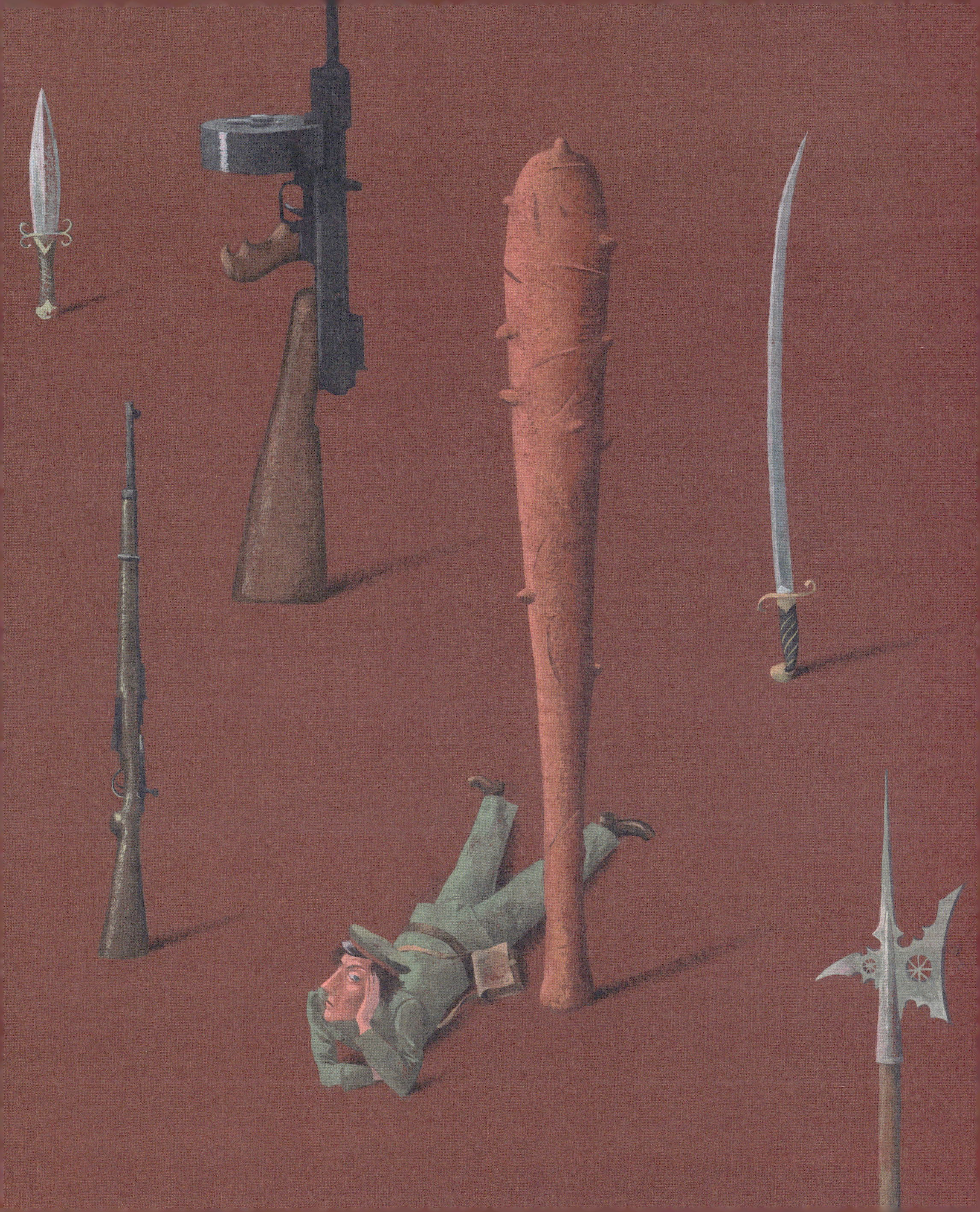

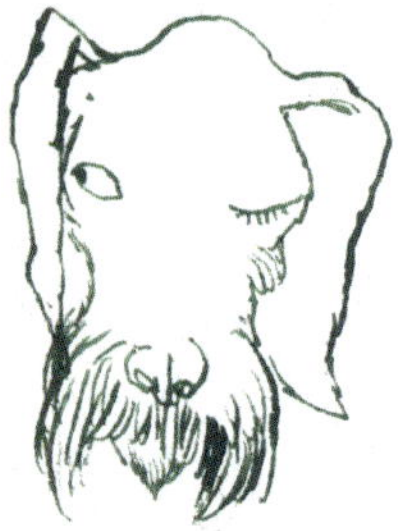

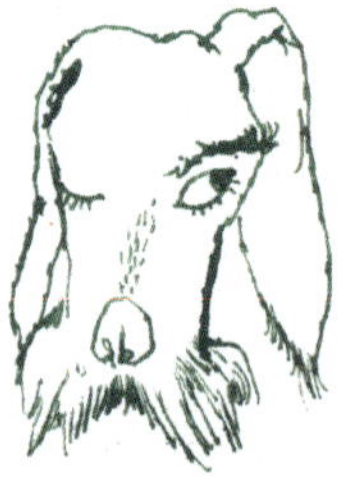

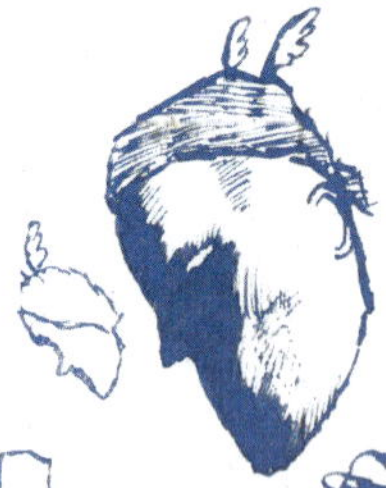

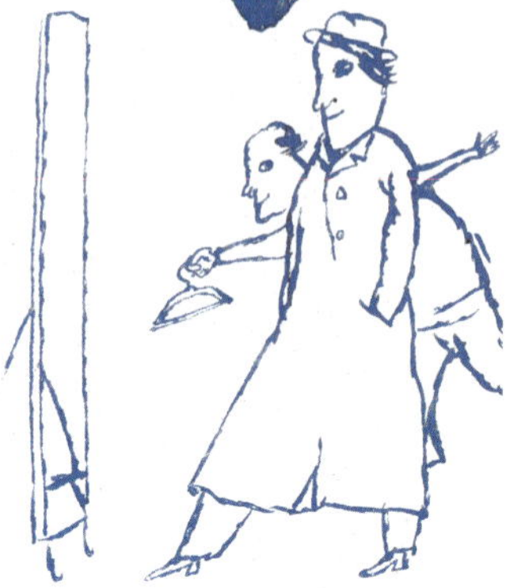

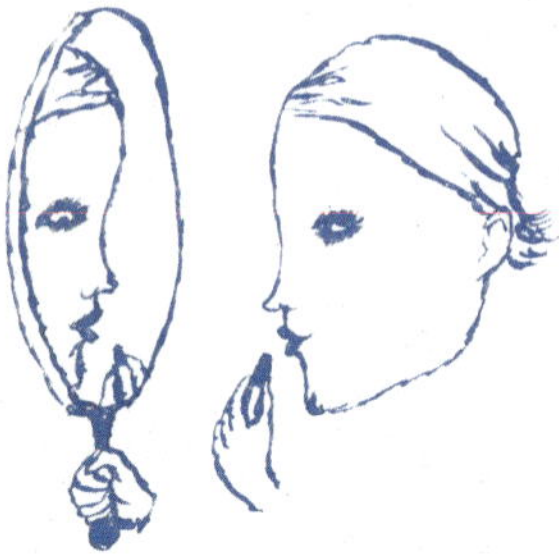

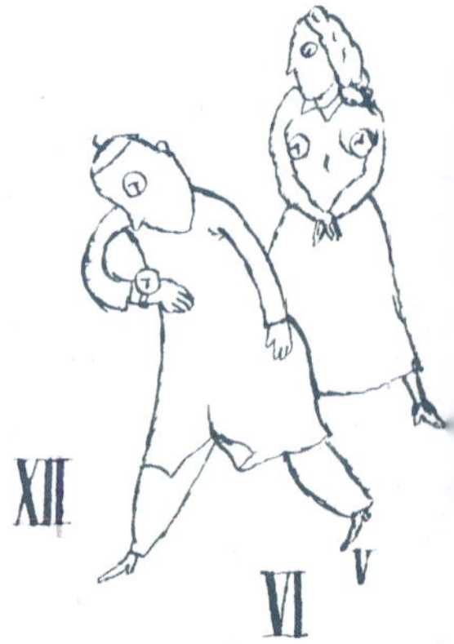

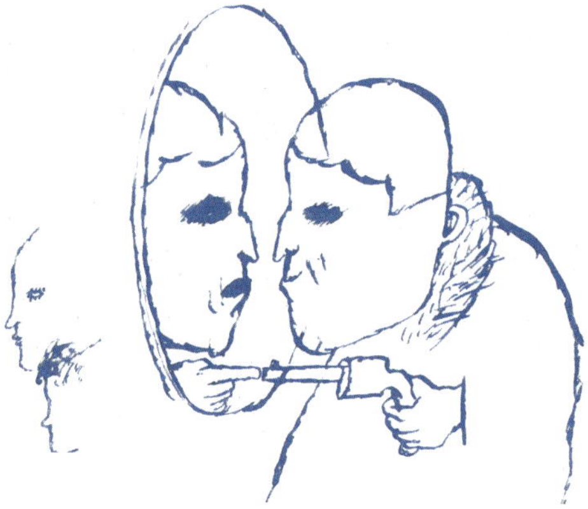

Sticking to the lines. Drawing with gouache

In the previous chapters we motioned different painting techniques that gouache enables us to do. So far, however, we have avoided one important application: Gouache is wonderful for drawing.

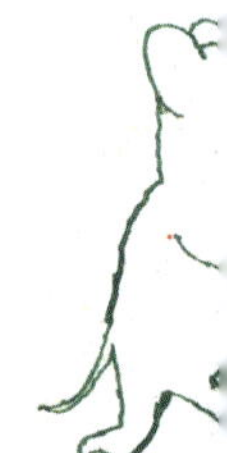

I got the idea when I was looking for a new technique for drawing pink figures on a dark background. I still remember very well the feeling of pure joy that arose during my first experiments. Unlike Indian ink, where the colour selection is limited to a few "usual suspects," black, sepia, umber and a few other paints, gouache can be mixed into any hue in no time. The drawing is very opaque, which is nice. And drawing with gouache works wonderfully with two tried and tested tools: drawing pens and reed pens.

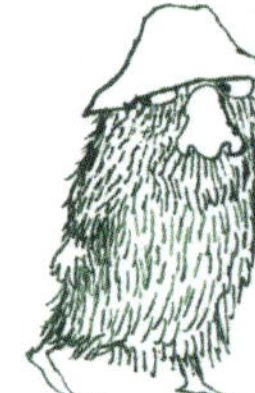

Drawing pens

They were invented in Aachen in 1748, but mass production only began decades later in England. It took almost exactly a hundred years for drawing and writing pens to return triumphantly to Germany and in 1842 the first Hamburg school abolished quills.

Drawing pens are well suited for small intricate drawings with fine hatching. In contrast to India ink, paints in the tube are heavily pigmented and too viscous for drawing. That is why we dilute them with water. And one more thing: Regardless of whether you work with drawing pens or reed pens, you'll need a brush to apply the paint to the pen. I work with the drawing pens in my right hand and the brush in my left hand.

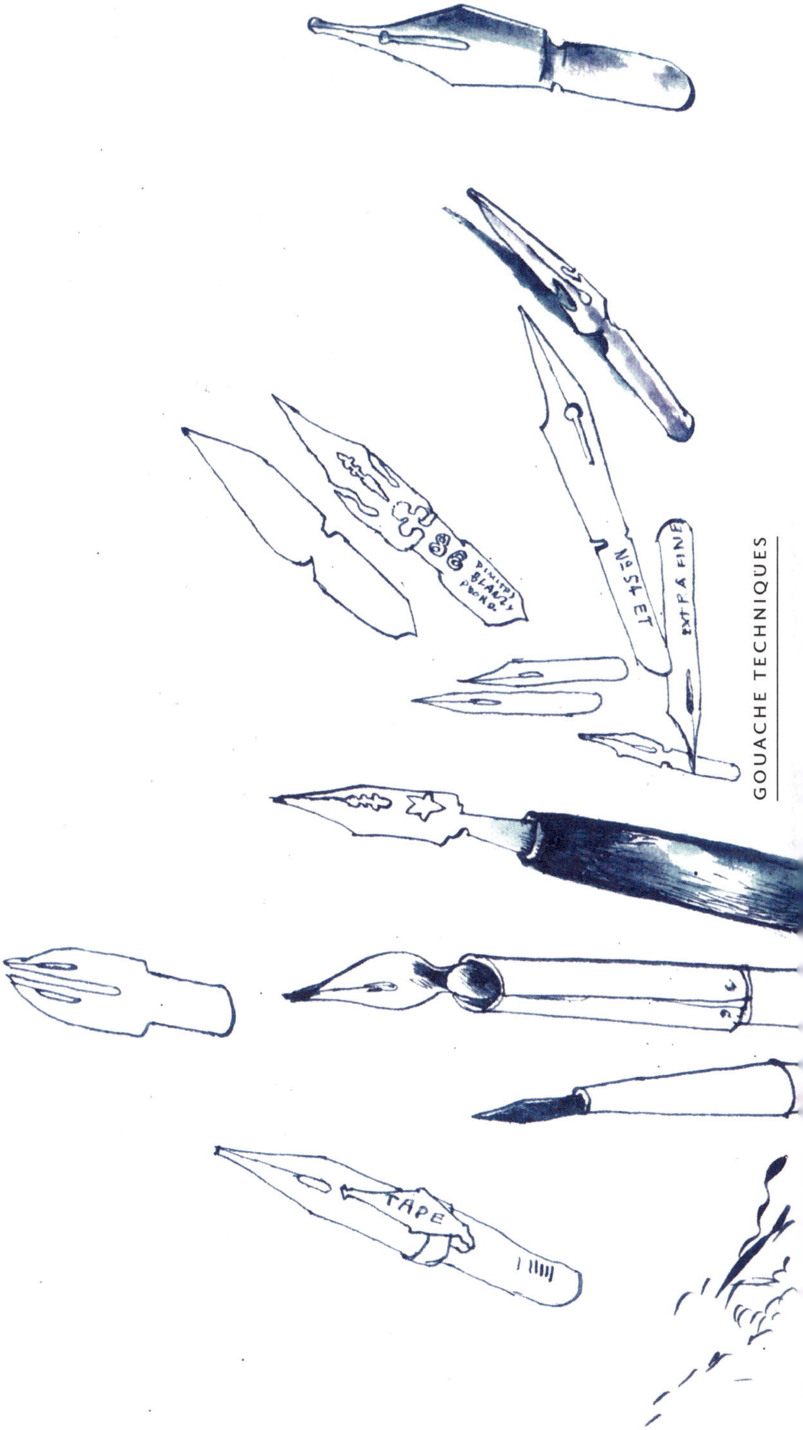

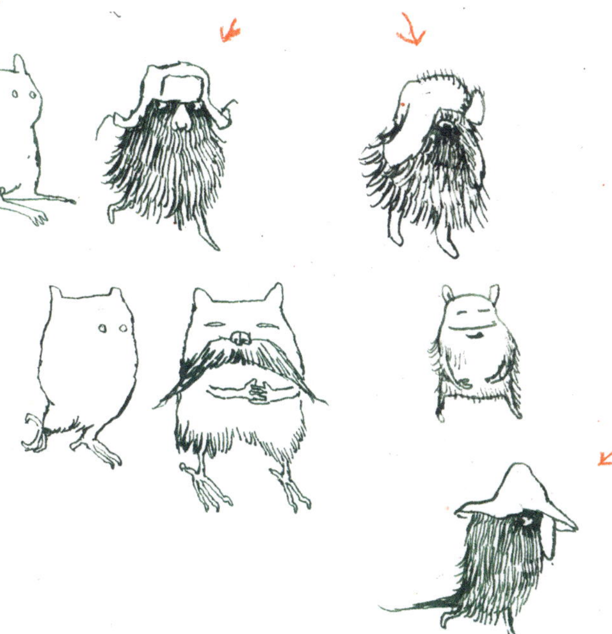

Reed pens

You won't find this drawing tool at the art supply shop. You'll have to find a lake or frog pond where Phragmites communis, the common reed, grows. (Unless you're sitting under thatched roof in Schleswig Holstein or Denmark, then you have it easier.) Don't confuse reeds with bamboo, which is hollow on the inside but very hard–you can just as easily draw with a twig.

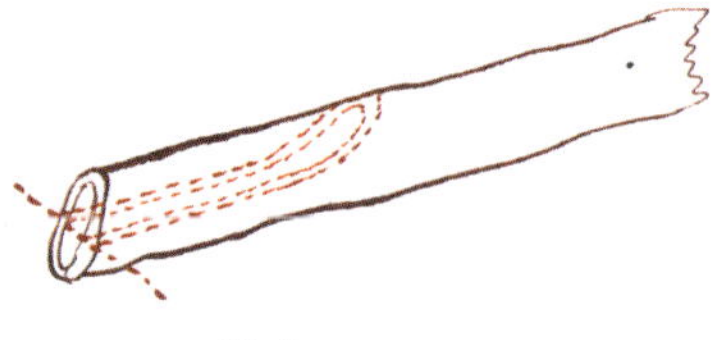

Cut

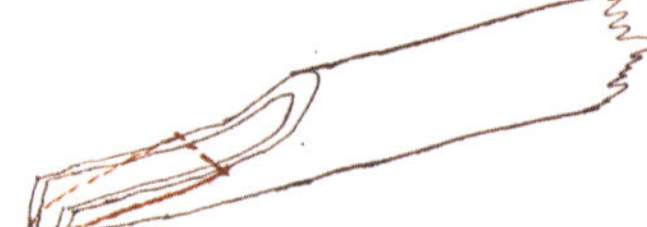

Taper on the right and left to a point

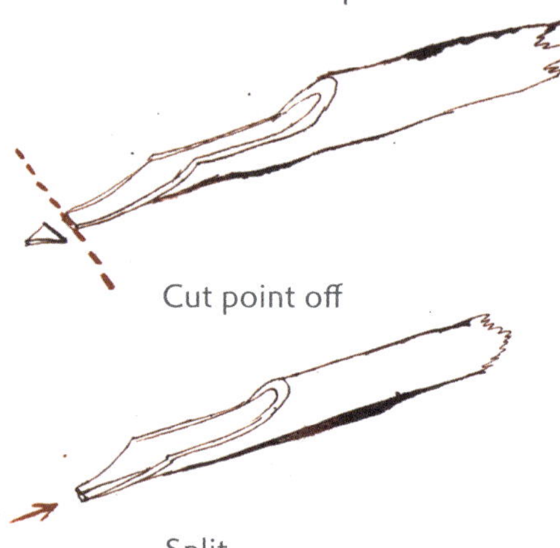

Cut point off

Split

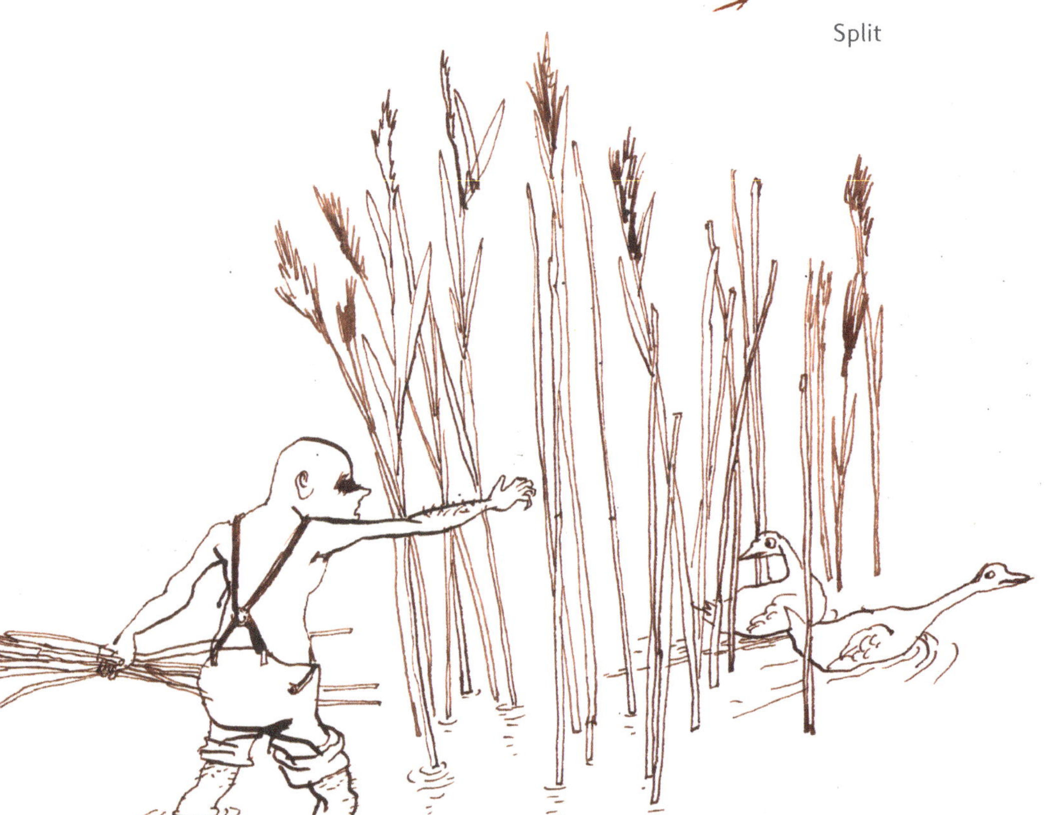

Try your reed pen right after sharpening. Whether you need to touch it up is decided when you draw. But give your freshly sharpened tool 1–2 minutes to "work itself in". Only then will you enjoy flowing lines, a large absorption capacity and, above all, the beautiful, smooth stroke of the pen. As modest as the reed pen looks, you're drawing with the great-grandmother of all writing and drawing utensils! The five books of Moses and classical ancient literature from Greece and Rome were brought to papyrus or parchment with it.

Drawing with a reed pen is wonderful for loose, "intuitive" sketches and for "blind drawing," drawing without looking at the paper. This is another advantage over the steel pens, which easily dig into the paper and cause small furrows (and therefore require far more control and precision).

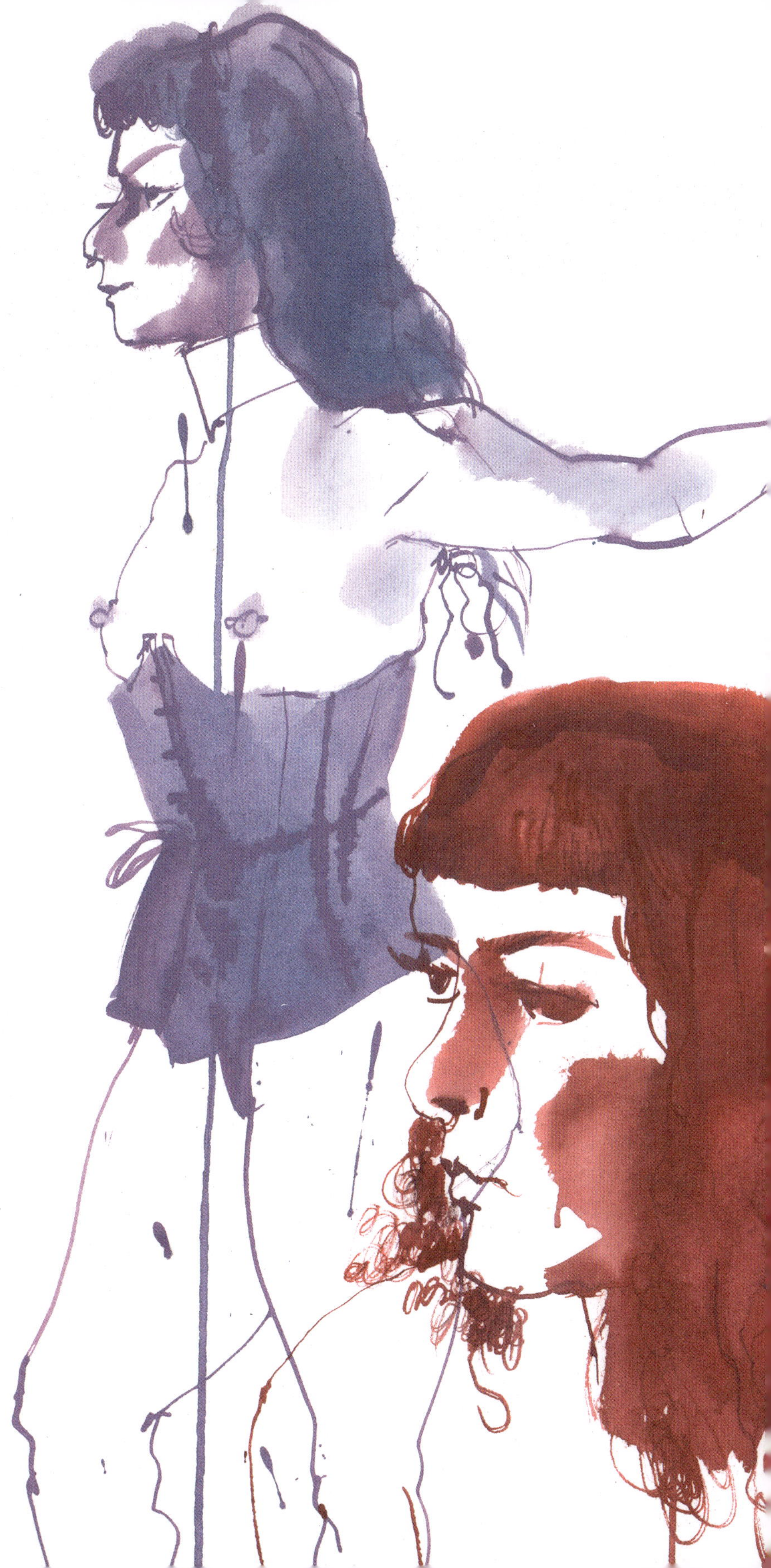

→ TIP: When collecting the reeds, be careful not to pick green plants. They are too fragile and won't last long when drawing. Choose floating or dry grasses from last year. The thicker the reeds, the more robust your drawing pens are!

→ TIP: In the raven picture, the black background was carefully wet with water and dabbed away until a dark grey appeared on the wings and head, including the beak. After that, the light areas were painted over into even brighter lights in a blue-grey.

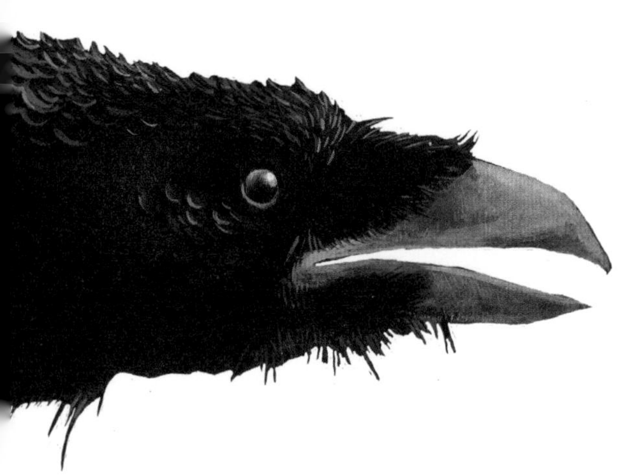

Two steps forward, one step back. Reworking technique

The be-all and end-all of gouache painting is that the paints remain water-soluble even after drying. Exactly this property is often considered a big shortcoming by beginners. Because when you put several colours on top of each other, it becomes increasingly difficult not to blur the lower layers. Just don't despair! What initially looks like a handicap is the strength of these paints. Because of the water solubility the undesired spots can almost always be corrected. You simply wet it and dab it away with a paper towel.

Here's the first application of the colour-reducing technique (another name for reworking) that I personally use a lot. When painting from dark to light, the lights can be applied with white to darker layers of paint. How to do this is described in the section "Pulling moods from the depths" on p. 94. But you can also wet the dark paint and dab it away with a paper towel or blotting paper until the paper shows through again! This tactic means that when you paint the subject, keep in mind that you will later rework parts of it. So in a way you're going two steps forward and one back.

You can also use the reworking technique to prepare the backgrounds. In this case, which surface you actually paint on is very important because the texture and grain of the paper play a major role in the result. First, the background is applied in one colour. Then – before the paint has dried completely – go over it with a cotton rag and take the paint away until the paper appears.

William Turner was undoubtedly a pioneer in colour-reducing techniques. While his contemporaries at the beginning of the nineteenth century painted in glazed layers and surpassed themselves in accuracy, he developed his very own eccentric methods. He dipped his pictures in water, washed away colours with a sponge or scraped out paint with his thumbnail.

All of these techniques are something you can try and experiment with. The result will depend very much on how hard you press when you wipe away the paint or whether, for example, you use an old rag or paper towels.

→ TIP: Invent other tools to remove the paint from the paper. Try a razor blade if the paper is strong enough. Even an eraser can take some paint away. Use sandpaper, pumice stone, rub the picture on a wall – there are no limits to your imagination!

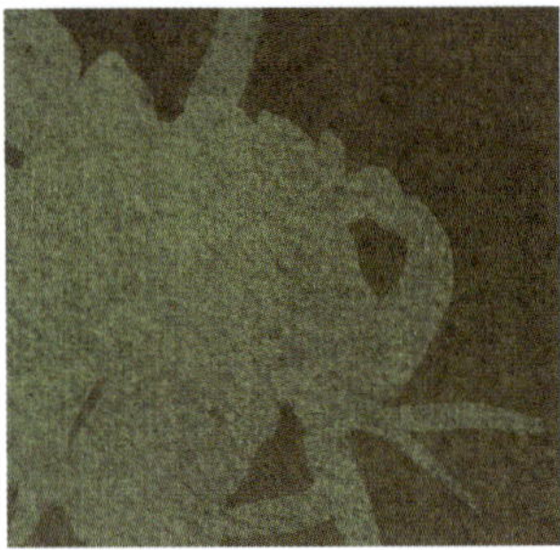

In this picture, the sepia brown on the eagle was carefully moistened and removed with a dry brush. The cool grey of the mountains below was also dabbed away so that the yellow shines through again.

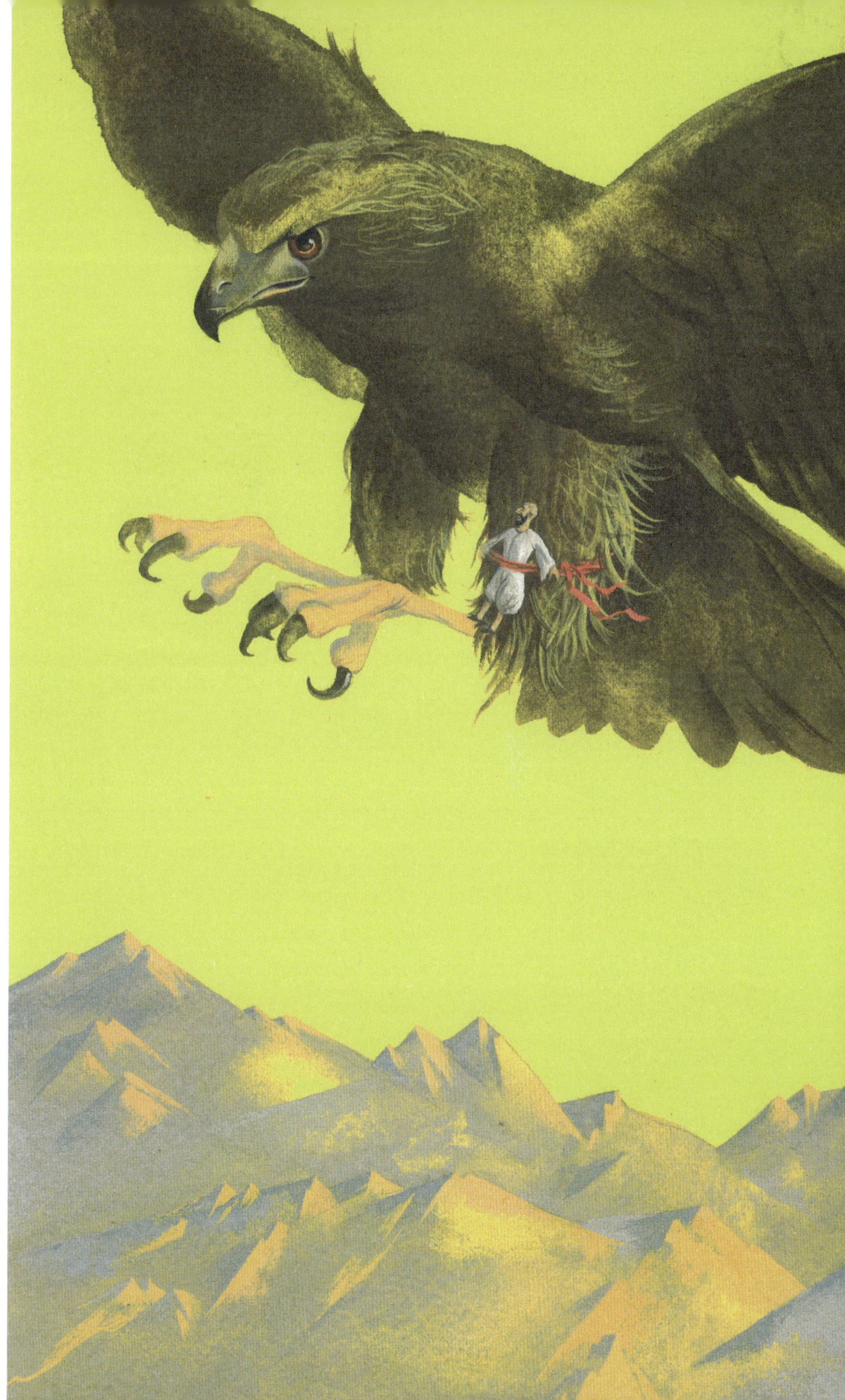

Spills and dribbles. Spray technique

The further you advance with techniques of gouache painting, the more you will discover your "wild" side. The same paints that go so well with small sizes and miniatures behave excellently if you spray them, pour them or apply them not at all precisely in any other conceivable way.

How it works? Spraying sounds simple, but needs to be practiced. The first thing you can try is to dip a large brush in paint and sweep it across the paper in wide movements. The streaks and splashes will remind you of Jackson Pollock's pictures. Another useful tool for spraying is an old toothbrush. Run your thumb over the bristled dipped in paint. With a little practice, you will soon create regular structures. The resulting splashes are reminiscent of a slightly blocked airbrush.

Once you've tried these methods, take a look around– everything that you think might create interesting structures, whether by spraying, dabbing, wagging, etc., can be used. Try twigs, grass, threads or crumpled paper, for example.

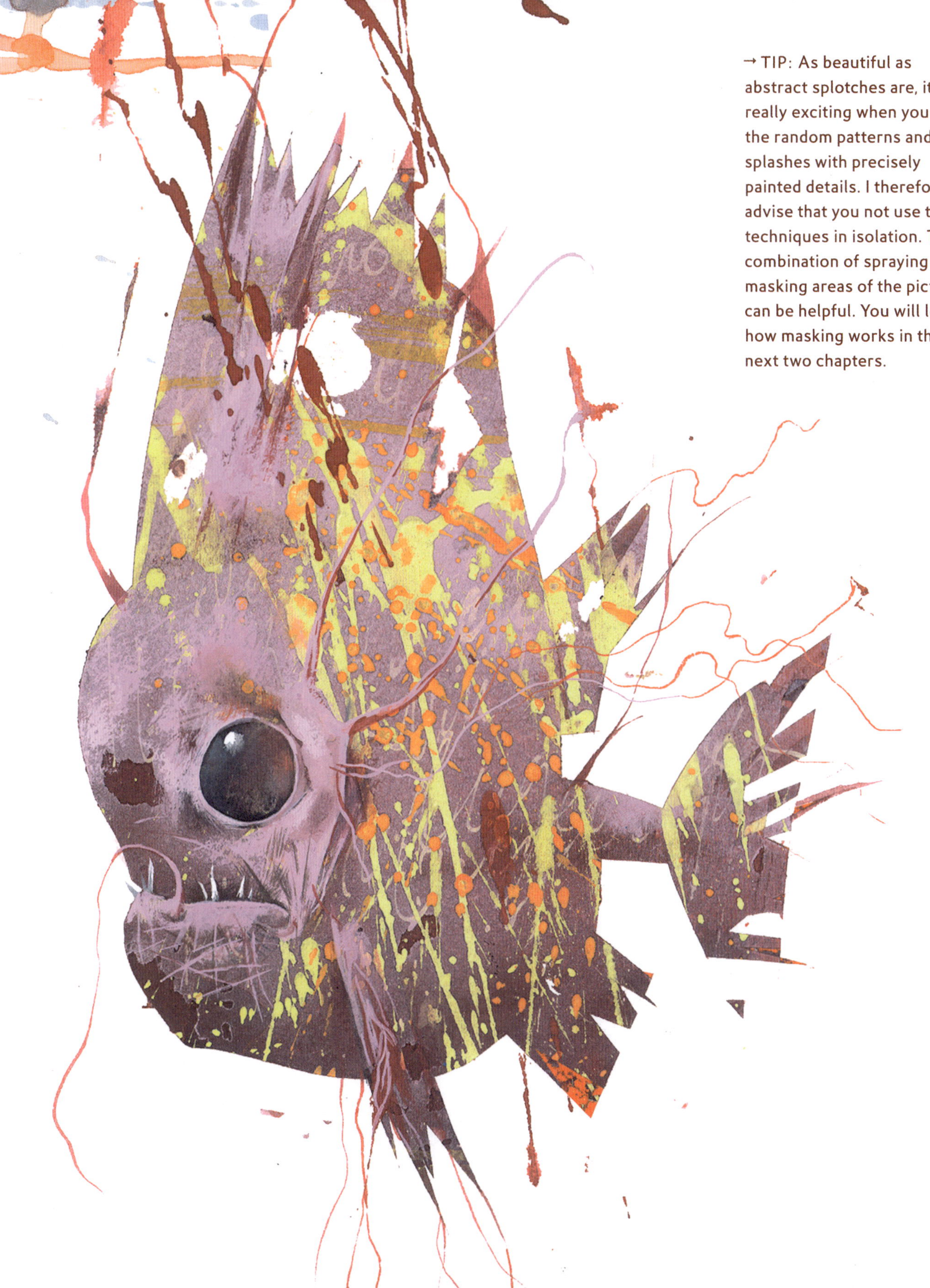

→ TIP: As beautiful as abstract splotches are, it gets really exciting when you pair the random patterns and splashes with precisely painted details. I therefore advise that you not use these techniques in isolation. The combination of spraying and masking areas of the picture can be helpful. You will learn how masking works in the next two chapters.

Gum arabic meets gum elastic. Using masking fluid

One of my favourite techniques is covering or masking parts of the picture. Masking works best with *tape* (more on this in the next chapter) or *masking fluid*. This is liquid rubber that dries on contact with the air to form a waterproof latex film. In this way, the underlying paper can no longer absorb paint. When the covering has served its purpose, the film can be pulled off more or less effortlessly or rubbed away with an eraser. This technique is not particularly difficult, the more interesting the possibilities it opens up. But you can only find out if you have tried it yourself. And please read the tips on important tricks, as this will save you some broken brushes and damaged originals!

As early as the eighteenth century, artists had thought about how to leave the white of paper blank. They cut stencils, prepared water-repellent pastes from beeswax and turpentine oil, applied them and later removed them with old bread. All of this was really time-consuming when compared to today's latex rubber solutions!

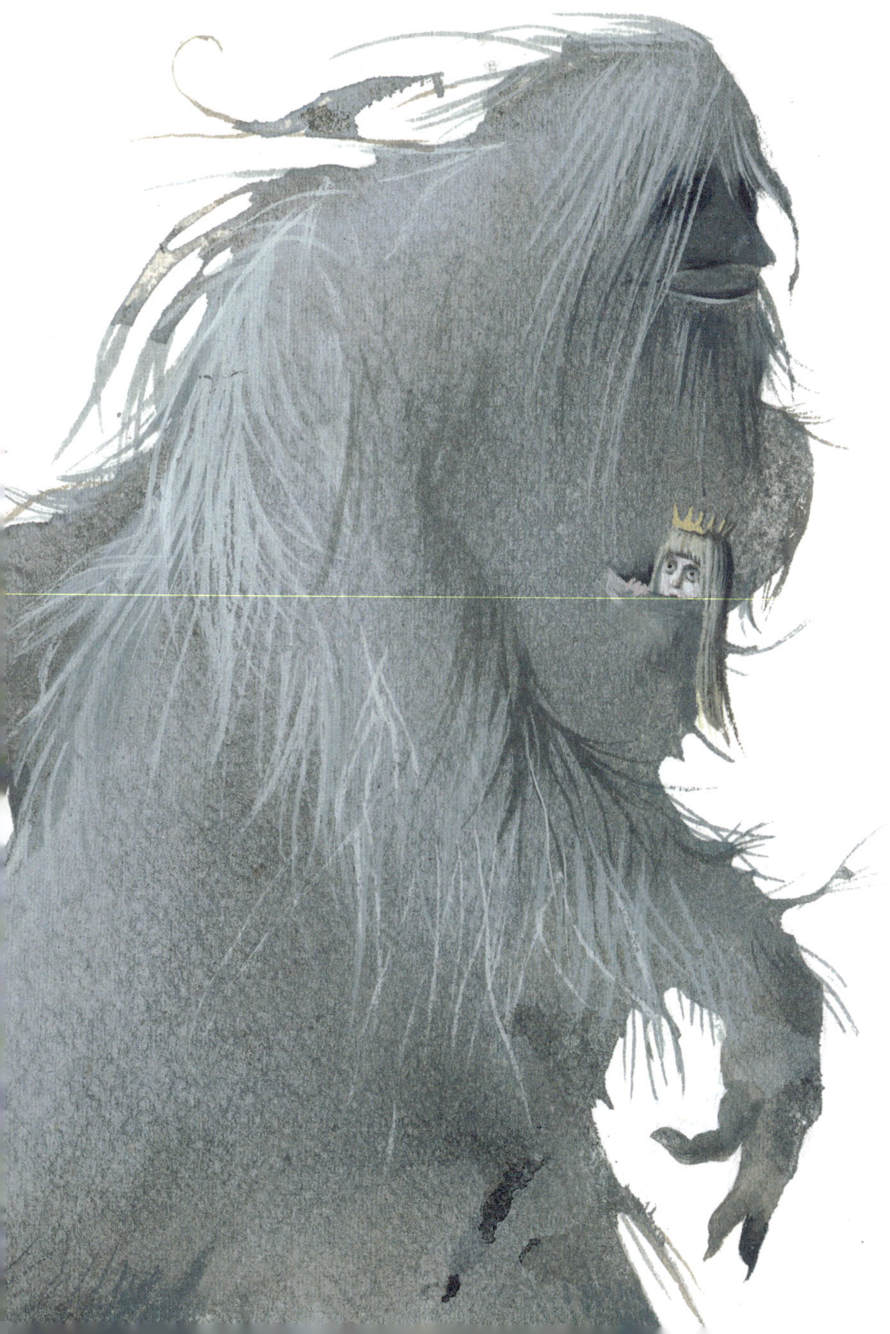

Masking is always suspenseful because you can never control exactly how the liquid rubber lies on the paper. So what comes to light after pulling off the film is always a little surprise!

Modern masking fluids are especially helpful when you want to take advantage of the randomness of watercolours. By masking, you hide elements of the picture, while other parts with different structures, shapes or splashes can be worked on separately. Thanks to this technique, you can frame this confusion with clearly defined empty spaces, or you can leave out white "islands of calm."

You already read about different masking fluids on p. 55 in the chapter "Other painting tools and what they're good for." Whichever brand you choose– the main difference will always be whether you use the strong smelling ammonia masking rubber made of latex or prefer the liquid frisket. For painting with gouache, I generally recommend the first type, because all latex-based masking fluids can be removed in one piece. This will prevent you from using an eraser, which can cause paints to smear. It's interesting that when masking with latex-containing masks two plant rubbers meet: gum arabic from the African acacia in the gouache and gum elastic (as latex is also called) from the rubber tree!

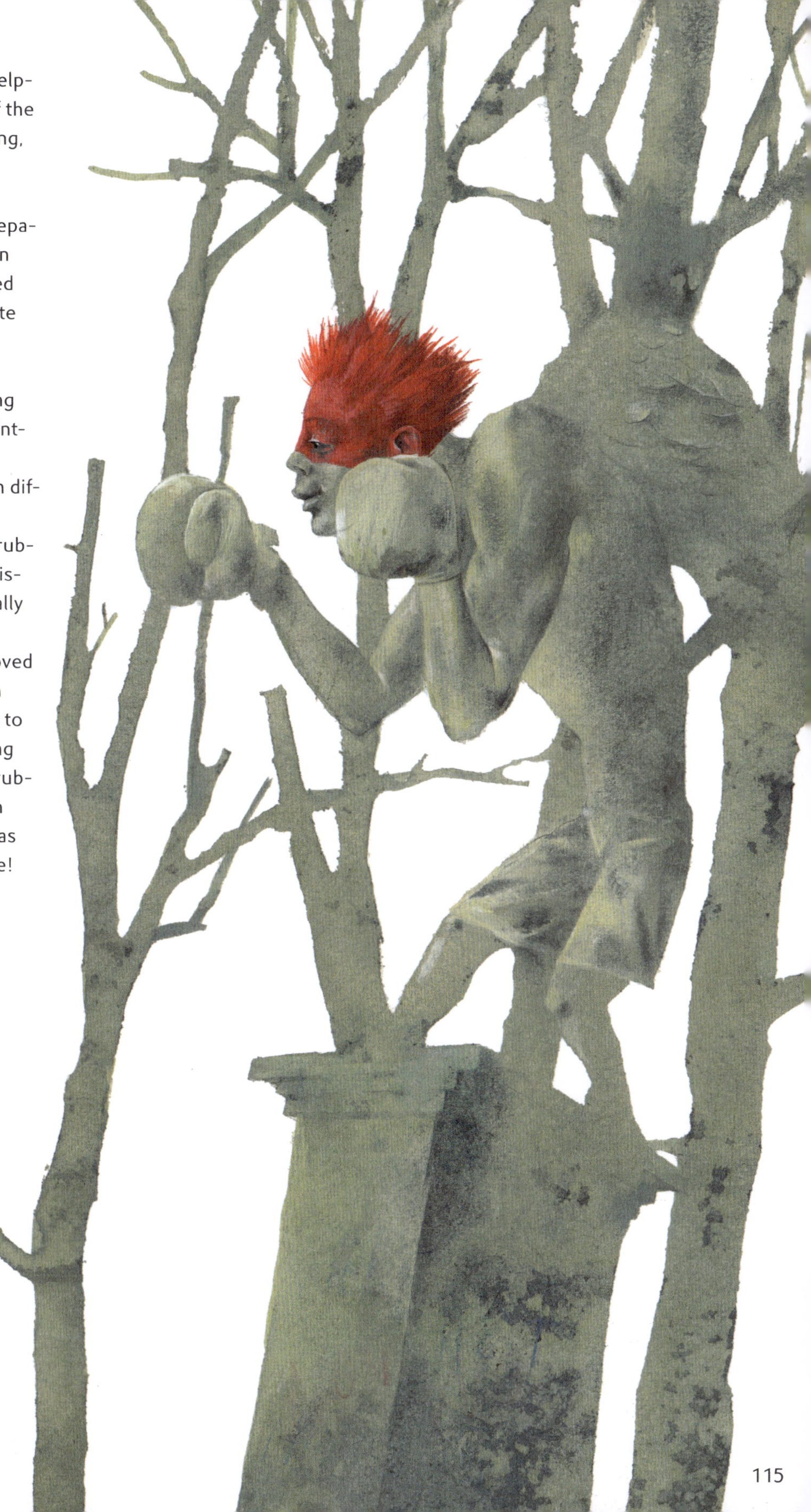

Layer for Layer

Masking with gum arabic

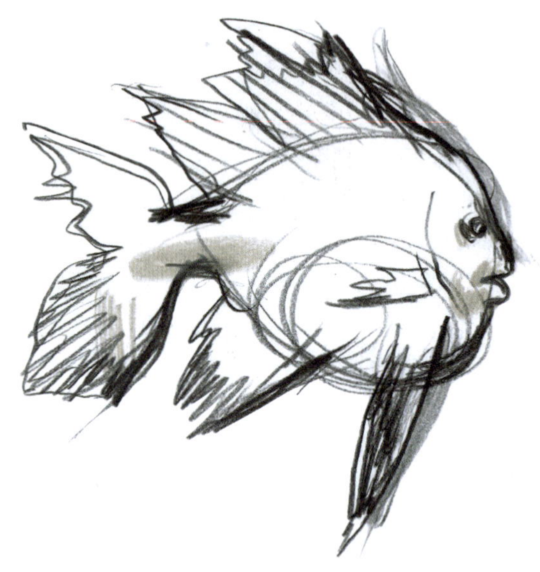

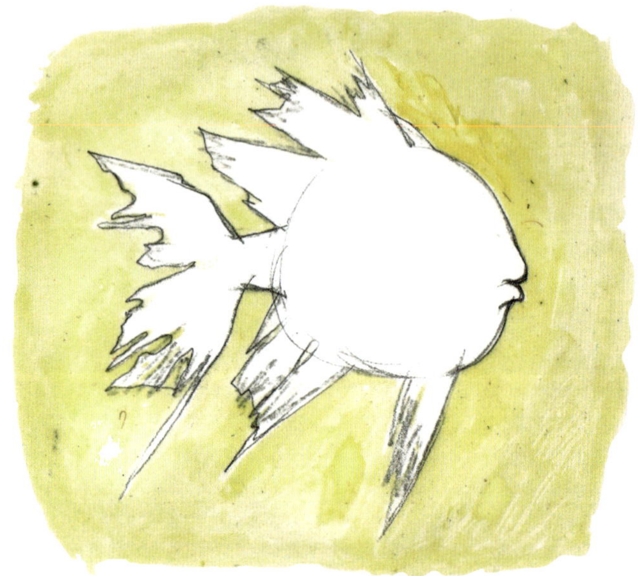

1.

First draw your subject in pencil. Once you have your sketch, trace it with carbon paper. If you don't have any on hand, you can make the perfect carbon paper yourself: take a 5B or 6B soft pencil and use it to create a graphite surface on the back of your sketch. Now turn it over and trace the subject.

2.

Now take the brush and apply the masking fluid. In this example it's yellow, but – depending on the brand – there are also blue, grey or transparent masking films. One thing is particularly important: the paper must be absolutely dry; otherwise the dried film will tear out ugly stripes when removed.

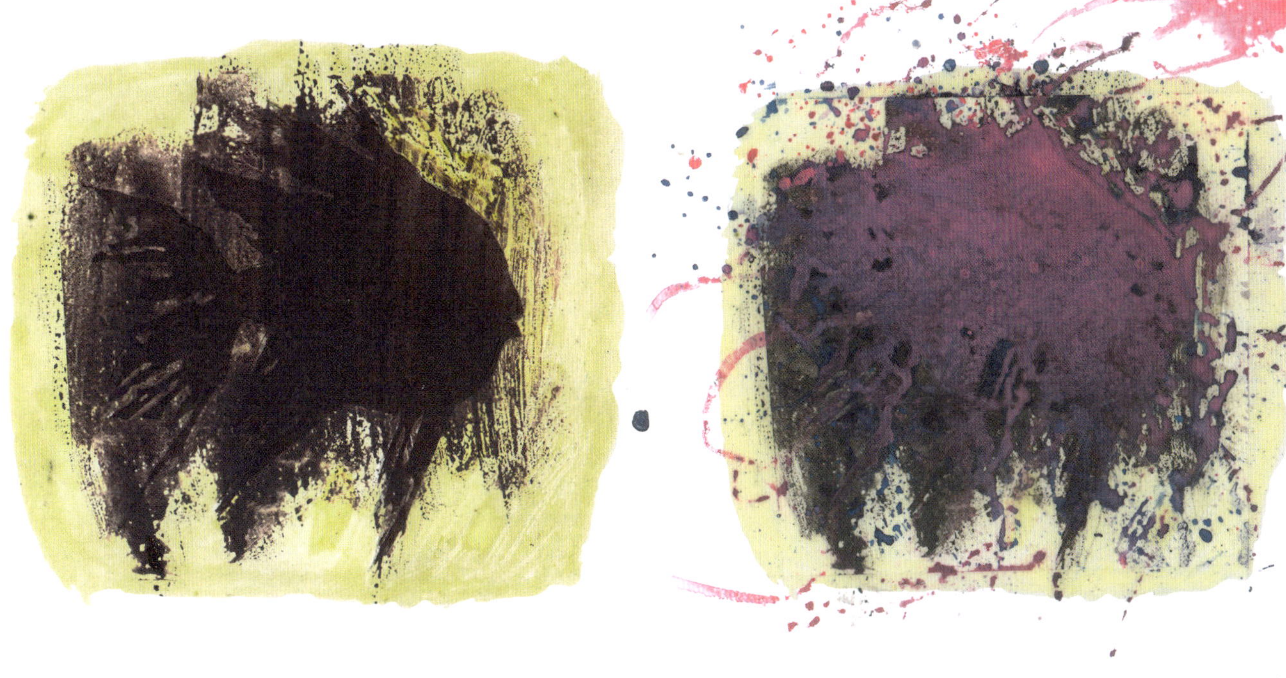

3.

Have a little patience and let the masking fluid dry nicely, it won't take long. Depending on the room temperature and humidity, it's usually ready in about 10 minutes. Now you can apply the first layer of paint, in our case I started with a dark brown shade.

4.

Let the gouache dry completely, then the second coat of paint follows. If you move the paper, you can let the paint flow in one direction or another and thus influence the distribution of the pigments. Try not to wash out the lower layer of paint!

→ TIP: Always close the masking tape jar tightly because it dries very quickly. If the paper is poor quality, the drying time is too short or the rubbing technique is incorrect, the picture may be damaged, i.e. the fibres or whole pieces of the picture are torn away! The better the paper (pure cotton paper is ideal), the less you run the risk of the liquid frisket tearing pieces when you pull it off.

Layer for Layer

Masking with gum arabic

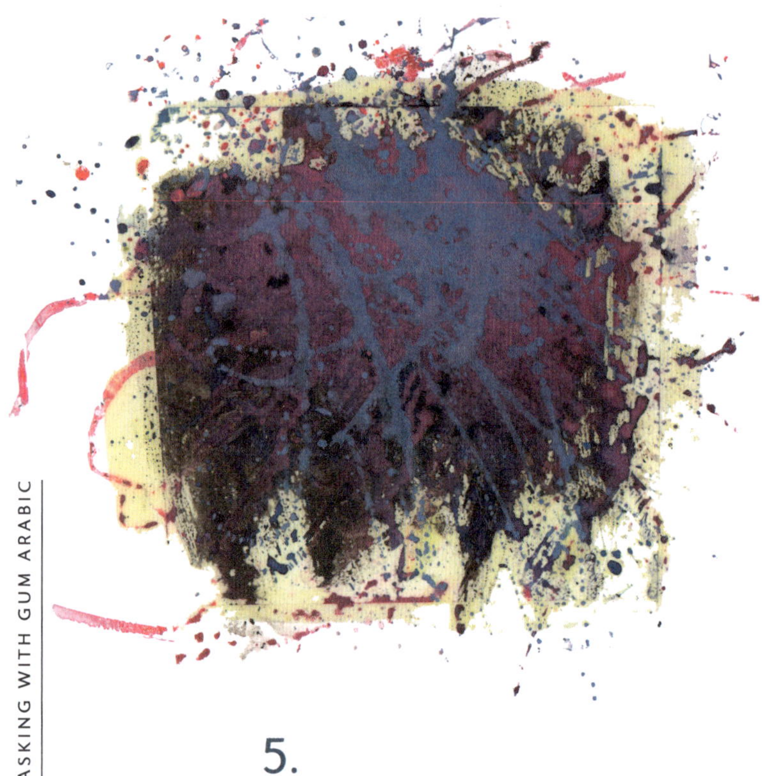

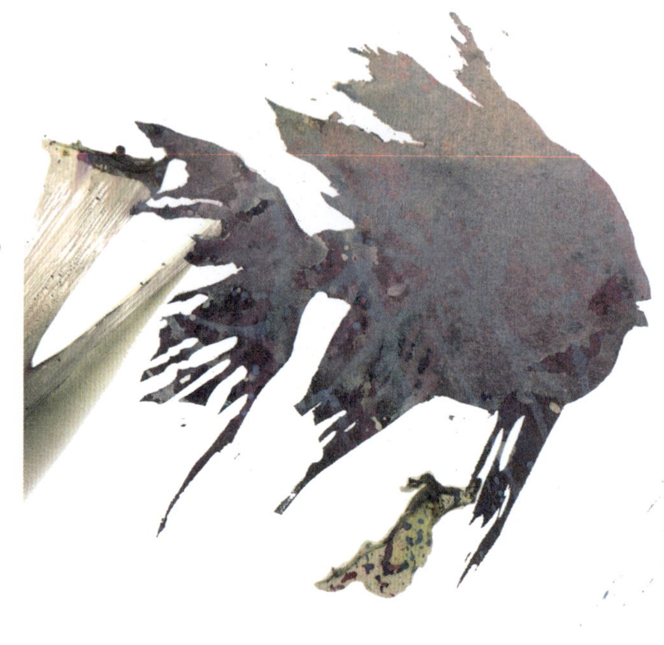

5.

After drying again, you can apply another (in this case blue) colour as a glaze. And so it can go on until about four to five layers lie on top of each other. More becomes difficult, because then you're unlikely to be able to avoid washing out the top layers of paint.

6.

If the colours are right, you can start peeling off the masking film. Now you can see the difference between the ammonia-containing masking rubbers and the liquid frisket. Basically, the former can be removed in one go, as in the illustration. The liquid frisket doesn't come off without an eraser.

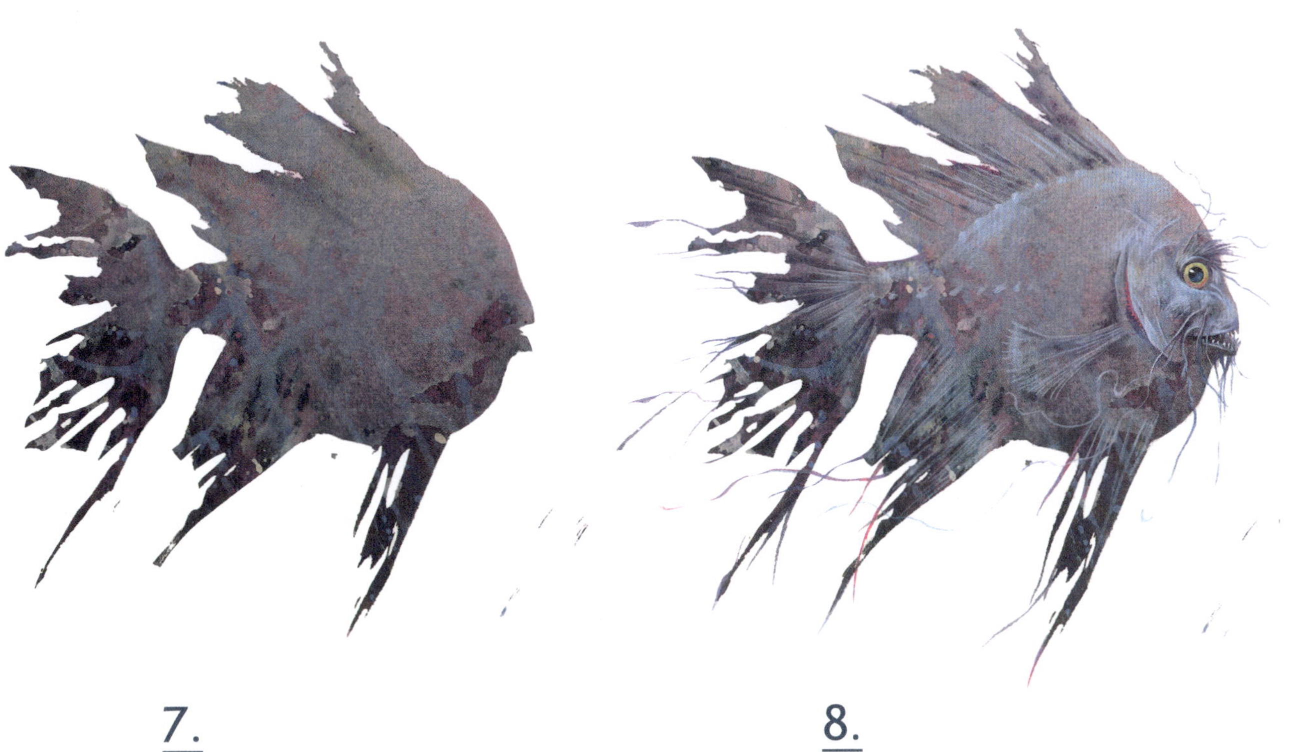

7.

Now the picture is exposed again, the remains of the masking film and the preliminary drawing have been erased. You can start with the finishing touches. Only the most important thing is missing, namely the details. The fish has a colourful body, but no face yet. So he gets one.

8.

With an even lighter shade of blue, the head section gets a few lights, and a few fin bones are also added. The eyes and mouth are very important for the expression; they are now painted in detail with a fine brush, for example size 3. At some point everything is correct and the picture is ready.

→ TIP: An important detail if you don't want your brushes to be gummed up right away. Place a strong soap solution next to your picture (washing up liquid, diluted 1:3 with water will do as well). Wash your brush in it every 30-40 seconds. Then you have a chance that your brush will survive the masking and can be used again at some point.

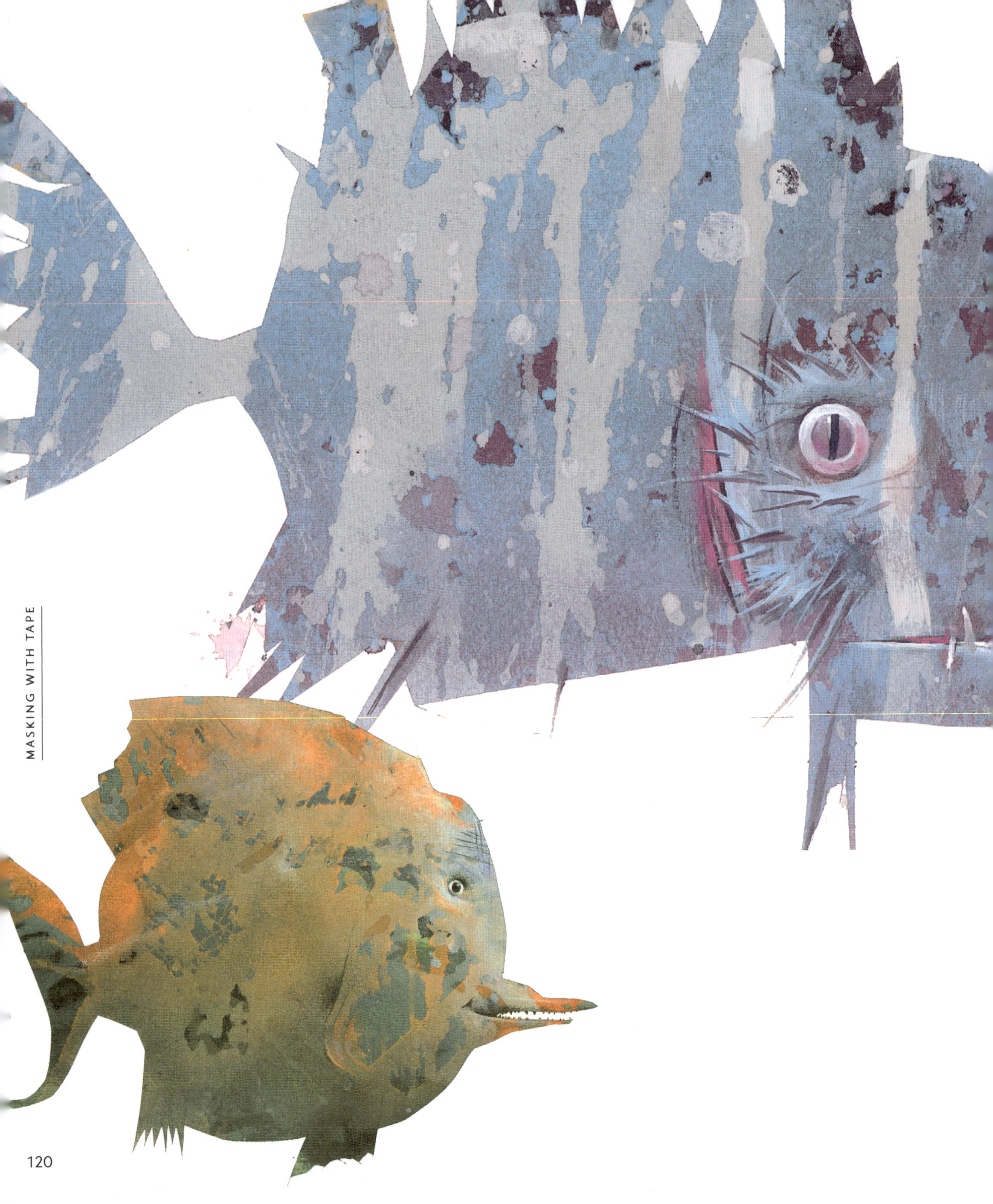

Masked ball. Masking with tape

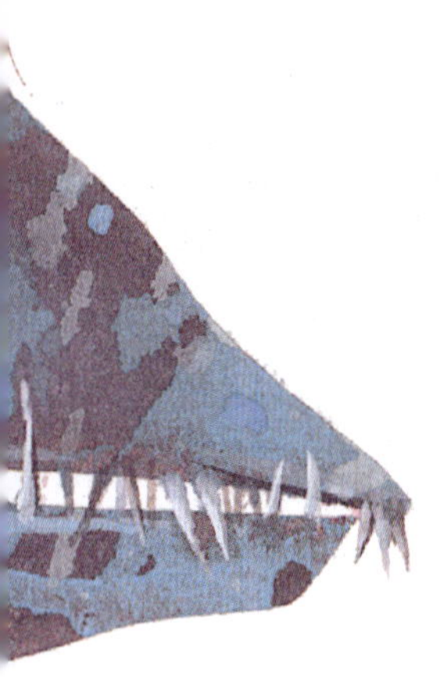

Every interesting subject possesses an inner tension. It arises when you manage to combine opposites in one picture. This masking technique is suitable for this– it allows you to set hard geometric shapes against soft, flowing structures within these shapes.

Masking with tape is relatively uncomplicated; apart from the tape itself and a knife, you won't need anything. You can start with a brown packing tape or transparent tape, or experiment with airbrush films or professional car paint films. There are also tapes specially made for masking, Nichiban is very good, for example. This technique really comes into its own when you want to integrate clearly defined geometric shapes into your painting. Because while masking fluid creates soft and irregular edges, the hard-cut edges of the picture masked with the tape look almost like collages and thus develop their very unique effect.

With an infinite number of different types of paper and tape available, you can't expect each of them to work perfectly together. On the one hand, the tape should stick enough so that the paint doesn't flow underneath. On the other hand, it's important that no strips are torn from the covered paper when peeling the tape off and that the background remains intact. So test how strongly the tape sticks to the paper and whether the paper is robust enough to survive the removal of the tape safely. From experience I know that well-gelled rag papers like Arches easily survive the masking.

→ TIP: Depending on the thickness of the tape, you might gash more or less deeply into the paper when cutting. No biggie! A little sensitivity is required to cut the mask. Before you start, try to see how hard you can push to avoid damaging the paper.

Layer for Layer

Masking with tape

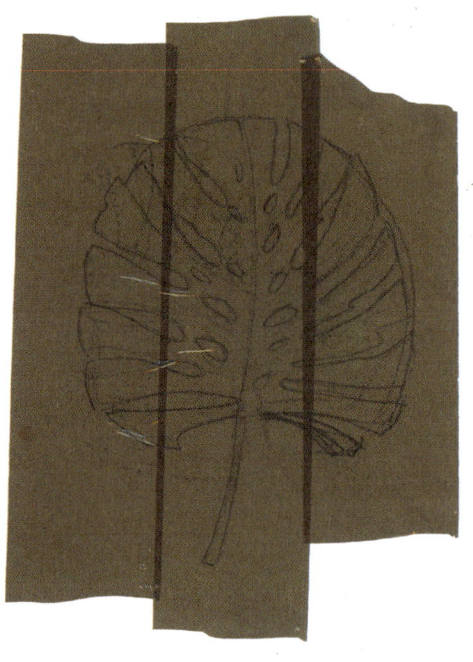

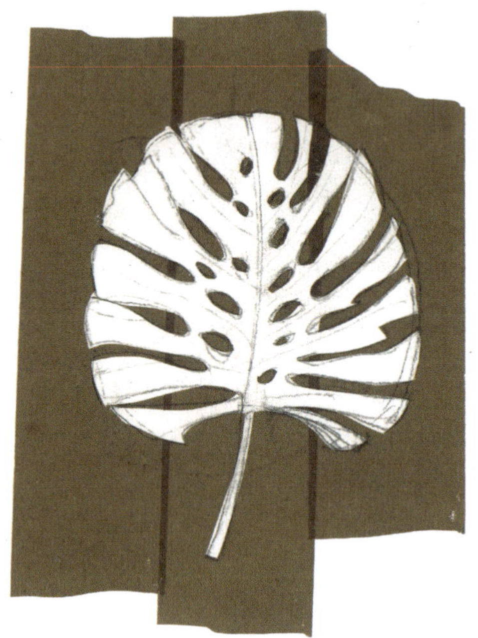

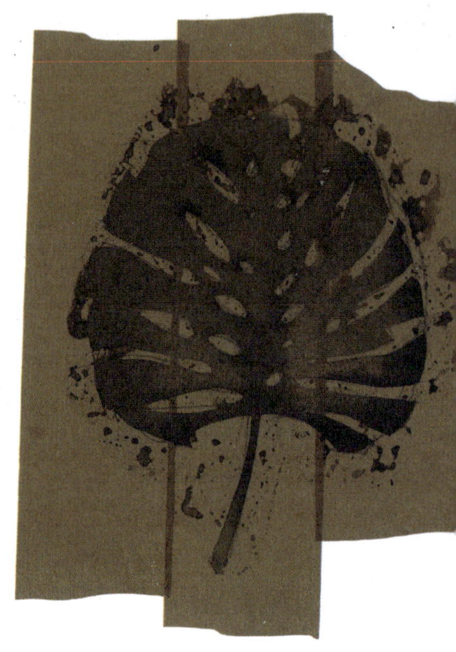

1.

First, make a pencil sketch directly on the paper. Then tape over the subject so that the tape overlaps your planned picture by at least 3-4 cm. If you plan to work with spraying and lots of water, I would tape the whole sheet!

2.

Since most tapes are not very thick, your preliminary drawing will probably remain visible. Now take a knife or cutter and cut out the leaf shape. Then carefully remove the tape.

3.

In the next phase, apply the first layer of paint. On the illustration it was sepia brown. Use a flat or round medium-sized brush from approximately size 10 with soft hair.

→ TIP: The technique of masking with tape works best if you cover the subject on white paper. Unfortunately, it's very difficult to do the same on a painted background. If the tape doesn't stick enough, the paint will flow underneath and if it sticks strong enough, it will very likely tear off the paint on the background when you peel it off. If you give it a try, work with a little water and look for adhesive tapes that are gentler.

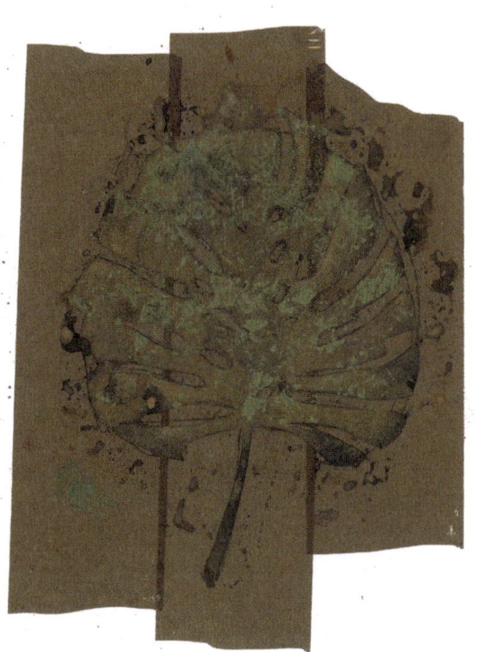

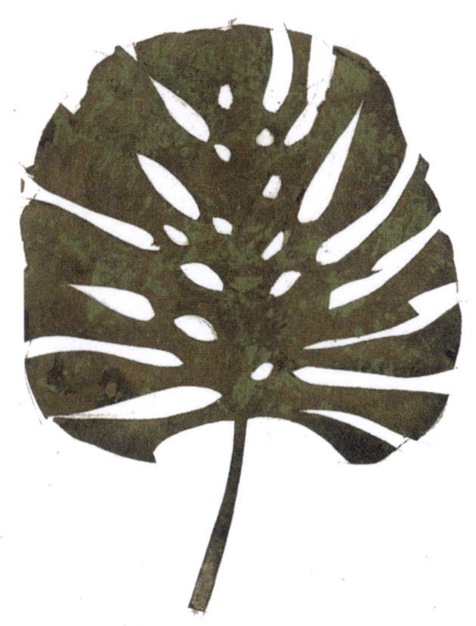

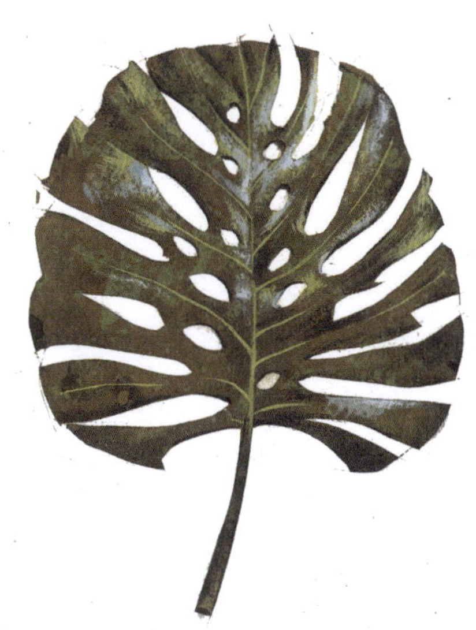

4.

Let the first layer of paint dry and apply the next layer or layers with a smaller brush approximately size 6. Make sure that your first coat is not completely painted over. Also check whether the tape is still sticking well.

5.

Now comes the moment of revelation, the tape is finally removed. Only now do you see how the edges turned out and where you may need to rework. Take the eraser in your hand and eliminate any visible remnants of the drawing.

6.

As a finishing touch, the subject gets depth and highlights at the crucial points. Try not to paint the sometimes randomly created patterns and edges "to death": put your brush aside sooner rather than later!

What can be combined with gouache? Watercolours, coloured pencils, pastels, etc.

After a dozen emails providing personal information and describing my request, in May 2019 I finally was standing in the study hall of Berlin's Museum of Prints and Drawings. In front of me were five cassettes containing gouaches by Adolf Menzel, which I now had all to myself. I already knew from books that the little man was very keen to experiment with these paints. But it was only when I held the originals in my hand that I noticed how differently Menzel handled his paints from picture to picture. For him, painting with gouache didn't mean a fixed technique with the same workflow. Sometimes he started to under-paint the background in ink, then built up the subjects from dark to light with gouache and later set the highlights with pastel chalk. Another time he painted with glazed gouache layers from light to dark and later washed away the paint with a cotton ball or his bare fingers.

Experience shows that as soon as an artist feels comfortable in his technique, he inevitably begins to expand its limits. It's in the nature of gouache that it can be wonderfully complemented by other techniques.

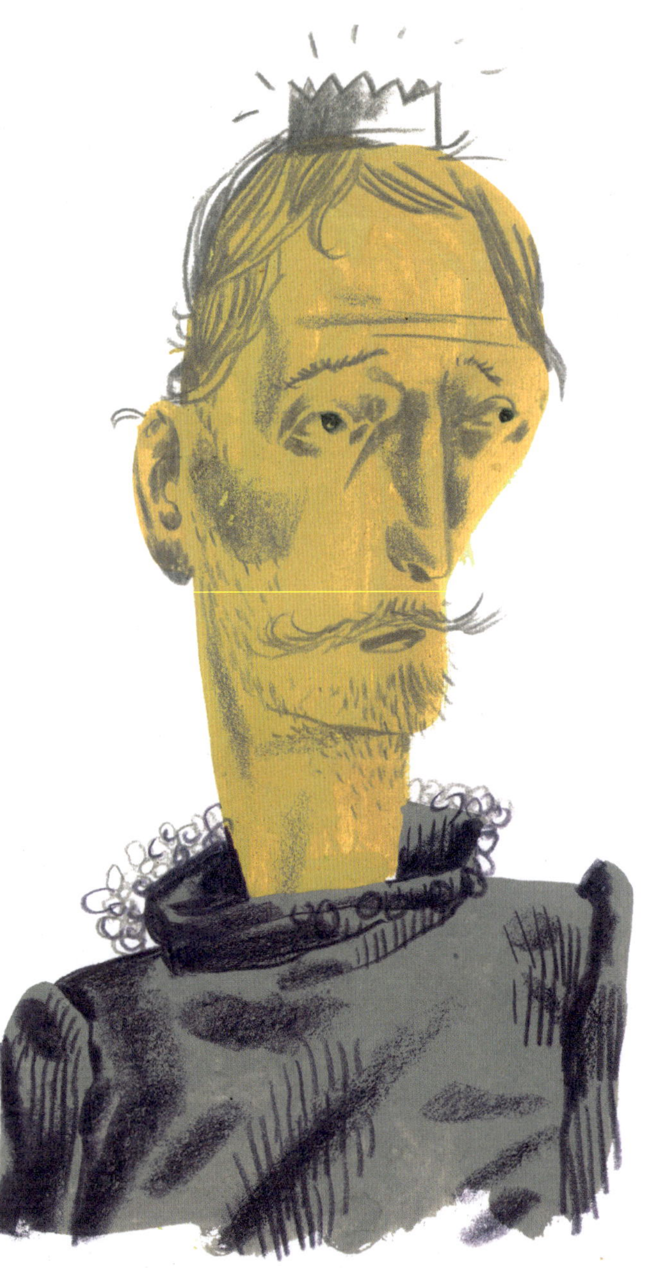

Her twin sister *watercolours* comes first, of course, because as you know, the modern separation between "transparent" and "opaque" watercolours has always been quite formal. The common binder gum arabic means that they mix easily with each other. Watercolours may be an option if you make your backgrounds very transparent as a wash. Then opaque gouache can be used.

Gouache is also closely related to *pastel chalks*. Both gum arabic, which is added to the chalk, and kaolin, which makes the paints appear softer in gouache and pastel, cause the two techniques to mix well with one another. Usually we use pastel on the painted gouache pictures, but the opposite is also possible, whereby a pastel drawing is created and then painted over. By the way, pastel chalk can also be dissolved with water.

Often minor corrections are necessary on finished gouache pictures or a shadow might be missing. *Coloured pencils* are used for this, preferably soft Polychromos or Prismacolor. It's great fun to draw on the slightly rough and sandy surface of a gouache picture with such pencils. You can be sure of a nice full stroke. Even bright colours or white on dark gouache backgrounds are often a nice addition to painting.

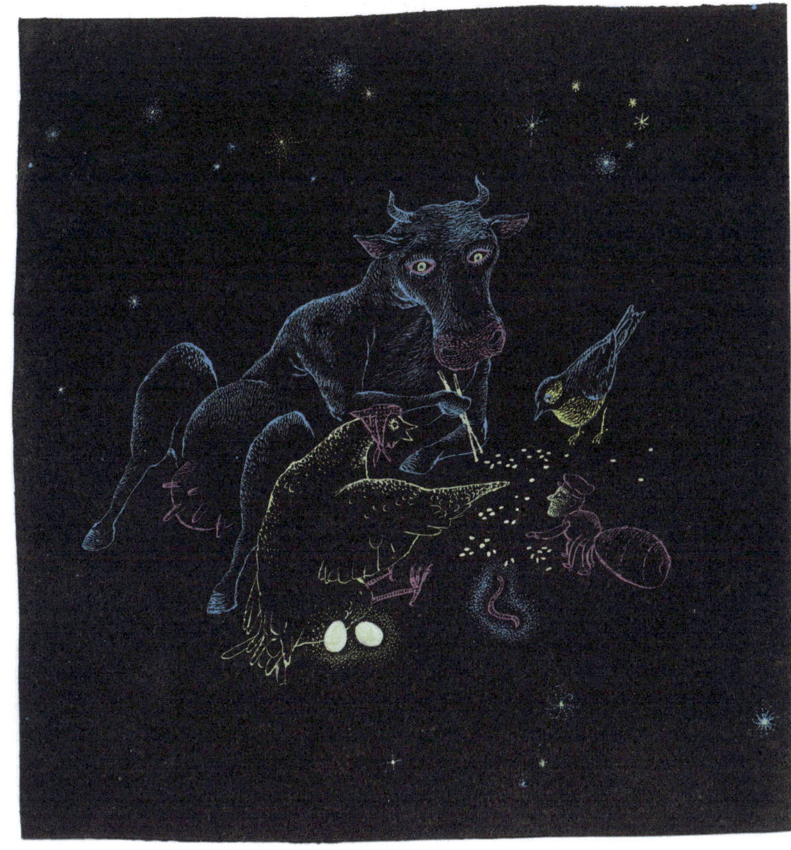

But not only "wet" (like watercolours) or "dry" (pastel chalks and coloured pencils) media can be combined with gouache. If you're interested in unusual liaisons, you can prime the paper with *oil paints*, for example, and try to draw on it with gouache. The oil is quickly absorbed by the paper, the turpentine evaporates. This enables gouache paints to hold well on a slightly shiny surface and not bead off.

→ **TIP: A gouache drawing on cardboard primed with oil paints would shine differently if it were drawn on a different background, for example on black paper.**

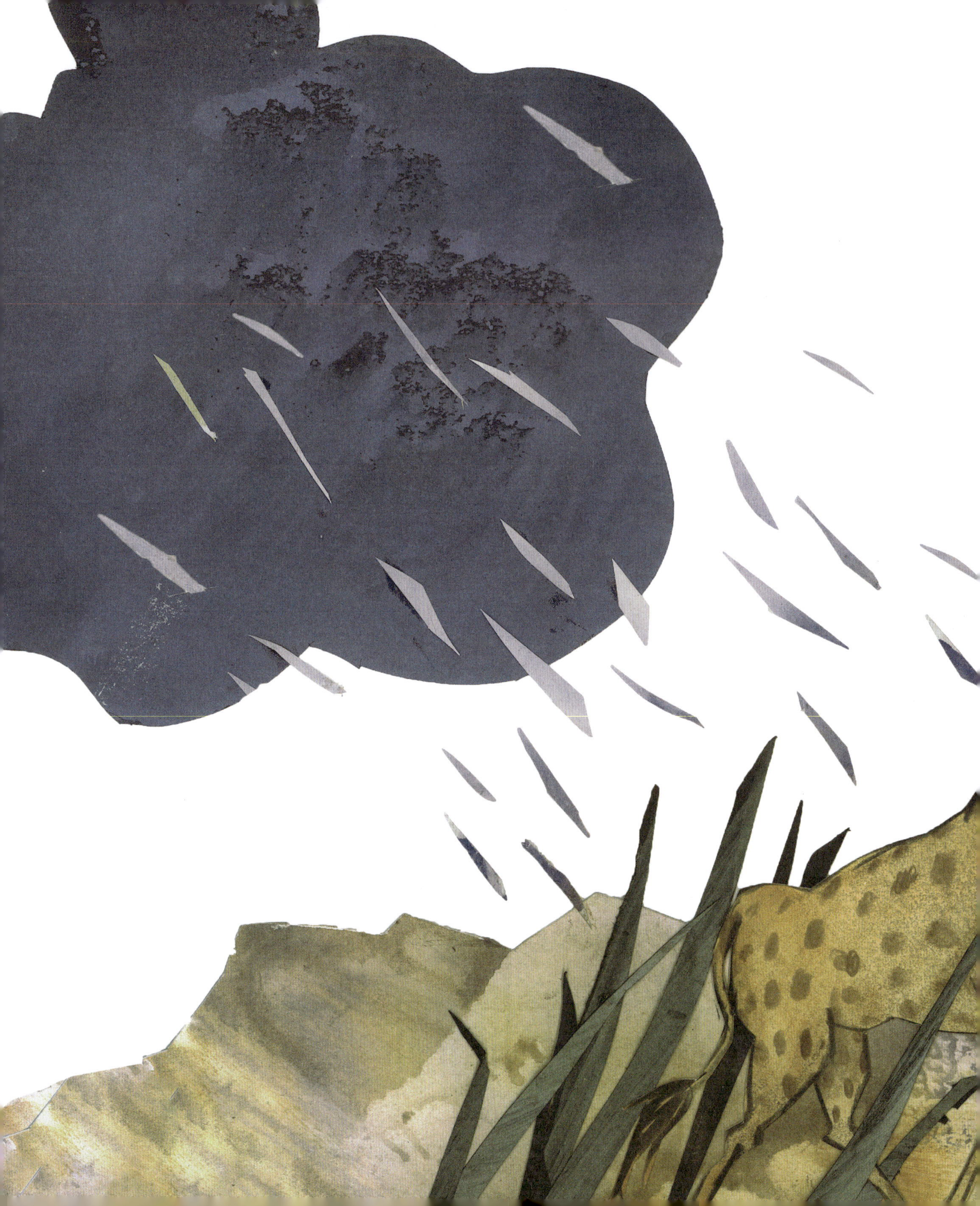

Controlled coincidences. Monotype

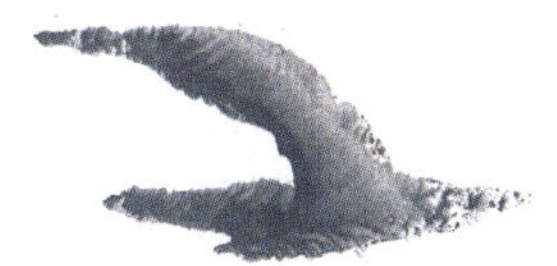

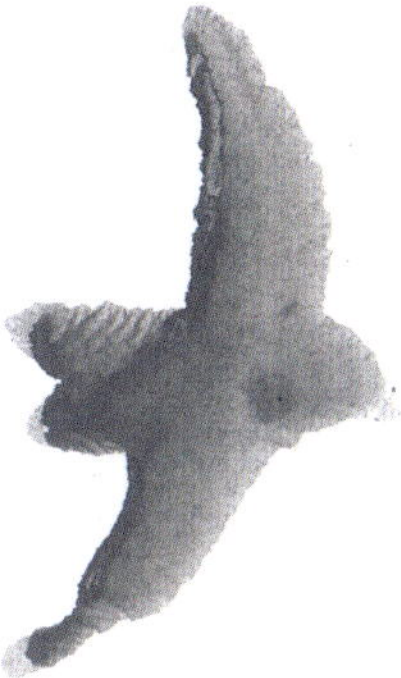

Monotype is a playful technique that is generally not considered suitable for gouache – mostly oil or printing ink is used. But if you want to get quick results or need interesting patterns for your collages, you can easily switch to gouache. For monotype, you need a glass or metal plate in addition to paints and brushes. First apply a thin layer. Then place a sheet of paper on the wet paint and lightly press it on with the palm of your hand. The colours appear on the paper in streaks and patterns, they vary depending on how wet and thick the paint was on the glass. And since the gouache paints dry very quickly, you shouldn't take too much time with the impression.

Since only one, at most two, prints are possible (that are anything but identical), we call it "monotype," as in a single print. If you don't have a glass plate at hand (if necessary, a glass from the picture frame on the wall would suffice), you can use a different surface. It's important that the board absorbs little water: like lacquered wood or laminated cardboard. A piece of plastic film is also adequate in a pinch.

Monotypes in gouache offer many great options. Different shapes can be cut out of the paper dyed in this way and processed into collages. Many illustrators work in this technique, for example Eric Carle. Remember his very *hungry caterpillar*? The pictures from that book were also created in monotype.

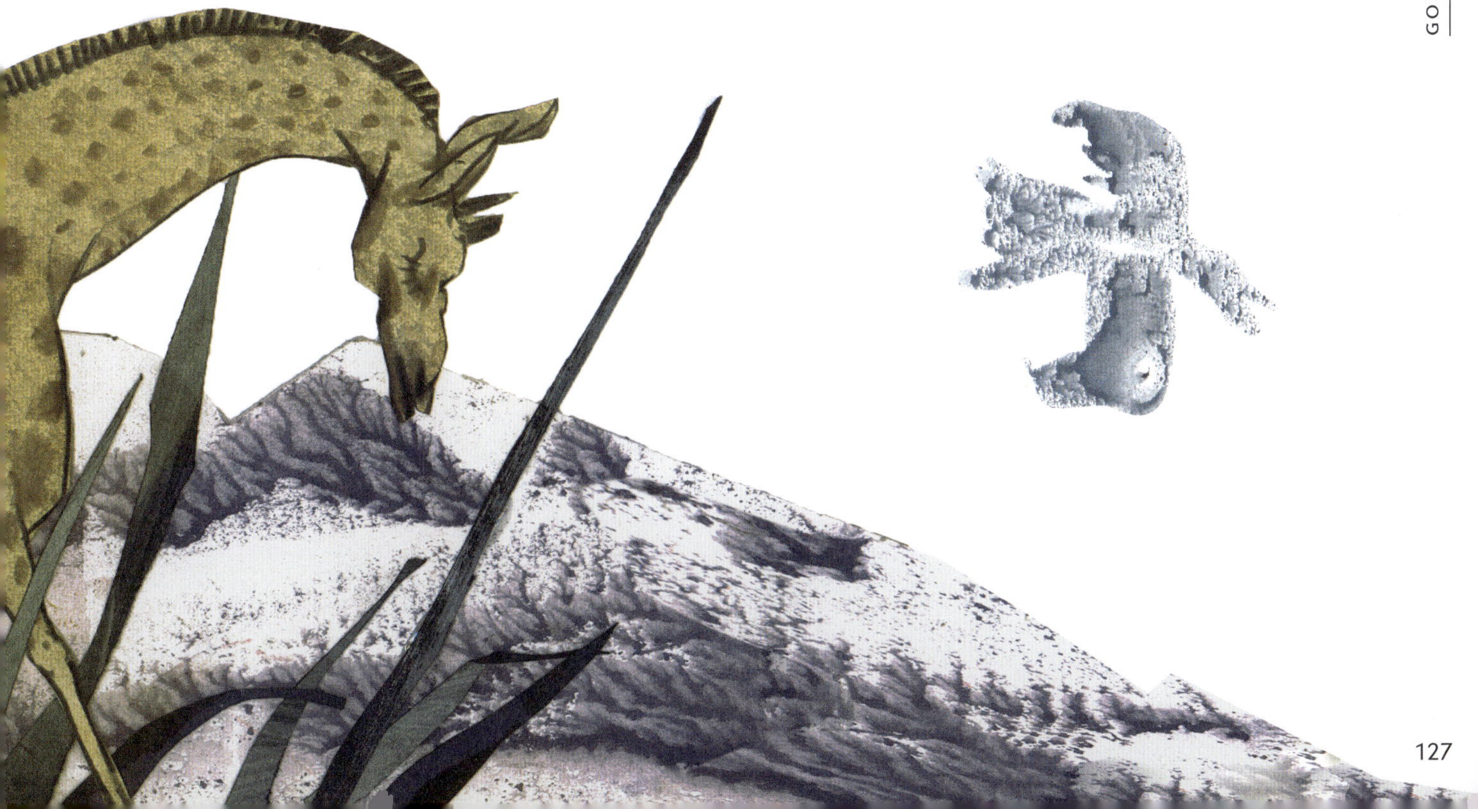

Portrait of a Banana Tree.
Apply and develop

This chapter is the last and actually the most important. It's about implementing everything we've learned about gouache so far. Because all materials, techniques and tricks presented in this book only become interesting when you use them. So here are some tips on the questions I once had myself. For example, how do I depict a human being, an animal or a plant in gouache? But since we artists ought not to be too dogmatic, use it as a guide for independent testing and further development.

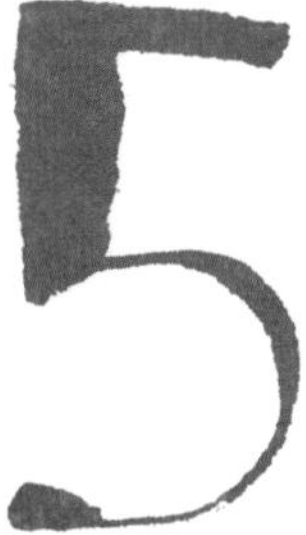

Let's get ready! Making sketches

Right at the beginning of the Soviet blockbuster The Adventures of Electronics two boys who look alike meet. One is a house robot named Electronic that has just been developed and has run away from the laboratory; the other is the schoolboy Sergey Syroezhkin, his human, all too chaotic prototype. The boy lives by the motto "live it up 'cause we got only one life" and sends Electronic to school in his place. The robot, whose dream it is to be a human being, has super powers, plans everything in advance, can sing beautifully and can calculate perfectly. The real Sergey is not very organized and mostly acts according to his feelings, but his sense of humour and good knowledge of human nature help him to master all the problems that crop up over the course of the film.

Why did I bring it up? Because there are also "Electronics" and "Sergeys" among us artists. The former plan everything in detail in their heads and only pick up their brushes when they have a precise picture in their minds. The others scribble. They don't stop until dozens of fully scribbled pieces of paper finally show the idea of the picture... I see myself more among the "Sergeys" who intuitively search while drawing or when painting, when it comes to a mood or atmosphere that I want to express in the picture. Because colours primarily convey moods and gouache paints are ideal for spontaneous searching and testing. Gouache has long been considered a particularly good sketching and drawing technique. What makes it so? First, the quick drying time. Secondly, the paints can be easily applied in large areas as well as nuanced. Third, when something goes wrong, we can always correct it. Because especially in a sketch, we aren't aiming for perfection.

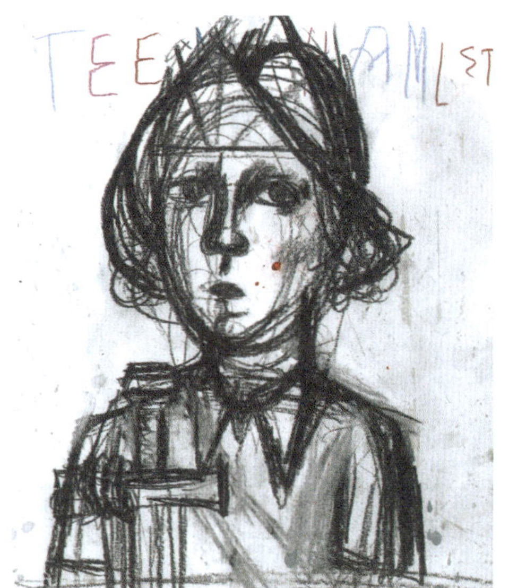

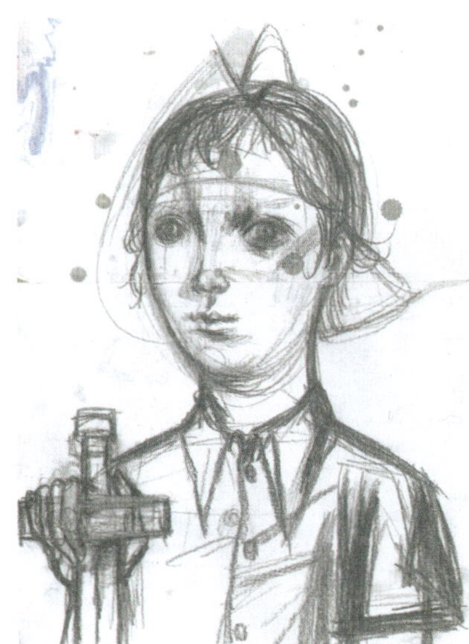

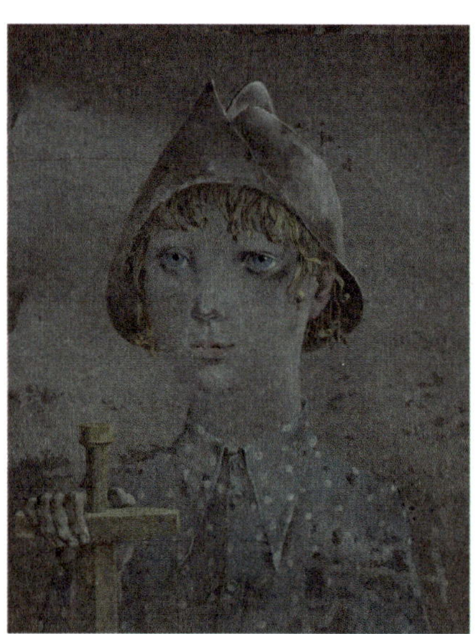

Finished illustration

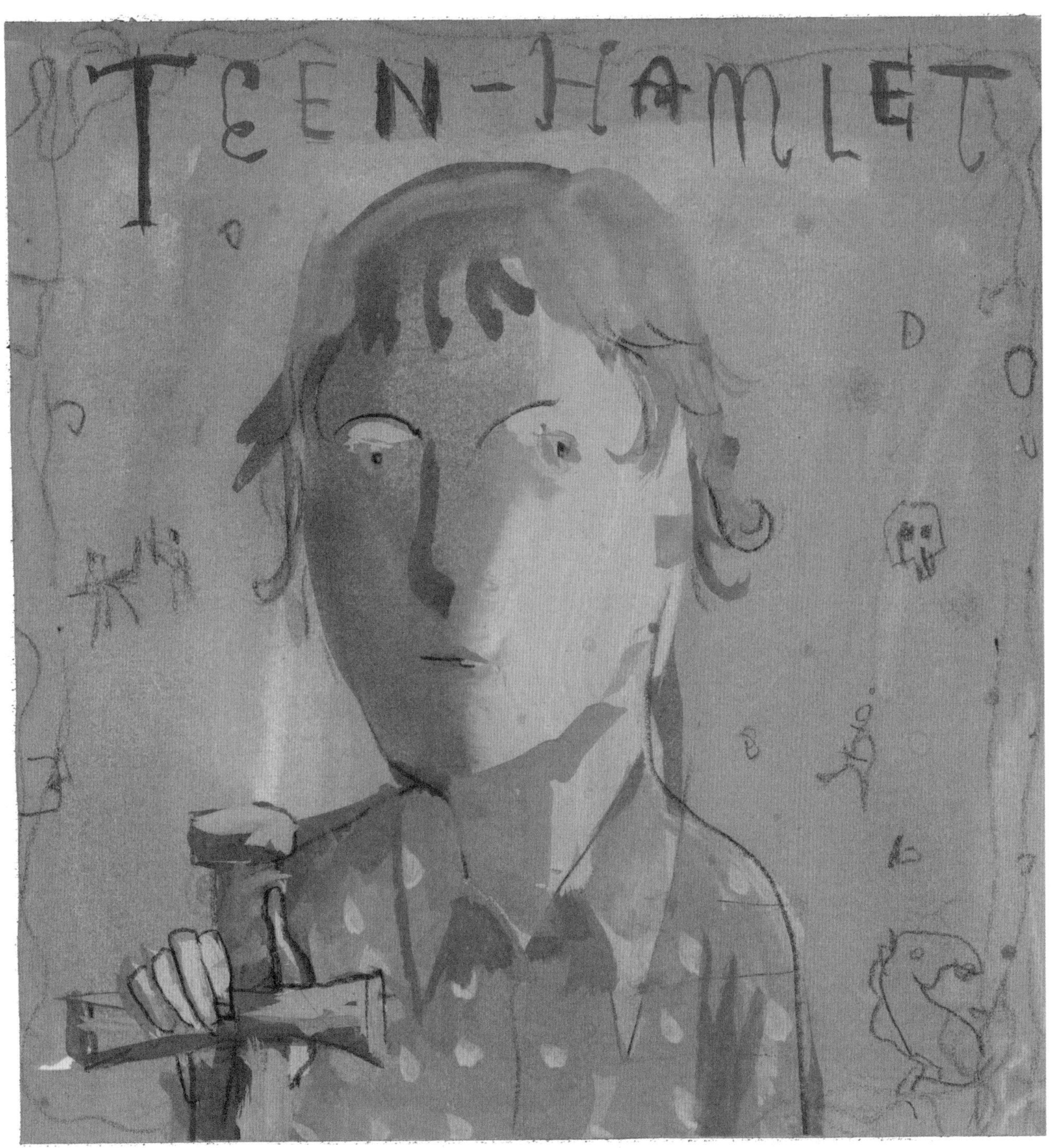
TEEN-HAMLET

When we look at a picture book, we have no idea how many sketches are behind each picture. Illustrators rarely just start painting, but thinks about their pictures in advance. A lot needs to be planned: it starts with colour mood and composition, then important details follow. This is why many sketches are made before you start painting. And for good reasons: Sometimes the sketches capture a colour mood that you have in mind for the picture. You can see such "mood sketches" on the previous double page. They illustrate the attempt to paint a restrained "tone-on-tone" picture in shimmering grey to create a slightly melancholic mood. Below you see the finished picture in small.

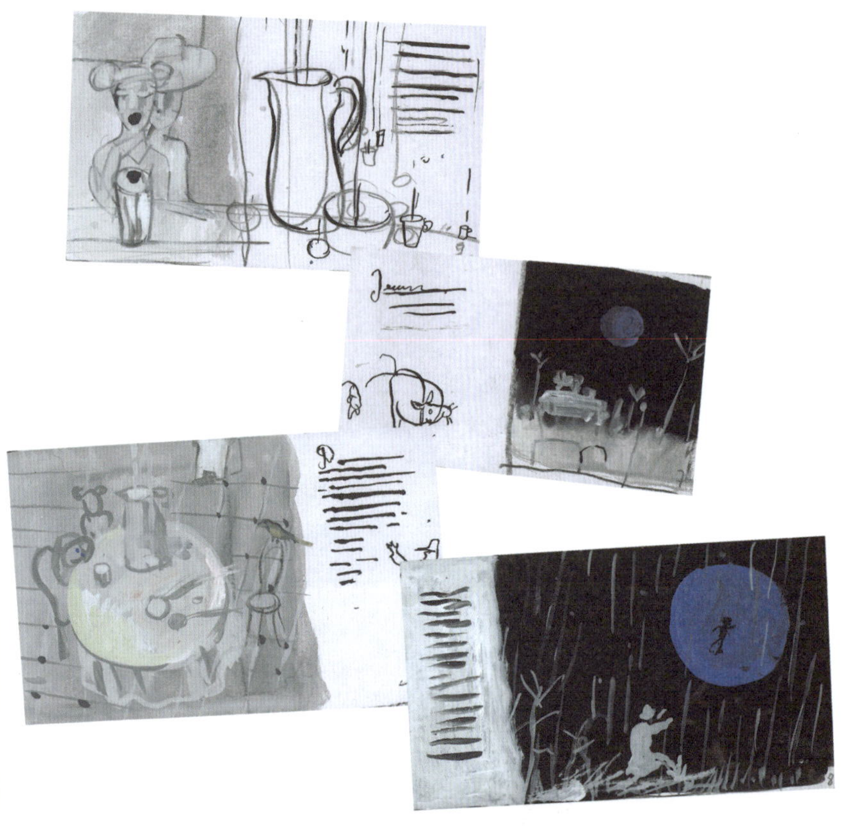

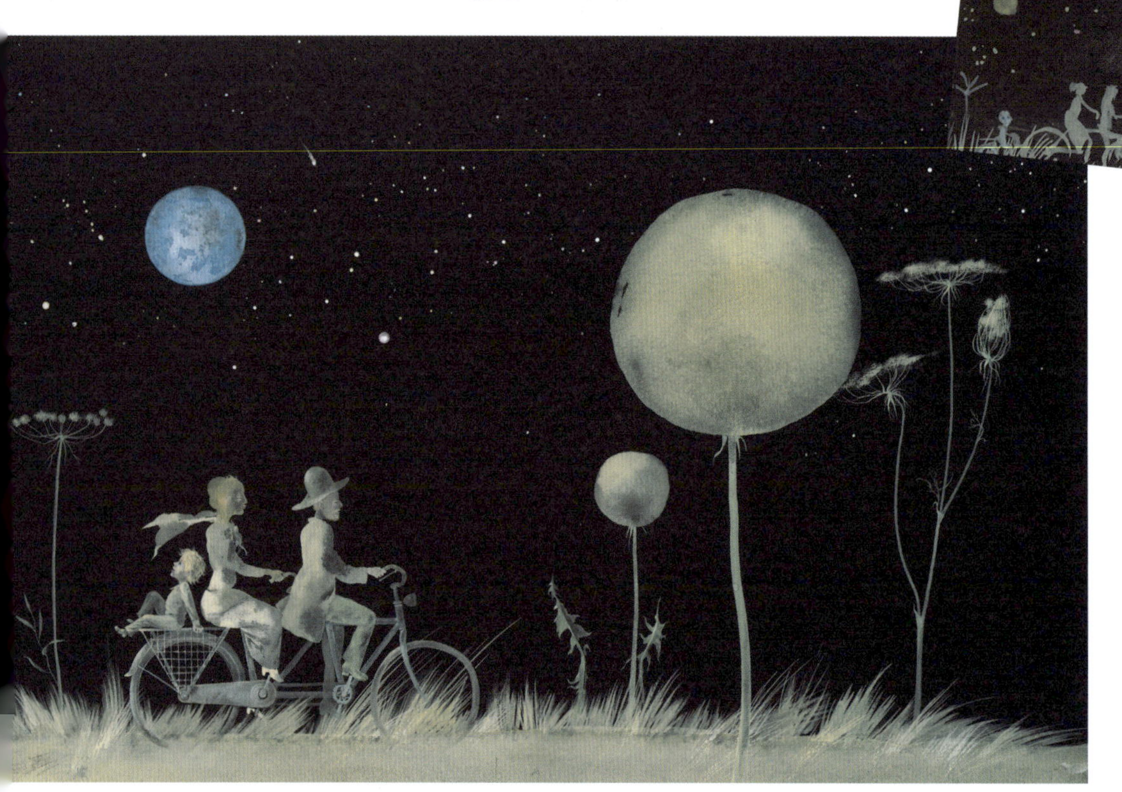

Sometimes it makes sense if the client (say, a publisher) can get an idea of what the finished picture will look like before you finish it. In addition, sketches help you to get a clearer vision of where your work is headed. Then the "thumbnails" emerge, little double-page sketches. The pictures on the left are an example of this. The black and grey preliminary sketches for a picture book set on the moon are almost monochrome. Here it was all about changing–from large to small shapes, from detail and close to total shots, similar to a movie. And from very black or white to grey double pages.

These sketches for the cover picture of a novel are much more detailed. Some of them are drawn with a steel pen to indicate details as precisely as possible in the sketch. I owe the fact that the final version in blue turned out differently to these sketches, which finally gave me the paper cutting idea.

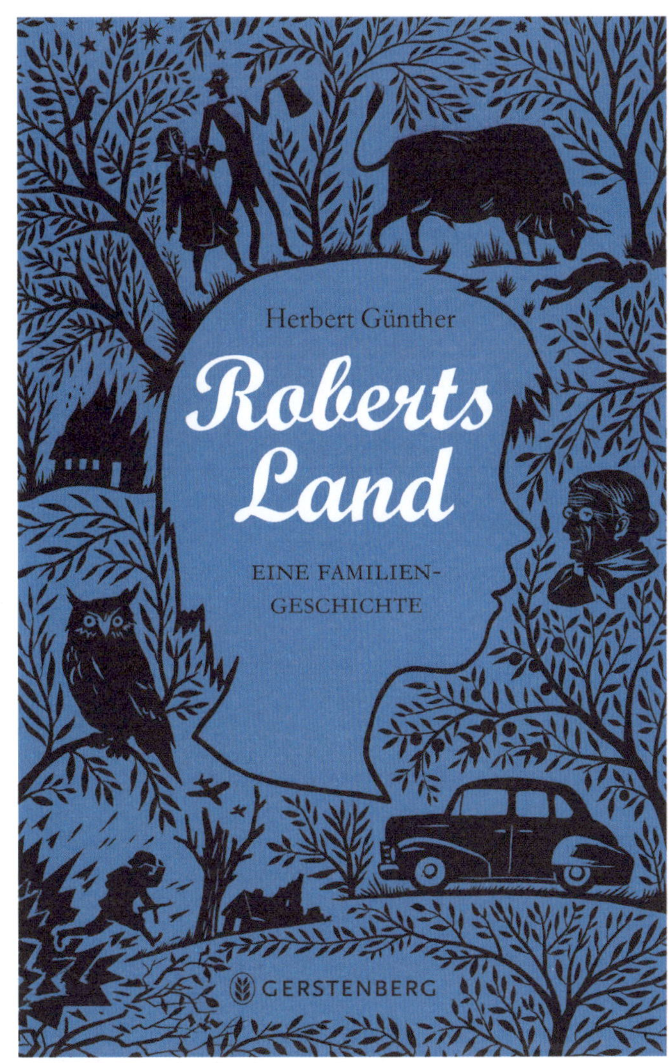

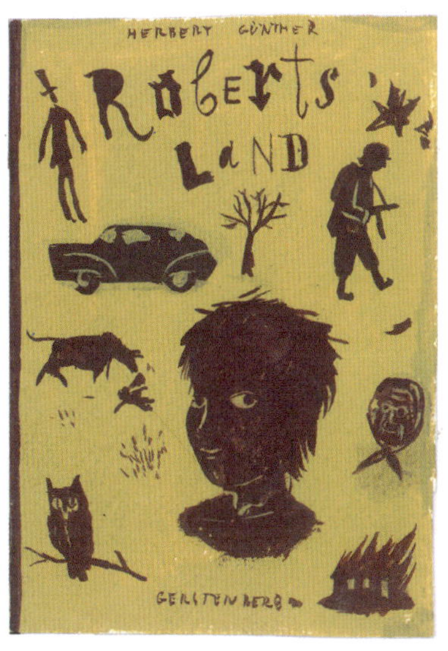

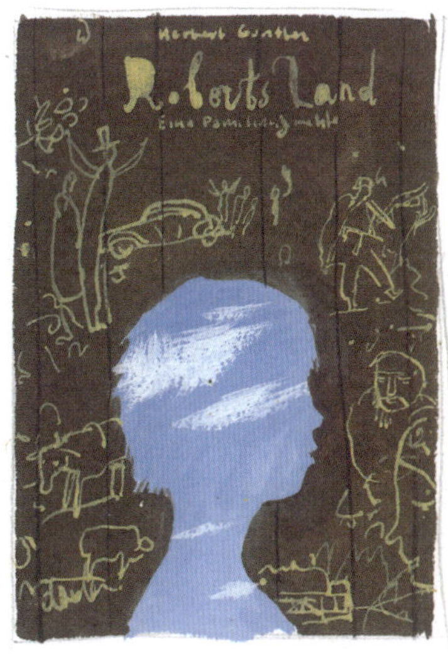

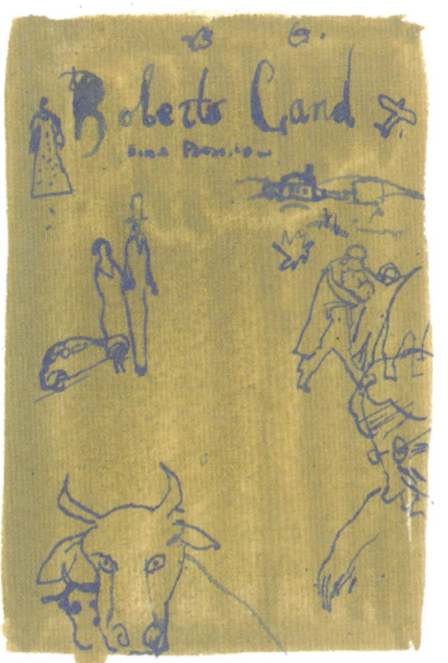

I made completely different sketches for a book of animal fables. When the decision was made to limit the palette to just five colours, the remaining colours had to be kept out of sight. For each new picture, I defined a key colour that dominated the respective picture. Some stories simply asked for a dark mood and were therefore more brown. The others, in turn, were more airy in terms of story content, so blue was better suited as a basic mood. Or sometimes dramatic– those had red as the main colour. The main aim of this series of pictures was to achieve maximum expression with a minimum of means (=colours). A change of colours from page to page was also very important. On the right you can see how one of the pictures turned out.

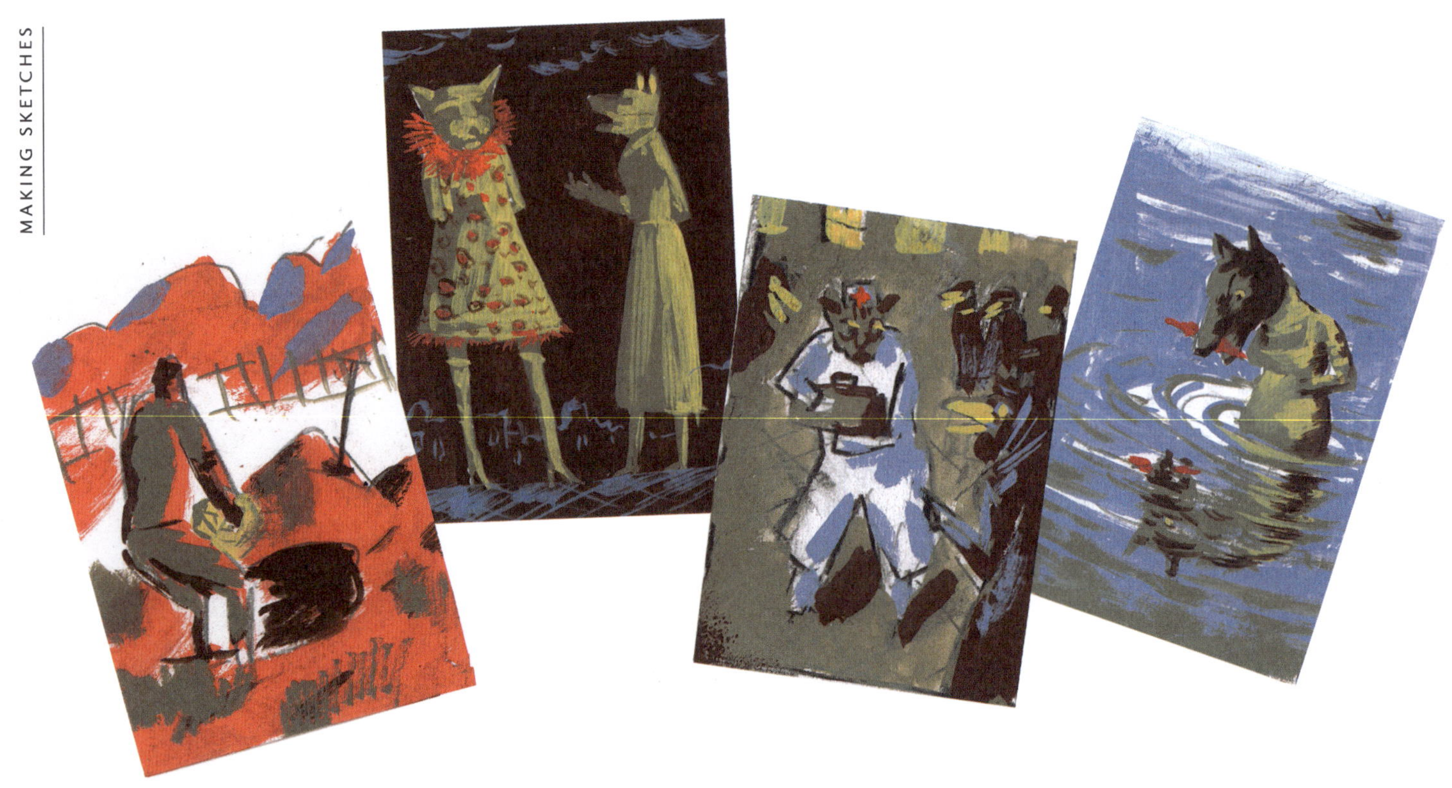

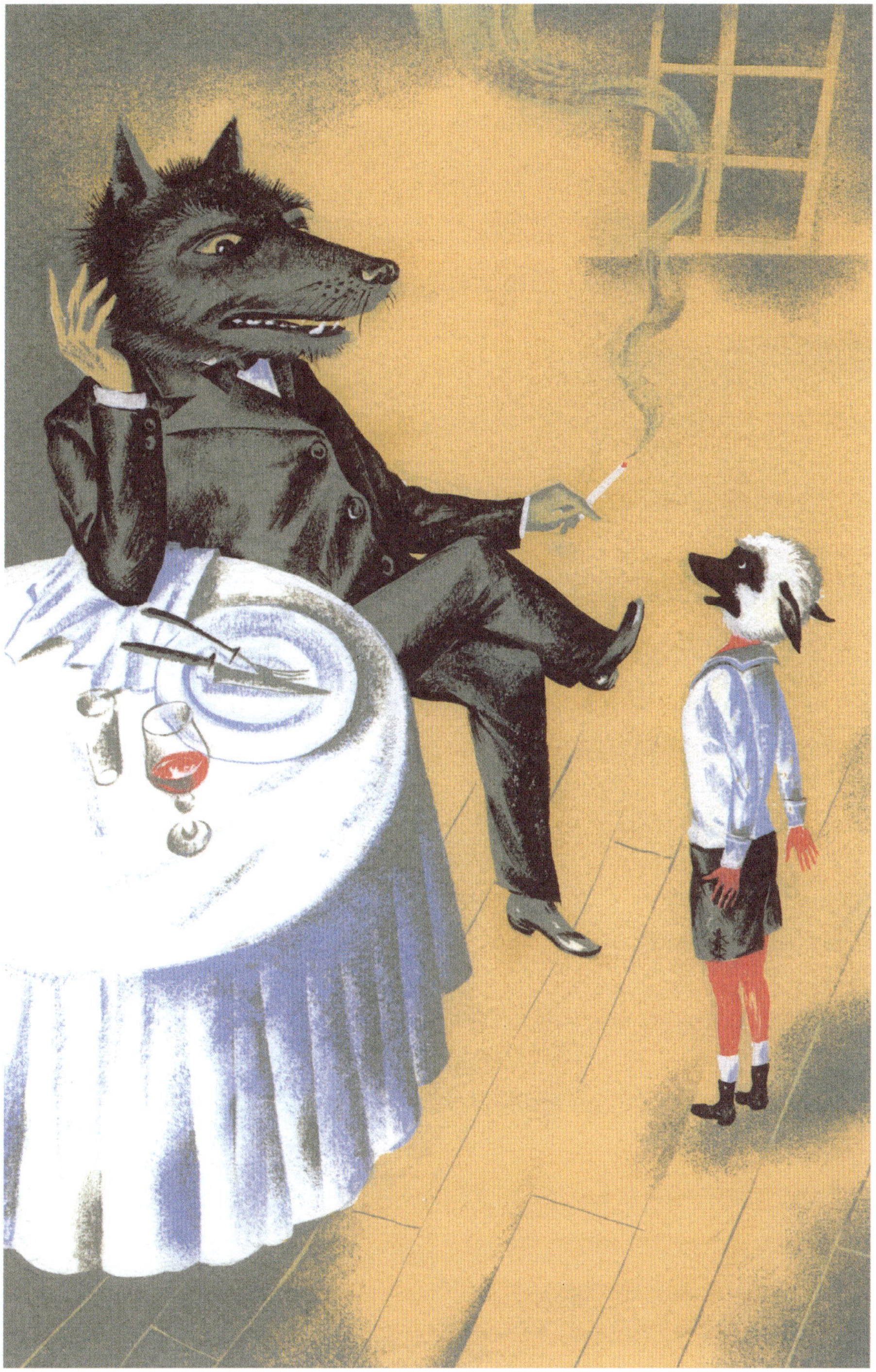

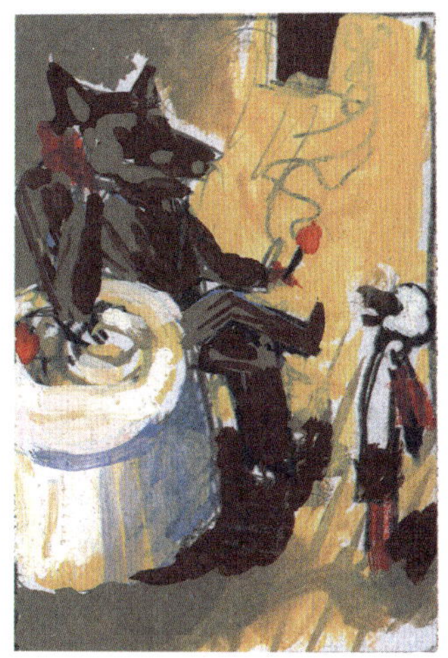

→ TIP: Which colours are applied first and which afterwards is important in the case of larger pictures, but you can just paint away with sketches. You can paint over black or dark brown with light tones. Good gouache paints are opaque enough and will easily manage it.

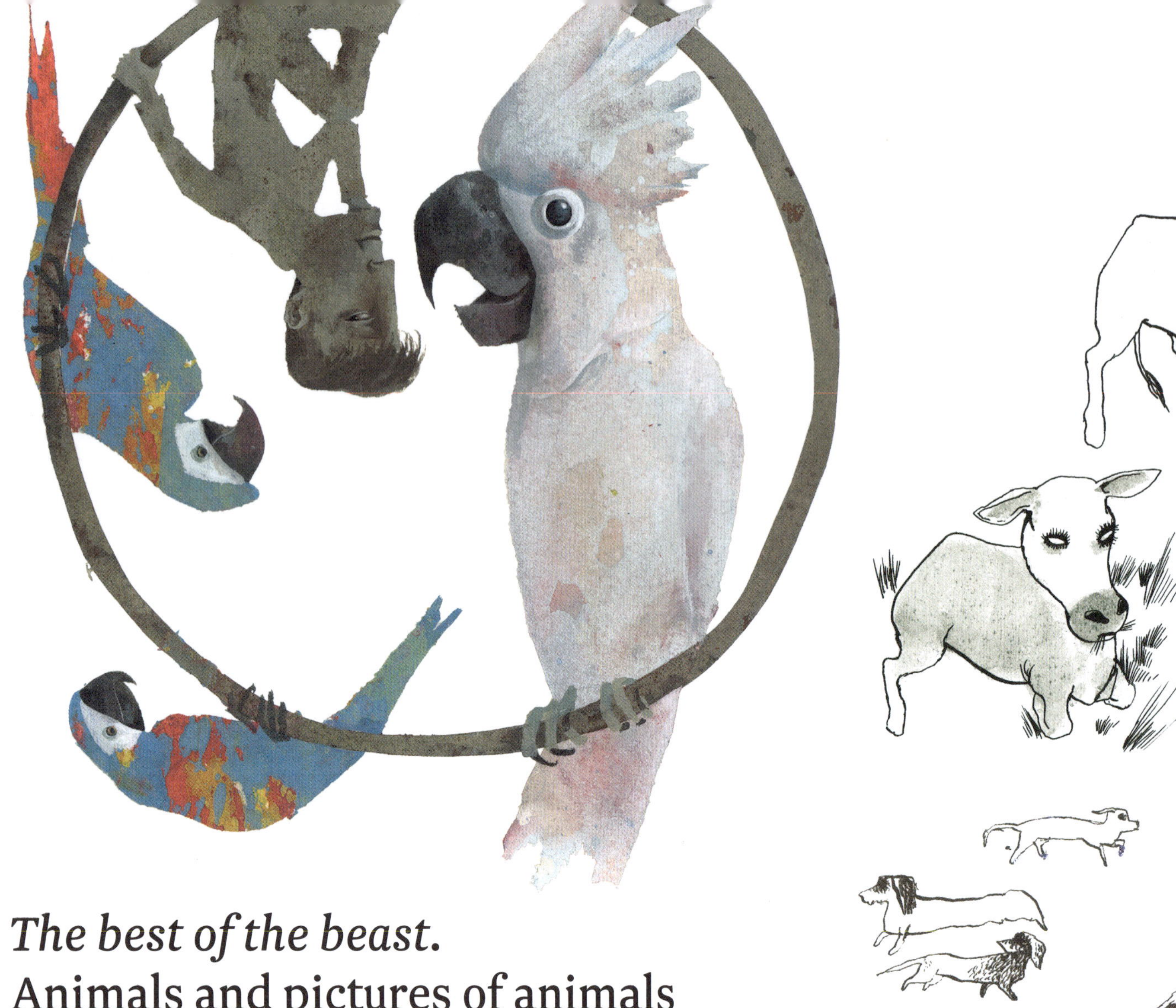

The best of the beast. Animals and pictures of animals

Why are animals so special, what makes them different from us? It's not just their cuddly appearance; I think the real reason is something else. An animal is immediate because it knows no social constraints and cannot pretend. So the giraffe will hardly wish to be a warthog and vice versa ... Maybe their directness is why animals have always magnetically attracted us. Children, in particular, who are being socialized and trying out their first roles in life, want to observe animals, stroke them and share in their honest nature. But most of all they want to take them home and keep them forever!

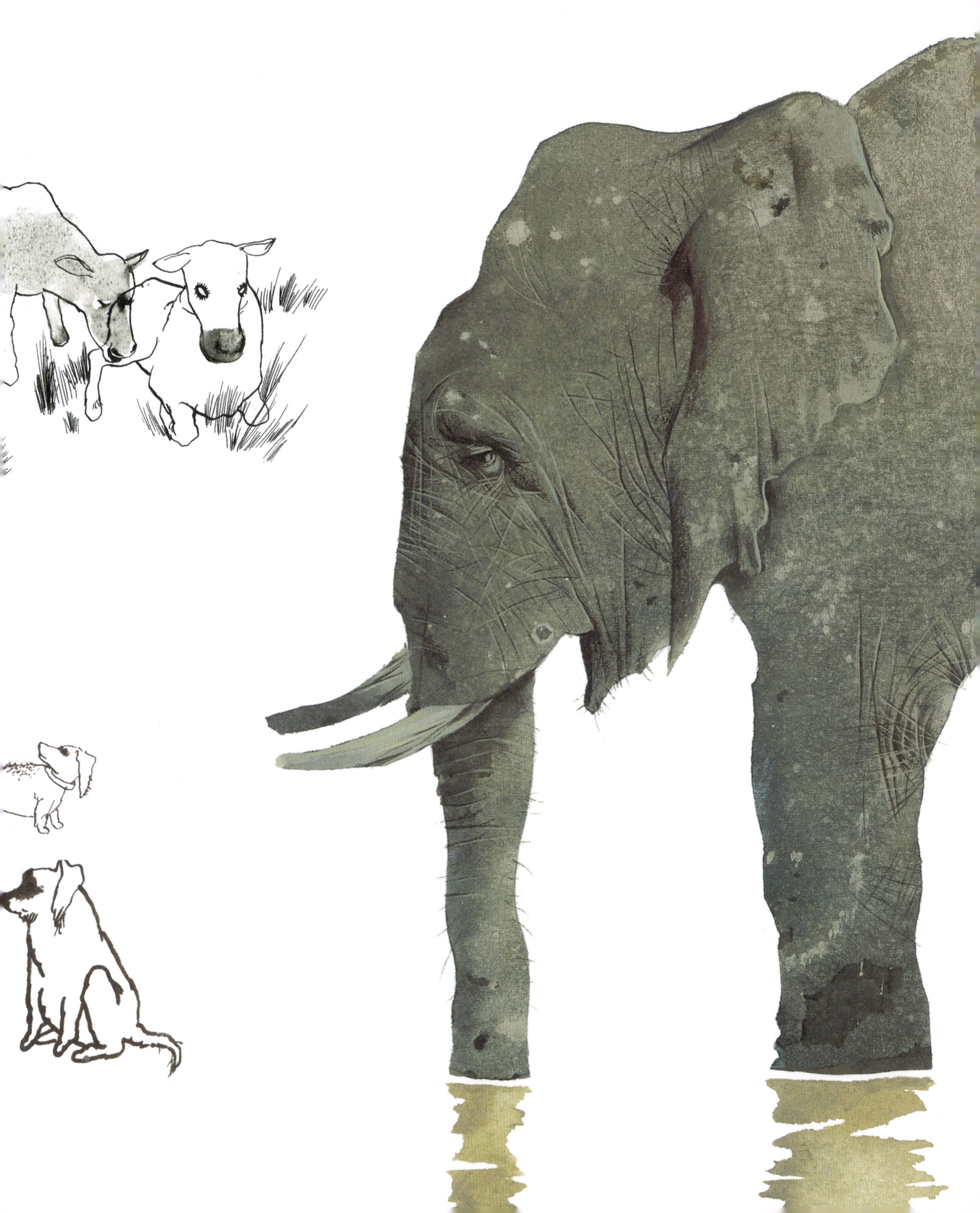

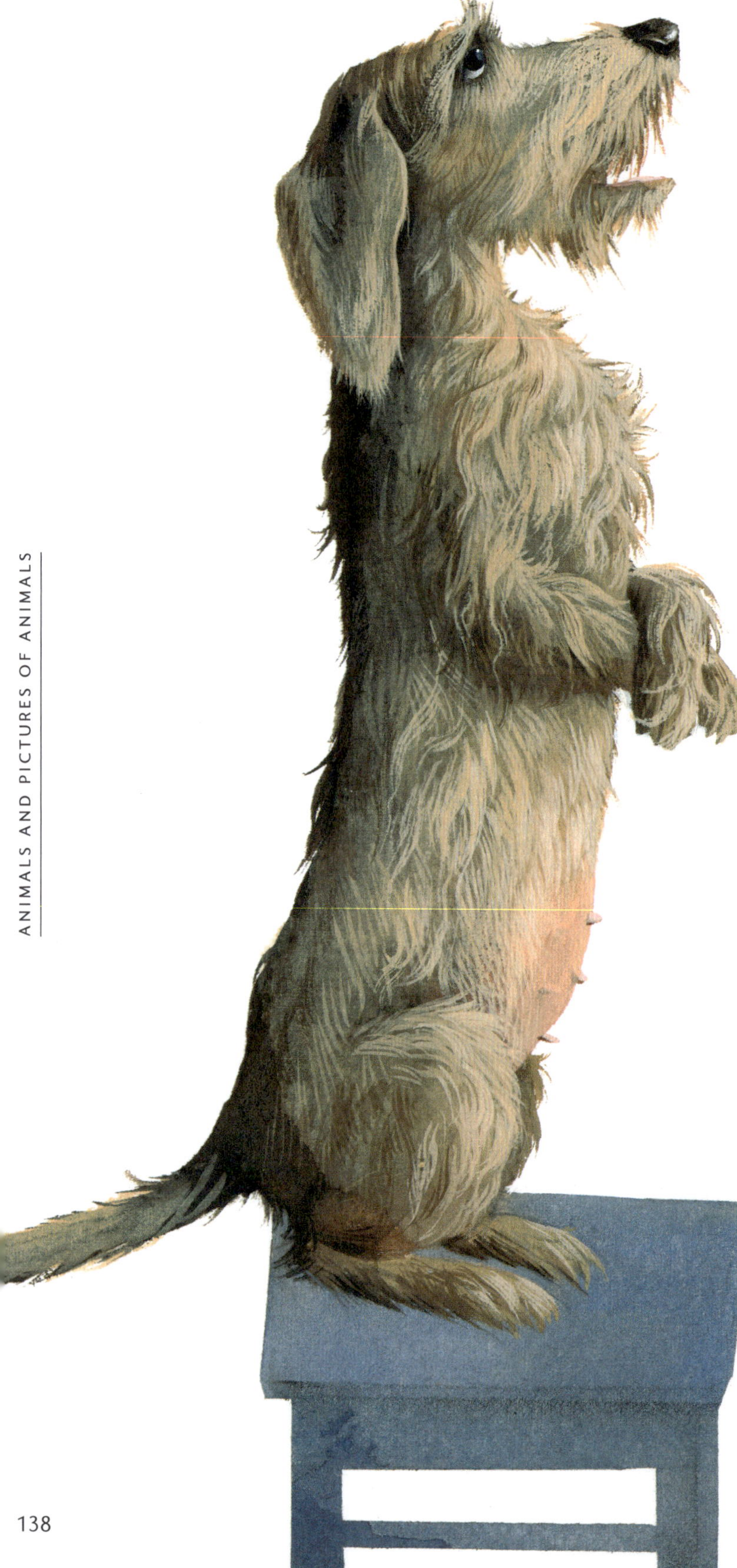

Today I have a lot of fun painting animals, but I used to find it very difficult. How do you get their anatomy right? What if the proportions are wrong? At some point, however, my feeling told me: Maybe you're looking in the wrong place; it's actually quite simple. Correct anatomy and realistic proportions are not so important. I noticed more and more that my animal pictures only became good when I managed, even at little, to lend the animals individuality and emotions.

Is there a rule about how to paint animals? What are the most important aspects? What really matters? As a possible answer to these questions, I wrote a "checklist" with four items. You can decide to what extent it's correct. In my opinion, an animal picture gains enormous expressiveness if all of these points are implemented consecutively or only one or two of them consistently. Experiment around a bit and see the results.

1. Proportions

Essential! Take in the animal's silhouette. How big is the head in relation to the body? How long are the legs? It's worth imagining the animal as an outline and laying it out as a surface. The more decisively you do this, the more expressive your picture will look.

2. Posture

Are the ears perked? Is the tail between its legs? From far away, long before you perceive anything else, you can roughly see how an animal feels from its posture. Put this knowledge into practice in your picture.

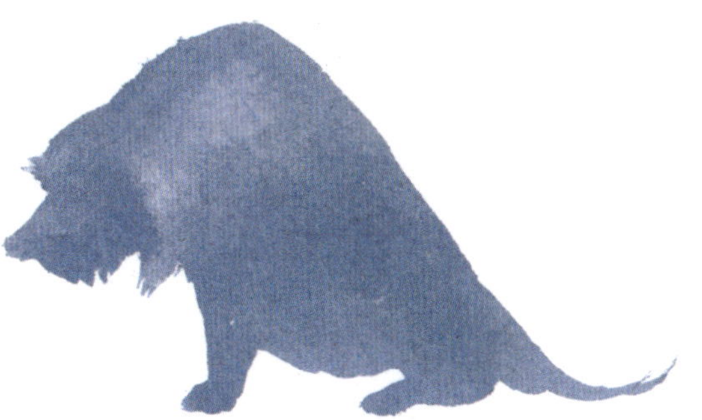

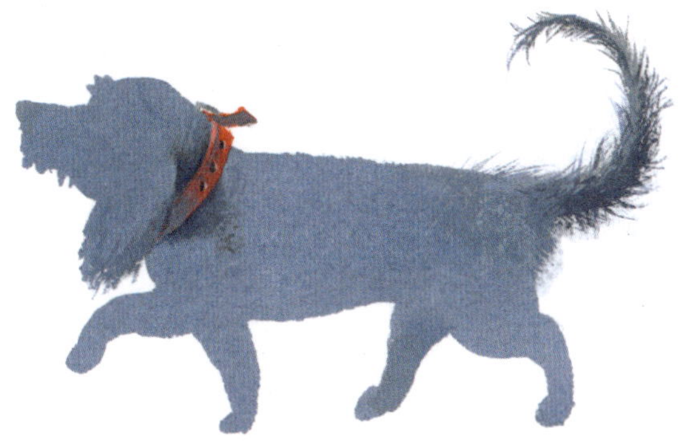

3. Details

A fancy collar or a bushy curled tail ... Choose one or two important details and paint them– they often speak volumes and say a lot about the animal portrayed.

4....and finally: Facial expression

Mood (even in animals!) is primarily reflected in the eyes. But also in how the animal "smiles" at us (which dogs actually do), or grumpily pulls the corners of its mouth down. Even the "face" of a fish, although it doesn't convey real fish feelings, will have an effect on us that can only be explained by an analogy with the human face. So think about what emotion the dog's snout, the fish or bird face triggers in you and show it in your picture!

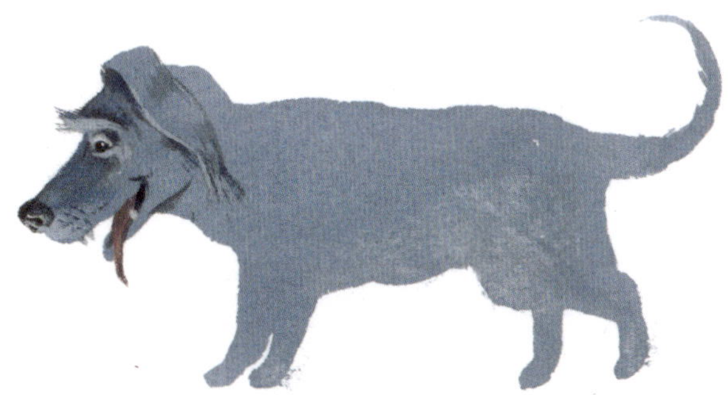

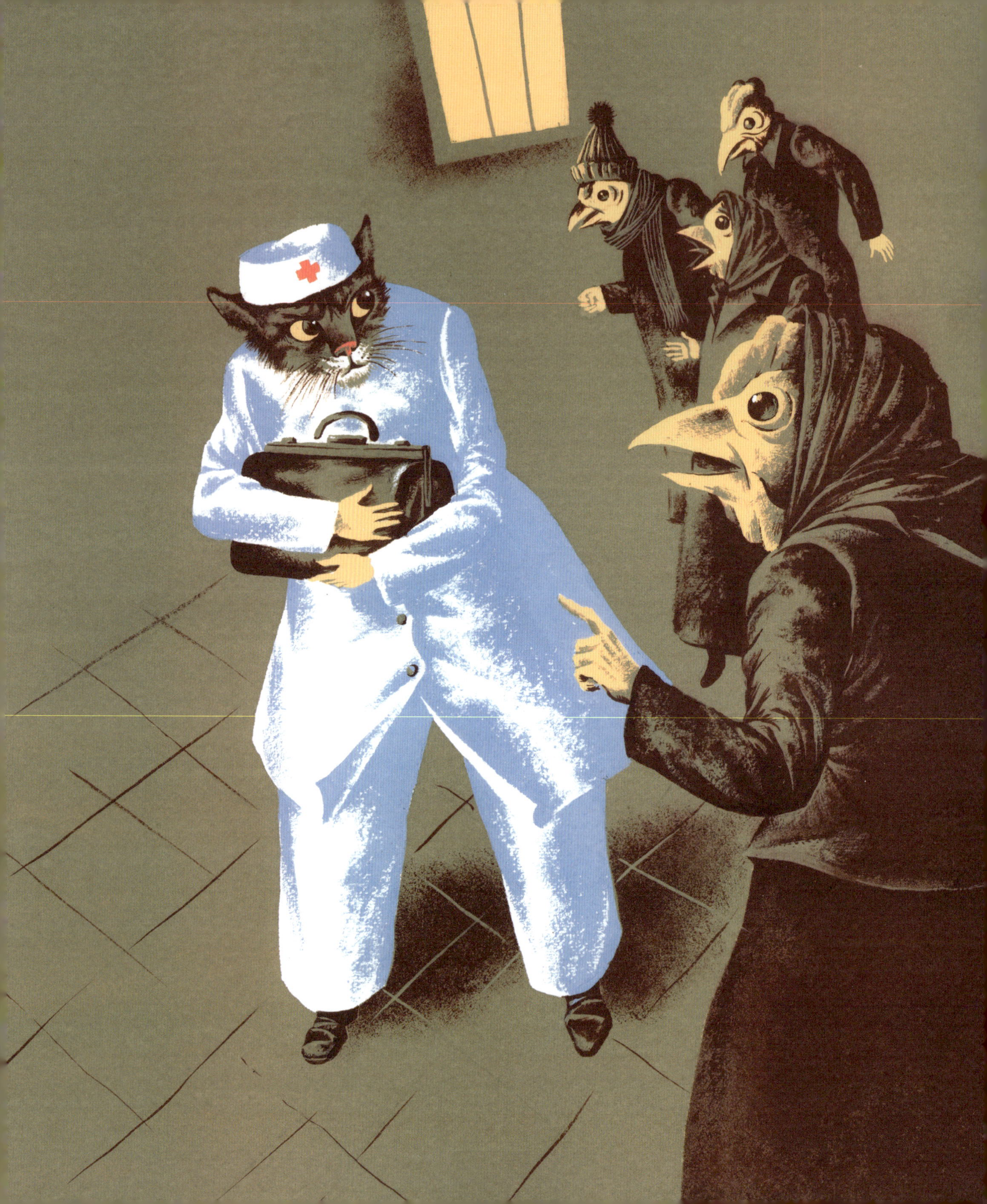

One technique I like to use to represent the animals is the dry brush as in the picture on the left. Painting with pasty paint applied in layers gives you very good control over details, and secondly the picture can be planned very precisely. Gouache doesn't flow here, but is applied in opaque layers. You can start with light tones and gradually go into the dark. Look at the example of the head of the big chicken in the picture: first came yellow, then grey and then brown. And then grey again to the light spots on brown (on the headscarf). And don't be too rigid about your tools! Instead of the dry brush you can dab with a dry sponge. That's how the shadow behind the cat was made in the picture.

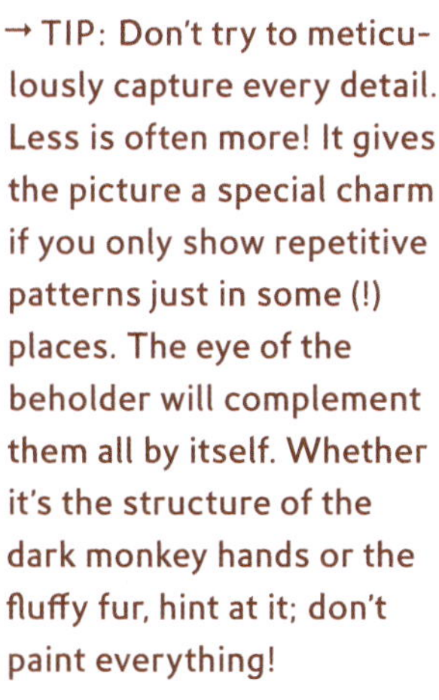

→ TIP: Don't try to meticulously capture every detail. Less is often more! It gives the picture a special charm if you only show repetitive patterns just in some (!) places. The eye of the beholder will complement them all by itself. Whether it's the structure of the dark monkey hands or the fluffy fur, hint at it; don't paint everything!

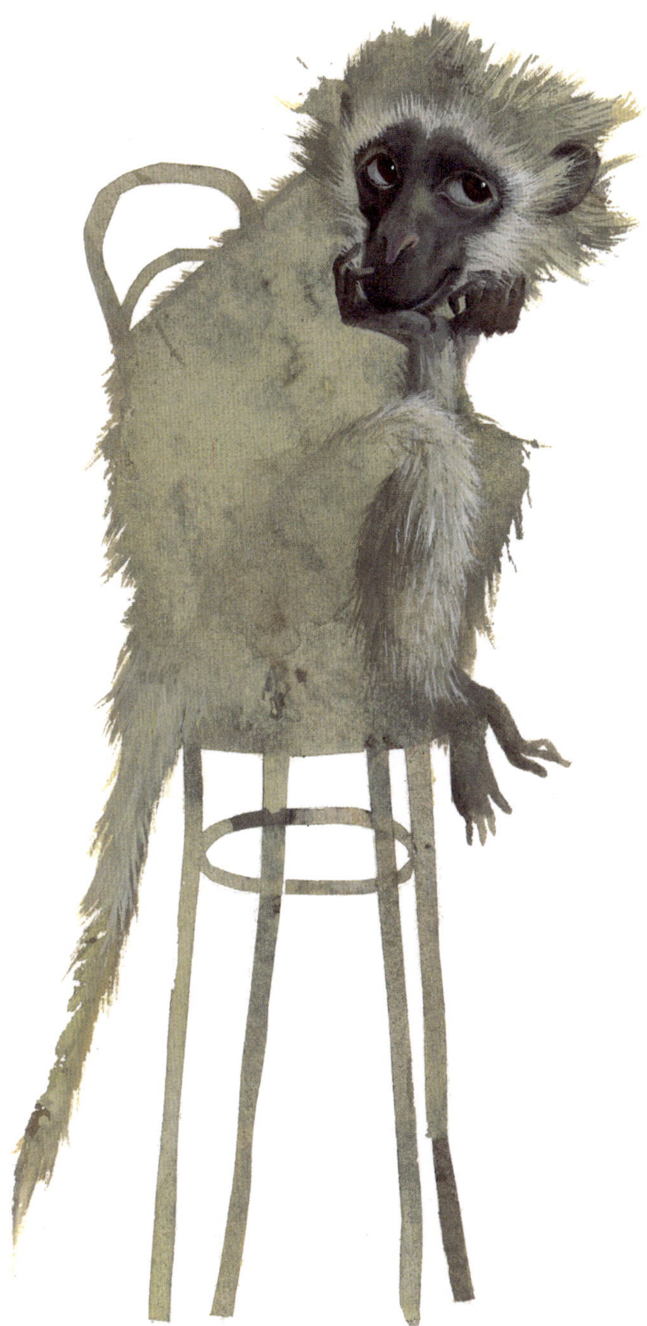

Layer for Layer

Animals

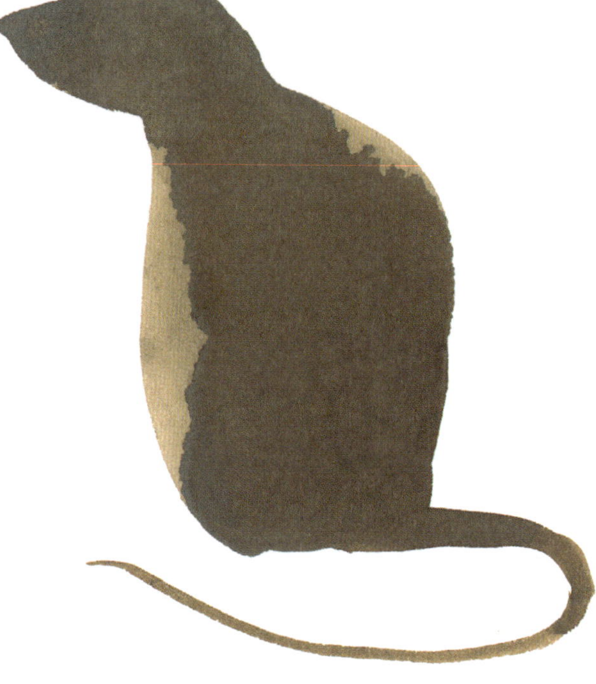

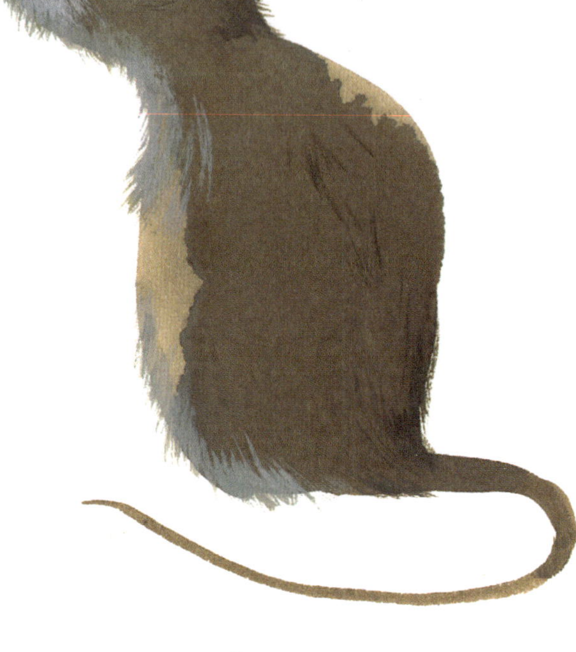

1.

The mouse is first quickly painted as a silhouette. You can use only one or two colours that mix within the contour. Depending on the size of the subject, a round medium-sized brush from number 10 is recommended.

2.

Then you'll need a finer brush to show the fur at important points on the head and belly of the mouse. A round sable-hair brush no. 3 would suit this well, so you can opaquely apply both the light grey and the dark brown colour with a little water.

→ TIP: Before you start painting, you can always make a drawing in pencil, then you're on the safe side. But the animal silhouette might even become much more interesting if you paint it spontaneously. Therefore my advice: Instead of sketching them meticulously, try to sketch several areas loosely, then choose the best one and continue working on it.

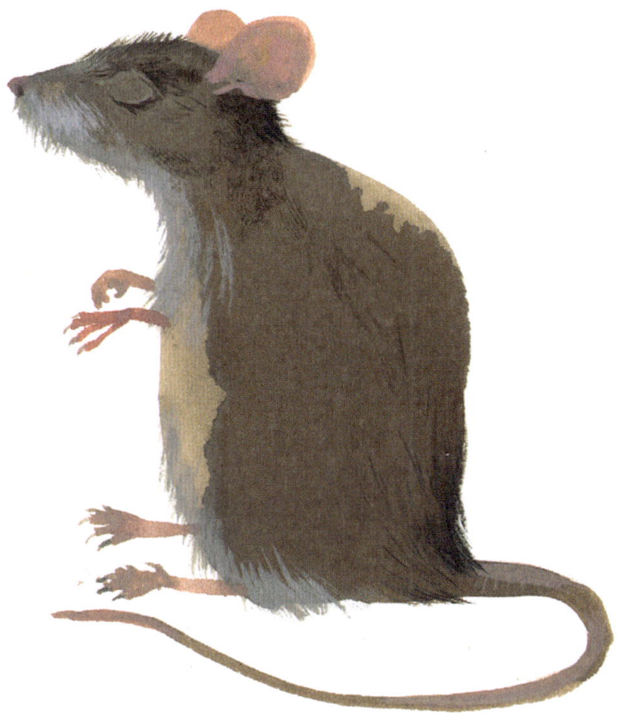

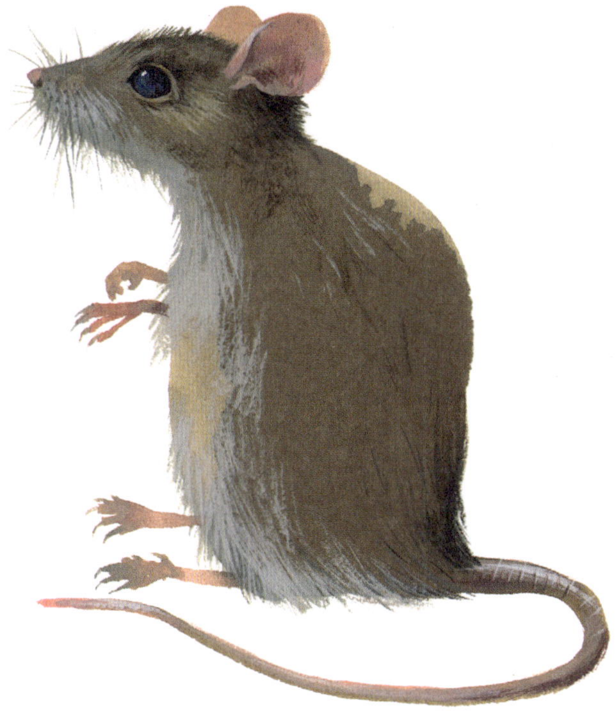

3.

At this point, the rodent gets more colour on its face: With the fine brush from before, pink ears and nose are applied. Don't forget the paws and the tip of the tail. By adding an even darker brown, you continue to model the head and the area around the eye.

4.

Finally, work out the ear, draw the moustache hair with the brush tip and add shadows and light to the tail. Then the dark eye, which you paint with blue and black, gets a light reflex on the side of the light. Now the good mouse is ready!

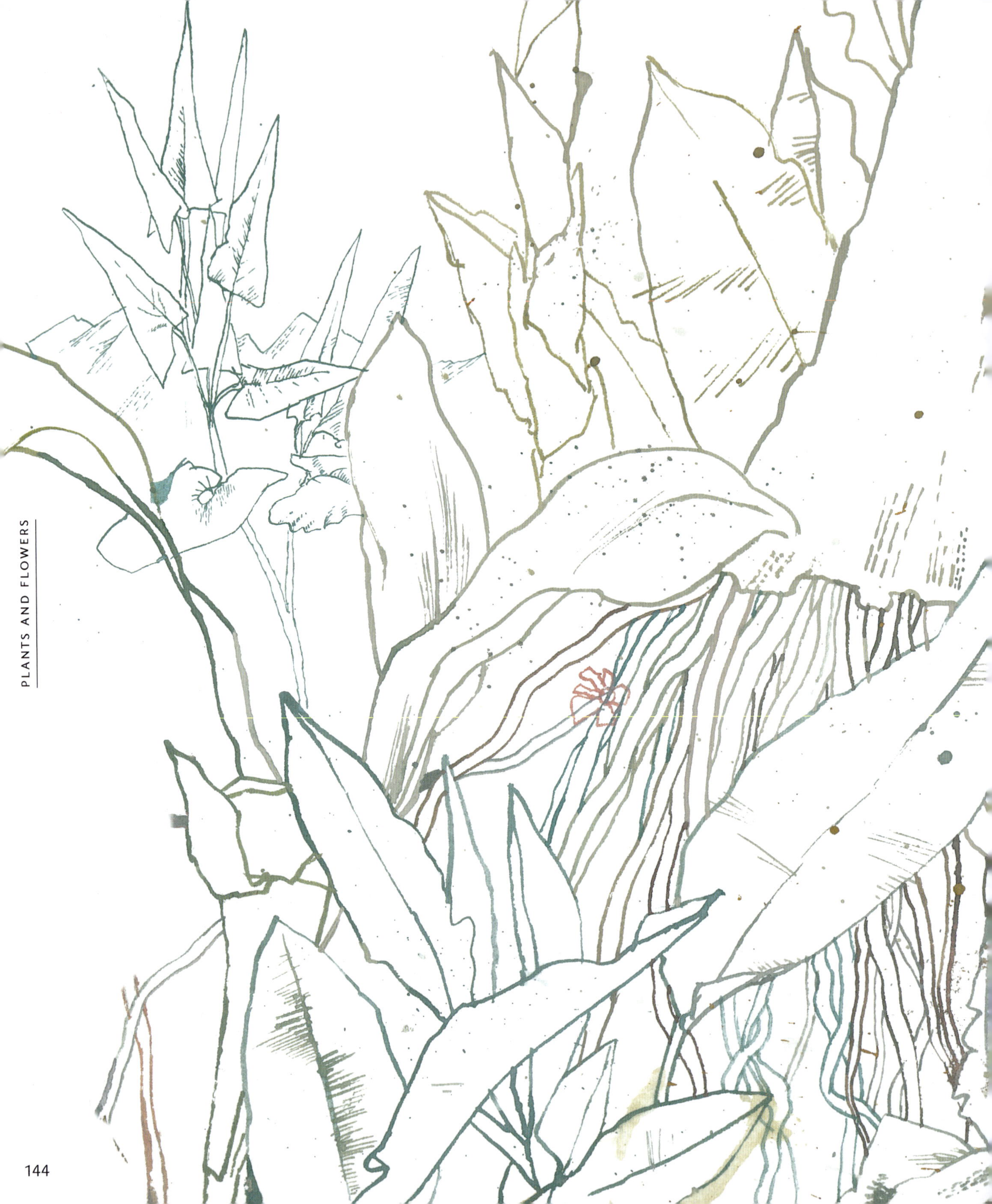

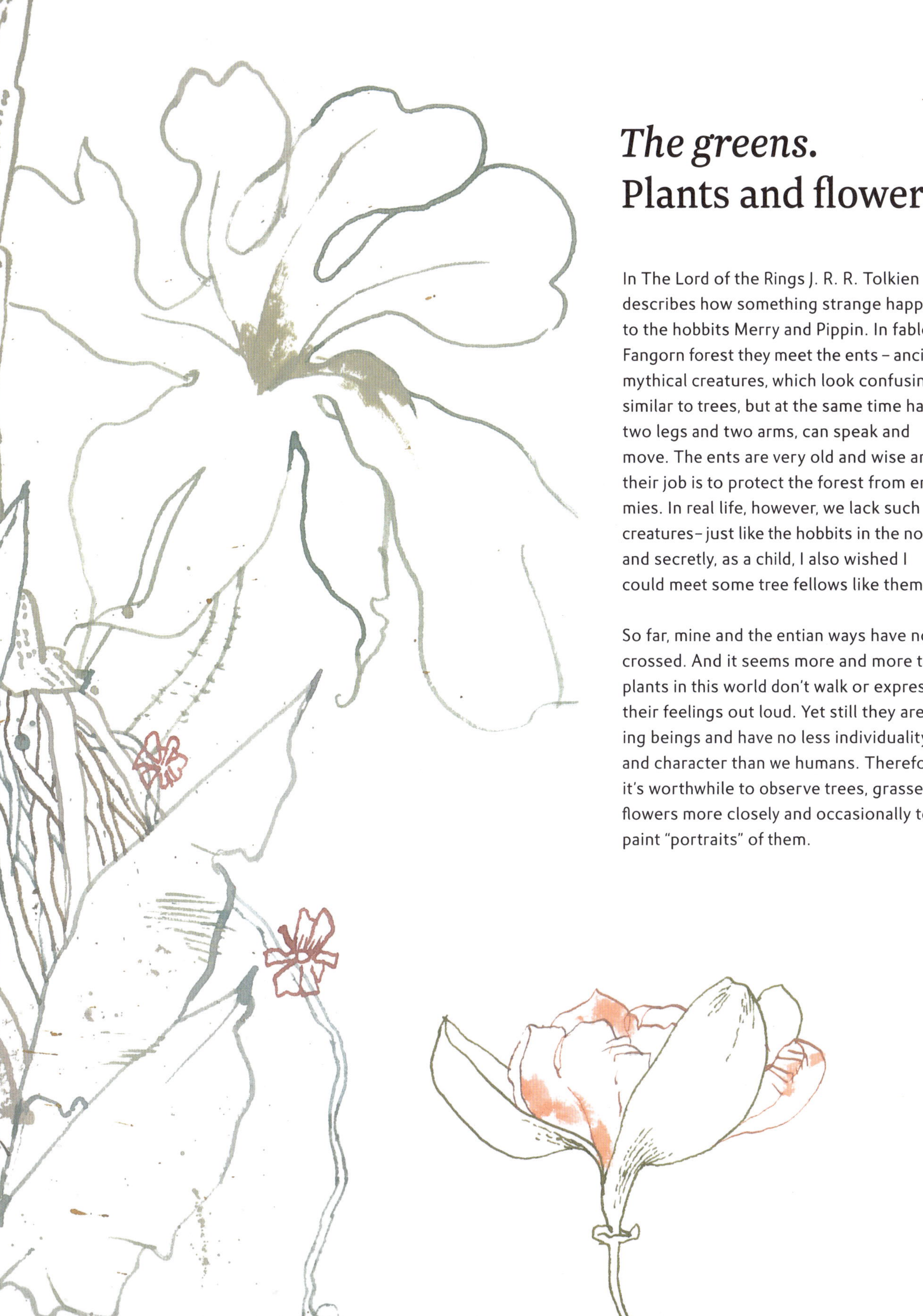

The greens. Plants and flowers

In The Lord of the Rings J. R. R. Tolkien describes how something strange happens to the hobbits Merry and Pippin. In fabled Fangorn forest they meet the ents – ancient mythical creatures, which look confusingly similar to trees, but at the same time have two legs and two arms, can speak and move. The ents are very old and wise and their job is to protect the forest from enemies. In real life, however, we lack such creatures– just like the hobbits in the novel– and secretly, as a child, I also wished I could meet some tree fellows like them.

So far, mine and the entian ways have not crossed. And it seems more and more that plants in this world don't walk or express their feelings out loud. Yet still they are living beings and have no less individuality and character than we humans. Therefore it's worthwhile to observe trees, grasses or flowers more closely and occasionally to paint "portraits" of them.

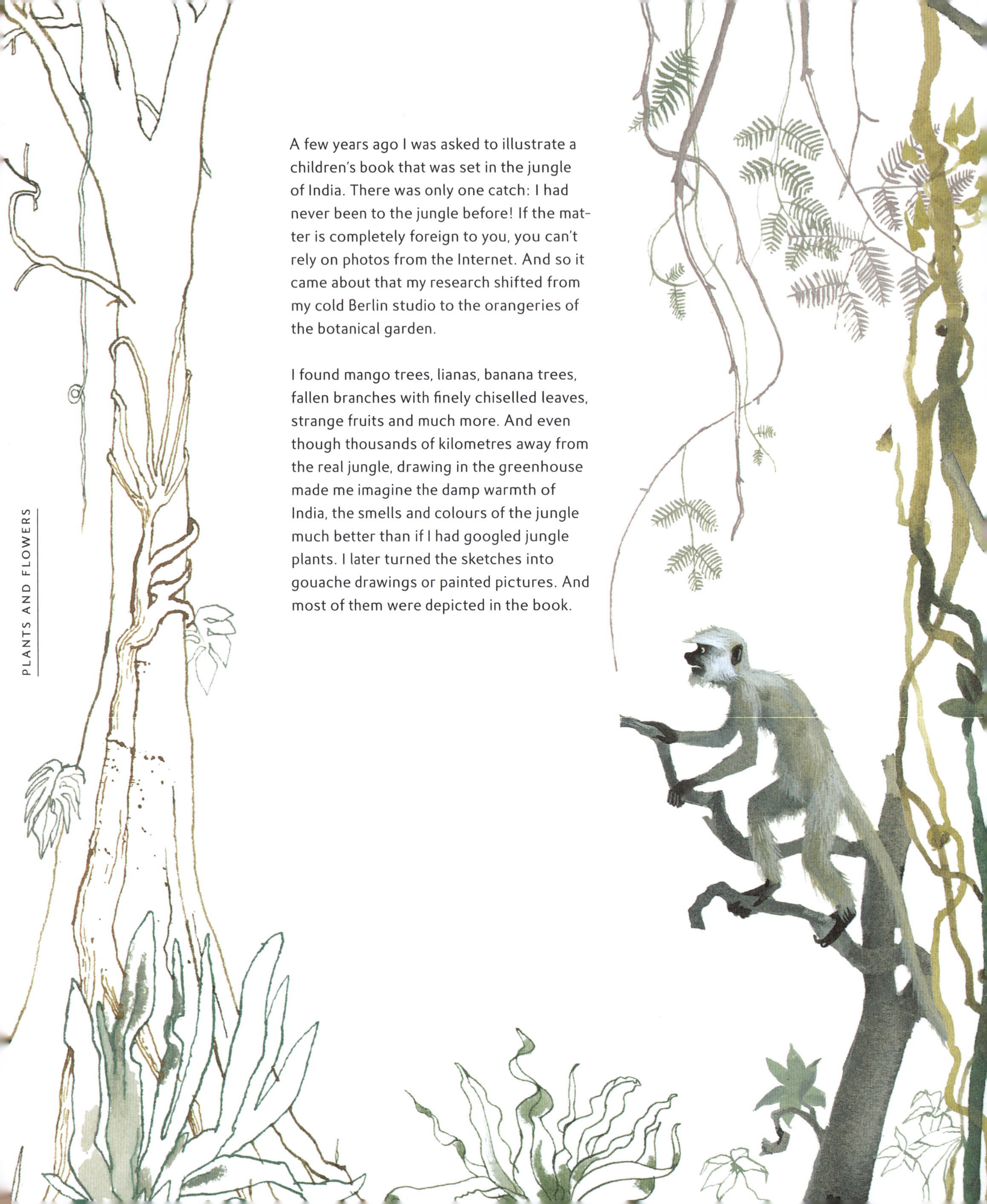

A few years ago I was asked to illustrate a children's book that was set in the jungle of India. There was only one catch: I had never been to the jungle before! If the matter is completely foreign to you, you can't rely on photos from the Internet. And so it came about that my research shifted from my cold Berlin studio to the orangeries of the botanical garden.

I found mango trees, lianas, banana trees, fallen branches with finely chiselled leaves, strange fruits and much more. And even though thousands of kilometres away from the real jungle, drawing in the greenhouse made me imagine the damp warmth of India, the smells and colours of the jungle much better than if I had googled jungle plants. I later turned the sketches into gouache drawings or painted pictures. And most of them were depicted in the book.

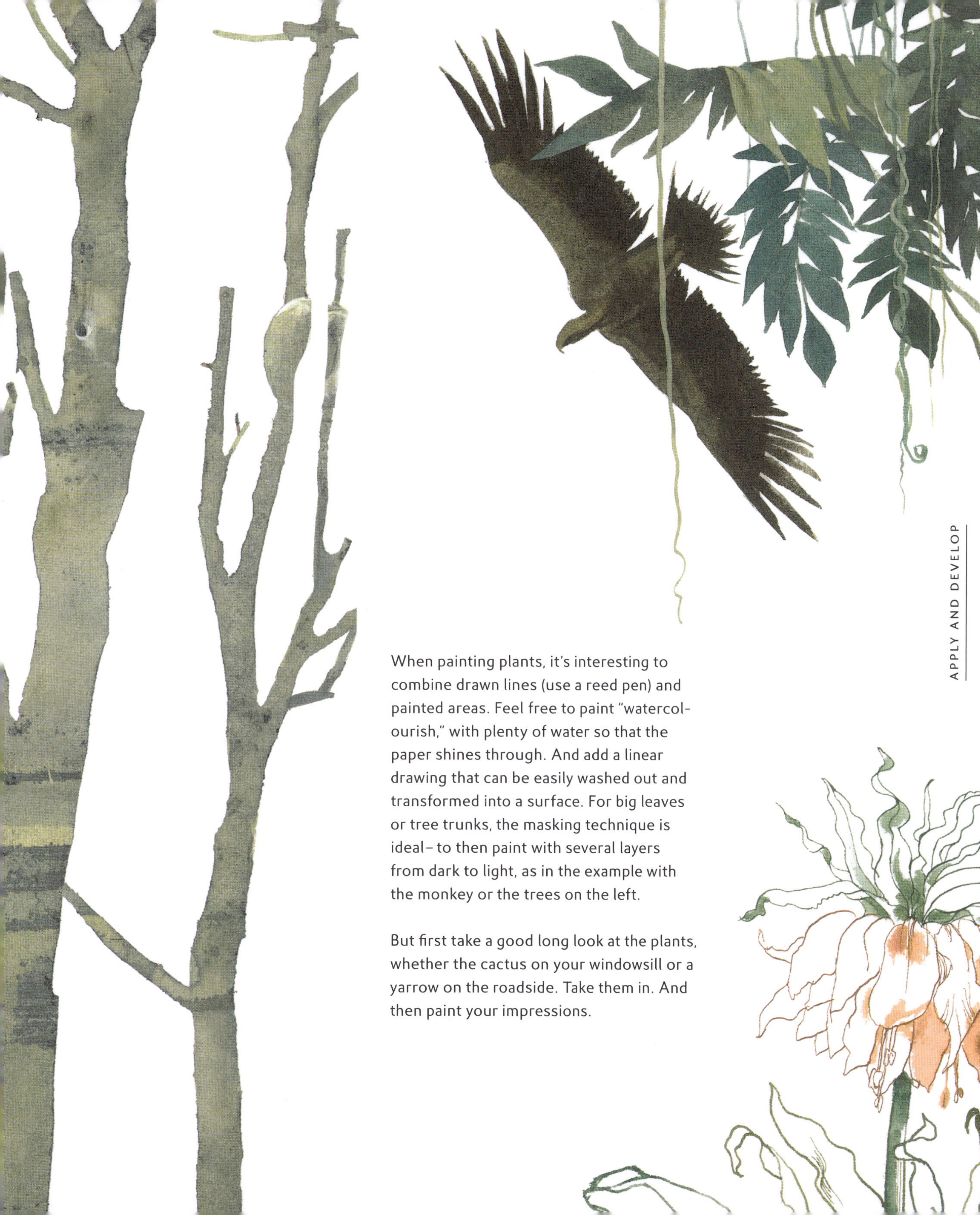

When painting plants, it's interesting to combine drawn lines (use a reed pen) and painted areas. Feel free to paint "watercolourish," with plenty of water so that the paper shines through. And add a linear drawing that can be easily washed out and transformed into a surface. For big leaves or tree trunks, the masking technique is ideal– to then paint with several layers from dark to light, as in the example with the monkey or the trees on the left.

But first take a good long look at the plants, whether the cactus on your windowsill or a yarrow on the roadside. Take them in. And then paint your impressions.

Layer for Layer

Flowers

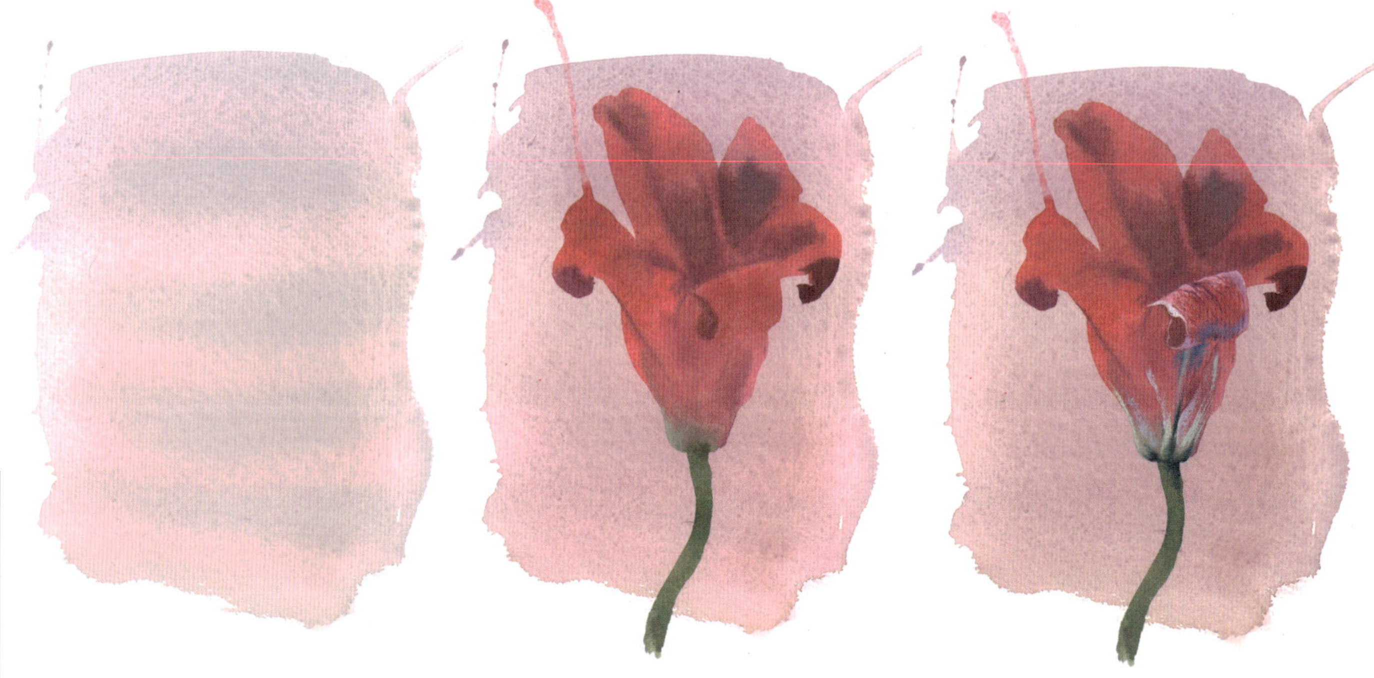

1.

First, create the background with a large round or flat brush (no. 10 or larger). Since you will glaze over it later, it will be a kind of primer for your flower. We build all other layers of paint on this hue. But let it dry thoroughly first.

2.

Now moisten the flower outline with water. Then paint the silhouette with diluted paints and quickly, wet-on-wet. You roughly create the shadow areas inside the flower and let the green of the stem flow into it.

3.

While the paint is drying, use the time to think about what details of the flower you'll work out. Accents are very important, especially with flowers! Often it's enough to focus just on the petal like this flower.

→ TIP: When you get to number 2, don't be too precise! At this point, the wild, unpredictable side of the watercolours should come into its own. It's worthwhile to make several backgrounds with loosely painted flower outlines in order to then choose the best ones for further elaboration.

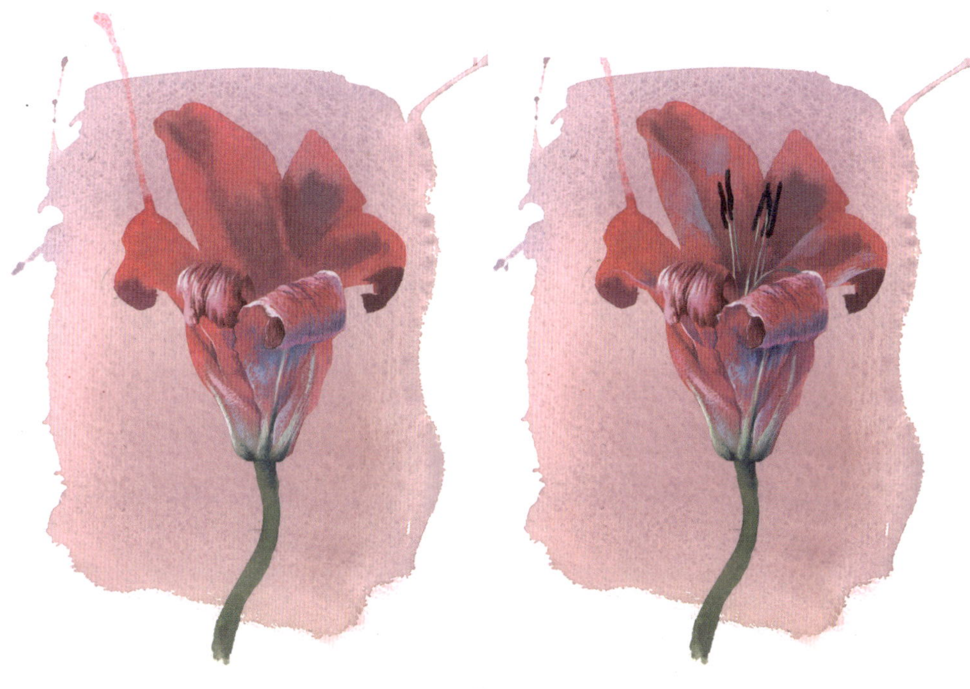

4.

You continue to paint with a fine sable-hair brush up to no. 4 on the two front petals and the flower base. Next, model the shadow areas and place the light areas with pink and opaque white on them. Don't touch the rest.

5.

Now add more depth to the inside of the flower and paint the fine stamens. Last but not least, the petals in the background get a little more contour, but just enough so that they don't come forward too much. The lily is done!

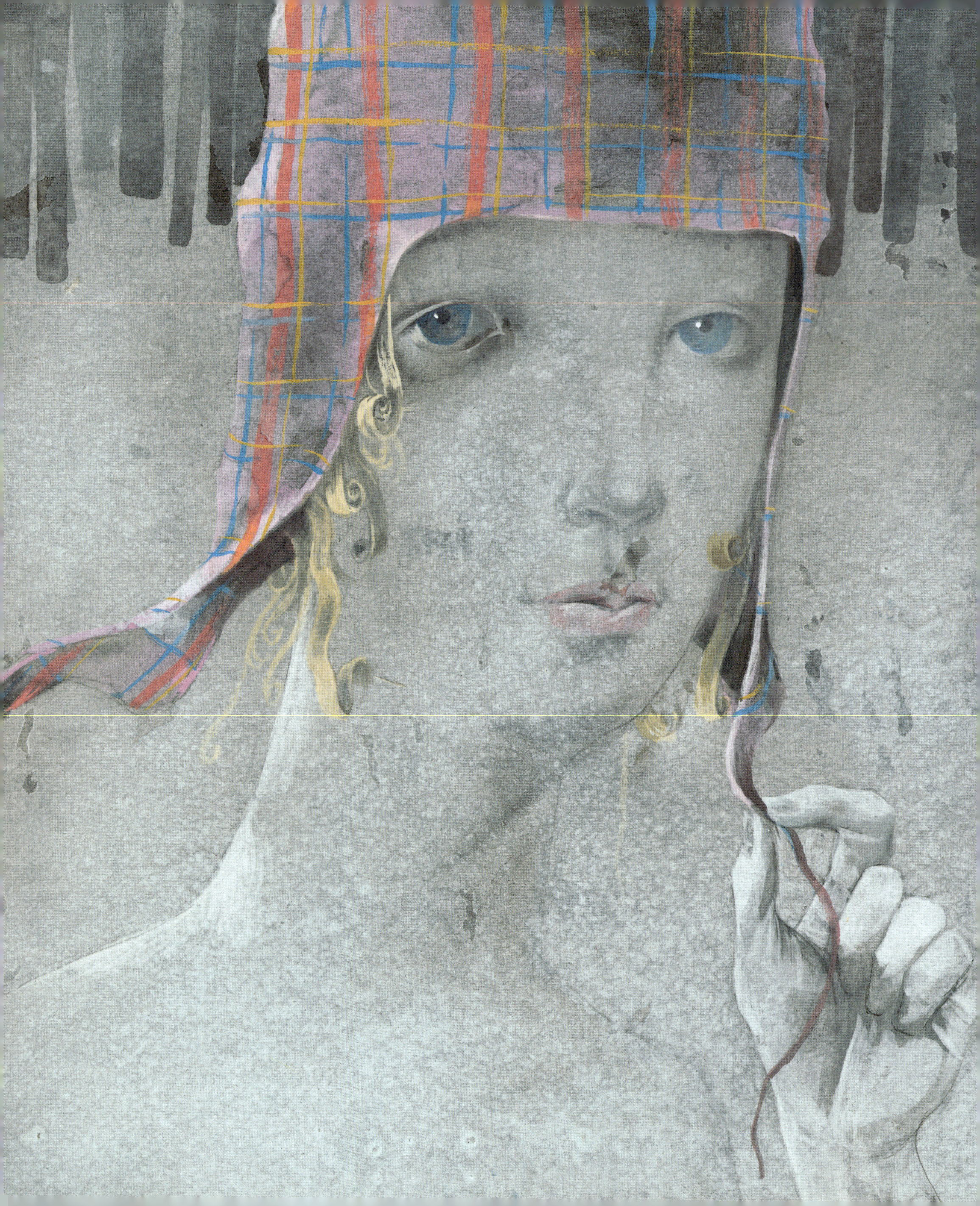

The eyes have it.
Pictures of people

Humans are social animals. From the delivery room to the grave, we are surrounded by other people. Their faces magically attract us and it seems essential to be able to read the moods of others. It's no coincidence that nature wanted a face to be the first thing a newborn child recognizes. As early as twelve days after birth, a baby can perceive and imitate facial expressions.

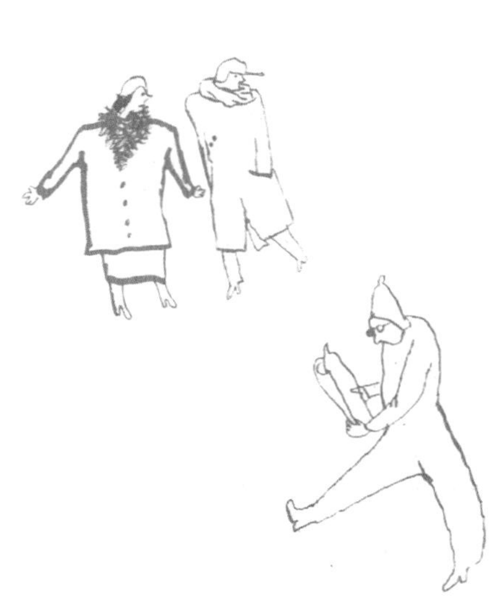

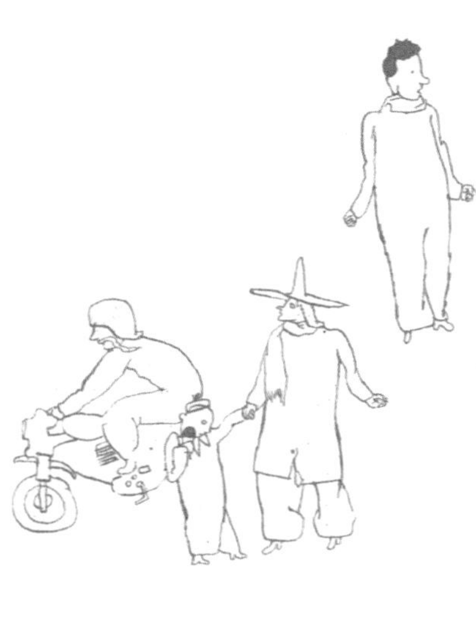

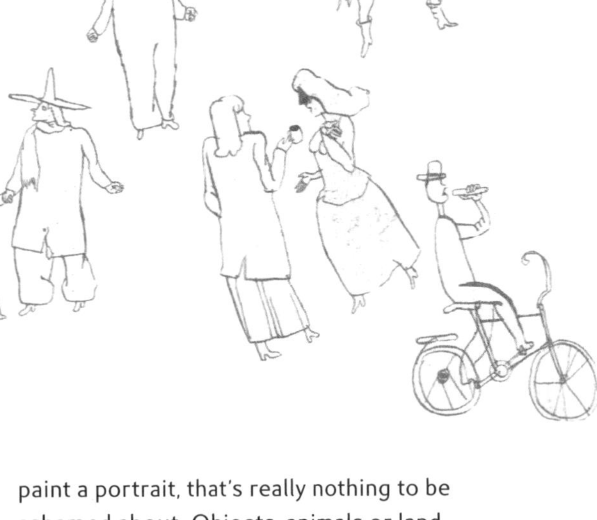

We live closely with family, neighbours, friends and colleagues. We're surrounded by their moods, stories and by lots and lots of faces. So it is not surprising that no other subject is as complex and contradictory as the face. If you get a little queasy sometimes when you're asked to quickly paint a portrait, that's really nothing to be ashamed about. Objects, animals or landscapes patiently sit for their portraits without expecting anything. A person, on the other hand, wants their image to give an insight into their soul and takes offence if the artist fails...

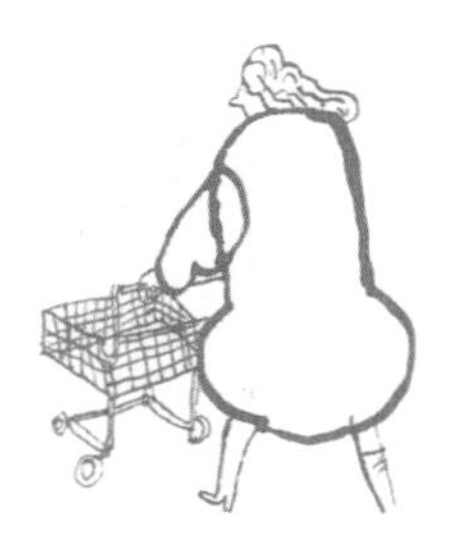

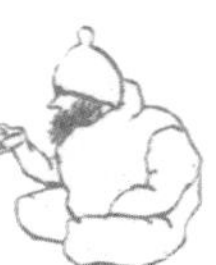

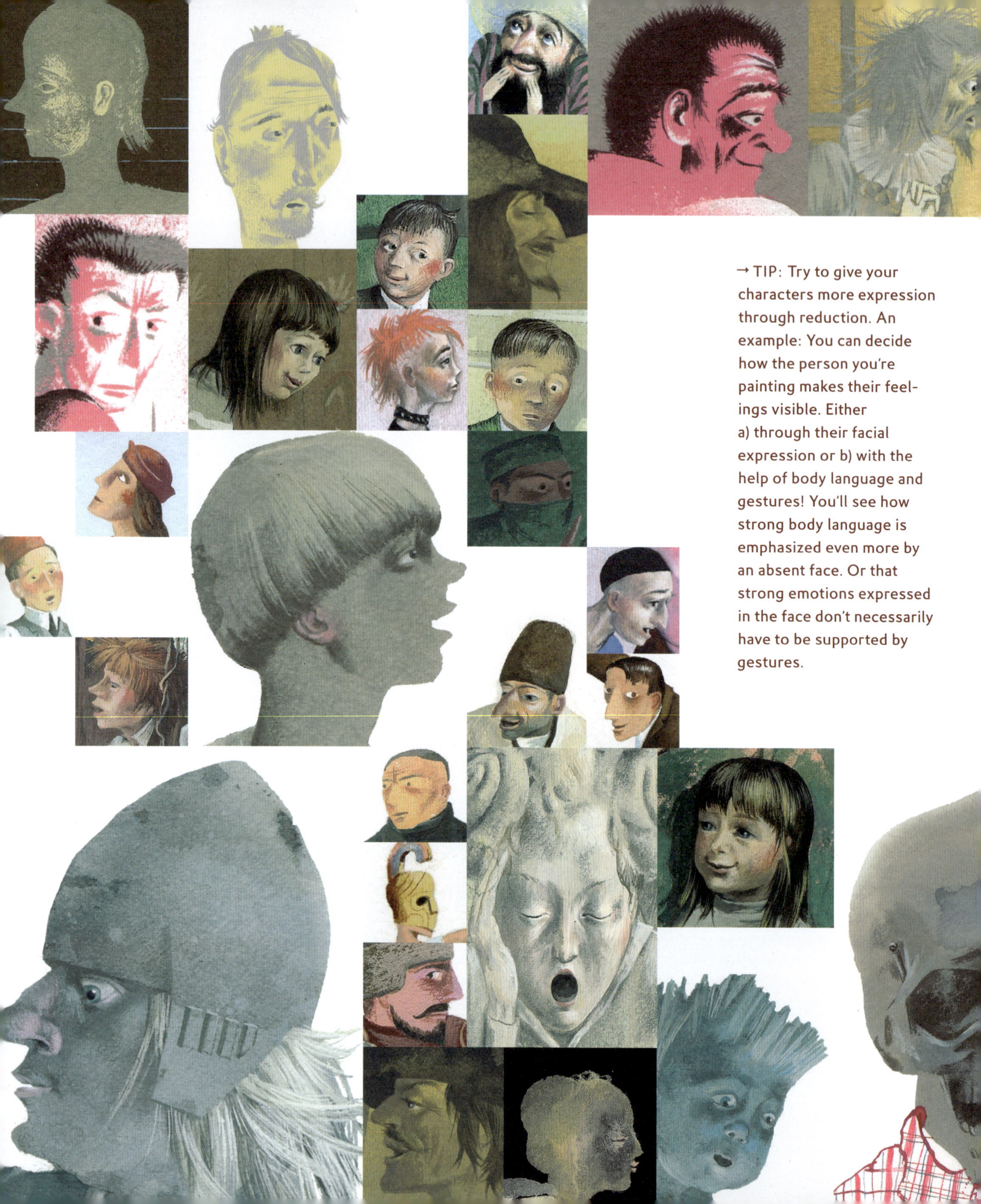

→ TIP: Try to give your characters more expression through reduction. An example: You can decide how the person you're painting makes their feelings visible. Either a) through their facial expression or b) with the help of body language and gestures! You'll see how strong body language is emphasized even more by an absent face. Or that strong emotions expressed in the face don't necessarily have to be supported by gestures.

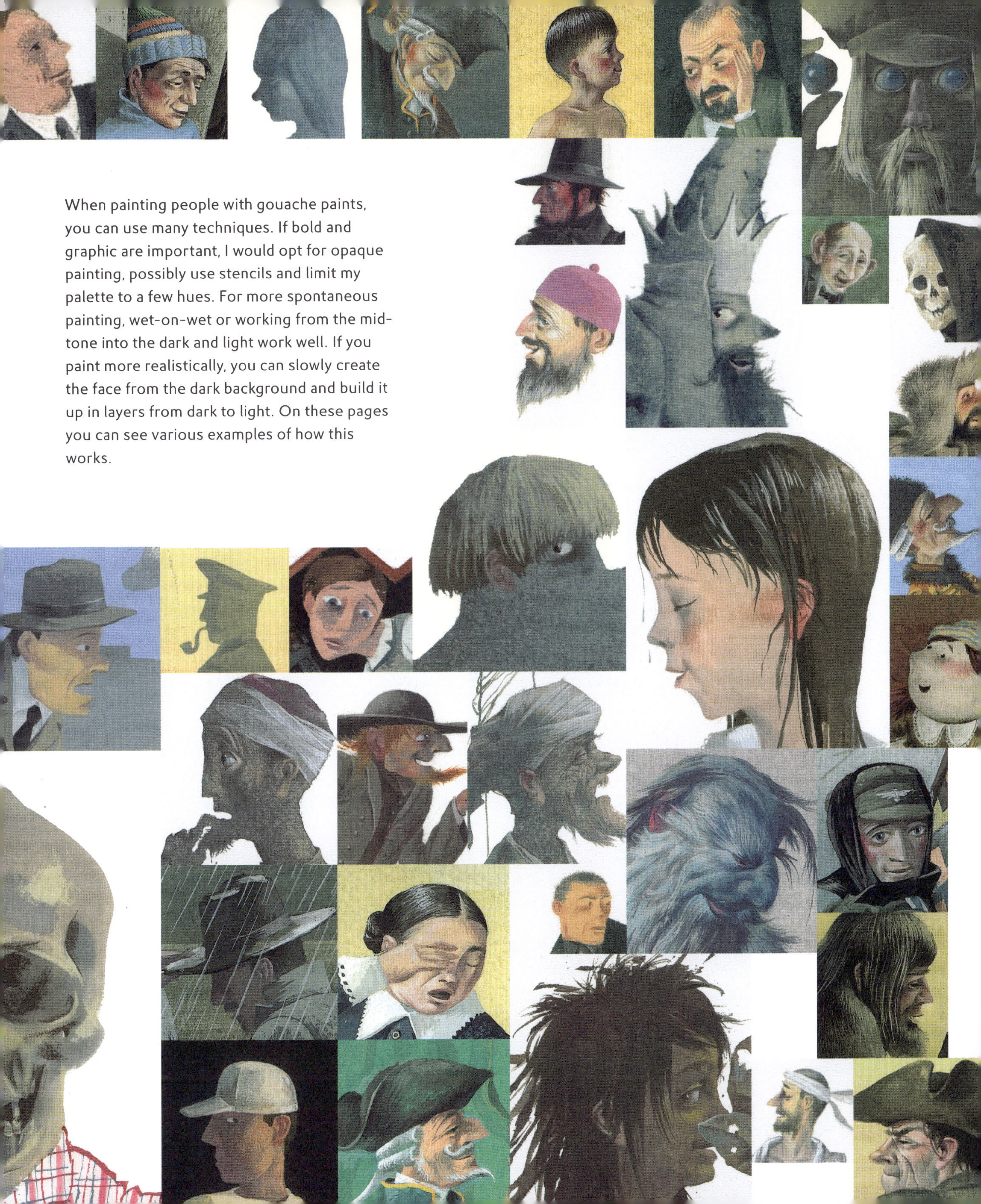

When painting people with gouache paints, you can use many techniques. If bold and graphic are important, I would opt for opaque painting, possibly use stencils and limit my palette to a few hues. For more spontaneous painting, wet-on-wet or working from the mid-tone into the dark and light work well. If you paint more realistically, you can slowly create the face from the dark background and build it up in layers from dark to light. On these pages you can see various examples of how this works.

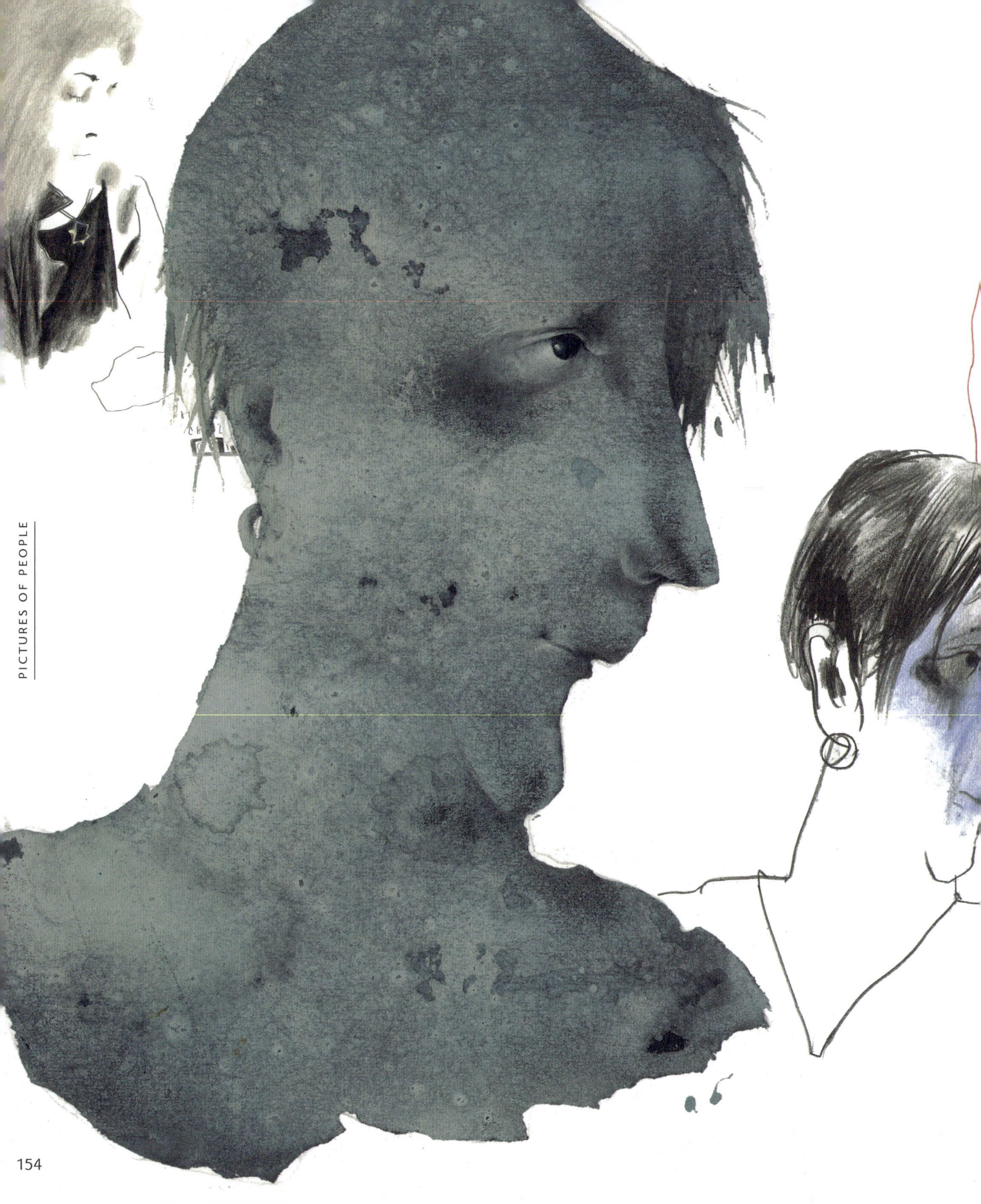

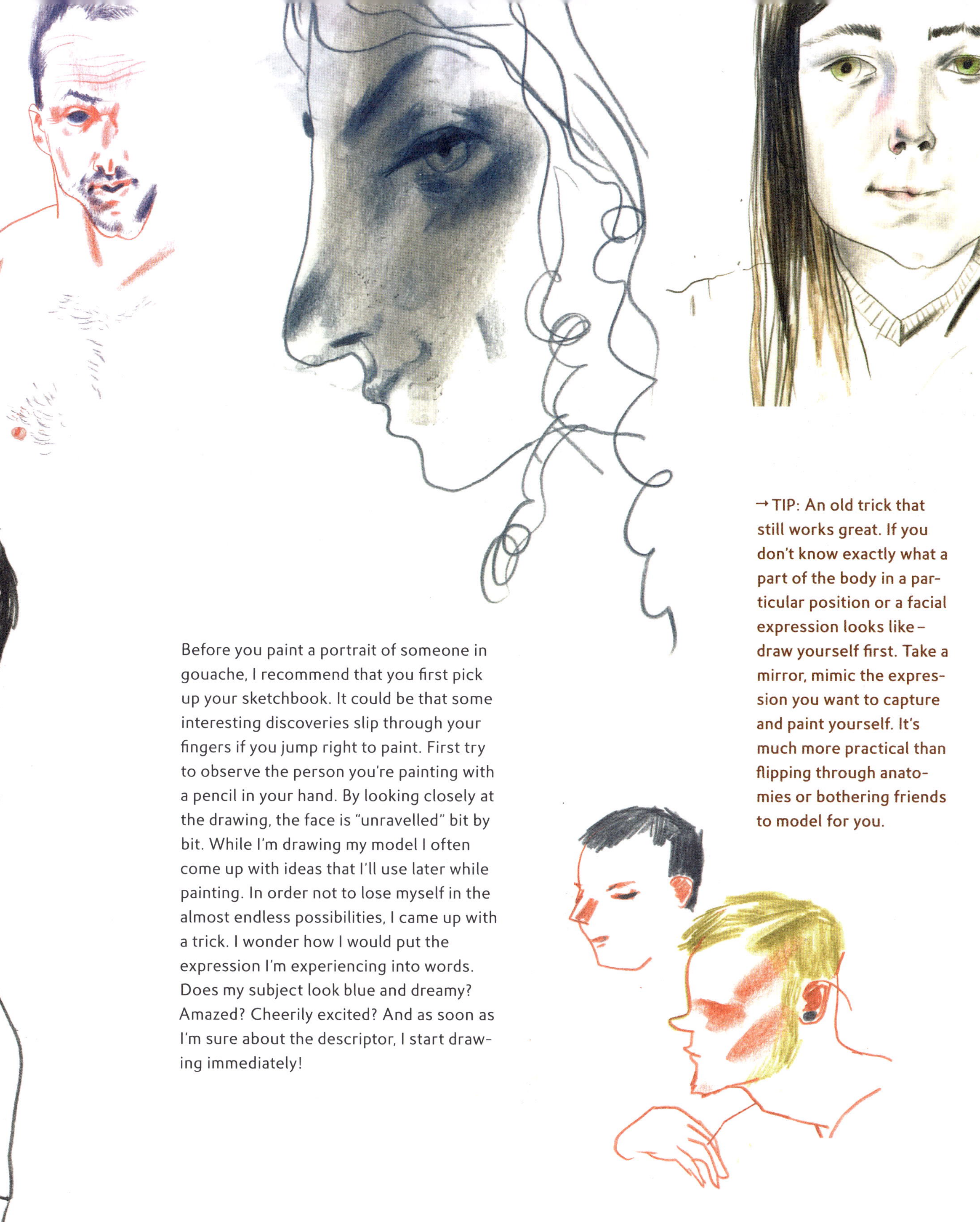

Before you paint a portrait of someone in gouache, I recommend that you first pick up your sketchbook. It could be that some interesting discoveries slip through your fingers if you jump right to paint. First try to observe the person you're painting with a pencil in your hand. By looking closely at the drawing, the face is "unravelled" bit by bit. While I'm drawing my model I often come up with ideas that I'll use later while painting. In order not to lose myself in the almost endless possibilities, I came up with a trick. I wonder how I would put the expression I'm experiencing into words. Does my subject look blue and dreamy? Amazed? Cheerily excited? And as soon as I'm sure about the descriptor, I start drawing immediately!

→ TIP: An old trick that still works great. If you don't know exactly what a part of the body in a particular position or a facial expression looks like – draw yourself first. Take a mirror, mimic the expression you want to capture and paint yourself. It's much more practical than flipping through anatomies or bothering friends to model for you.

Layer for Layer

The face

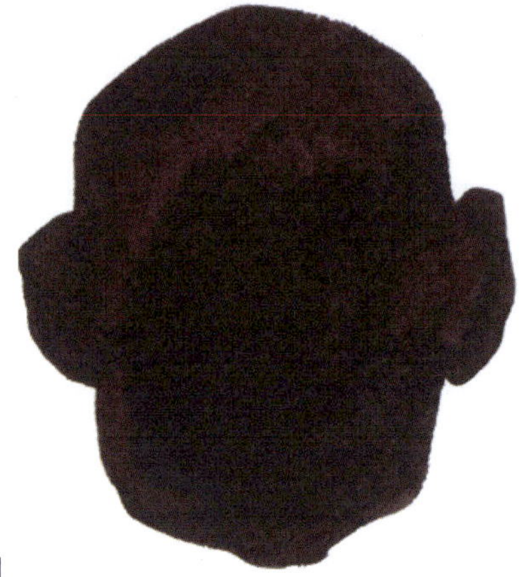

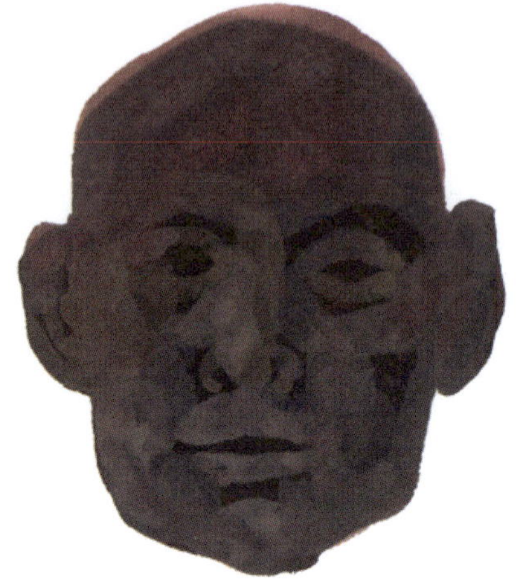

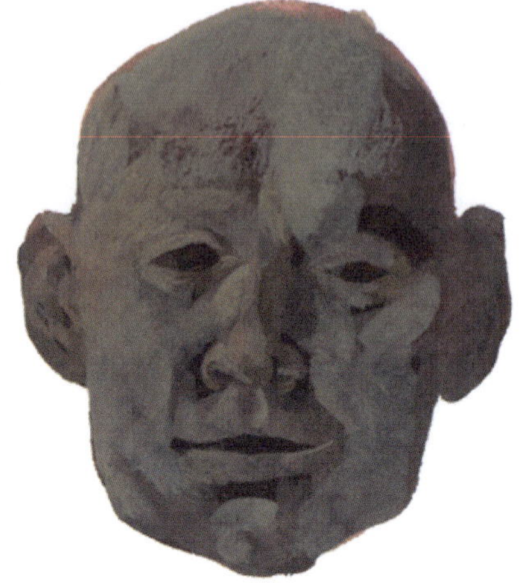

1.

Apply the silhouette in a dark hue. The outline should be expressive, but try not to apply the first layer of paint too thickly!

2.

Take a lighter shade mixed with white and start roughly modelling the facial features. It's enough to mark the approximate position of the mouth, nose and eyes.

3.

With the next layer of paint, cover both the lighted and shadowed side of the face. Leave only the very darkest places untouched. Don't paint too accurately in this phase!

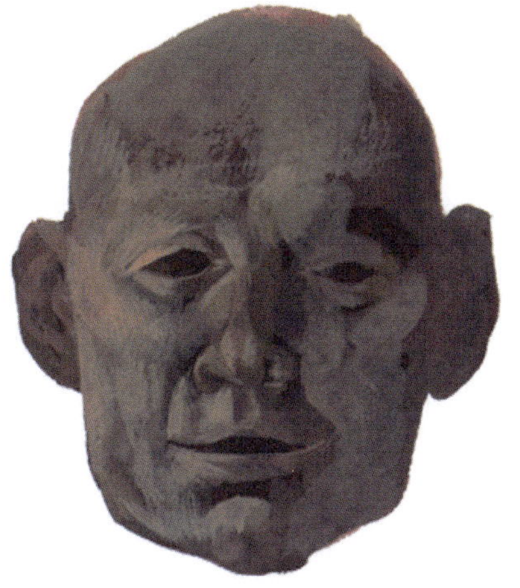

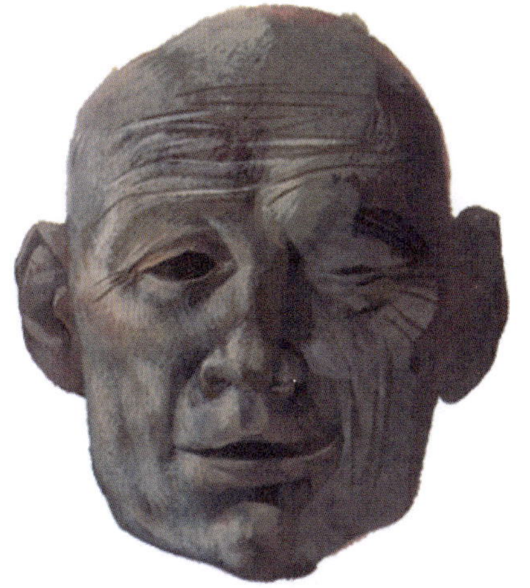

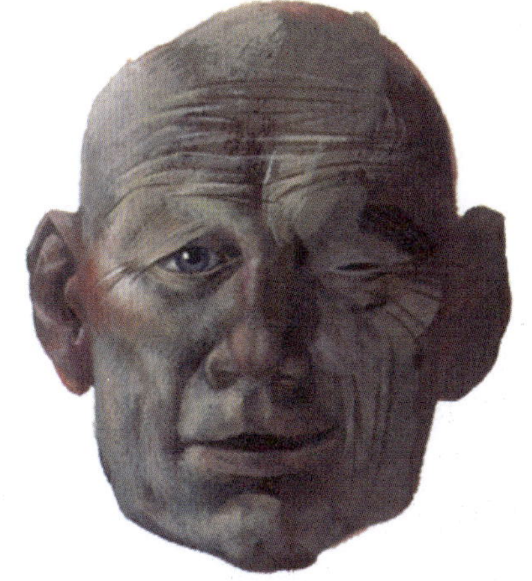

4.

Every new layer of paint has to dry. Increase the amount of white in your next glaze. Since colours generally look cooler with the addition of white, add a warm tone, say yellow.

5.

Now you start in on the details, wrinkles or eyelids and give the face even more expression. The folds and dimples are first painted dark and later heightened with a light colour.

6.

Now paint the crucial details such as the eye, red cheeks and nose. Lend the face sharpness and character.

→ TIP: Don't try to carefully work out every square inch of the face. Sometimes what's omitted says more than too many details. Don't forget that the eye of the beholder will quickly add what's missing.

Bundle up!
Clothing and textiles

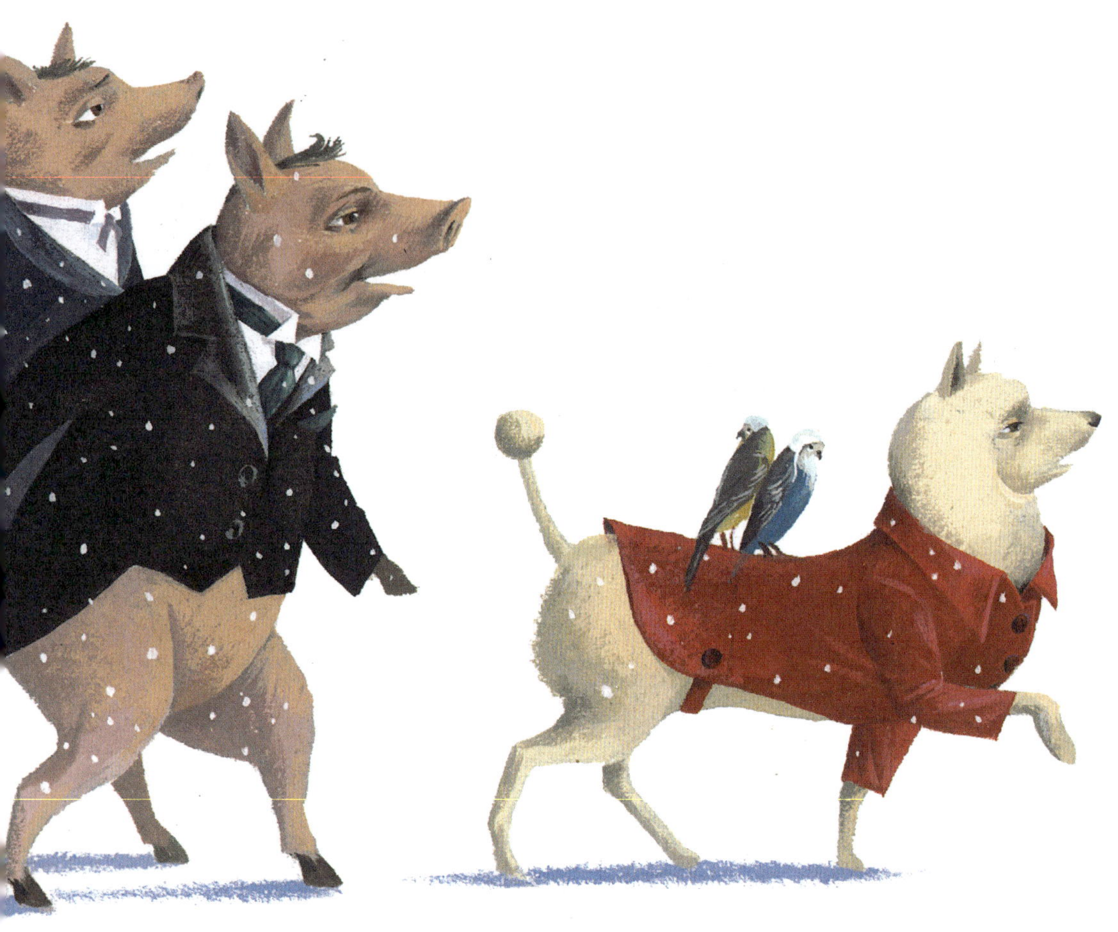

The people around us rarely walk about naked. Our “second skin” has become an important part of our personality. With it, we make visible what would otherwise remain hidden: our tastes, temperament, even our current mood. With it, we show we belong to a social group, a profession or, quite the contrary, we show that we don’t want to be associated with anything.

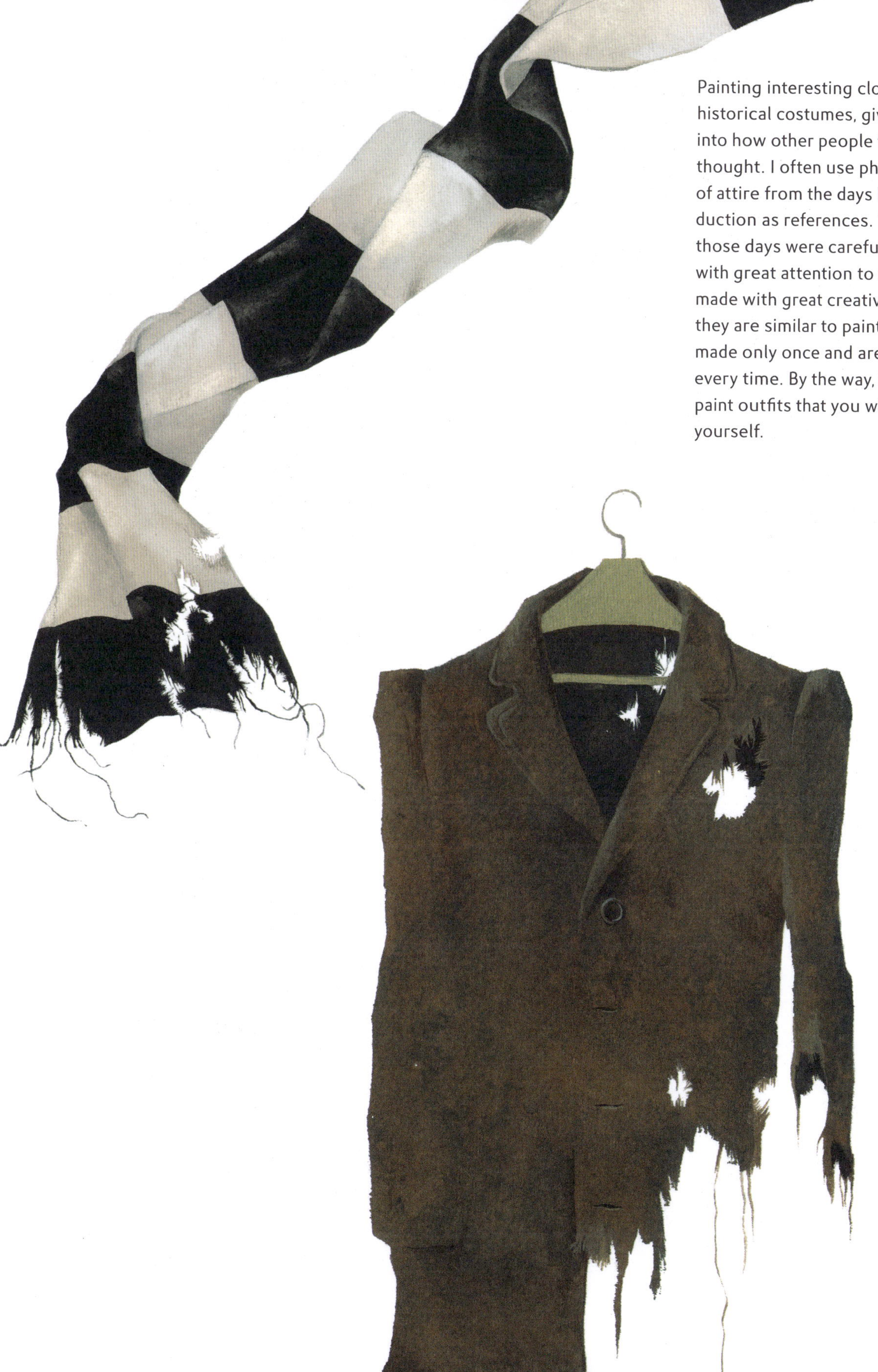

Painting interesting clothing, especially historical costumes, gives us an insight into how other people felt, what they thought. I often use photos or engravings of attire from the days before mass production as references. The garments from those days were carefully handcrafted, with great attention to detail and often made with great creativity. In this respect, they are similar to painted pictures that are made only once and are "tailor-made" every time. By the way, it's great fun to paint outfits that you wish you could wear yourself.

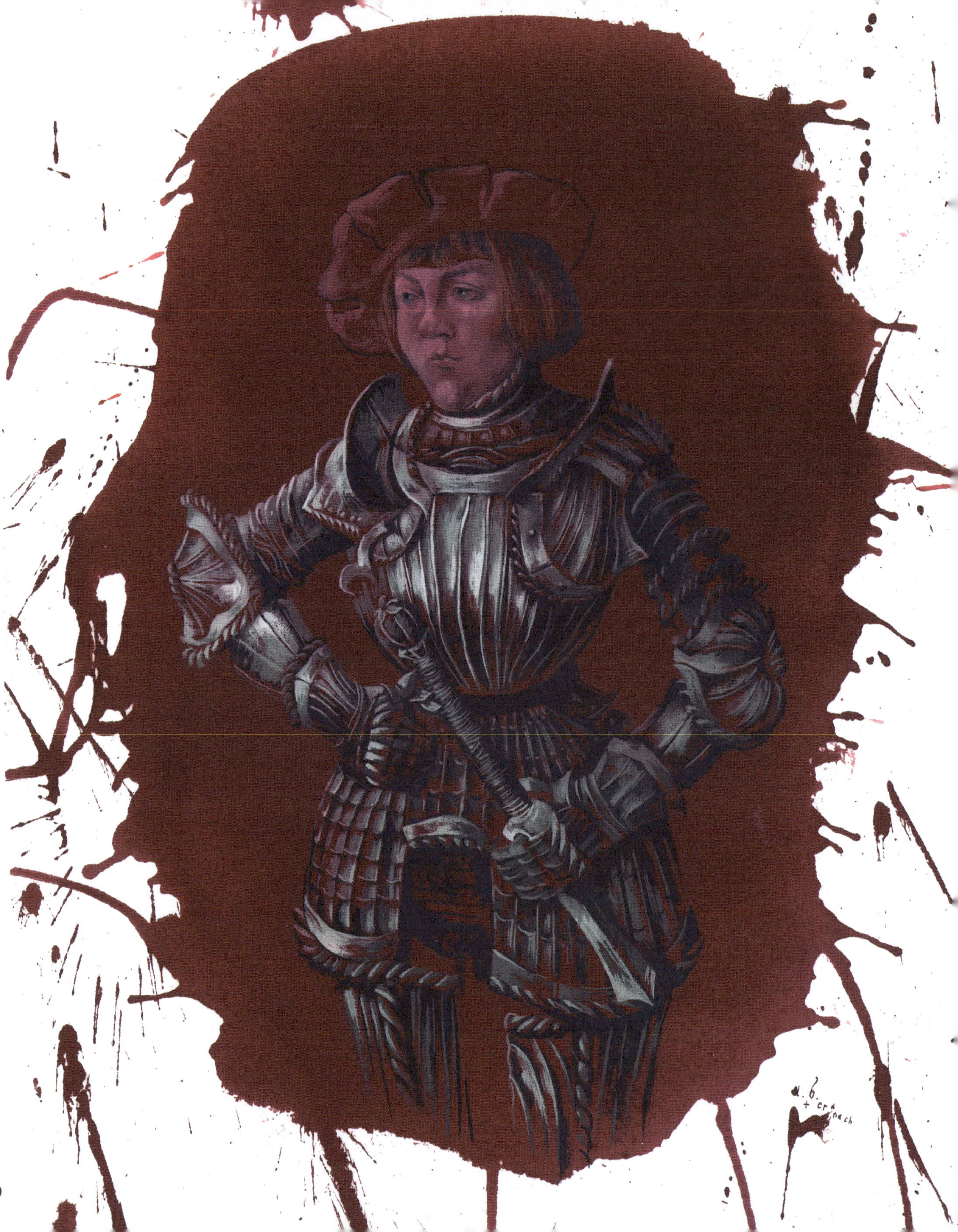

I wouldn't have liked to spend my days in a suit of armour, but the austere elegance and dignity that this combat gear exudes impressed me as a child. The Knights' Room at the Hermitage, where dozens of suits of armour for horses and riders is on display, was the long-awaited highlight of every museum visit for me. Not everyday wear, but work wear, the more ludicrous a suit of armour is, the more interesting it is to paint. To get the shiny reflective metal with its rivets and ornaments, you should definitely integrate the colour in the background, in this case red. Use it as your mid-tone, paint the shadowed areas with dark grey and add targeted white highlights on the chest and the areas where direct light falls.

When we're painting old combat wear, it is only right and proper to show a comparably great item of clothing from today. The dress on the right is based on models by Alexander McQueen, one of the flashiest contemporary artists who sadly died young. I tried to convey the hypnotic effect of the red and black stripes. I also wanted to express different shades of red in the dress in contrast to the pallor of the skin.

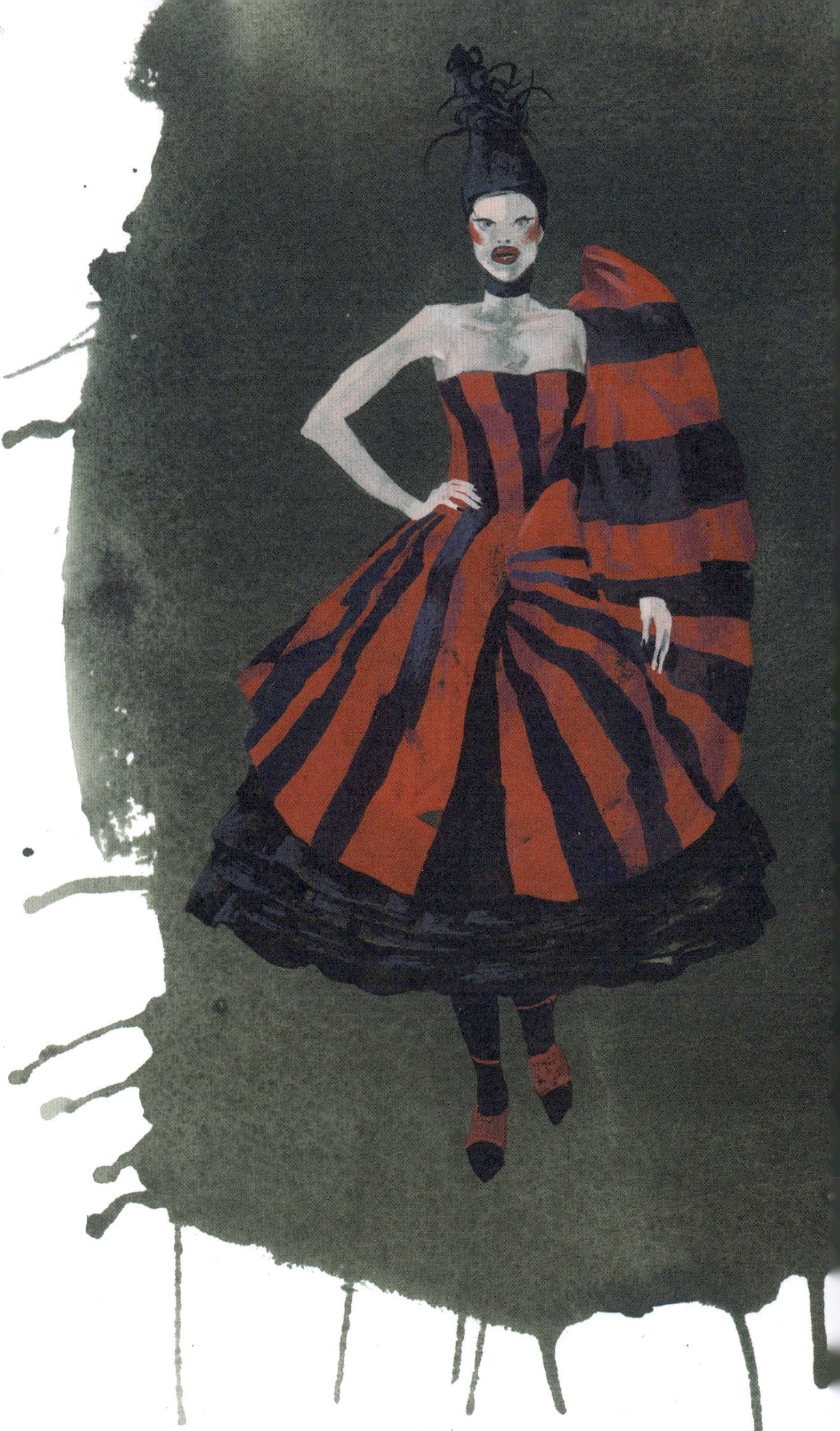

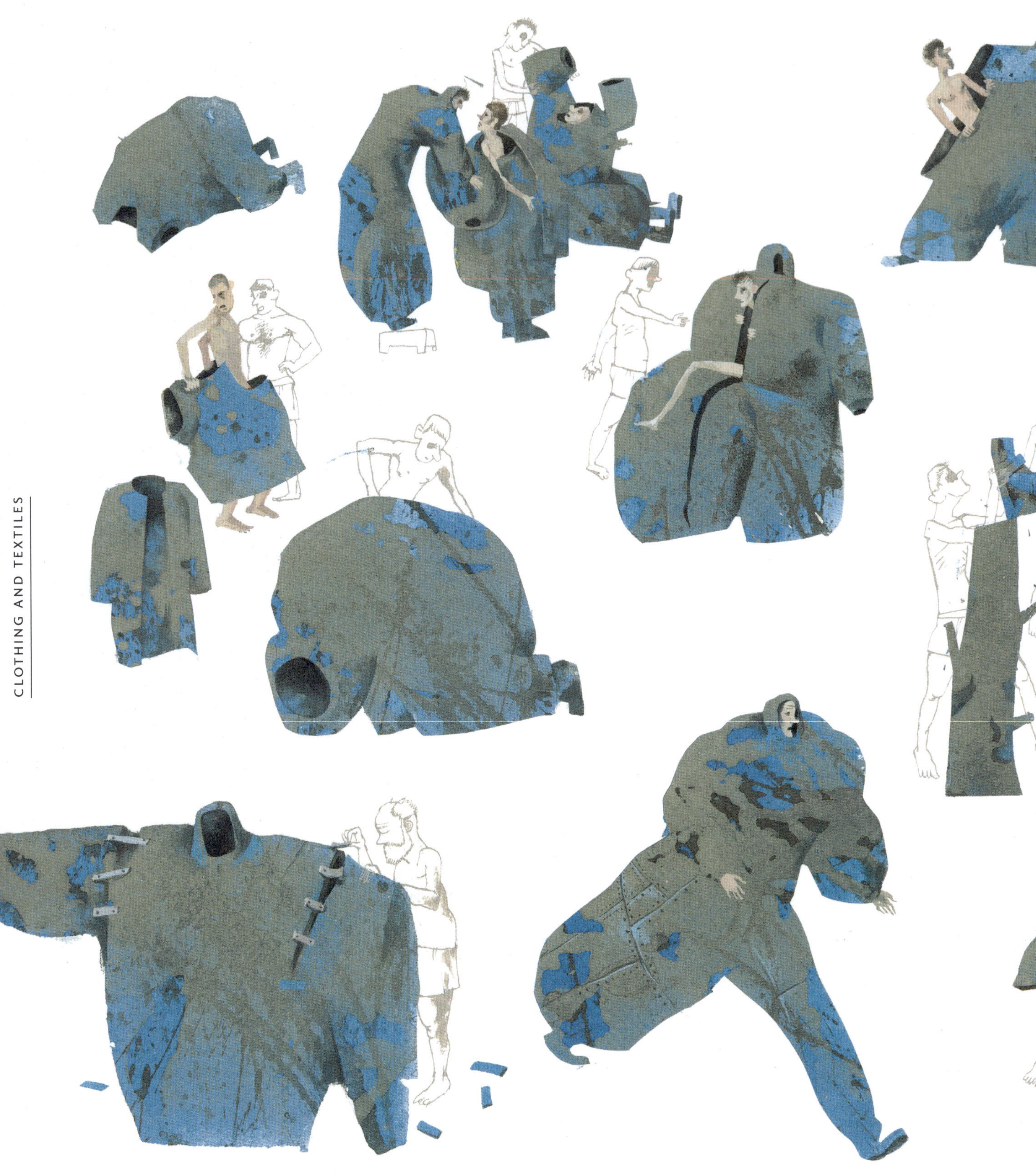

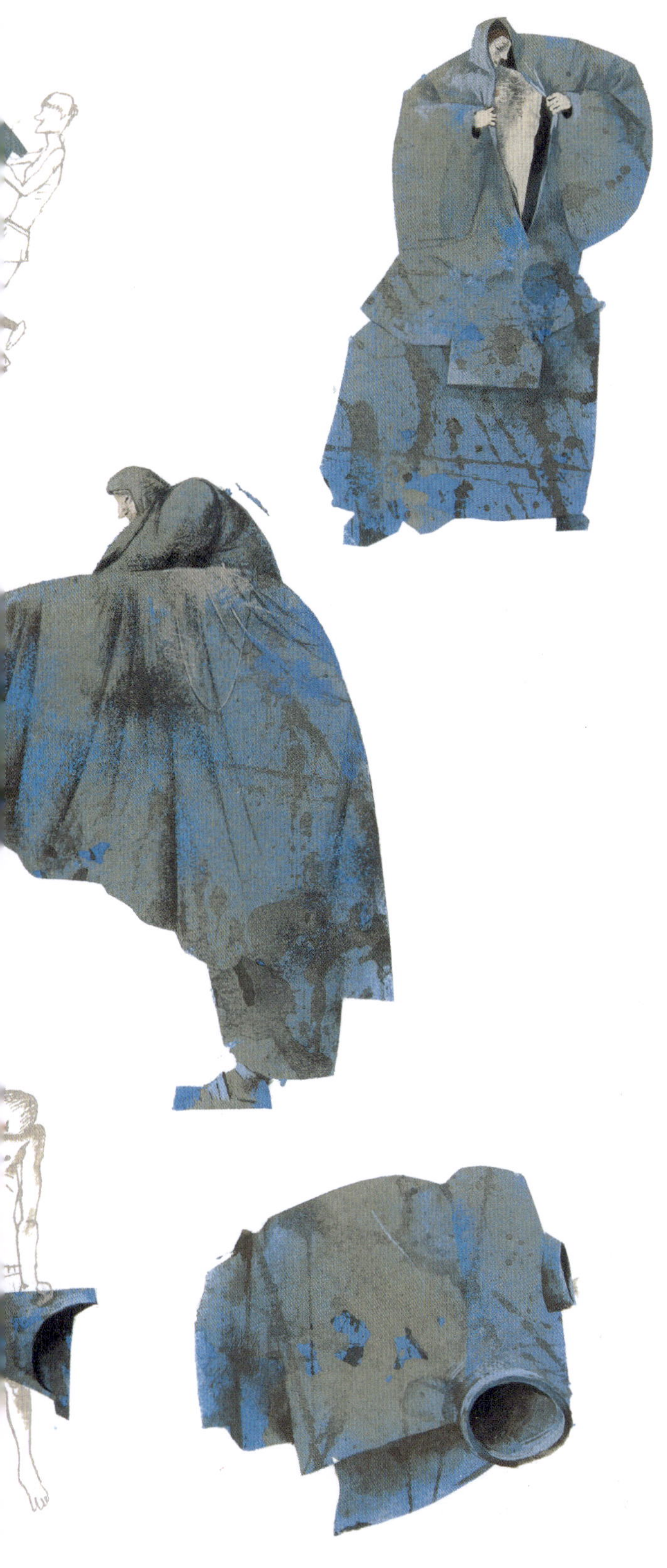

Clothing can play various roles in your pictures. Garments often display something. But the opposite also happens when the clothes hide unfavourable details or the fact that something is missing. This is the function of the costumes on this double page. The otherwise skinny, vulnerable little men are going to war disguised in martial armour. The costumes are based on grotesque suits of armour from other eras and intentionally designed to be as uncomfortable as possible. This is because in this story, the soldiers tear off their armour as soon as the battle starts.

→ TIP: Use clothing in your pictures even if you're not quite certain about representing the human body. The nice thing about dressing up your own figures is being able to cover the proportions and show little of your protagonists. This way, your clothes really will make the man!

Nature morte, the world of things. Objects of glass, stone, metal and wood

It's no coincidence that the golden age of the Flemish still life was during the sixteenth to seventeenth centuries. That was the time that John Calvin's teachings were most popular in the Netherlands. The famous moralist himself had a special relationship with commodities and believed that each of them had a secret meaning. Thus, they painted fully laden tables bending under the weight of meticulously portrayed game, fruit, wine glasses and mussels. But the overwhelming realism of these still lifes was not an end in itself. The real meaning was in their symbolism, which may not seem so natural to us today.

The educated viewer of that time saw many hidden allegories and metaphors in this feast for the eyes. Silver cutlery was a symbol of earthly riches and their transience; hams, liverwursts and other butchery products meant carnal delights and a lemon (which is pretty on the outside but sour on the inside) represented betrayal. An extinguished candle symbolized the brevity of human existence; a tall fluted glass was an indication of life's fragility, but also of abstinence and the ability to control one's emotions.

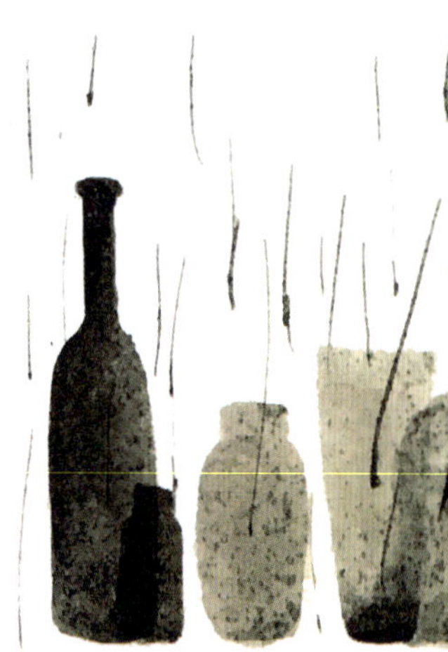

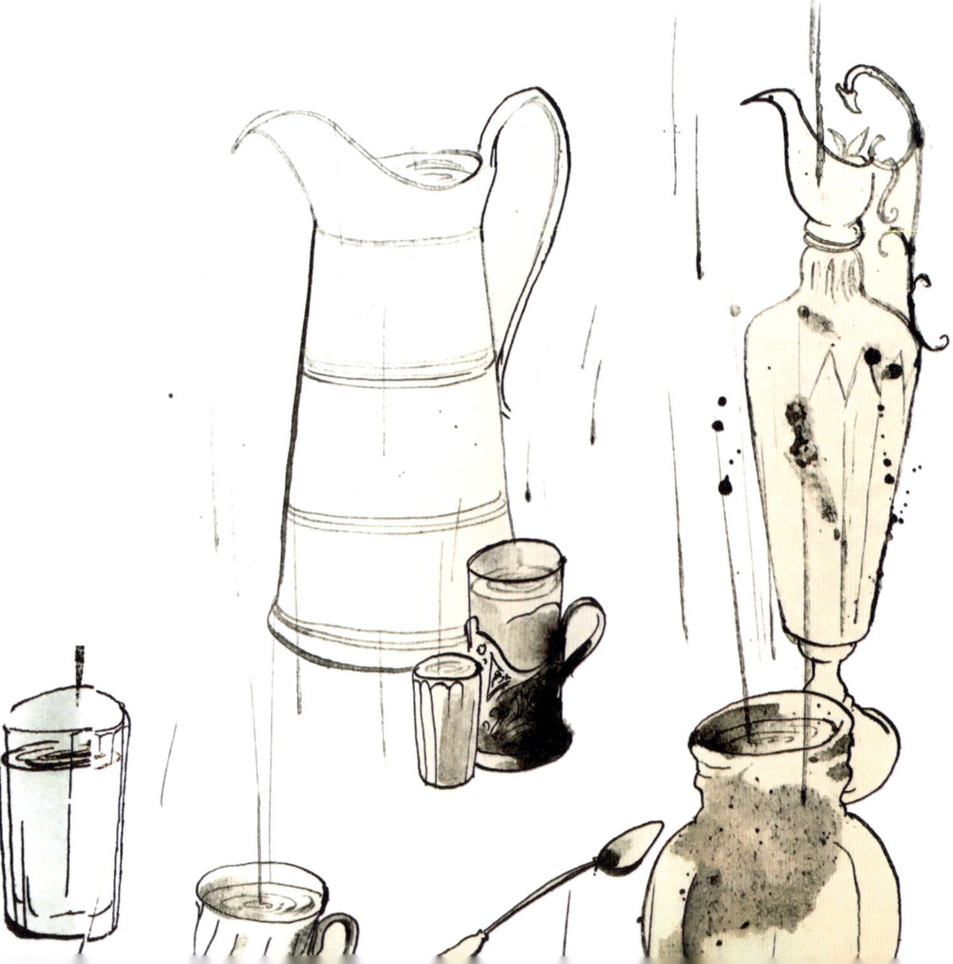

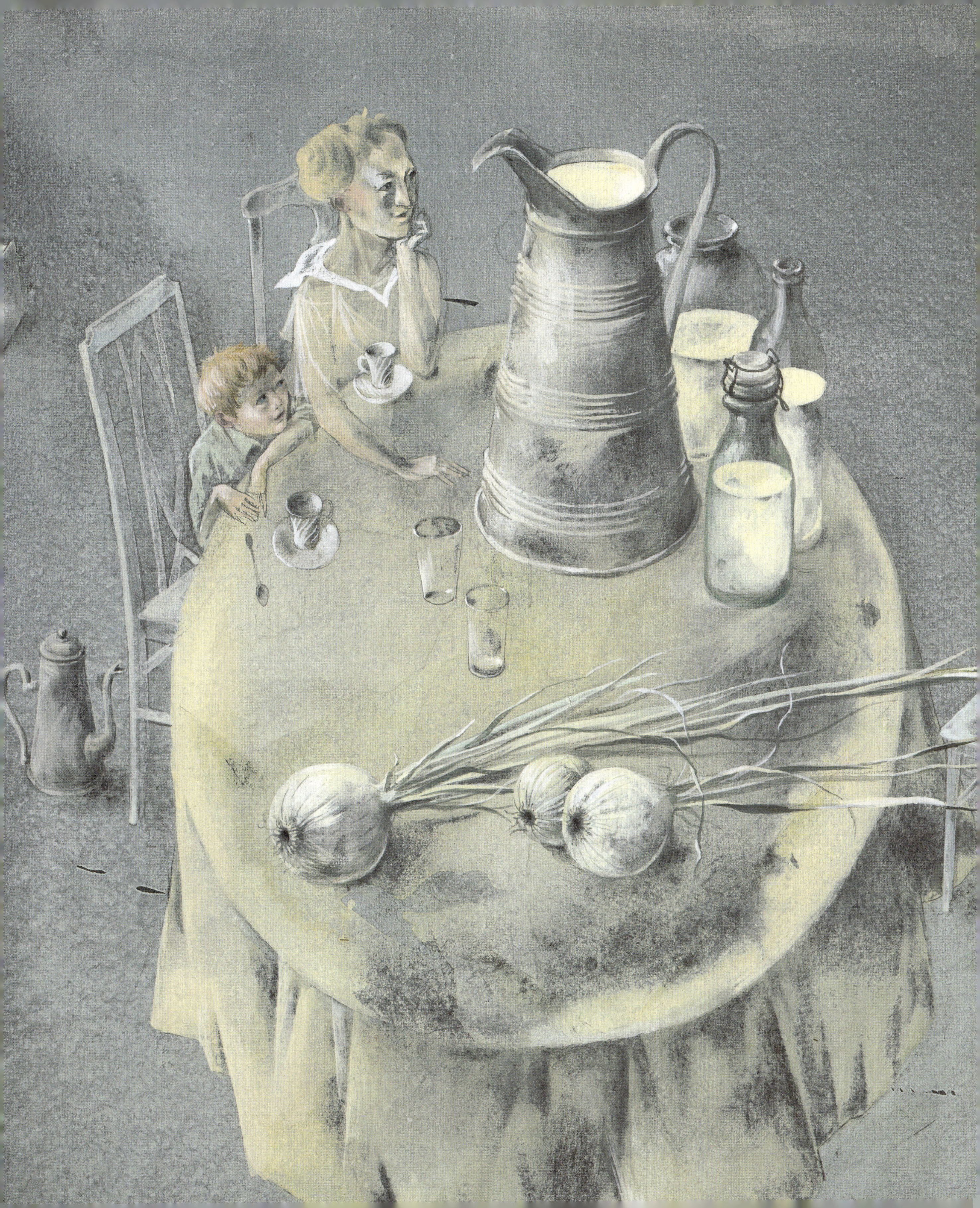

But even without all the symbolism: We own many things around us simply because they're practical and some others simply because of their beauty. We are reflected in it, use it to better estimate other people or to protect ourselves from strangers. And sometimes we want to impress our contemporaries with them. Objects permeate our lives; they influence it and often make the invisible visible. So it's not surprising that objects appear in so many pictures.

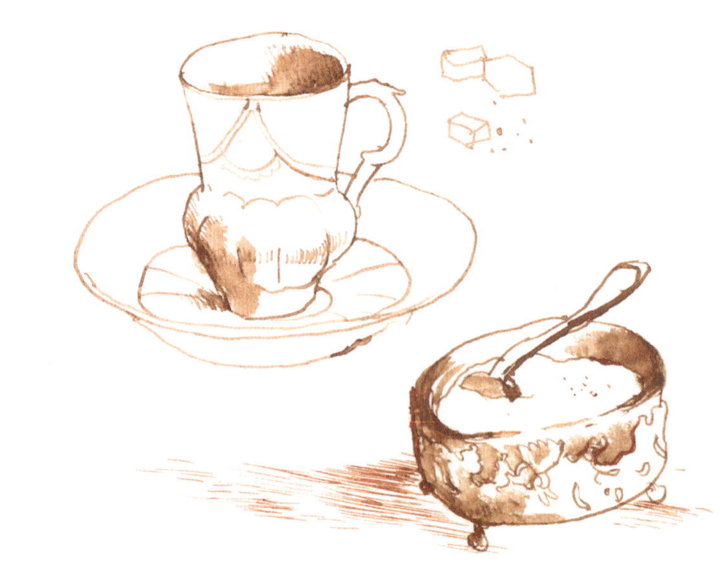

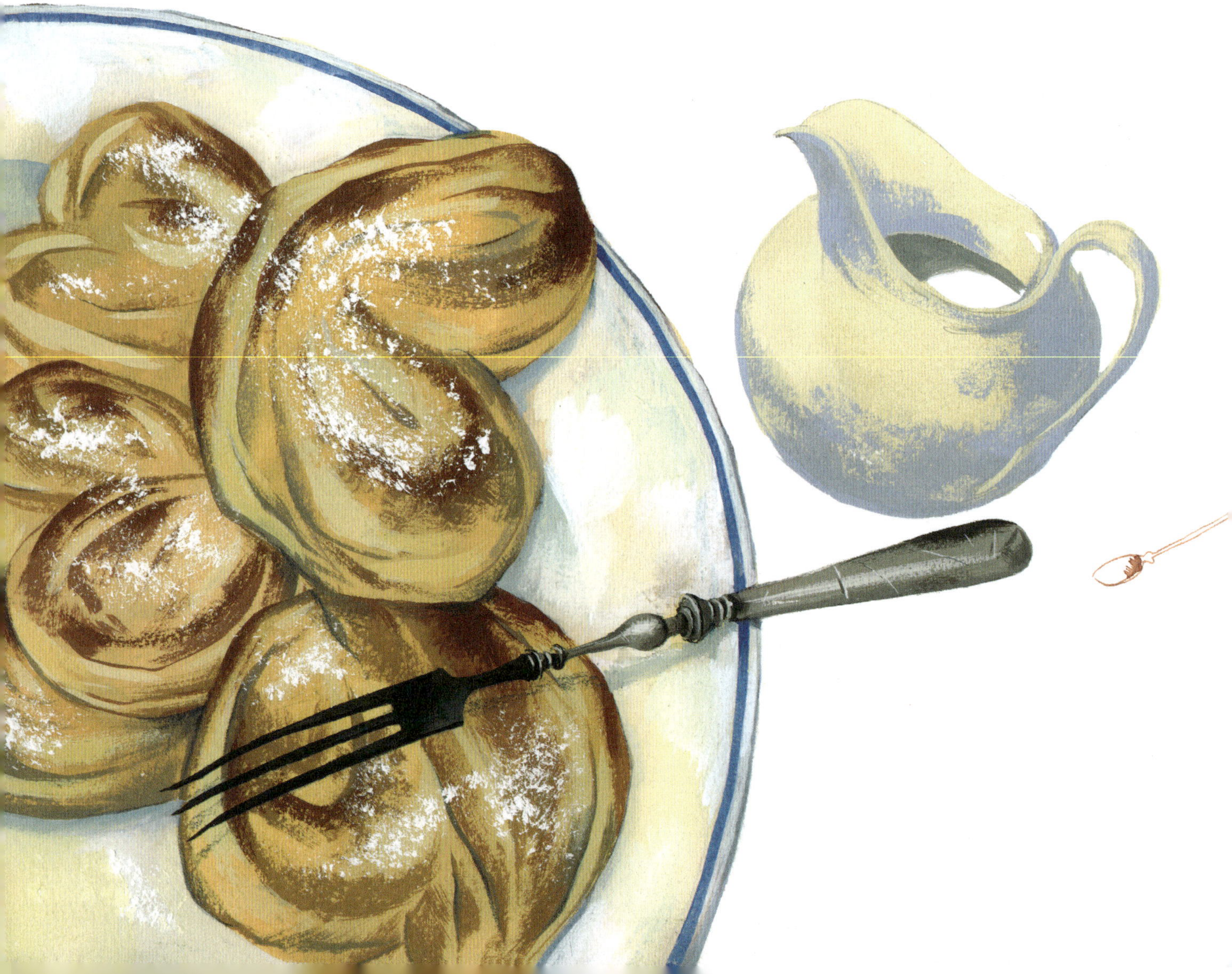

For me, it's always wonderful when a painting manages to combine objects of different materials – whether a bottle, an apple or a teaspoon – in one picture. I'd like to give you some tips and ideas for how you can master this in gouache.

The first example shows how to make the food you paint look even more delicious. The pastries on the left and the plate don't contrast by chance. If you paint the porcelain with cool colours and keep the food on it in warmer tones, this increases the contrast. And when you get it right, you should get hungry just looking at it!

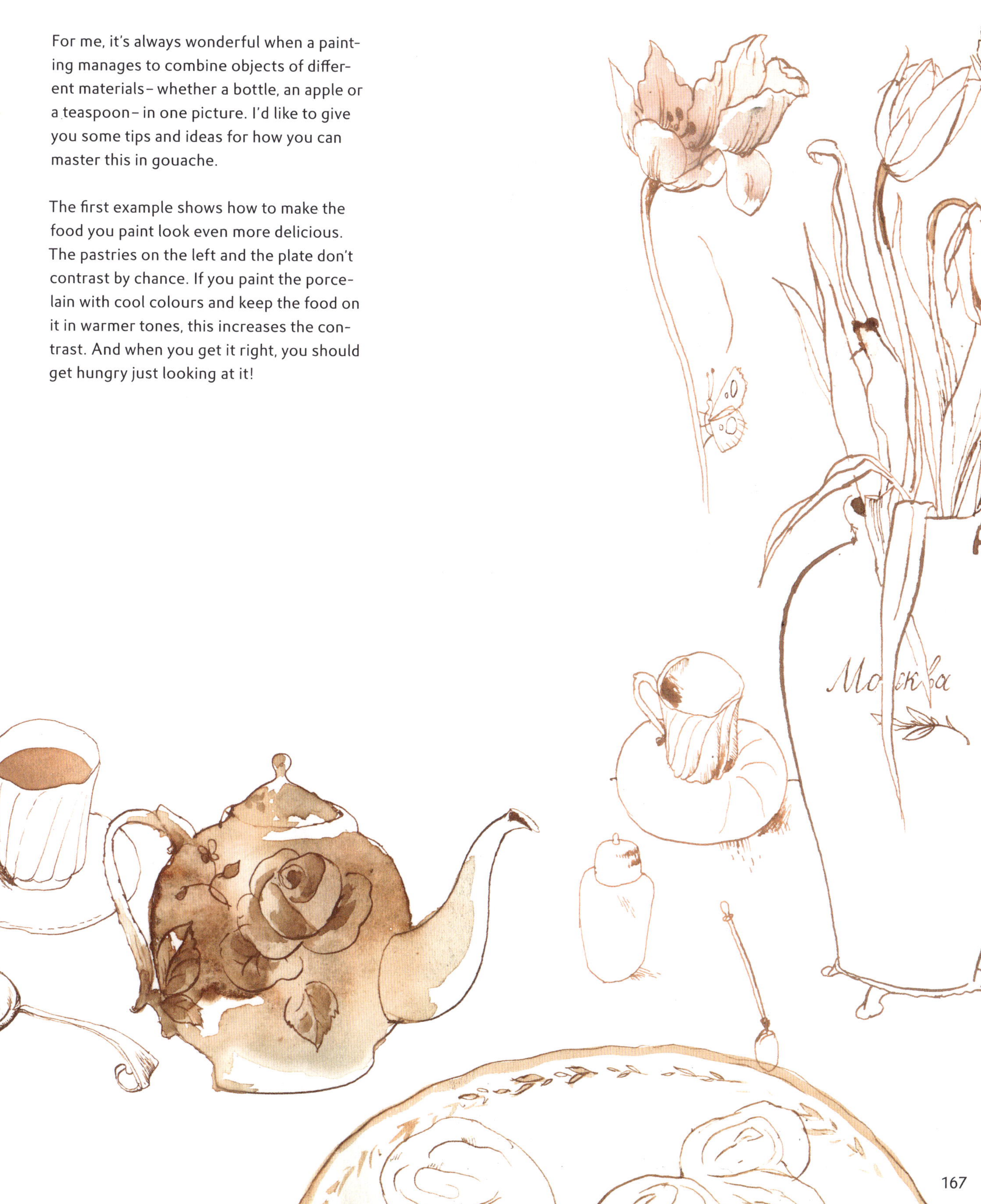

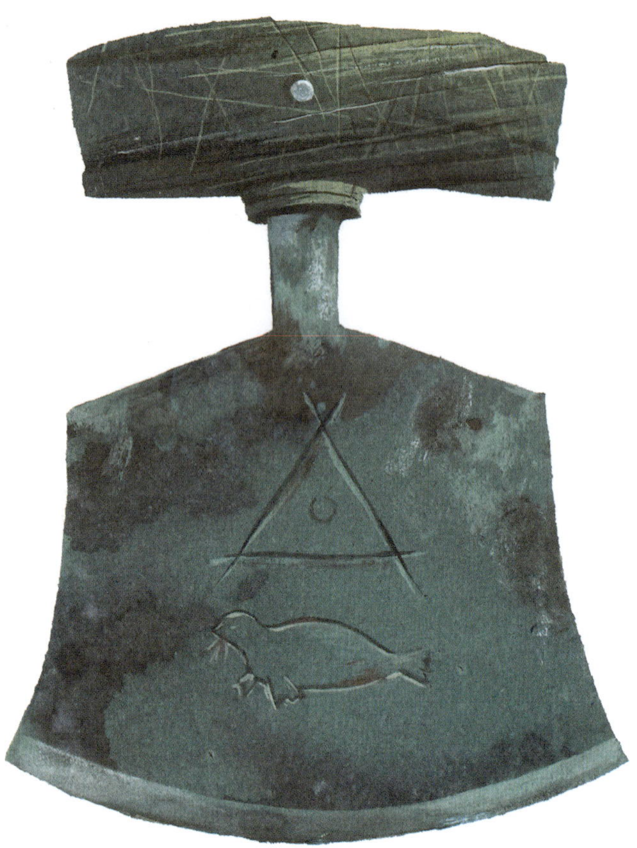

Silver

Anyone who paints the family silver should work with a lot of white (including opaque) and know whether the silver is going to be dull or shiny. Because the shinier the metal, the higher the contrast of the light reflections. The two teaspoons in the picture had not been cleaned for a long time and therefore only shine with restraint.

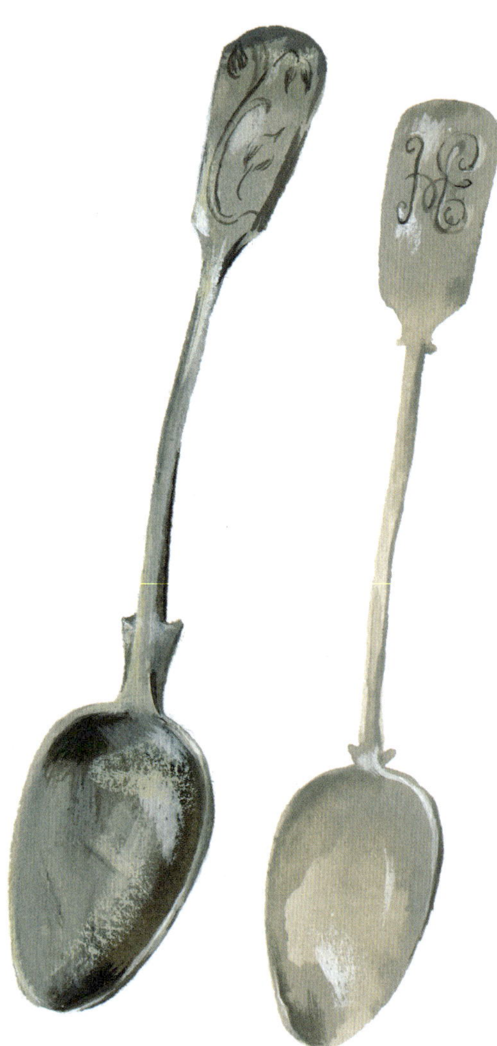

Iron

Since iron rusts easily and acquires a patina, but shines again when polished, it's important to show these two properties. The Inuit knife is painted so that the dark rusty layer was applied first, then gone over with the "steely" grey wash. Then I painted the polished metal with light grey and only then the hallmark: first the dark pits, then the light reflections.

Wood

This wooden board comes from the northernmost tip of Denmark, found on the beach in Skagen. Sanded by the sea and with two rusty nails, it reminds me a little of a thoughtful crocodile... To ensure that the wood grain comes out well, I used light ochre yellow as the first layer and immediately allow a reddish-brown for rust to bleed through the wet paint. The shadowed areas come next in light grey. This gives the board three-dimensionality. The wood grain comes last– it's light grey at the light spots, but darker than the background. In the shadowed areas, the grain should also be painted correspondingly darker.

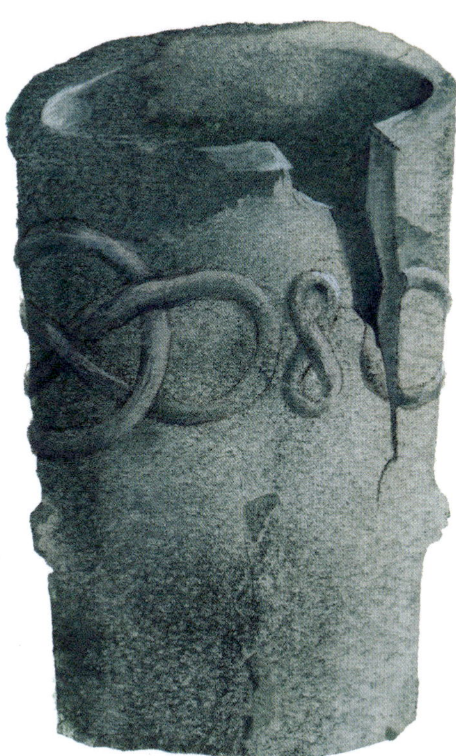

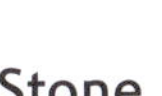

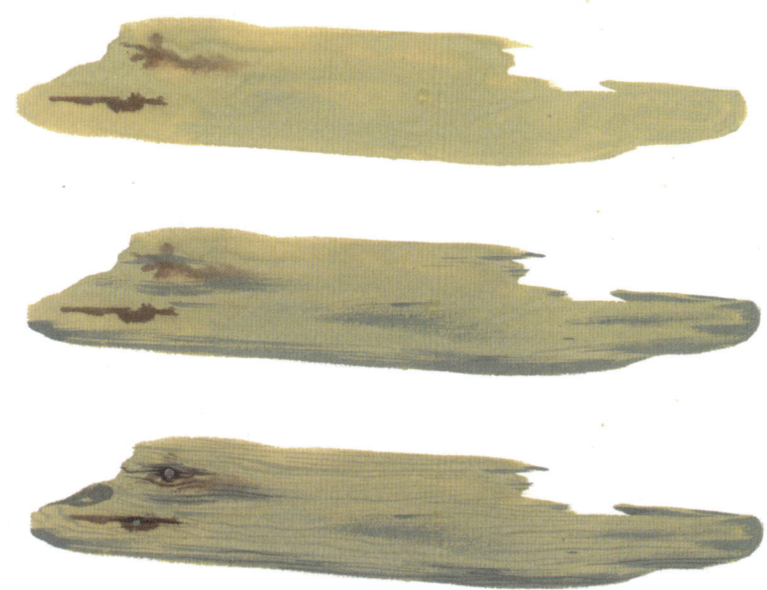

Stone

The masking technique is particularly suitable for expressing the materiality of a stone. To do this, you mask the negative shape (more on this in the chapter "Using masking fluid"). Then work your way from dark to light grey. It's important that you give the last light glaze "free rein" and apply the paint very fluidly with generous brush strokes.

Layer for Layer

Glass

→ TIP: A glass bottle was originally poured into its shape, so it's not wrong to work with a lot of water in the first layer – this way, you can better render the irregularities in the glass by the more or less uncontrolled flow of the paint.

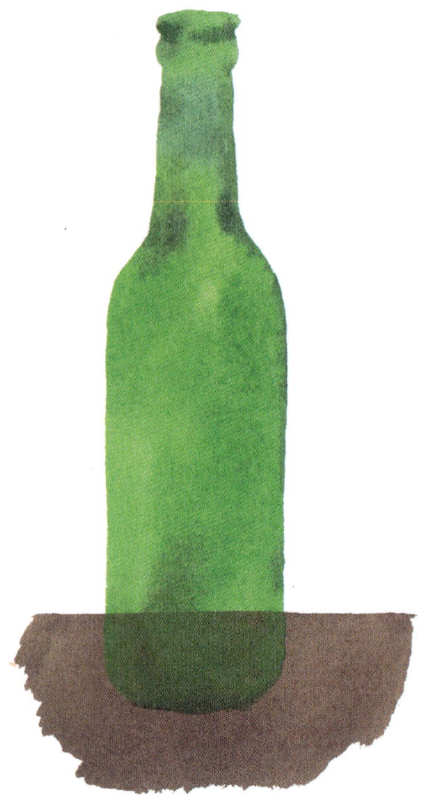

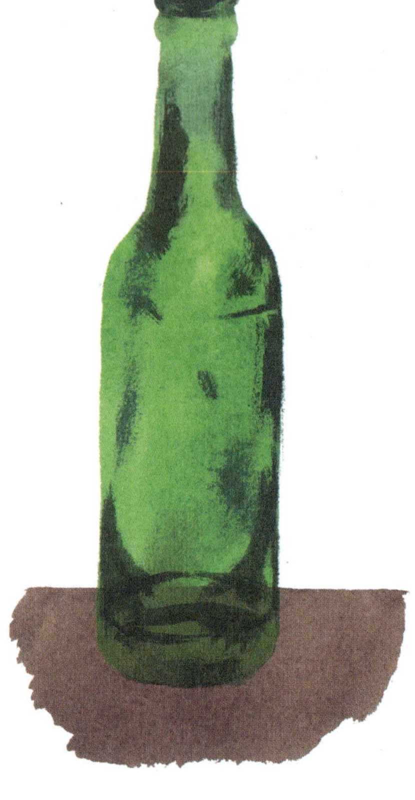

1.

Before you start with the empty beer bottle you need a background. Paint with thin paint, a larger soft brush from number 8 and apply the paint as quickly as possible. Then let it dry well.

2.

The first glaze should consist of two or three hues. Dilute the paints very transparently with plenty of water so that the brown surface also shines through. Paint with a soft squirrel or sable-hair brush about no. 6.

3.

The phenomenon of refraction causes the light to refract differently when it passes through glass of different thicknesses. Therefore the background will appear crooked through the glass. Use a darker green to paint the thick glass walls, for example on the bottleneck.

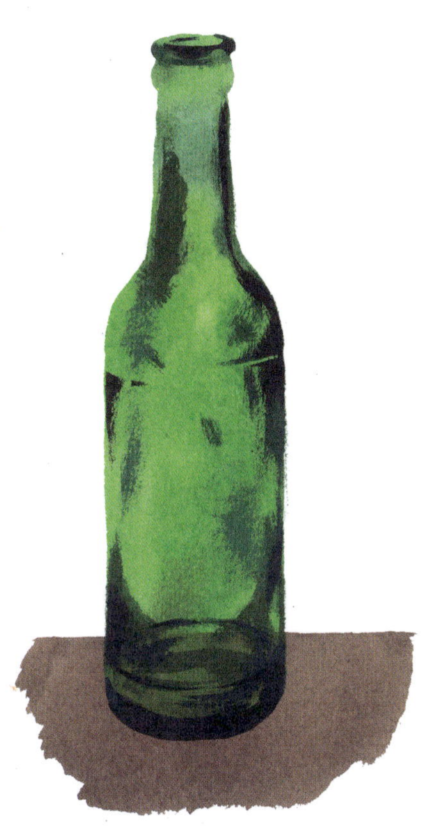

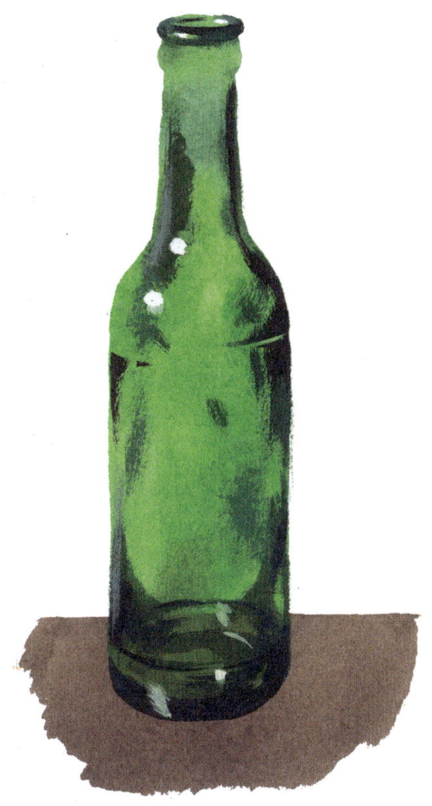

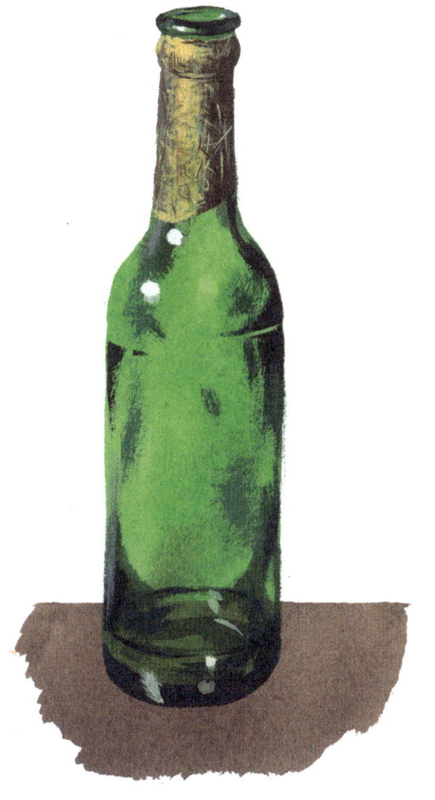

4.

Continue to paint the darkest areas, that is, wherever the glass is thickest – like the bottom of the bottle or the sides – with a thinner brush about no. 4. This lends the bottle the necessary contrast and shapes it.

5.

Now you can add light reflections on the side facing you completely in light and weaker and darker in the bottle bottom and the bottle interior. Incidentally, reflections usually occur where the shape changes.

6.

And one more thing: Don't forget the golden aluminium foil on the bottleneck. Since it's made of a different material than the bottle, it's best to paint it with the "dry brush." And your beer bottle is finished!

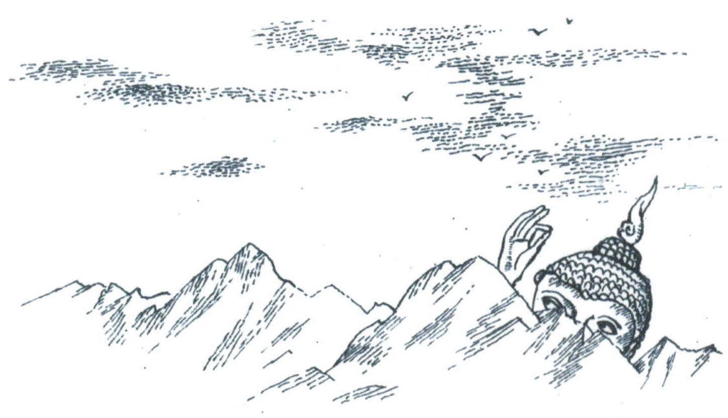

A question of perspective. Landscapes with gouache

Whatever a landscape painting depicts – the sunrise on Mars or a dog meadow in the next city park – it opens windows to another world. And since this world is above all an inner world, the landscape becomes an image of our feelings. It is therefore very important that you are clear about which atmosphere you want to create and what feelings you convey to the viewer through your picture.

But how is an atmosphere made? First: with colours. Open, clear hues are perceived as friendly and cheerful. Broken and dark colours are gloomier. Second, it can be helpful to think of the symbolism of different landscapes. If we questioned psychologists and dream researchers they would probably associate a landscape by the sea with the subconscious because of the great depths below sea level. Foggy and cloudy landscapes can stand for negative thoughts and mountains or boulders for individual problems.

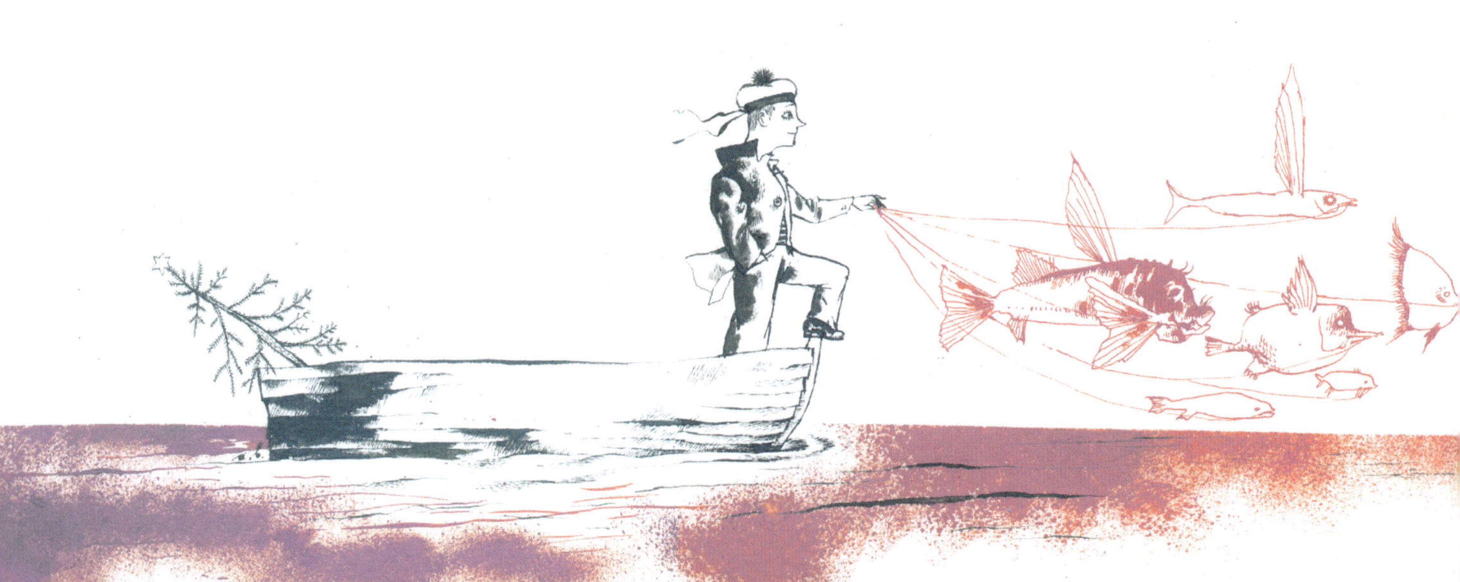

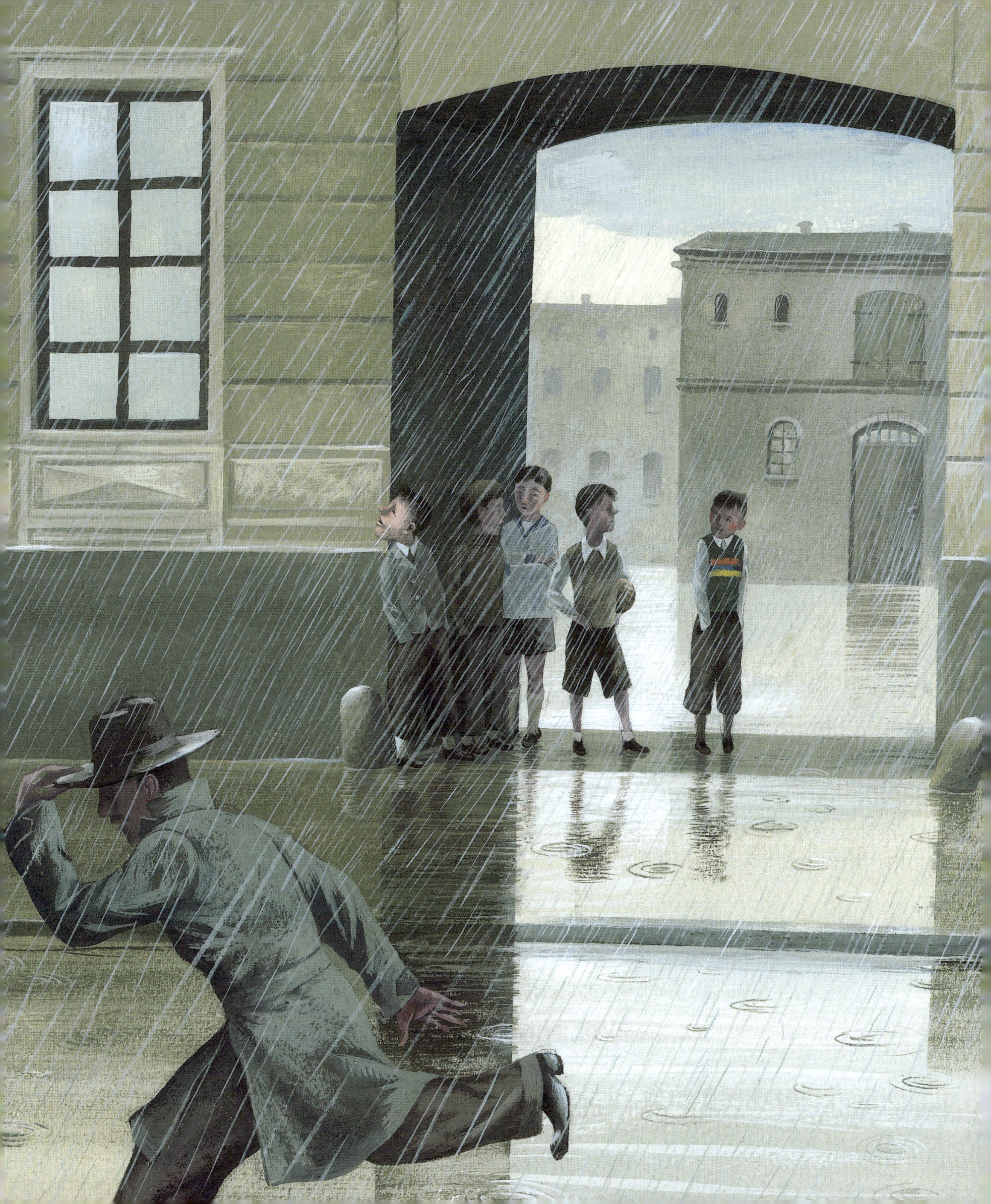

You will only succeed with a landscape if you manage to bring spatial depth to it. To understand how this works, consider perspective and the foreground and background of an image. Perspective first of all requires that you are sure of your own point of view. It's no coincidence that the further away they are, the smaller they become, only when we look at them from a clearly defined location. This first basic rule is expanded to include the fact that we see things clearly in the vicinity while everything in the distance gets more and more blurry. That is the rule two. And then rule number *three*: Since air is not completely transparent and air molecules mainly reflect blue light, everything that is in the distance will appear more bluish.

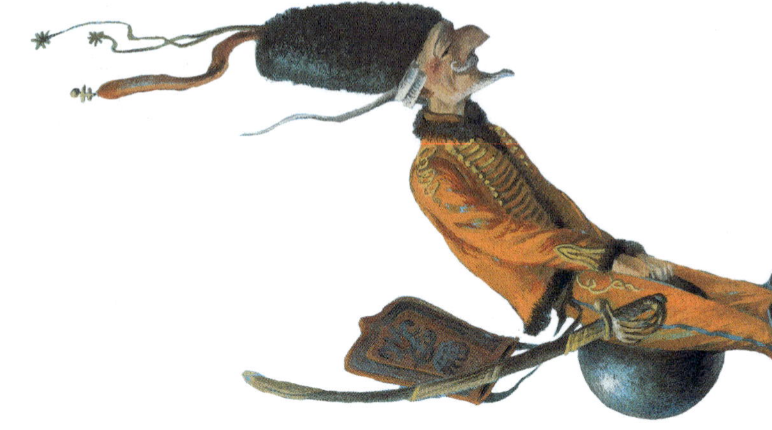

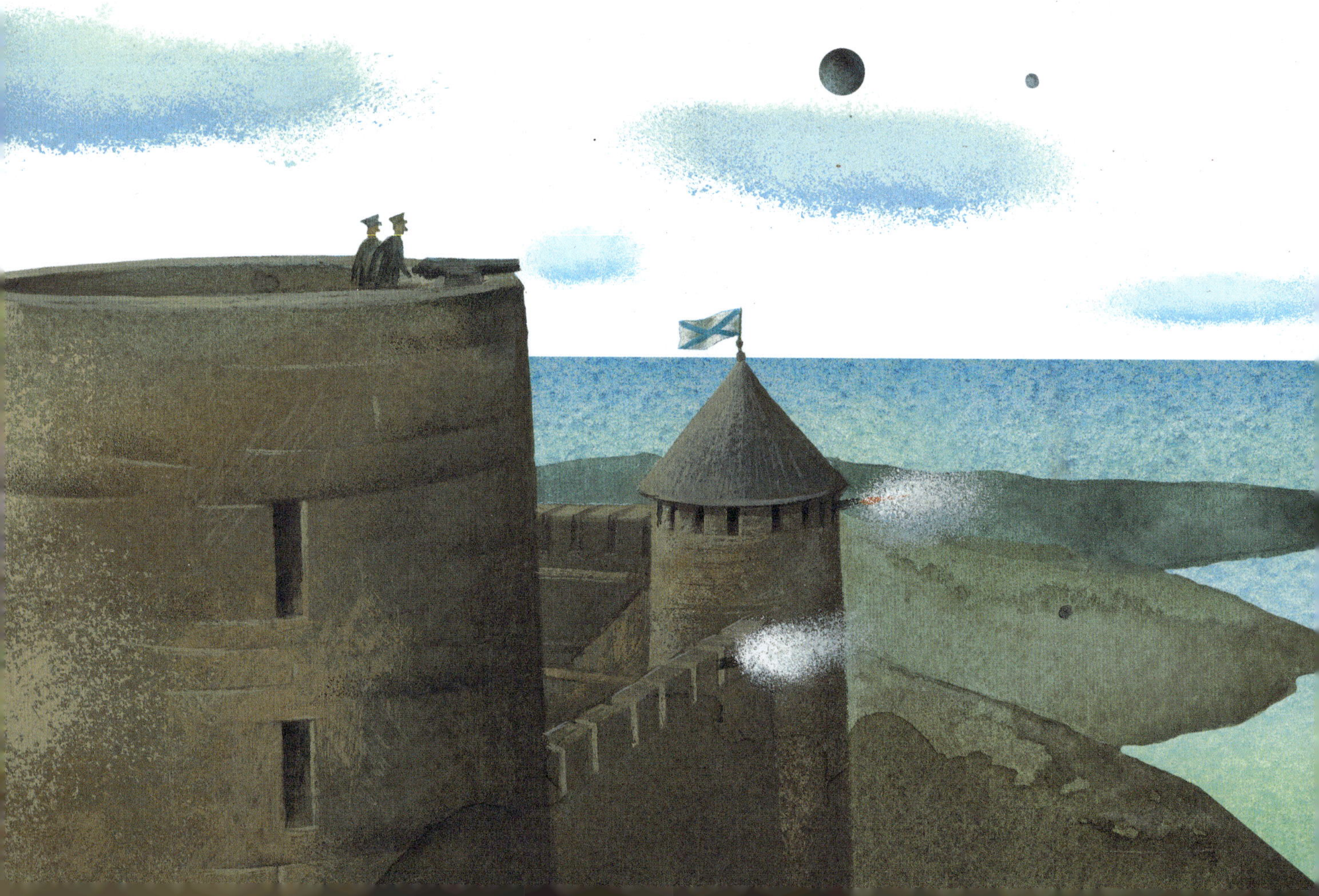

The interesting thing is that you don't have to apply all three of these rules at the same time. It may be enough if one or two objects of the same size become smaller in the distance. In this way, the headlands in the picture become ever narrower and at the same time they become bluish. How much things "blur" can depend, among other things, on what you want to focus on. Sometimes weather also comes into play, for if you want to display heavy rain for example, you really shouldn't be able to see the background clearly (see the large rain picture on the previous double page).

→ TIP: Clouds can be very helpful to give the picture more depth. A few large clouds in the foreground against a few smaller ones in the background and the blue area becomes a sky.

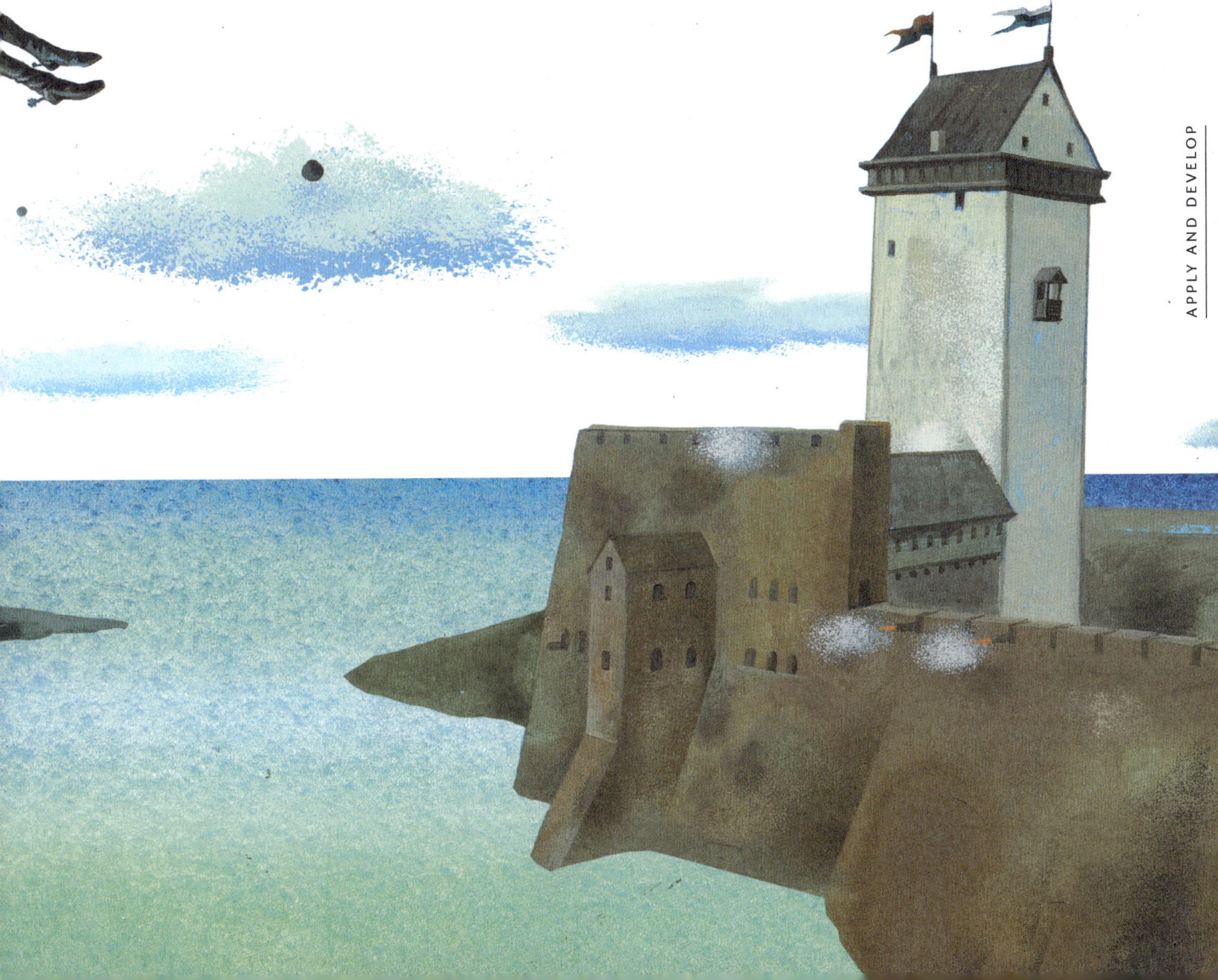

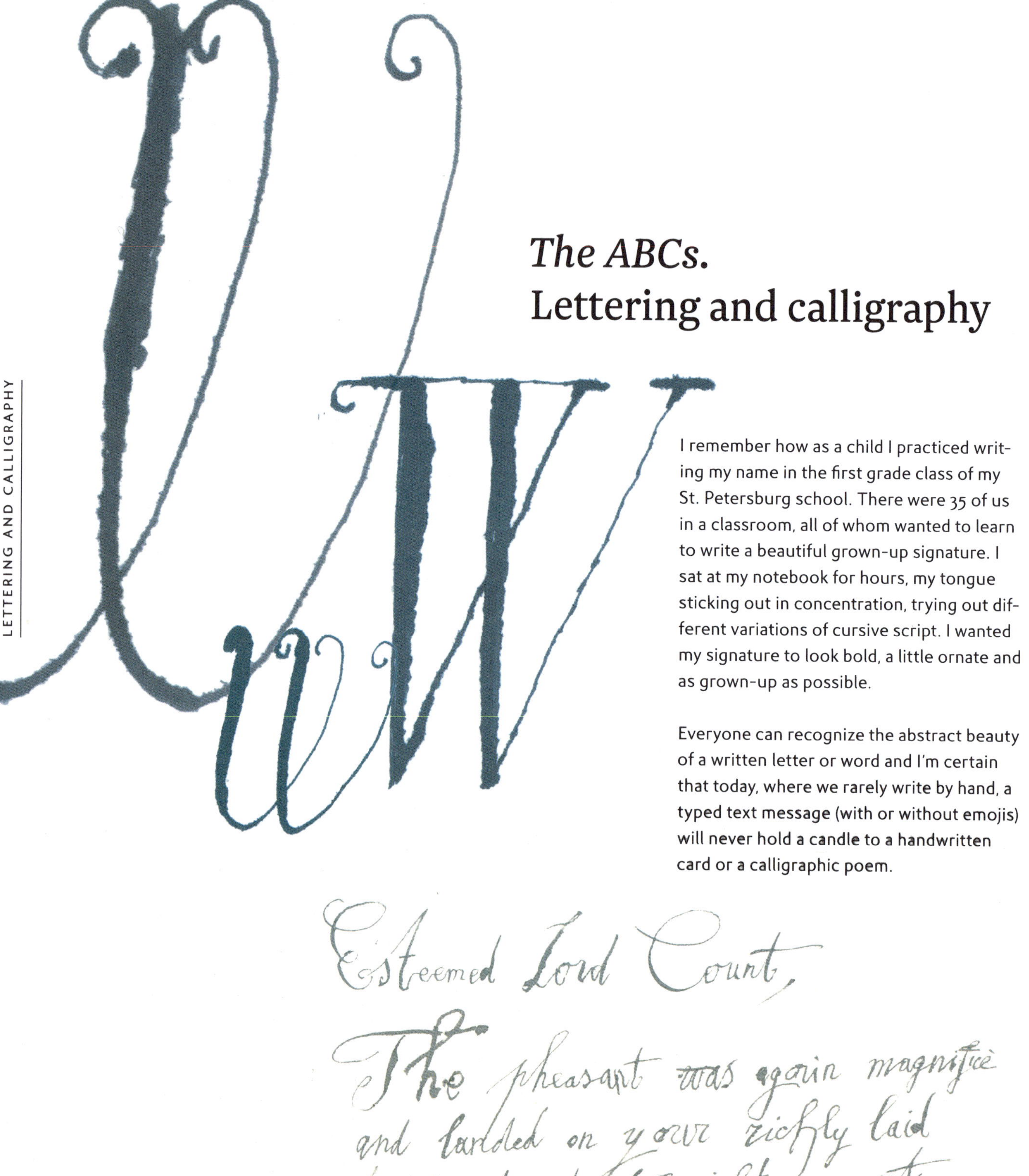

The ABCs. Lettering and calligraphy

I remember how as a child I practiced writing my name in the first grade class of my St. Petersburg school. There were 35 of us in a classroom, all of whom wanted to learn to write a beautiful grown-up signature. I sat at my notebook for hours, my tongue sticking out in concentration, trying out different variations of cursive script. I wanted my signature to look bold, a little ornate and as grown-up as possible.

Everyone can recognize the abstract beauty of a written letter or word and I'm certain that today, where we rarely write by hand, a typed text message (with or without emojis) will never hold a candle to a handwritten card or a calligraphic poem.

It's no different in printed media. Whether illustrated books or magazines, we find a feast for the eyes in drawn script. Handwritten headlines or text passages simply lend the text you set extra character! But single illustrated initial letters also have a great effect. Initials, decorative initial letters of a chapter or paragraph, are still used to this day. When Johannes Gutenberg printed his first incunabula in the middle of the fifteenth century, initials were often the only illustrations that adorned "the book of books." I really like this genre of illustration. The drawn or painted letters give a kind of foretaste and reveal something of the story before you start reading.

Universal as it is, gouache is wonderful for writing. The initials on this double page were drawn with a writing pen; they imitate a fine, slightly antique English script. In the chapter "Drawing with gouache," you read about the technique of putting the paint on the drawing or reed pen. The high pigment content of the gouache even makes it possible for the paints to shine on a dark or black background; you can't do that with watercolours or acrylic paints.

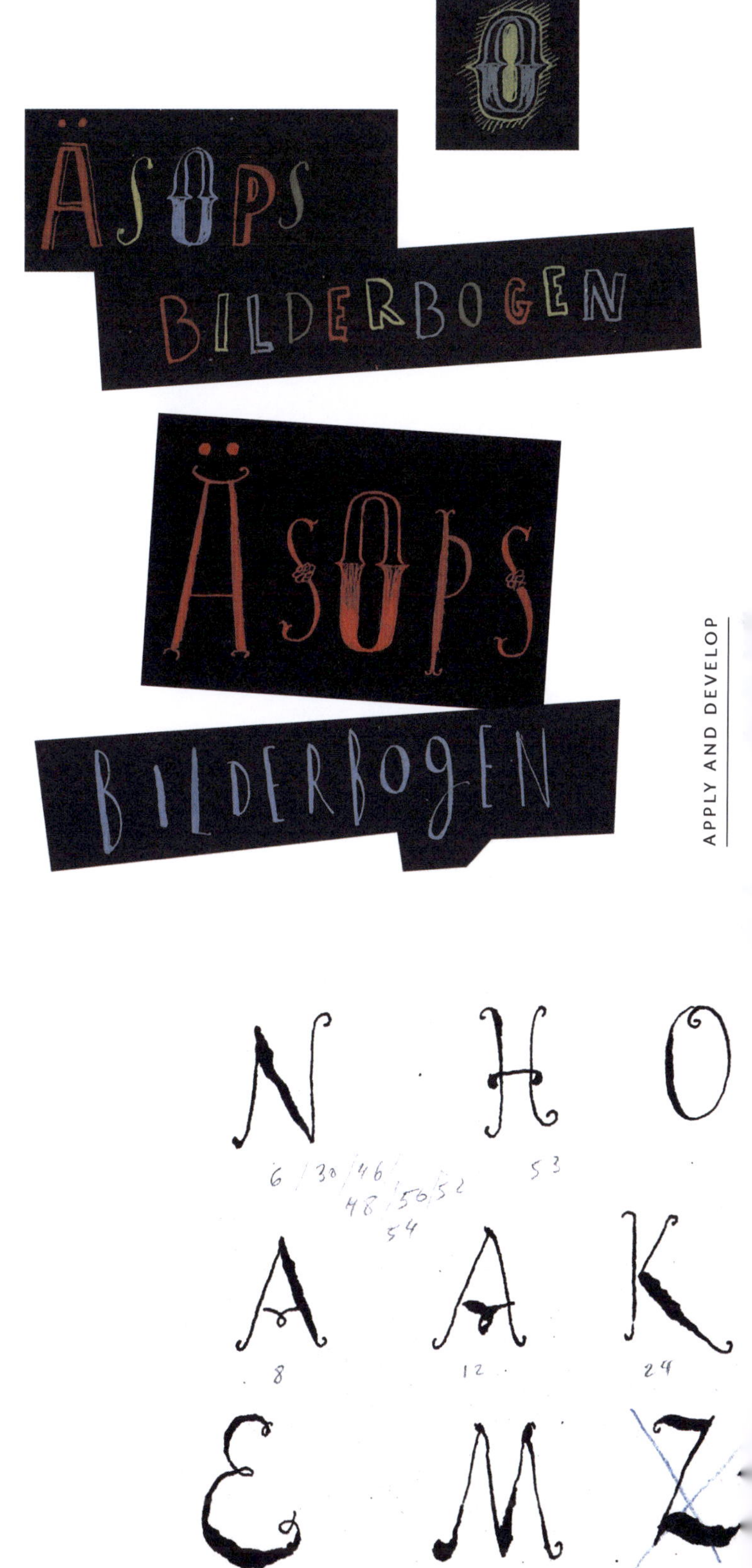

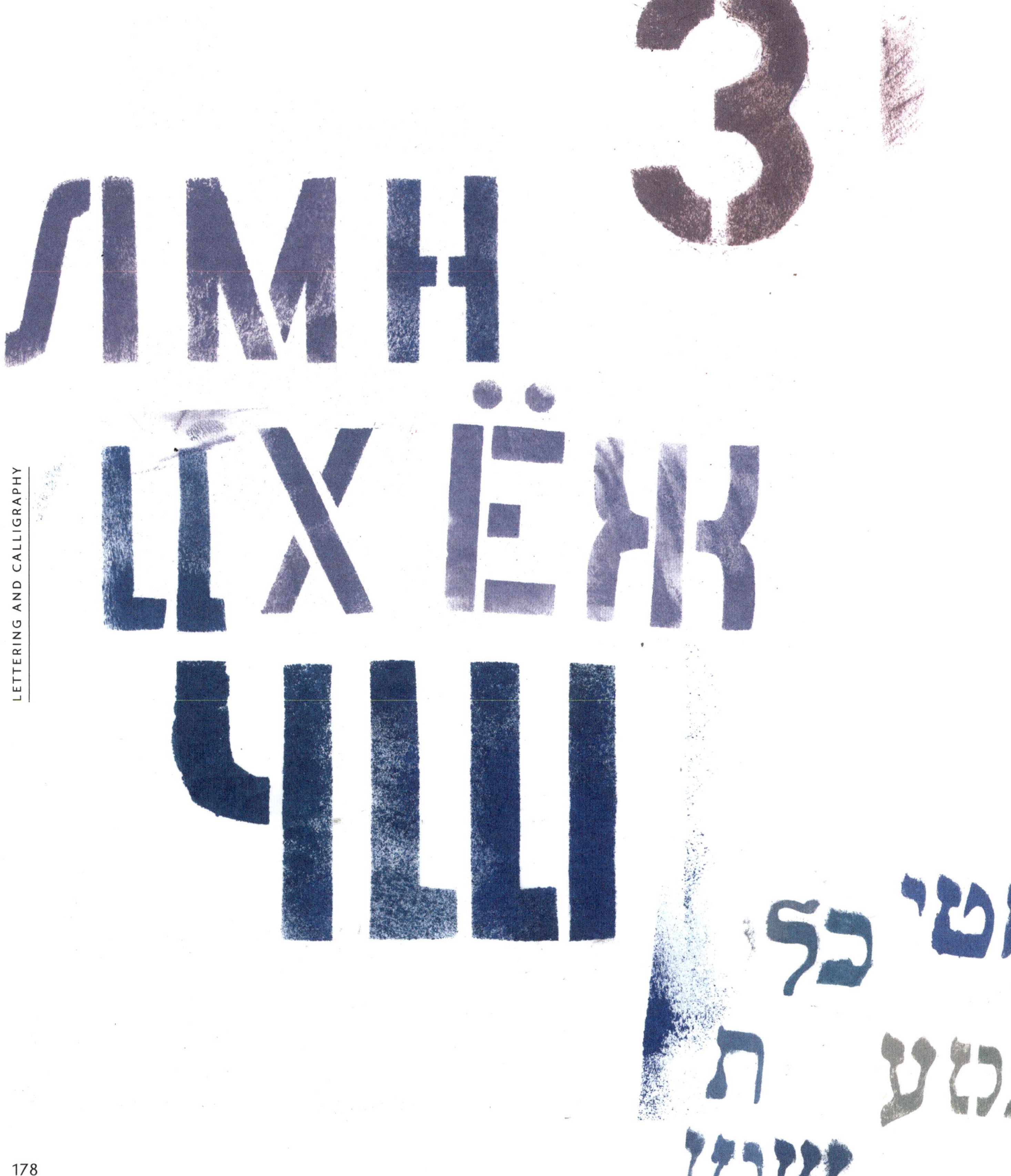
3
ЛМН
ЦХЁЖ
ЧШ
כל
ת

Stencilling is a tried and tested method of painting letters. There are many ready-made stencils, for example for schoolchildren (I used one for Hebrew letters on this page). You can also make your own stencils, from coarse and chunky to refined and delicate– just as you like it. All you have to do is select a font of your choice on the computer, type a word and then print it out in the desired size. Next, use a cutter or knife to cut out the letters (don't forget to leave little bridges so that the inside of the letters doesn't fall out). Now stamp the paint with a sponge or stencil brush.

Another possibility is the mixture of analogue painted backgrounds and digital fonts. To do this, you must be digitally equipped and, in addition to gouache paints, have an image-editing program like Adobe Photoshop. Here are a few examples of what such decorative letters can look like. How it works? The structures are first painted in gouache and then scanned. Then you convert your favourite font into pixels, cut out the outline of the letter and highlight your painted area. Finished. The illustrated E's and A's on this double page were created in this way.

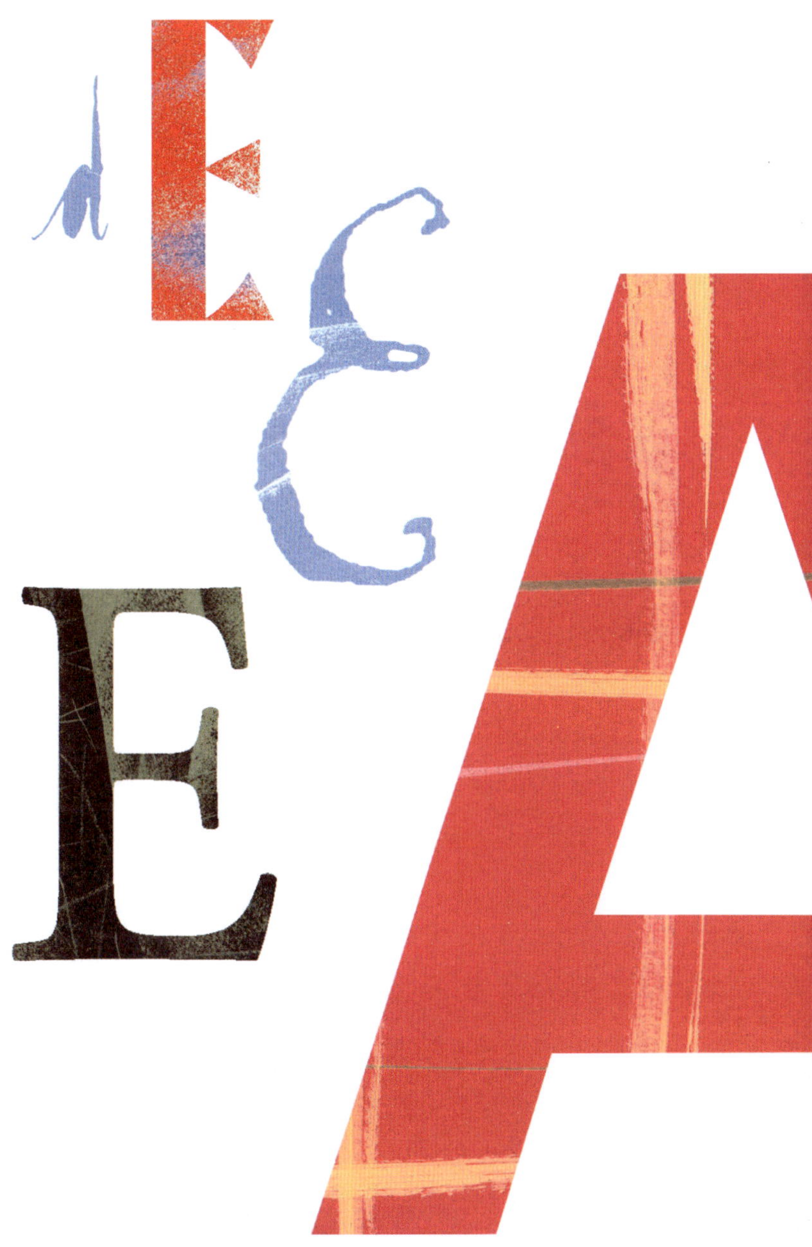

And initials can do much more. In some books you'll even find proper picture letters that represent things, plants or animals. C, T, E and A are initials based on Nordic legends and fairy tales. Old stone sculptures from the Viking era were the inspiration for these pictures and influenced their appearance. Some of them are reminiscent of stylized mythical creatures or plants and were created by using masking fluid and glazing the paint from dark to light (more on this in the chapter "Using masking fluid").

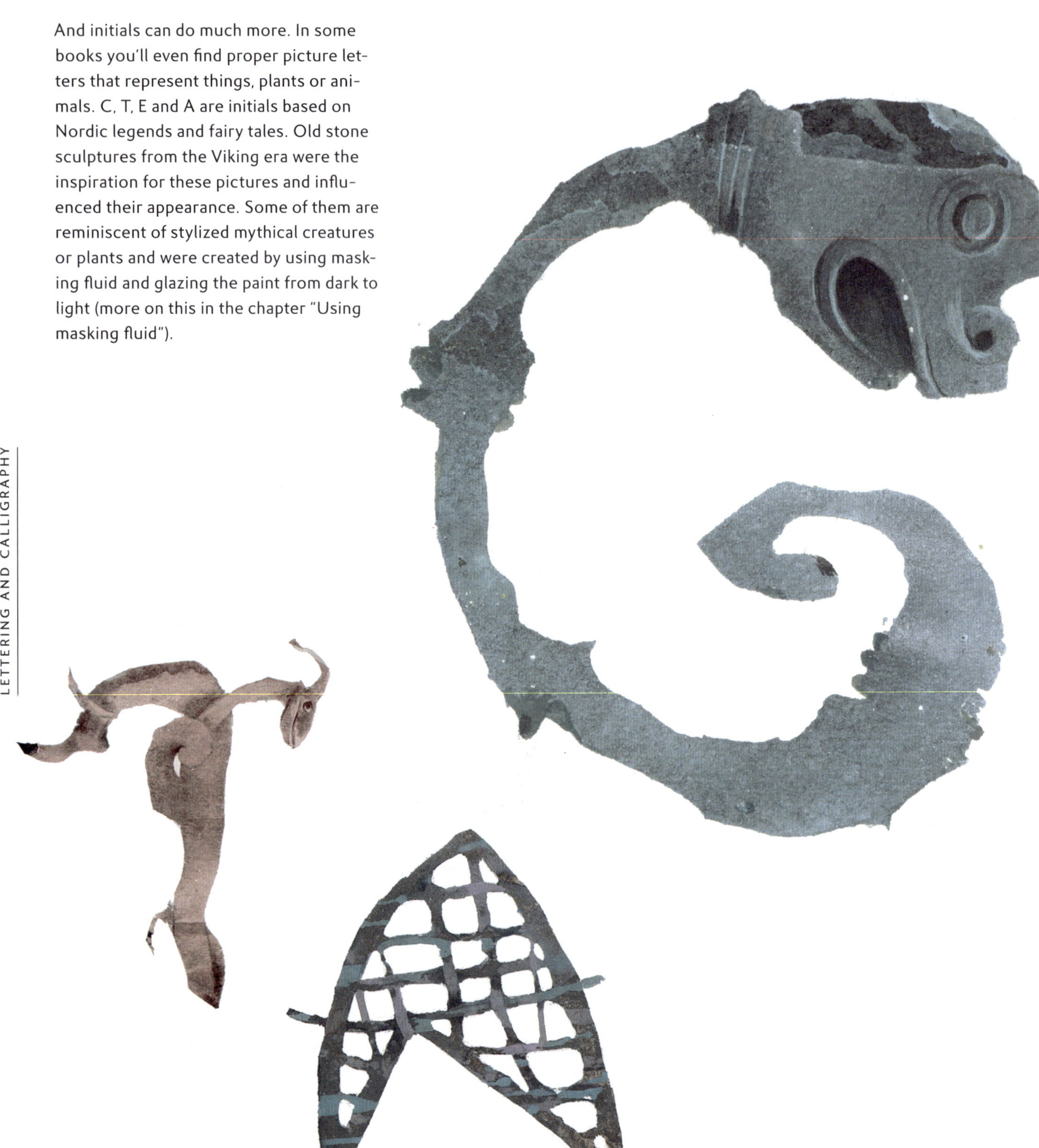

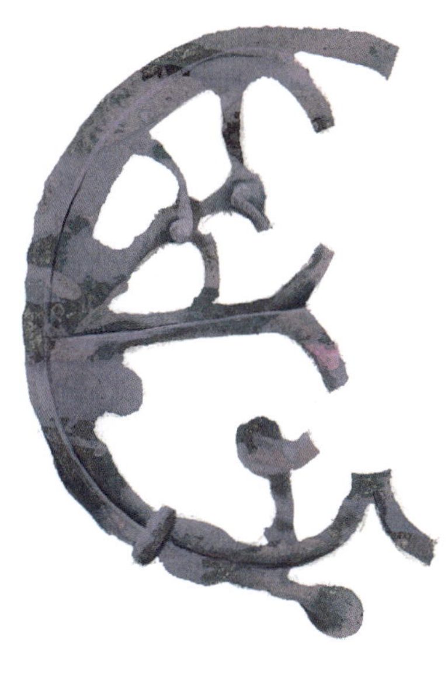

→ TIP: In order to come up with interesting ideas, it's worth your while to study and copy writings from all eras. Great new script ideas often emerge from the mix of personal "imperfect" handwriting and well-proportioned font templates. Try it!!

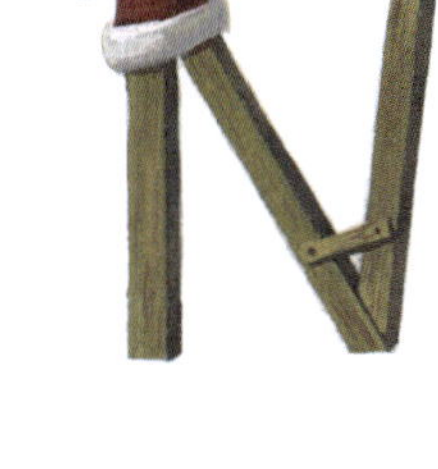

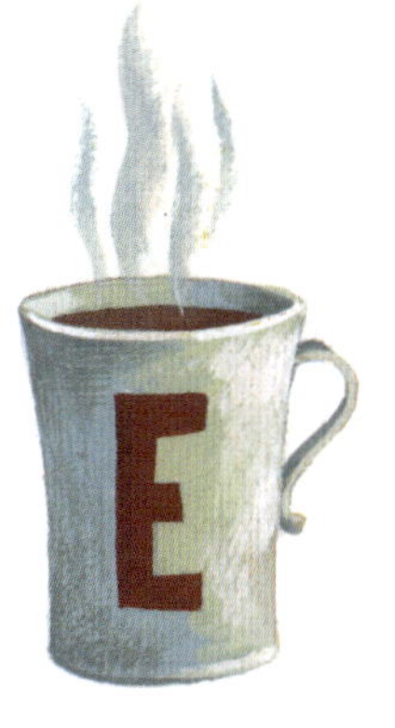

Another example: Painted objects as characters– packages, notes, bows– can also be picture letters. They illustrate a fairy tale and only look like proper letters when they're in front of the typeset text. Only then will many of them be perceived as initials!

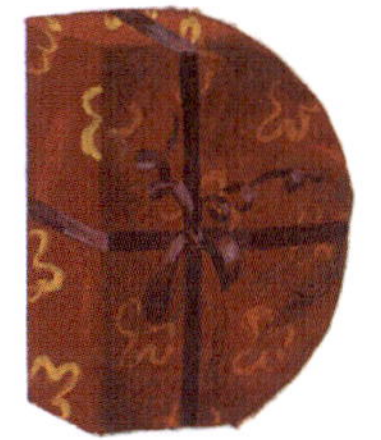

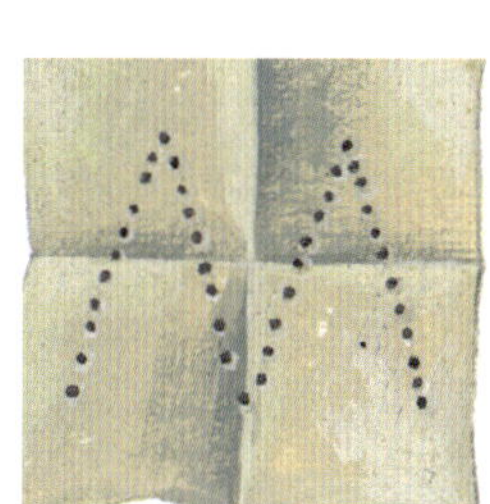

Working with letters takes me back to my school days. The same enthusiasm that I first experienced when I tried my signature and got lost in the poetry of the painted script emerged when I painted the letters. Try it for yourself. Letters are more than information carriers. With the right script, you can also convey your feelings.

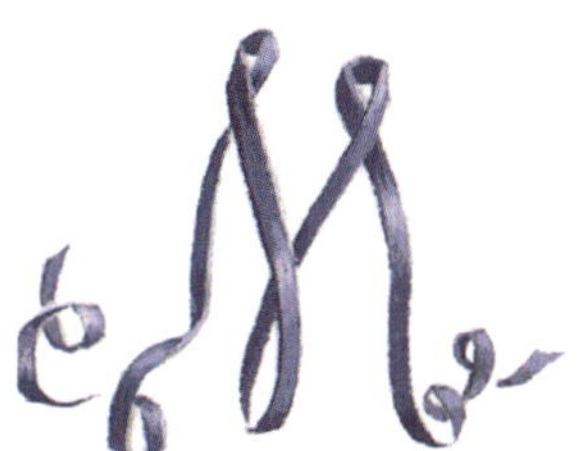

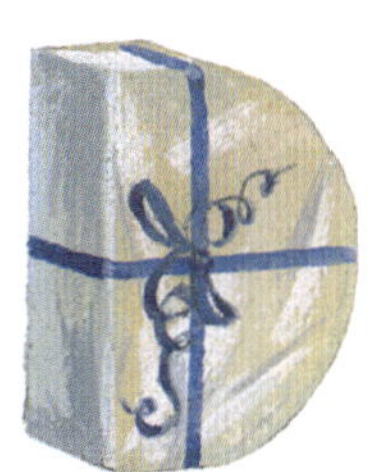

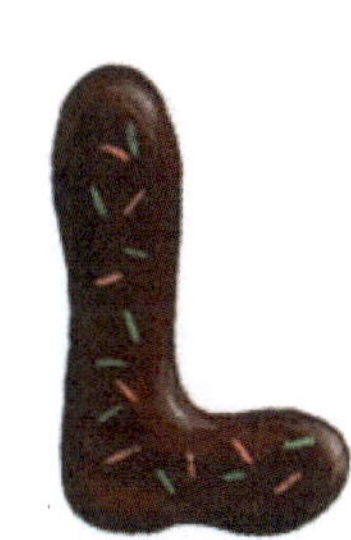

And now...

... paint a few pictures with gouache yourself to see if it becomes "your" technique, just as it became "mine." If so, then this whole endeavour will have been worth it. Try it, make your own discoveries, and make your own mistakes. After all, every experience worthy of the name must be our own. Or as Oscar Wilde put it, "Experience is simply the name we give our mistakes." There's a reason that this book is called *Rediscovering Gouache: A New Approach to a Versatile Technique for Contemporary Artists and Illustrators* these paints adapt perfectly to very different tasks, working conditions, and even temperaments. I hope they will adapt to yours as well. And if you want to do more with gouache, you can find more information, ideas and tips, as well as links to my workshops at www.aljoschablau.com.

This book grew out of a loose collection of images and ideas, thanks in large part to my friends and other great people I was able to share my ideas with. At this point I would like to express my gratitude to all of them. I would like to thank Natascha Schwarz for her help with the layout and Felix Scheinberger for his tips on writing. And I would also like to thank the Museum of Prints and Drawings (Kupferstichkabinett) in Berlin and its head restorer Georg Dietz for the insightful hours that we spent over the original gouaches of Menzel, Dürer, and Botticelli.

Aljoscha Blau

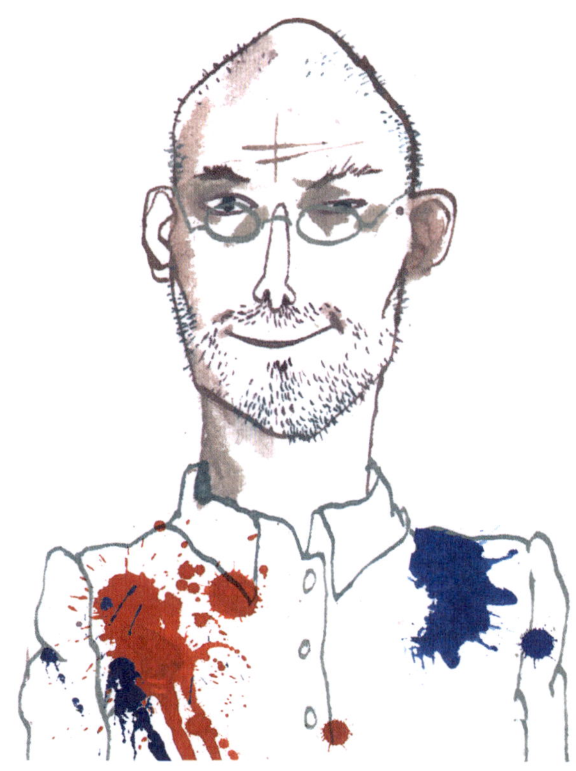

Aljoscha Blau, born in St. Petersburg in 1972, grew up there in an artist family and came to Germany half a year after the fall of the wall in 1990. He studied illustration and free graphic arts at the HAW Hamburg and published his first books as a student. Today, Aljoscha Blau lives in Berlin and works as an illustrator for German and international publishers. He has illustrated over 60 books, many of which have won major German and international awards. These include the German Youth Literature Prize, German Design Award Gold, Bologna Ragazzi Award, Austrian State Prize and others. In addition to his artistic work, Aljoscha Blau teaches as a visiting professor at art academies in Germany, Denmark, Switzerland and Italy.

All illustrations in this book were either newly gouached by Aljoscha Blau or come from books he has illustrated:

We would like to thank the following publishers for permission to reprint:

ATLANTIS, an imprint of Orell Füssli Verlag, Orell Füssli Sicherheitsdruck AG, © 2018, *Die Schlacht von Karlawatsch*
AUFBAU VERLAG GMBH & CO. KG, © 2007, *Der Ritt auf dem Seepferd*, © 2011, *Hinter der roten Sonne*
BELTZ & GELBERG of the Verlagsgruppe Beltz, © 2002/2005, 2007, *Geschichte der Wirtschaft*
S. FISCHER VERLAG GMBH, © 2005, *Der Winterzirkus*
GERSTENBERG VERLAG, © 2010, *Roberts Land*
CARL HANSER GMBH & CO. KG, © 2014, *Abends will ich schlafen gehen*
INSEL VERLAG, © 2012, *Sankt Nikolaus in Not*
NORDSÜD VERLAG AG, © 2015, *Das Dschungelbuch*
PETER HAMMER VERLAG, © 2013, *Das Kind im Mond*
ROWOHLT BERLIN VERLAG GMBH, © 2006, *Tagesschau erklärt die Welt*
VERLAGSHAUS JACOBY & STUART, © 2016, *Was ist los vor meiner Tür?*

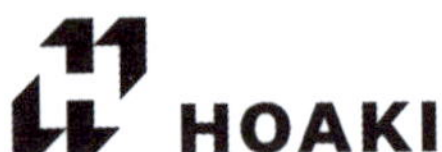

C/ Ausiàs March, 128
08013 Barcelona, Spain
T. 0034 935 952 283
F. 0034 932 654 883
info@hoaki.com
www.hoaki.com

hoakibooks

Rediscovering Gouache
A New Approach to a Versatile Technique for Contemporary Artists and Illustrators

ISBN: 978-84-17656-62-1
Reprint: 2024

Text: Aljoscha Blau
Editing: Bertram Schmidt-Friderichs
Translation: Faith Gibson, Philadelphia.
Design: Aljoscha Blau. Basic design by Eva Finkbeiner
Cover design: Eva Finkbeiner
Typesetting: Laura Eckes, Anna-Maria Koptenko
Proofreading: Sandra Mandl
Fonts used Prell Regular, Newzald Book

D.L.: B 12401-2021
Printed in China

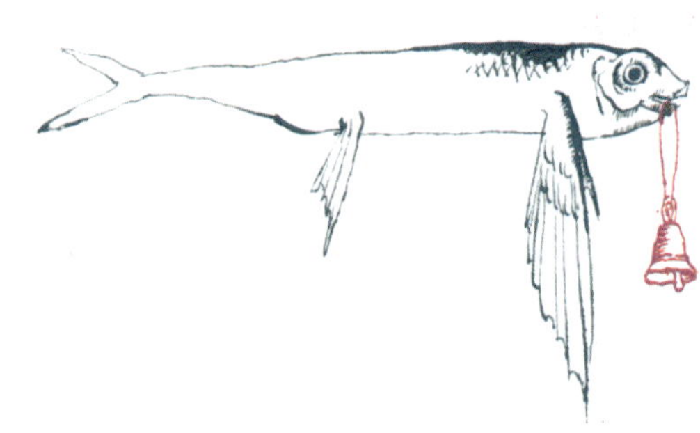